**Principles of Soft Computing Using Python
Programming**

Principles of Soft Computing Using Python Programming

Learn How to Deploy Soft Computing Models in Real World Applications

Gypsy Nandi
Assam Don Bosco University
Guwahati, India

IEEE PRESS

WILEY

Published by John Wiley & Sons, Inc., Hoboken, New Jersey.
Published simultaneously in Canada.

No part of this publication may be reproduced, stored in a retrieval system, or transmitted in any form or by any means, electronic, mechanical, photocopying, recording, scanning, or otherwise, except as permitted under Section 107 or 108 of the 1976 United States Copyright Act, without either the prior written permission of the Publisher, or authorization through payment of the appropriate per-copy fee to the Copyright Clearance Center, Inc., 222 Rosewood Drive, Danvers, MA 01923, (978) 750-8400, fax (978) 750-4470, or on the web at www.copyright.com. Requests to the Publisher for permission should be addressed to the Permissions Department, John Wiley & Sons, Inc., 111 River Street, Hoboken, NJ 07030, (201) 748-6011, fax (201) 748-6008, or online at http://www.wiley.com/go/permission.

Trademarks: Wiley and the Wiley logo are trademarks or registered trademarks of John Wiley & Sons, Inc. and/or its affiliates in the United States and other countries and may not be used without written permission. All other trademarks are the property of their respective owners. John Wiley & Sons, Inc. is not associated with any product or vendor mentioned in this book.

Limit of Liability/Disclaimer of Warranty: While the publisher and author have used their best efforts in preparing this book, they make no representations or warranties with respect to the accuracy or completeness of the contents of this book and specifically disclaim any implied warranties of merchantability or fitness for a particular purpose. No warranty may be created or extended by sales representatives or written sales materials. The advice and strategies contained herein may not be suitable for your situation. You should consult with a professional where appropriate. Neither the publisher nor author shall be liable for any loss of profit or any other commercial damages, including but not limited to special, incidental, consequential, or other damages.

For general information on our other products and services or for technical support, please contact our Customer Care Department within the United States at (800) 762-2974, outside the United States at (317) 572-3993 or fax (317) 572-4002.

Wiley also publishes its books in a variety of electronic formats. Some content that appears in print may not be available in electronic formats. For more information about Wiley products, visit our web site at www.wiley.com.

Library of Congress Cataloging-in-Publication Data Applied for:

Hardback ISBN: 9781394173136

Cover Design: Wiley
Cover Image: © Tuomas A. Lehtinen/Getty Images

Set in 9.5/12.5pt STIXTwoText by Straive, Chennai, India

Contents

About the Author   *xi*
Preface   *xiii*

1   **Fundamentals of Soft Computing**   *1*
1.1   Introduction to Soft Computing   *1*
1.2   Soft Computing versus Hard Computing   *2*
1.3   Characteristics of Soft Computing   *4*
1.4   Components of Soft Computing   *7*
1.4.1   Fuzzy Computing   *7*
1.4.2   Neural Network   *10*
1.4.3   Evolutionary Computing   *12*
1.4.4   Machine Learning   *19*
1.4.5   Other Techniques of Soft Computing   *29*
          Exercises   *31*

2   **Fuzzy Computing**   *35*
2.1   Fuzzy Sets   *37*
2.1.1   Features of Fuzzy Membership Functions   *38*
2.2   Fuzzy Set Operations   *41*
2.3   Fuzzy Set Properties   *42*
2.4   Binary Fuzzy Relation   *45*
2.5   Fuzzy Membership Functions   *46*
2.6   Methods of Membership Value Assignments   *49*
2.7   Fuzzification vs. Defuzzification   *58*
2.8   Fuzzy c-Means   *62*
          Exercises   *71*

3   **Artificial Neural Network**   *75*

3.1   Fundamentals of Artificial Neural Network (ANN)   *76*

3.2   Standard Activation Functions in Neural Networks   *81*

3.2.1   Binary Step Activation Function   *81*

3.2.2   Linear Activation Function   *83*

3.2.3   Sigmoid/Logistic Activation Function   *84*

3.2.4   ReLU Activation Function   *85*

3.2.5   Tanh Activation Function   *87*

3.2.6   Leaky ReLU Activation Function   *88*

3.2.7   SoftMax Activation Function   *90*

3.3   Basic Learning Rules in ANN   *91*

3.3.1   Hebbian Learning Rule   *93*

3.3.2   Perceptron Learning Rule   *93*

3.3.3   Delta Learning Rule   *94*

3.3.4   Correlation Learning Rule   *94*

3.3.5   Competitive Learning Rule   *95*

3.3.6   Outstar Learning Rule   *95*

3.4   McCulloch–Pitts ANN Model   *96*

3.5   Feed-Forward Neural Network   *98*

3.5.1   Single-Layer Perceptron   *99*

3.5.2   Multilayer Perceptron   *103*

3.5.3   Radial Basis Function Network   *107*

3.6   Feedback Neural Network   *111*

3.6.1   Self-Organizing Map (SOM)   *111*

3.6.2   Hopfield Neural Network (HNN)   *116*

    Exercises   *119*

4   **Deep Learning**   *123*

4.1   Introduction to Deep Learning   *123*

4.2   Classification of Deep Learning Techniques   *125*

4.2.1   Convolutional Neural Networks   *125*

4.2.2   Recurrent Neural Network (RNN)   *137*

4.2.3   Generative Adversarial Network (GAN)   *144*

4.2.4   Autoencoders   *149*

    Exercises   *155*

5   **Probabilistic Reasoning**   *159*

5.1   Introduction to Probabilistic Reasoning   *159*

5.1.1   Random Experiment   *160*

5.1.2   Random Variables   *160*

5.1.3   Independence   *161*

5.1.4   Sample Space   *162*

5.1.5   Odds and Risks   *162*

5.1.6   Expected Values   *165*

5.2   Four Perspectives on Probability   *165*

5.2.1   The Classical Approach   *166*

5.2.2   The Empirical Approach   *166*

5.2.3   The Subjective Approach   *167*

5.2.4   The Axiomatic Approach   *167*

5.3   The Principles of Bayesian Inference   *168*

5.4   Belief Network and Markovian Network   *171*

5.4.1   Syntax and Semantics   *172*

5.4.1.1   Belief Network   *172*

5.4.1.2   Markovian Network   *172*

5.4.2   Conditional Independence   *172*

5.4.3   Learning Methods of the Networks   *177*

5.5   Hidden Markov Model   *178*

5.6   Markov Decision Processes   *186*

5.7   Machine Learning and Probabilistic Models   *191*

     Exercises   *194*

6   **Population-Based Algorithms**   *197*

6.1   Introduction to Genetic Algorithms   *197*

6.2   Five Phases of Genetic Algorithms   *198*

6.2.1   Population Initialization   *198*

6.2.2   Fitness Function Calculation (Evaluation)   *199*

6.2.3   Parent Selection   *200*

6.2.4   Crossover   *204*

6.2.5   Mutation   *205*

6.3   How Genetic Algorithm Works?   *207*

6.4   Application Areas of Genetic Algorithms   *212*

6.4.1   Using GA in Travelling Salesman Problem   *212*

6.4.2   Using GA in Vehicle Routing Problem   *216*

6.5   Python Code for Implementing a Simple Genetic Algorithm   *221*

6.6   Introduction to Swarm Intelligence   *225*

6.7   Few Important Aspects of Swarm Intelligence   *227*

6.7.1   Collective Sorting   *228*

6.7.2   Foraging Behavior   *228*

6.7.3   Stigmergy   *229*

6.7.4   Division of Labor   *229*

6.7.5   Collective Transport *230*
6.7.6   Self-Organization *231*
6.8   Swarm Intelligence Techniques *233*
6.8.1   Ant Colony Optimization *233*
6.8.1.1 How ACO Technique Works? *233*
6.8.1.2 Applying ACO to Optimization Problems *235*
6.8.1.3 Using ACO in Travelling Salesman Problem *236*
6.8.1.4 Python Code for Implementing ACO in TSP *239*
6.8.2   Particle Swarm Optimization *241*
6.8.2.1 How PSO Technique Works? *242*
6.8.2.2 Applying PSO to Optimization Problems *243*
6.8.2.3 Using PSO in Job-Shop Scheduling Problem *246*
6.8.2.4 Python Code for Implementing PSO *247*
         Exercises *251*

7   **Rough Set Theory** *255*
7.1   The Pawlak Rough Set Model *255*
7.1.1   Basic Terms in Pawlak Rough Set Model *256*
7.1.2   Measures of Rough Set Approximations *260*
7.2   Using Rough Sets for Information System *262*
7.3   Decision Rules and Decision Tables *263*
7.3.1   Parameters of Decision Tables *264*
7.3.1.1 Consistency Factor *264*
7.3.1.2 Support and Strength *265*
7.3.1.3 Certainty Factor *265*
7.3.1.4 Coverage Factor *266*
7.3.2   Probabilistic Properties of Decision Tables *266*
7.4   Application Areas of Rough Set Theory *268*
7.4.1   Classification *268*
7.4.2   Clustering *271*
7.4.3   Medical Diagnosis *273*
7.4.4   Image Processing *276*
7.4.5   Speech Analysis *278*
7.5   Using ROSE Tool for RST Operations *280*
7.5.1   Attribute Discretization *280*
7.5.2   Finding Lower and Upper Approximations *281*
         Exercises *285*

8   **Hybrid Systems** *289*
8.1   Introduction to Hybrid Systems *289*
8.2   Neurogenetic Systems *291*

8.2.1   GA-based Weight Determination of Multilayer Feed-forward Net   *292*
8.2.2   Neuroevolution of Augmenting Topologies (NEAT)   *298*
8.3   Fuzzy-Neural Systems   *302*
8.3.1   Fuzzy Neurons   *303*
8.3.2   Adaptive Neuro-fuzzy Inference System (ANFIS)   *307*
8.4   Fuzzy-Genetic Systems   *311*
8.5   Hybrid Systems in Medical Devices   *315*
         Exercises   *322*

         Index   *327*

About the Author

Dr. Gypsy Nandi currently holds the position of Associate Professor and Head of the Department of Computer Applications at Assam Don Bosco University, located in Assam, India. With a profound educational background that includes a PhD in computer science, she has amassed nearly two decades of invaluable experience within the academic sphere. Driven by a fervent passion for cutting-edge technologies, she has been instrumental in advancing the fields of machine learning, data science, and social network analysis through her significant contributions.

Her accomplishments extend to successfully managing various government-sanctioned consultancy and research-based projects. Additionally, she has authored two impactful books that delve into the domains of data science and soft computing. She has also secured an Indian patent grant for her innovative design of a versatile, multi-functional robot.

Over the course of her illustrious academic career spanning 18 years, she has been a sought-after speaker for both national and state-level events, where she shares her expertise in her respective fields. Her extensive research output is evident in her numerous publications, which include esteemed journal articles, conference papers, and book chapters.

Beyond her academic pursuits, she remains actively engaged in social commitment activities. She serves as the coordinator of VanitAgrata, a women empowerment cell at Assam Don Bosco University. Through this initiative, she provides free digital literacy training to girls and women in rural areas, contributing to the advancement of society. She has also received international recognition from a university in the Philippines for her dedication to service-learning at the institutional level. Her commitment extends to offering free digital literacy training to various underprivileged communities in rural Assam.

In summary, she stands as a distinguished scholar and educator who has left an indelible mark on the fields of computer science and technology. Her accomplishments showcase not only academic excellence but also a profound dedication to social development and enriching the lives of students and communities alike.

Preface

In an era defined by rapid technological advancements, the field of soft computing has emerged as a powerful paradigm for solving complex real-world problems. Soft computing leverages the principles of human-like decision-making, allowing machines to handle uncertainty, vagueness, and imprecision in data and reasoning. This interdisciplinary field encompasses a variety of computational techniques, each with its unique strengths and applications.

This comprehensive textbook, *Principles of Soft Computing Using Python Programming*, is designed to provide students, researchers, and practitioners with a solid foundation in the core concepts and techniques of soft computing. With a focus on clarity and accessibility, this book takes you on a journey through the fundamental principles and methods that underpin soft computing.

Chapter 1 – Fundamentals of Soft Computing initiates our exploration, setting the stage by introducing soft computing and distinguishing it from its counterpart, hard computing. It delves into the key characteristics of soft computing and explores its essential components, including fuzzy computing, neural networks, evolutionary computing, machine learning, and other techniques. Engaging exercises at the end of the chapter invite you to apply your newfound knowledge.

Chapter 2 – Fuzzy Computing delves deeper into one of the cornerstone techniques of soft computing. It covers fuzzy sets, operations on fuzzy sets, properties, and more. You will also explore the practical aspects of fuzzy computing, such as membership functions, fuzzification, defuzzification, and the application of fuzzy c-means clustering.

Chapter 3 – Artificial Neural Network introduces the fundamentals of artificial neural networks (ANNs), a powerful tool inspired by the human brain. You will learn about standard activation functions, basic learning rules, and various types of neural network architectures, including feedforward and feedback networks. Engaging exercises will help reinforce your understanding of ANN concepts.

Chapter 4 – Deep Learning delves into the realm of deep neural networks, which have revolutionized fields such as computer vision, natural language processing, and speech recognition. This chapter provides an overview of deep learning techniques, including convolutional neural networks (CNNs), recurrent neural networks (RNNs), generative adversarial networks (GANs), and autoencoders.

Chapter 5 – Probabilistic Reasoning explores the world of probability and its applications in soft computing. You will delve into random experiments, random variables, and different perspectives on probability. Bayesian inference, belief networks, Markovian models, and their applications in machine learning are also covered.

Chapter 6 – Population Based Algorithms introduces genetic algorithms and swarm intelligence techniques. You will discover how genetic algorithms work and explore their applications in optimization problems. Additionally, you will dive into swarm intelligence methods, including ant colony optimization (ACO) and particle swarm optimization (PSO), with practical Python code examples.

Chapter 7 – Rough Set Theory delves into the Pawlak Rough Set Model and its applications in information systems, decision rules, and decision tables. You will explore the use of rough sets in various domains such as classification, clustering, medical diagnosis, image processing, and speech analysis.

Chapter 8 – Hybrid Systems concludes our journey by discussing hybrid systems that combine different soft computing techniques, including neuro-genetic systems, fuzzy-neural systems, and fuzzy-genetic systems. You will also explore their applications in medical devices.

Each chapter in this book is carefully structured to provide a clear understanding of the topic, with practical exercises to reinforce your learning. Whether you are a student, researcher, or practitioner, "Principles of Soft Computing Using Python Programming" equips you with the knowledge and skills to tackle complex real-world problems using the power of soft computing. So, let us embark on this enlightening journey through the world of soft computing.

16 October 2023

Dr. Gypsy Nandi
Guwahati, Assam, India

1

Fundamentals of Soft Computing

Soft computing is a vital tool used for performing several computing operations. It uses one or more computational models or techniques to generate optimum outcomes. To understand this concept, let us first clarify our idea about computation. In any computation operation, inputs are fed into the computing model for performing some operations based on which results are accordingly produced. In the context of computing, the input provided for computation is called an *antecedent*, and the output generated is called the *consequence*. Figure 1.1 illustrates the basics of any computing operation where computing is done using a *control action* (series of steps or actions). Here, in this example, the control action is stated as $p = f(q)$, where "q" is the input, "p" is the output, and "f" is the mapping function, which can be any formal method or algorithm to solve a problem.

Hence, it can be concluded that computing is nothing but a mapping function that helps in solving a problem to produce an output based on the input provided. The control action for computing should be precise and definite so as to provide accurate solution for a given problem.

1.1 Introduction to Soft Computing

Many a time, it has been noticed that no fixed solution can be found for a computationally hard task. In such a case, a precisely stated analytical model may not work to produce precise results. For this, the soft computing approach can be used that does not require a fixed mathematical modeling for problem solving. In fact, the uniqueness and strength of soft computing lie in its superpower of fusing two or more soft computing computational models/techniques to generate optimum results.

The concept of soft computing was evolved by Prof. Lofti A. Zadeh (University of California, USA) in the year 1981. Soft computing, as described by Prof. Zadeh,

Principles of Soft Computing Using Python Programming: Learn How to Deploy Soft Computing Models in Real World Applications, First Edition. Gypsy Nandi.
© 2024 The Institute of Electrical and Electronics Engineers, Inc. Published 2024 by John Wiley & Sons, Inc.

Figure 1.1 Basic concepts of computing.

is "*a collection of methodologies that aim to exploit the tolerance for imprecision and uncertainty to achieve tractability, robustness, and low solution cost.*" Prof. Zadeh also emphasized that "*soft computing is likely to play an increasingly important role in many application areas, including software engineering. The role model for soft computing is the human mind.*" Soft computing mimics the notable ability of the human mind to reason and make decisions in an environment of improbability and imprecision. The principal components of soft computing include fuzzy logic, neurocomputing, and probabilistic reasoning (PR).

If you are wondering in which areas soft computing is being used in our day-to-day lives, the simplest and most common examples include kitchen appliances (rice cookers, microwaves, etc.) and home appliances (washing machines, refrigerators, etc.). Soft computing also finds its dominance in gaming (chess, poker, etc.), as well as in robotics work. Prominent research areas such as data compression, image/video recognition, speech processing, and handwriting recognition are some of the popular applications of soft computing.

1.2   Soft Computing versus Hard Computing

If we consider computing from the perspective of computer science, it is considered a certain task that can be accomplished using computers. Such computing may require certain software or hardware systems to accomplish the task(s) and to derive a certain outcome or output. To understand this easily, let us take a simple example of a self-driving car (named, say, *Ziva*). Now, the car *Ziva* is given the instructions to start moving (say, from point A) and to arrive at a destination point B. To accomplish this task, two possible cases can be considered, as discussed below:

Case A: The car *Ziva* uses a software program to make movement decisions. The path coordinates for movement decisions are already included in the software program with the help of which *Ziva* can take a predefined path to arrive at its destination. Now, suppose, while moving, *Ziva* encounters an obstacle in the path. In such a case, the software program can direct it to move to either to the right, or to the left, or to take a back turn. In this case, the self-driving car is not modeled to identify the nature and complexity of the obstacle to make a meaningful and proper decision. In this situation, the computation model used for the car is deterministic in nature, and the output is also concrete. Undoubtedly, there is less complexity in solving the problem, but the output is always fixed due to the rigidness of the computation method.

Case B: The car *Ziva* uses a software program to make movement decisions. However, in this case, the complexity of the program is more compared to the complexity of the program defined in Case A. This is so as the car is much more involved in complex decision-making. *Ziva* can now mimic the human brain in making decisions when any kind of obstacle is met in between its travel.

Ziva, first of all, assesses the type of the obstacle, then decides whether it can overcome the obstacle by any means, and finally, it keeps track of if any other alternate path can be chosen instead of overcoming the obstacle found in the same path. The decision to be taken by *Ziva* is not very crisp and precise, as there are many alternative solutions that can be followed to reach destination point B. For example, if the obstacle is a small stone, *Ziva* can easily climb up the stone and continue on the same path, as it will lead to a computationally less-expensive solution. However, if the obstacle is a big rock, *Ziva* may choose an alternative to choose another path to reach the destination point.

Case C: Now, let us consider Case C, in which the software program is written to let the self-driving car reach its destination by initially listing out all the possible paths available to reach from source A to destination B. For each path available, the cost of traveling the path is calculated and accordingly sorted to reach at the fastest time possible. Finally, the optimum path is chosen, considering the minimum cost as well as considering avoidance of any major obstacle. It can be realized that Case C appends both the cases of Case A and Case B to inherit approaches from both cases. It also adds some functionalities to tackle complex scenarios by choosing an optimum decision to finally reach destination point B.

The above three cases can be summarized (as listed in Figure 1.2) to check the points of differences among each of these cases. From each of the above three cases, it can be observed that the nature of computation in each of the three cases is not similar.

Notice that emphasis is given on reaching the destination point in the first case. As the result is precise and fixed, the computation of the Case A type is termed *hard computing*. Now, in the second case, the interest is to arrive at an approximate result, as a precise result is not guaranteed by this approach. The computation of the Case B type is termed *soft computing*. The third case inherits the properties of both Case A and Case B, and this part of computing is referred to as *hybrid computing*. Thus, computing in perspective of computer science can be broadly categorized, as shown in Figure 1.3.

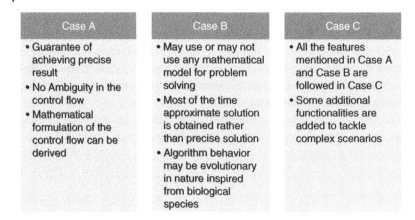

Figure 1.2 Summarization of three varying cases of a self-driving car.

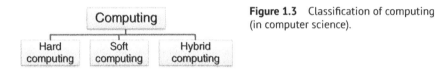

Figure 1.3 Classification of computing (in computer science).

The choice on which classification of computing should be used relies mainly on the nature of the problem to be solved. However, it is important that before choosing any of the computing techniques for problem solving, we should be clear about the main differences between hard computing and soft computing. Table 1.1 lists a few notable differences between hard computing and soft computing to deal with real-world problems.

The points of differences listed in Table 1.1 clear out the fact that soft computing methods are more suitable for solving real-world problems in which ideal models are not available. To name a few applications that may be solved using soft computing techniques include signal processing, robotics control, pattern recognition, business forecasting, speech processing, and many more. Recent research has given a lot of importance to the field of computational intelligence (CI). While traditional artificial intelligence (AI) follows the principle of hard computing, CI follows the principle of soft computing.

1.3 Characteristics of Soft Computing

As we understood that soft computing can deal with imprecision, partial truth, and uncertainty, its applications are varied, ranging from day-to-day applications to various applications related to science and engineering. Some of the dominant

Table 1.1 Important points of differences between soft computing and hard computing.

Sl. no.	Hard computing	Soft computing
1	Requires a precisely stated analytical model	Can deal with imprecise models
2	Often requires a lot of computation time to solve a problem	Can solve a problem in reasonably less time
3	These techniques commonly use arithmetic, science, and computing	It mostly imitates the model from nature
4	Cannot be used in real-world problems for which an ideal model is not present	Suitable for real-world problems for which an ideal model is not present
5	Requires full truth to produce optimum result	Can work with partial truth to produce optimum result
6	Needs a precise and accurate environment	Can work in an environment of improbability and imprecision
7	The programs that are written using these techniques are deterministic	The soft computing techniques are developed mainly to get better results for any nondeterministic polynomial (NP)-complete problems
8	Usually, high cost is involved in developing solutions	Low cost is involved in developing solutions

characteristics of soft computing are listed in Figure 1.4, and a brief discussion on each of these characteristics is given next:

(a) **Human expertise:** Soft computing utilizes human expertise by framing fuzzy if–then rules as well as conventional knowledge representation for solving real-world problems that may consist of some degree of truth or false. In short, where a concrete decision fails to represent a solution, soft computing techniques work best to provide human-like conditional solutions.

(b) **Biologically inspired computational models:** Computational learning models that follow the neural model of the human brain have been studied and framed for complex problem solving with approximation solutions. A few such popular neural network models include the artificial neural network (ANN)-, convolutional neural network (CNN)-, and the recurrent neural network (RNN)-based models. These models are commonly used for solving classification problems, pattern recognition, and sentiment analysis.

(c) **Optimization techniques:** Complex optimization problems that are inspired by nature are often used as soft computing techniques. For example,

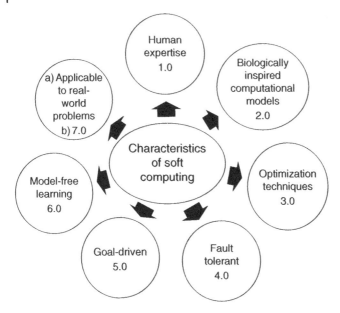

Figure 1.4 Soft computing characteristics.

genetic algorithms (GA) can be used to select top-N fit people out of a human population of a hundred people. The selection of the most fit people is done by using the mutation properties inspired by biological evolution of genes.

(d) **Fault tolerant:** Fault tolerance of a computational model indicates the capacity of the model to continue operating without interruption, even if any software or hardware failure occurs. That is, the normal computational process is not affected even if any of the software or hardware components fail.

(e) **Goal-driven:** Soft computing techniques are considered to be goal-driven. This indicates that emphasis is given more on reaching the goal or destination than on the path considered to be taken from the current state to reach the goal. Simulated annealing and GA are good examples of goal-driven soft computing techniques.

(f) **Model-free learning:** The training models used in soft computing need not be already aware of all the states in the environment. Learning of a step takes place in due course of actions taken in the present state. In other words, it can be said that there is a teacher who specifies beforehand all the precise actions to be taken per condition or state. The learning algorithm indirectly only has a critic that provides feedback as to whether the action taken can be rewarded or punished. The rewards or punishments given help in better decision-making for future actions.

(g) **Applicable to real-world problems:** Most of the real-world problems are built on uncertainties. In such circumstances, soft computing techniques are often used to construct satisfactory solutions to deal with such real-world problems.

1.4 Components of Soft Computing

The three principal components of soft computing include fuzzy logic-based computing, neurocomputing, and GA. These three components form the core of soft computing. There are a few other components of soft computing often used for problem solving, such as machine learning (ML), PR, evolutionary reasoning, and chaos theory. A brief summary of all these components of soft computing techniques is explained next, along with an illustrative diagram, as given in Figure 1.5.

While fuzzy computing involves understanding fuzzy logic and fuzzy sets, neural networks include the study of several neural network systems such as artificial neural network (ANN) and CNN. Evolutionary computing (EC) involves a wide range of techniques such as GA and swarm intelligence. Techniques for ML are categorized mainly as supervised learning (SL), unsupervised learning, and reinforcement learning (RL). Soft computing also involves a wide variety of techniques such as chaos theory, PR, and evolutionary reasoning.

1.4.1 Fuzzy Computing

The idea of fuzzy logic was first familiarized by Dr. Lotfi Zadeh of the University of California at Berkeley in the 1960s. While Boolean logic allows evaluation of output to either 0 (*false*) or 1 (*true*), and no other acceptance values in between, fuzzy logic, on the other hand, is an approach to computing that works on the basis of the "*degrees of truth*" that can consider any values between 0 and 1. That is, fuzzy logic considers 0 and 1 as extreme values of a fact or truth (value "0" represents *absolute false*, and value "1" represents *absolute true*). Any value between 0 and 1 in fuzzy logic indicates the various levels or states of truth.

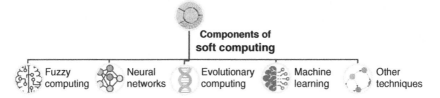

Figure 1.5 Components of soft computing.

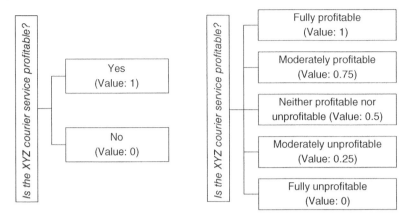

Figure 1.6   (a) Boolean (nonfuzzy) and (b) fuzzy logic-based solutions for a problem.

Let us understand this simple concept with the help of an example. For instance, if we consider the question, *"Is the XYZ Courier Service Profitable?"* the reply to this question can be simply stated as either *"Yes"* or *"No."* If only two close-ended choices are provided for this question, it can be considered as value 1 if the answer given is *"Yes"* or 0 if the answer given is *"No."* However, what if the profit is not remarkably well, and only a moderate profit is incurred from the courier service? If we have a deeper look at the question, there is a possibility that the answer can be within a range between 0 and 1, as the amount of profitability level may be not totally 100% profitable or 100% unprofitable. Here, the role of fuzzy logic comes into play where the values can be considered in percentages (say, neither profit nor loss, i.e., 0.5). Thus, fuzzy logic tries to deal with real-world situations, which consider partial truth as a possible solution for a problem.

Figure 1.6(a) illustrates the two outcomes provided for the question *"Is the XYZ Courier Service Profitable?"* The solution provided for the question in this case is Boolean logic based, as only two extreme choices are provided for responses. On the other hand, Figure 1.6(b) illustrates the various possibilities of answers that can be provided for the same question *"Is the XYZ Courier Service Profitable?"* Here, the concept of fuzzy logic is applied to the given question by providing a few possibilities of answers such as *"fully unprofitable," "moderately unprofitable," "neither profitable nor unprofitable," "moderately profitable,"* and *"fully profitable."* The class membership is determined by the fuzzy membership function. As seen in Figure 1.6(b), the membership degree (e.g., 0, 0.25, 0.5, 0.75, and 1) is taken as output value for each response given.

One common example of using fuzzy sets in computer science is in the field of image processing, specifically in edge detection. Edge detection is the process of identifying boundaries within an image, which are areas of rapid-intensity changes. Fuzzy logic can be used to make edge detection more robust and accurate, especially in cases where the edges are not clearly defined. Let us consider a grayscale image where each pixel's intensity value represents its brightness. To detect edges using fuzzy logic, one might define a fuzzy set for "*edgeness*" that includes membership functions like "*definitely an edge*," "*possibly an edge*," and "*not an edge*". In such a case, the membership functions can be defined as follows:

(a) **Definitely an edge:** If the intensity difference is high, the pixel is more likely to be on an edge.
(b) **Possibly an edge:** If the intensity difference is moderate, the pixel might be on an edge.
(c) **Not an edge:** If the intensity difference is low, the pixel is unlikely to be on an edge.

Using these membership functions, you can assign degrees of membership to each pixel for each of these fuzzy sets. For instance, a pixel with a high-intensity difference would have a high degree of membership in the "*definitely an edge*" fuzzy set.

A crisp set, as you may know, is a set with fixed and well-defined boundaries. For instance, if the universal set (U) is a set of all states of India, a crisp set may be a set of all states of North-East India for the universal set (U). A crisp set (A) can be represented in two ways, as shown in Equations (1.1) and (1.2)

$$A = \{a_1, a_2, a_3, \dots, a_n\} \tag{1.1}$$

$$A = \{x|P(x)\} \tag{1.2}$$

Here, in Equation (1.2), the crisp set "A" consists of a collection of elements ranging from a_1 to a_n. Equation (1.2) shows the other way of representing a crisp set "A," where "A" consists of a collection of values of "x" such that it has got the property $P(x)$.

Now, a crisp set can also be represented using a characteristic function, as shown in Equation (1.3):

$$\mu_{A'}(x) = \begin{cases} 1, & \text{if } x \text{ belongs to } A \\ x, & \text{if } x \text{ does not belong to } A \end{cases} \tag{1.3}$$

A fuzzy set is a more general concept of the crisp set. It is a potential tool to deal with uncertainty and imprecision. It is usually represented by an ordered pair where the first element of the ordered pair represents the element belonging to a set, and the second element represents the degree of membership of the element to the set. The membership function value may vary from 0 to 1. Mathematically, a fuzzy set A' is represented as shown in Equation (1.4).

$$A' = \{x, \mu_{A'}(x)| x \in X\} \tag{1.4}$$

Here, the membership function value indicates the degree of belongingness and is denoted by $\mu_{A'}(x)$. Here, in Equation (1.4), "X" indicates the universal set, which consists of a set of elements "x." A membership function can either be any standard function (for example, the Gaussian function) or any user-defined function in requirement to the problem domain. As this membership function is used to represent the degree of truth in fuzzy logic, its value on the universe of discourse "X" is defined as:

$$\mu_{A'}(x) = [0, 1] \tag{1.5}$$

Here, in Equation (1.5), each value of "X" represents an element that is mapped to a value between 0 and 1.

The above explanations lead us to the understanding that a fuzzy set does not have a crisp, clearly defined boundary; rather it contains elements with only a partial degree of membership. Some of the standard properties of fuzzy sets include commutative property, associative property, distributive property, transitivity, and idempotent property. There are few other properties of fuzzy sets that will be elaborately discussed in Chapter 2.

Also, there are three standard fuzzy set operators used in fuzzy logic – fuzzy union, fuzzy intersection, and fuzzy complement. In case of complement operation, while a crisp set determines "*Who do not belong to the set?*," a fuzzy set determines "*How many elements do not belong to the set?*" Again, in case of union operation, while a crisp set determines "*Which element belongs to either of the set?*," a fuzzy set determines "*How much of the element is in either of the set?*" Lastly, in case of intersection operation, while a crisp set determines "*Which element belongs to both the sets?*," a fuzzy set determines "*How much of the element is in both the sets?*" These fuzzy operations will also be elaborately discussed in Chapter 2.

Fuzzy logic systems have proved to be extremely helpful in dealing with situations that involve decision-making. As some problems cannot be solved by simply determining whether it is True/Yes or False/No, fuzzy logic is used to offer flexibility in reasoning in order to deal with uncertainty in such a situation. The applications of fuzzy logic are varied, ranging from domestic appliances to automobiles, aviation industries to robotics.

1.4.2 Neural Network

The human brain consists of billions of interconnected neurons. These neurons are cells that use biochemical reactions to receive data, and accordingly process and transmit information. A typical neuron consists of four main parts – *dendrites* (receptors that receive signals from other neurons), *soma* (the cell body that sums up all the incoming signals to create input), *axon* (the area through which neuron signals travel to other neurons when a neuron is fired), and *synapses* (point of

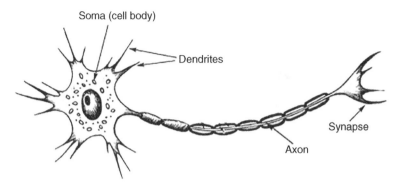

Figure 1.7 Parts of a neuron.

interconnection of one neuron with other neurons). The different parts of a neuron are illustrated in Figure 1.7. A neuron gets fired only if certain conditions are met.

The signals received on each synapse may be of excitatory or inhibitory type. When the excitatory signals exceed the inhibitory signals by certain quantified threshold value, the neuron gets fired. Accordingly, either positive or negative weights are assigned to signals – a positive weight is assigned to excitatory signals, whereas a negative weight is assigned to inhibitory signals. This weight value indicates the amount of impact of a signal on excitation of the neuron. The signals multiplied by the weight in all the incoming synapse is summed up to get a final cumulative value. If this value exceeds the threshold, then the neuron is excited. This biological model has been mathematically formulated to accomplish optimal solutions to different problems and is technically termed as *"Artificial Neural Network* (ANN)." ANN has been applied in a large number of applications such as pattern matching, pattern completion, classification, optimization, and time-series modeling.

A simple example of an ANN is given in Figure 1.8. The nodes in ANN are organized in a layered structure (input layer, hidden layer, and output layer) in which each signal is derived from an input and passes via nodes to reach the output. Each black circular structure in Figure 1.8 represents a single neuron. The simplest artificial neuron can be considered to be the threshold logic unit (TLU). The TLU operation performs a weighted sum of its inputs and then outputs either a "0" or "1." An output of "1" occurs if the sum value exceeds a threshold value and a "0" otherwise. TLU thus models the basic *"integrate-and-fire"* mechanism of real neurons.

The basic building block of every ANN is the artificial neuron. At the entrance section of an artificial neuron, inputs are assigned weights. For this, every input value is multiplied by an individual weight (Figure 1.9). In the middle section of the artificial neuron, a sum function is evaluated to find the sum of all the weighted

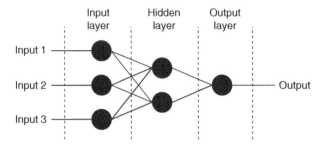

Figure 1.8 A simple example of neural network.

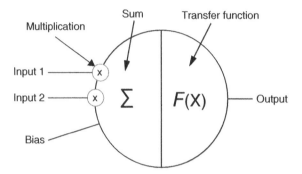

Figure 1.9 The design of an artificial neuron.

inputs and bias. Next, toward the exit of the artificial neuron, the calculated sum value is passed through an activation function, also called a transfer function.

ANN provides a simplified model of the network of neurons that occur in the human or animal brain. ANN was initially found with the sole purpose of solving problems in the same way that a human or animal brain does. However, more and more research on ANN has led to the deviation of ANN from biology to solve several challenging tasks such as speech recognition, medical diagnosis, computer vision, and social network filtering.

1.4.3 Evolutionary Computing

EC is a distinct subfield of soft computing that has gained wide popularity in the past decade in various areas of research related to natural evolution. In the case of natural evolution, an environment consists of a population of individuals that struggle for survival and strive for reproduction. The fitness of each individual decides its probability of being able to survive in a given environment. Evolutionary algorithms (EA) follow heuristic-based approach to problem solving, as these algorithms cannot be solved in polynomial time. Many variants of EC have evolved

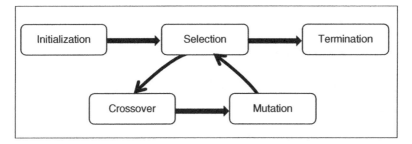

Figure 1.10 Basic steps of evolutionary algorithms.

over time, and each variant is suitable for more specific types of problems and data structures. At times, two or more evolutionary algorithms (EA) are applied together for problem solving in order to generate better results. This makes EC very popular in computer science, and a lot of research is explored in this area.

In general, *EA* mimic the behavior of biological species based on Darwin's theory of evolution and natural selection mechanism. The four main steps involved in EA include – *initialization, selection, use of genetic operators (crossover* and *mutation),* and *termination*. Each of these chronological steps makes an important contribution to the process of natural selection and also provides easy ways to modularize implementations of EA. The four basic steps of EA are illustrated in Figure 1.10, which begins with the *initialization* process and ends with the *termination* process.

The *initialization* step of EA helps in creating an initial population of solutions. The initial population is either created randomly or created considering the ideal condition(s). Once the population is created in the first step, the *selection* step is carried out to select the top-N population members. This is done using a fitness function that can accurately select the right members of the population. The next step involves use of two genetic operators – *crossover* and *mutation* – to create the next generation of population. Simply stated, these two genetic operators help in creating new offspring from the given population by introducing new genetic material into the new generation. Lastly, the EA involve the *termination* step to end the process. The termination step occurs in either of the cases – the algorithm has reached some maximum runtime, or the algorithm has reached some threshold value based on performance.

Independent research work on EA led to the development of five main streams of EA, namely, the evolutionary programming (EP), the evolution strategies (ES), swarm intelligence, the GA, and the differential evolution (DE) (as shown in Figure 1.11). A brief discussion on each of these subareas of EA is discussed in the later part of this section.

- **Evolutionary programming:** The concept of EP was originally conceived by Lawrence J. Fogel in the early 1960s. It is a stochastic optimization strategy

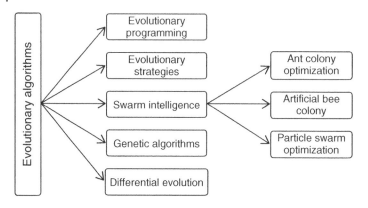

Figure 1.11   Main families of evolutionary algorithms.

similar to GA. However, a study is made on the behavioral linkage of parents and offspring in EP, while genetic operators (such as crossover operators) are applied to produce better offspring from given parents in GA. EP usually involves four main steps, as mentioned below. Step 1 involves choosing an initial population of trial solutions. Step 2 and Step 3 are repeated either until a threshold value for iteration exceeds or an adequate solution for the given problem is obtained:

○ **Step 1**: An initial population of trial solutions is chosen at random.
○ **Step 2**: Each solution is replicated into a new population. Each of these off-spring solutions is mutated.
○ **Step 3**: Each offspring solution is assessed by computing its fitness.
○ **Step 4**: Terminate.

The three common variations of EP include the *Classical EP* (uses Gaussian mutation for mutating the genome), the *Fast EP* (uses the Cauchy distribution for mutating the genome), and the *Exponential EP* (uses the double exponential distribution as the mutation operator). A few of the common application areas of EP include path planning, traffic routing, game learning, cancer detection, military planning, combinatorial optimization, and hierarchical system design.

• **Evolution strategies:** Evolution strategies (ES) is yet another optimization technique that is an instance of an evolutionary algorithm. The concept of ES was proposed by three students, Bienert, Rechenberg, and Schwefel, of the Technical University in Berlin in 1964. ES is also inspired by the theory of evolution. In fact, it is inspired mainly by the species-level process of evolution (phenotype, hereditary, and variation). The main aim of ES algorithm is to maximize the fitness of a group of candidate solutions in the context of an objective function from a domain. ES usually involves six main steps as mentioned below, out of which Steps 2–5 are repeated until convergence:

- **Step 1**: Randomly choose n population of individuals.
- **Step 2**: Create n population of parameters $\theta_1, \theta_2, \ldots, \theta_n$ by adding Gaussian noise to the best parameter (θ is the parameter vector).
- **Step 3**: Evaluate the objective function for all the parameters, and select the top-N best-performing parameters (elite parameters).
- **Step 4**: Find the best parameter (best parameter = mean(top-N elite parameters)).
- **Step 5**: Decay (minimize) the noise by some factor.
- **Step 6**: Terminate.

Mutation and selection are two main operations performed in evolution strategies. These two operations are applied continuously until a termination criterion is met. While selection operation is deterministic and based on fitness rankings, mutation is performed by adding a normally distributed random value to each vector component. The simplest case of ES can be a population of size two – the parent (current point) and the result of its mutation. In such a case, if the fitness of the mutant is either equal or better than the fitness of the parent, the mutant then becomes the parent for the next iteration. If not, the mutant is discarded.

- **Swarm intelligence:** Swarm intelligence (SI) algorithms are a special type of EA. The concept of SI was first introduced by Beni and Wang in *"swarm intelligence in cellular robotic system."* SI algorithms adapt to the concept of the behavior of swarms. A swarm is a dense group of homogenous agents that coordinate among themselves and the environment for an interesting, combined clustered behavior to emerge. The term swarm is mostly used in biological concepts to explain the coordinated behavior of a group of animals, fish, or birds. For example, a colony of ants marching together in search of food is a remarkable example of clustered behavior found in biological environment. SI algorithms mainly include particle swarm optimization (PSO), ant colony optimization (ACO), and artificial bee colony (ABC).

  (a) **Particle swarm optimization:** Particle swarm optimization (PSO) is a nature-inspired population-based stochastic optimization technique developed by Kennedy and Eberhart in 1995. PSO algorithms mimic the social behavior of animals, such as fish schooling and bird flocking, in which fish or birds move collectively to solve a task. The PSO technique works on the same principle of foraging behavior of biological species. PSO is easy to implement, as it requires adjustment of only a few parameters. This is the reason why PSO has been successfully applied in many application areas, such as the traveling salesman problem, scheduling problem, sequential ordering problem, and vehicle routing problem.

  (b) **Ant colony optimization:** Ant colony optimization (ACO) is a population-based metaheuristic mainly used to find an approximate solution to a given

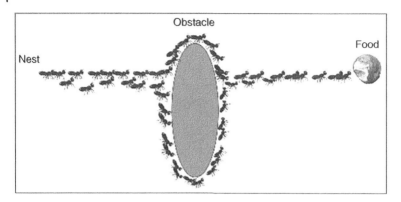

Figure 1.12 Colony of ants marching toward food source.

challenging optimization problem. ACO uses a set of software agents called *artificial ants*, which help find good solutions to a given optimization problem. Figure 1.12 shows the concept of how a colony of ants marches together to reach the food source. In between, if any obstacle is met for the first time, the ants divide among themselves to travel in both directions. However, the shorter route is noted and followed by the rest of the ant based on the pheromone (chemical substance produced and released into the environment) deposit concentration.

The pheromone smell deposited by the ant on the pathway provides an indication to the other worker ants about the presence of food in a nearby area. The pheromone trails help create indirect communication between all the nearby ants, which helps in finding the shortest path between the food source and the nest.

(c) **Artificial bee colony:** Artificial bee colony (ABC) is a computing technique that is based on the intelligent foraging behavior of honey bee swarms. This concept was first proposed by Dervis Karaboga of Erciyes University in the year 2005. The ABC model considers three types of bees: the employed bees, the onlooker bees, and the scout bees. Usually, only one artificial employed bee is hired for a food source. The artificial employed bee targets the food source and performs a dance after returning to its hive. Once the target food source is over, the employed bee shifts its position to a scout and starts hunting for a new food source. The role of onlookers is to watch the dance of employed bees and choose food sources based on the performance of the dances. The onlookers and the scouts are considered unemployed bees.

ABC accomplishes the task of hunting for food through social cooperation. In the ABC problem, each food source signifies a possible solution to the optimization problem, and the amount of nectar in the food sources decides the quality or fitness of the given solution. In fact, the quality of a food source depends on many factors, such as the amount of food source available, the ease of extracting its nectar, and also its distance from the nest. Depending on the number of food sources, the same number of employed bees is chosen to solve a problem. It is the role of employed bees to carry on the information about the quality of the food source and share this information with the other bees.

The unemployed bees also play an active role in the food hunt. One type of unemployed bee is the scout, which explores the environment near the nest in search of food. The other type of unemployed bee is the onlooker, which waits in the nest to get information about the quality of food sources from the employed bees and establish the better food sources. Communication among bees related to the quality of food sources takes place through the famous "*waggle dance*" of honey bees. This exchange of information among the three types of bees is the most vital occurrence in the formation of collective knowledge.

- **Genetic algorithms:** The concept of genetic algorithms (GA) was proposed by John Holland in the 1960s. Later, Holland along with his colleagues and students developed the concepts of GA at the University of Michigan in the 1960s and 1970s as well. A genetic algorithm is a metaheuristic that is inspired by Charles Darwin's theory of natural evolution. GA are a part of the larger class of EA that emphasize on selecting the fittest individuals for reproduction in order to produce offspring. The generated offspring inherit the characteristics of their parents and is therefore expected to have better fitness if the parents do have good fitness values. Such offspring, in turn, will have a better chance of survival. If this process continues to repeat multiple times, at some point in time, a generation of the fittest individuals will be formed.

There are basically five main phases of GA (as illustrated in Figure 1.13): population initialization, fitness function calculation, parent selection, crossover, and mutation. Initially, a random population of size "n" consisting of several individual chromosomes is chosen. Next, the fitness value of each of the individual chromosomes is calculated based on a fitness function. The fitness value plays a vital role in the decision-making of the selection of chromosomes for crossover.

In the crossover phase, every two individual chromosomes selected are reproduced using a standard crossover operator. This results in the generation of two offspring from each pair of chromosomes. The new offspring generated are then mutated to produce a better set of individual chromosomes in the newly generated population. These entire five phases of GA are repeated until a termination condition is met. Each iteration of the GA is called a *generation*, and the entire

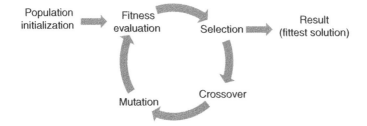

Figure 1.13 Steps followed in genetic algorithms.

set of *generations* is called a *run*. The final output (result) is the generation of the fittest individuals that have the greatest chance of survival.

- **Differential evolution:** Differential evolution (DE) is a common evolutionary algorithm stimulated by Darwin's theory of evolution and has been studied widely to solve diverse areas of optimization applications since its inception by Storn and Price in the 1990s. The various steps involved in DE include population initialization, mutation, crossover, selection, and result generation (illustrated in Figure 1.14). Prior to applying these basic steps, the parameters of DE need to be defined, such as the population size, the selection method, the crossover method, and the perturbation rate (the weight applied to random differential).

There are various popular variants of DE, some of which are mentioned below:

- The standard differential evolution (DE)
- The self-adaptive control parameters differential evolution (JDE)
- The adaptive differential evolution with optional external archive (JADE)
- The composite differential evolution (CODE)
- The self-adaptive differential evolution (SADE)

The applications of DE are varied, including synthesis and optimization of heat-integrated distillation system, optimization of an alkylation reaction, digital

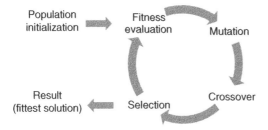

Figure 1.14 Steps followed in differential evolution.

filter design, optimization of thermal cracker operation, batch fermentation process, estimation of heat transfer parameters in bed reactor, engineering system design applied in multiobjective context, and parameter estimation in fed-batch fermentation process.

1.4.4 Machine Learning

ML is an emerging area in the field of computer science, and its applications are varied, be in medical diagnosis or speech recognition, stock market predictions or gaming, and Google translation or recommendation systems. In fact, ML is a branch of AI that allows systems to learn through experience rather being explicitly controlled through programs. Thus, the core approach in ML is to train a machine for developing the capability of learning without being explicitly programmed to provide optimum output.

ML initially follows the procedure of feeding the machine with required input data and then training the machine to a certain level so that it is able to learn and adapt to the ability of predicting the output based on the training acquired. Let us try to understand and analyze this approach with the help of a suitable example, as given in Figure 1.15. Imagine input data of various objects of different shapes and colors are fed into the computer system. The ML technique can be applied to cluster the objects based on the colors, shapes, and sizes. Figure 1.15 shows the output in which four clusters have been formed after training the model based on input provided.

Let us consider another example of ML, as shown in Figure 1.16. The emails received by a user are trained by ML algorithm to classify these emails as either legitimate mail (sent to inbox folder) or spam emails (sent to spam folder). The ML algorithm initially uses a dataset that has a list of emails classified either as spam

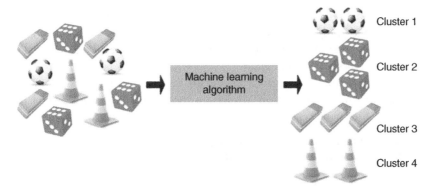

Figure 1.15 Machine learning algorithm used for training data to form clusters.

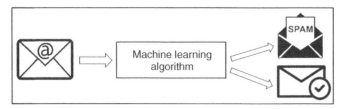

Figure 1.16 Machine learning algorithm used for classifying email as spam or legitimate.

or not spam. Once the algorithm gets fully trained and shows high accuracy in prediction, this algorithm is now all ready to be used for such similar predictions for the future.

The contribution of ML right from solving day-to-day tasks to solving complex real-life problems is tremendous. In fact, many home appliances, health care monitoring systems, mobile apps, and internet services heavily rely on using ML. Also, popular virtual personal assistants such as *Alexa*, *Siri*, and *Google Now* rely dominantly on the techniques of ML. These popular virtual assistants are a perfect example of the usage of advanced ML, as it has a number of capabilities that include voice interaction, playing audio, answering the door, dimming the lights of a room, and reading the latest headlines. Again, traffic predictions using GPS navigation services use ML techniques to provide live data to users regarding traffic congestion while traveling. ML algorithms also help companies develop chatboxes to solve user queries. It is expected that the contribution of ML in the near future will continue exceeding, and researchers have to extensively depend on such ML algorithms to build innovative tools and techniques.

There are mainly four types of ML – SL, unsupervised learning, semi-supervised learning, and RL. Under the umbrella of SL are classification and regression, which use a dataset having known inputs and outputs. Unsupervised learning, on the other hand, uses a dataset to identify hidden patterns. Under the umbrella of unsupervised learning falls clustering and association analysis. Semi-supervised learning lies between SL and unsupervised learning and handles the drawbacks of both these types of ML techniques.

Figure 1.17 illustrates the various types of ML used for different variety of data and problems. All these types of ML have a special role to perform, which is explained in brief next. Let us now try to understand these four types of ML in brief.

- **Supervised learning (SL):** Most of the ML techniques are based on SL, which works on the basis of supervision. Basically, supervised learning techniques train machines using "labeled" datasets. Such datasets have input variables that are used by a mapping function to derive the output variable(s). This can be mathematically expressed as $P = f(Q)$, where Q is the input data, and P is the

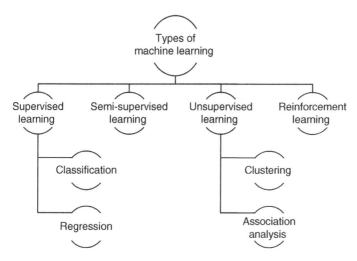

Figure 1.17 Types of machine learning.

output. SL thus uses the input variables and the corresponding output having "labeled" data to train machines by approximating the mapping function. The training is carried out accurately to an extent such that when a new input data ($q1$) is fed, a perfect prediction can be made to display the output variable (P) for that data ($q1$).

To clear the idea of SL, let us consider a simple example. Let us assume that a dataset that consists of images of three varying animals – say, *dog*, *goat*, and *cat*, which are provided as input to the machine. The output variable, also called the labeled variable, stores the values as either "*dog*," "*goat*," or "*cat*." Now, a SL model is trained with this labeled dataset that can differentiate among these three animals and correctly predict the output. This learning model is illustrated in Figure 1.18, in which the labeled data are trained, and the model is tested with a test dataset (unlabeled data) to check the accuracy of the predicted output once the training is completed. If the accuracy of prediction is very high, the model can be set to be trained and ready for use for future predictions.

There are two main notable techniques of supervised ML – classification and regression. Both these techniques have a similar goal of predicting the output (dependent attribute) based on the series of input data provided. Classification deals with prediction of discrete class label(s), whereas regression deals with prediction of continuous quantity. Also, a classification problem is mainly evaluated using accuracy as the evaluation metric, whereas a regression problem is usually evaluated using root mean square error (RSME).

(a) **Classification:** Classification is a type of supervised ML as it considers "labeled" data to perform the task of prediction of output. The "labeled"

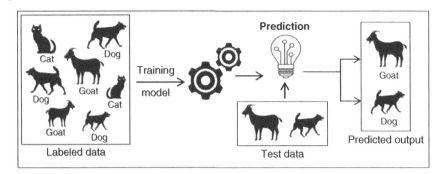

Figure 1.18 Supervised learning.

variables are termed as *classifiers*, which play a major role in training the algorithm. It approximates a mapping function (f) from input variables (Q) to discrete output variables (P). For a given observation, the primary task of classification is to predict the value of class. The technique of classification is applied in many significant areas where new observations are needed to be categorized, such as spam filtering, face detection, credit approval, fraud detection, optical character recognition, market segmentation, and so on.

For a given observation, the primary task of classification is to predict the value of class.

As shown in Figure 1.18, the problem given is of classification in which the output to be obtained belongs to any of the three classes – *cat*, *dog*, or *goat*. Another example of a problem of classification would be if the output to be predicted is either Yes or No, such as "Diabetes" or "No Diabetes," "Provide Loan" or "Do not Provide Loan," "Spam Mail" or "Legitimate Mail," and so on.

Classification techniques are further classified under two models – the *lazy learners* and the *eager learners*. In the case of *lazy learning* model, the training time taken is comparatively less; however, the prediction time is more compared to the *eager learning* model. Examples of lazy learners include the k-Nearest Neighbor (kNN) classification model, and case-based learning model. Eager learners construct the classification model from the given training data even before receiving any test data. Examples of eager learners include decision trees, Naïve Bayes, and ANNs.

(b) **Regression:** In regression, the main task is to approximate a mapping function (f) from input variables (X) to a continuous output variable (Y). The continuous output variable (Y) should denote a quantity and has to be a real value, such as an integer or floating-point value. Given a new set of input values, regression can make a prediction of the corresponding quantitative output (y), based on the study of previous corresponding (x, y)

paired values. Thus, regression analysis is a predictive modeling technique that analyses the relationship between a dependent variable (the new y value) based on the independent variable (the given x value). For example, given a series of values of the number of sales of tea cups per month at a tea stall, a prediction on the amount of sale of tea can be made for any near-future months.

There are various types of regression models, which differ mainly on three factors – the number of independent variables considered, the shape of the regression line, and the type of dependent variable being used. If only one independent variable is used, it is a case of simple regression, whereas if more than one independent variable is used, it is a case of multiple regression. Moreover, both simple and multiple regressions can be either linear or nonlinear. Figure 1.19 mentions the various standard regression models used for SL for continuous variables.

i. **Linear regression:** The most common type of regression used is the linear regression in which a linear relationship is maintained between the dependent and independent variables. Here, the dependent variable is continuous, whereas the independent variable(s) can be either discrete or continuous.

ii. **Logistic regression:** In logistic regression, the dependent or target variable can belong to only one of the possible binary values, such as 1 or 0, True or False, Positive or Negative, and so on. Its probability value ranges between 0 and 1.

iii. **Polynomial regression:** When the relationship between the dependent and the independent variables is nonlinear in nature, polynomial regression is used.

iv. **Ridge regression:** If two or more independent variables are used that have high intercorrelations among them, it is the case of multicollinearity. Ridge regression is a type of regression that can be best used for dealing with multicollinearity in multiple regression data.

v. **Lasso regression:** LASSO stands for least absolute shrinkage and selection operator. Lasso regression, also called penalized regression, uses the shrinkage technique to determine the coefficients. Shrinkage

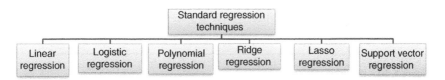

Figure 1.19   The two main types of regression.

is a concept in which the data values are shrunk toward a central or middle point.

vi. **Support vector regression (SVR):** This method supports both linear and nonlinear regressions. It uses the concepts of hyperplanes, kernels, boundary lines, and support vectors that are also used in the case of support vector machines (SVM).

- **Unsupervised learning:** Many of the real-time datasets are not provided with any labels. Such datasets are not classified beforehand and hence have no class labels. SL fails to handle such datasets to solve a ML-based task. This is where unsupervised learning is used to find commonalities among its input data without the help of any labels or classifications. The primary goal of unsupervised learning is to discover hidden patterns from the input data provided.

To understand unsupervised learning, let us consider the same example given in Figure 1.18. In this Figure, all the data in the dataset are labeled "*cat*," "*dog*," and "*goat*." Now, imagine that the dataset is not provided with any label. The primary task of unsupervised learning is to group similar data based on some features of input data, such as color, size, pattern, and so on. Figure 1.20 illustrates a case of unsupervised learning in which a dataset without having any labels is fed into the training model to generate similar clusters as output. As can be seen in Figure 1.20, the dataset consists of several different images of cats, dogs, and goats. The results obtained are the three clusters that are grouped based on the common features (similarities) among each animal.

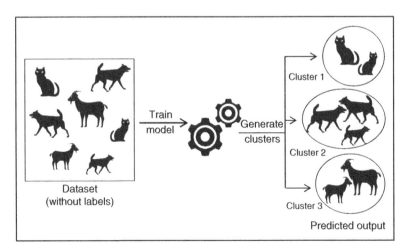

Figure 1.20 Unsupervised learning.

There are two main notable techniques of unsupervised ML – clustering and association rule mining. As these are unsupervised learning techniques, the models are not supervised using any training dataset. Let us now discuss the concepts of clustering and association rule mining in brief:

(a) **Clustering:** Clustering is a simple method in which items or objects are grouped into clusters based on similarities. The similarities are generated based on the presence or absence of some features among the objects. A real-time example where clustering is used is in recommender systems of e-commerce sites, which groups items of similar tastes for a user based on his/her previous purchasing experiences.

There are various clustering algorithms, and a choice of which algorithm is to be chosen relies on whether the algorithm can scale to the given input dataset. The four types of clustering are explained next:

    i. **Centroid-based clustering:** This clustering approach works by repeatedly finding the centroid of each cluster until the results become stable. A classic way to apply centroid-based clustering is the K-means clustering, where "k" refers to the number of clusters to be formed. Initially, "k" number of points are chosen at random for selection of centroids. The rest of the data points are measured and grouped to the nearest centroid based on a distance measure. The centroids are then again determined based on the cluster formed. The steps are repeated iteratively until convergence.

    ii. **Density-based clustering:** This clustering approach connects areas of high density into clusters. While doing so, the outliers are often left out and may not be included in any of the clusters formed. The distributions can be of arbitrary shape or size, as the primary approach is to consider all objects in the same cluster if they belong to dense areas or connectivities.

    iii. **Distribution-based clustering:** This clustering approach uses the concepts of probability distribution such as Gaussian distribution or binomial distribution to form clusters. The basic idea is that as the distance from the center of the distribution increases, the probability of a point belonging to that distribution decreases.

    iv. **Hierarchical clustering:** This clustering approach creates a hierarchy of clusters in the form of a tree. The tree-like structure that is formed to create several clusters is called *dendrogram*. The hierarchical clustering may follow either of the two approaches: agglomerative or divisive. The *agglomerative approach* is a bottom-up approach that initially begins by considering each data item as a single cluster and then proceeds by merging the closest pair of clusters. The *divisive approach*, on the other hand, works just the opposite of the *agglomerative approach*. The *divisive approach* initially begins by considering only one big cluster that consists of all the data points. It gradually then splits the big cluster into smaller clusters based on nonsimilarity of data points.

An example of clustering is well explained and illustrated in Figure 1.19. The example explains how three clusters have been formed based on the similarity of animal species by using an unsupervised clustering technique.

(b) **Association analysis:** This unsupervised learning approach was introduced by Rakesh Agrawal, Tomasz Imieliński, and Arun Swami. The basic idea was to make a market basket analysis of the products sold in a supermarket. This approach helps in finding the itemsets that are frequently purchased together so as to understand the customer purchasing patterns. This is done by generating more and more new rules by analyzing the dataset. Usually, the dataset considered is large, and the final goal of association rule learning is to train a machine to be able to mimic the human brain for feature extraction and abstract association capabilities.

Let us understand the concept better with the help of an example. For example, a rule $\{milk, coffee\} \Rightarrow \{sugar\}$ that is discovered based on the transaction sales of a supermarket indicates that customers have shown a strong tendency to buy the product *sugar* when *milk* and *coffee* have been bought together. Such kind of rules generated can help a supermarket increase its sales through better product placements and promotional pricing of items when bought together.

If we consider Table 1.2, we find that there are seven transaction details being considered. In each transaction, it shows what the lists of items purchased by a customer are. Now, the interestingness of a rule can be

Table 1.2 Transaction details of a supermarket store.

TID	Purchased items
1	Milk, coffee, butter
2	Eggs, butter, jam
3	Milk, coffee, sugar
4	Spices, rice, juice
5	Milk, coffee, eggs, cake, cream, sugar
6	Milk, coffee, biscuits, sugar
7	Milk, juice, soap, butter

evaluated by using the standard constraints called *support* and *confidence*. While support determines how frequently itemsets appear in a dataset, confidence indicates how often a rule has been found to be true.

To understand how *support* is calculated for association analysis, let us consider a rule. If a rule $X \Rightarrow Y$ holds with support S, it means $S\%$ of the transactions in the dataset contain $X \cup Y$. This support value S is compared with the threshold support value, and if S is found to be greater than the threshold support value, it is said to have the *minimum support*. Again, if the rule $X \Rightarrow Y$ holds with confidence C, it means $C\%$ of the transactions in the dataset that contain X also contains Y. This confidence value C is compared with the threshold confidence value, and it is said to have the *minimum confidence* if C found to be greater than the threshold confidence value.

Let us proceed to find *support* and *confidence* for the rule *{milk, coffee}* $\Rightarrow$ *{sugar}* by considering Table 1.2. The support value for this rule will be calculated from the given seven transactions as 3/7, which is 0.43. This is calculated by finding out how many transactions contain the items *milk, coffee,* and *sugar* out of a total of seven transactions. This calculated support value is compared with the minimum support value (a threshold value) to determine the strength of the rule. Now, if we consider the threshold support value as 30%, the rule exceeds this value as the calculated support value is 43%.

Another measure of interestingness of a rule is confidence. The confidence value that can be calculated from the given seven transactions is 3/4, which is 0.75. This is calculated by finding out how many transactions contain all the items *milk, coffee,* and *sugar* out of a total of four transactions that contain only items *milk* and *coffee*. This calculated confidence value is compared with the minimum confidence value (a threshold value) to determine the strength of the rule. Now, if we consider the threshold confidence value as 50%, the rule exceeds this value as the calculated confidence value is 75%. Based on the calculations of support and confidence, the determination of *frequent itemsets* is made for market basket analysis for any departmental store.

- **Semi-supervised learning:** This learning falls between SL and unsupervised learning, and is an approach often used to deal with partially labeled data and mostly unlabeled data. Semi-supervised learning tries to handle the disadvantages of both supervised and unsupervised learning to solve real-time applications. At times, data need to be hand-labeled by human, especially by a data engineer, data scientist, or ML specialist to carry out SL. However, this is a costly process and requires huge time for labeling all data. This is where semi-supervised learning balances the disadvantage of SL by carrying out training with mostly unlabeled data and only a few labeled data. Also, unsupervised learning, owing to its limitations of dealing with only unlabeled data, cannot handle a variety of applications. Semi-supervised learning also resolves this issue, as it considers a few labeled data during the training process.

As semi-supervised learning is more effective, it is used to solve a variety of real-world ML problems. In cases where 100% of the dataset is unlabeled, this learning technique considers manual labeling of a small amount of data to train the model, also called the base model. Only a small portion of data is manually labeled, as it is a very tedious and time-consuming process. The next step is the process of pseudo-labeling that uses the partially trained base model and makes predictions for the rest of the unlabeled data. In each iteration the unlabeled data gets labeled, thereby increasing the number of labeled data for the entire dataset. Such unlabeled data are separately trained, and given labels are called pseudo-labels, as these labels will not be fully accurate. With more number of iterations, the accuracy of the model is increased, and the model is then considered ready for any new predictions to be made.

- **Reinforcement learning (RL):** RL is a feedback-based ML technique that relies on a software agent for performing some actions. The agent behaves in an environment by performing some actions and accordingly produces results. If the agent performs a correct action in the learning environment, the environment in turn sends feedback to the agent in the form of an award. However, if the agent performs an incorrect action, the environment sends a penalty as a reward to the agent. Figure 1.21 illustrates this simple feedback system of RL. Based on the feedback, the agent accordingly tries to adapt or improve to the environment. One advantage of this technique is that the agent need not be pretrained about the environment, as it can learn about it through the feedback it receives during the training phase.

  RL has recently gained much importance, as its applications have increased over time in the last decade. The concept of RL is applied in playing games (such as chess), robot decision-making, self-driving cars, operations research, GA, swarm intelligence, and many more. The primary difference between SL

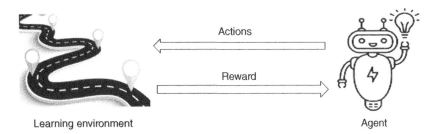

Actions

Reward

Learning environment   Agent

Figure 1.21 Reinforcement learning.

and RL is that SL makes a decision based on the initial input provided, whereas RL makes a decision sequentially by considering the inputs generated at every new phase of RL. The decisions made in RL at each level are independent of each other, whereas the decisions made in SL rely on the decisions made at the previous level.

1.4.5 Other Techniques of Soft Computing

There are several other soft computing techniques such as PR, chaos theory, and evidential reasoning (ER). A brief description of all of these techniques is given next:

- **Probabilistic reasoning (PR):** Real-world situations many a times deal with uncertainty. In such cases, PR may be used to indicate the degree of uncertainty involved. As we know, probability is the chance that an uncertain event will occur, and its value is between 0 and 1. PR uses this concept of probability to handle uncertain situations. Generally, the probability of occurrence of an uncertain event is calculated as:

$$\text{Probability of occurrence } (P) = \frac{\text{number of desired Outcomes } (N)}{\text{total number of outcomes } (T)}$$

A belief network, also known as a Bayesian network or Bayes network, is a probabilistic graphical model used to represent a set of variables and their conditional dependencies via a directed acyclic graph (DAG). The nodes in a DAG represent variables (can be unknown parameters, latent variables, observable quantities, etc.), and the edges represent conditional dependencies. If two nodes are not connected in the graph, it indicates that the two variables are conditionally independent of each other. A belief can be considered as the occurrence of a state. For instance, a switch can have two states – either *on* or *off*. The probability of the occurrence of the state {switch = "on"} is 50%. Similarly, the belief in the state {switch = "off"} is also 50%. In this way, for a given problem, all beliefs of all possible states of a node are stored in a table called *Conditional Probability Table*.

To define conditional probability using a traditional approach, the concept of joint probability is used. For instance, for an uncertain event Q, the probability $P(Q|R)$ represents a belief in P, assuming that R is known. The conditional probability formula $P(Q|R)$ can be equated using the concept of joint probability $P(Q, R)$ as given below.

$$P(Q|R) = \frac{P(Q, R)}{P(R)}$$

However, it is also possible to define $P(Q \mid R)$ without referring to the joint probability as follows:

$$P(Q|R) = \frac{P(R|Q)P(Q)}{P(R)}$$

This is called Bayes rule and is often used for updating a belief about a hypothesis Q in the light of new evidence R.

Bayesian networks provide a natural representation of (casually induced) conditional independence. It has replaced many rule-based systems by being less rigorous and more robust. However, one major limitation of a Bayesian network is that it typically requires initial knowledge of many probabilities. Another issue is that the output is also largely dependent on the quality and extent of prior knowledge.

- **Chaos theory:** Chaos theory is well-suited to be used for problems that are highly sensitive to initial conditions. In such a case, a slight difference in initial conditions (for example, a change in initial value in the second place after the decimal point) leads to highly diverging outcome. The chaotic behavior can be experienced in our nature, such as changes in weather. Robert L. Devaney has classified a dynamic system as chaotic based on the following three properties:
  - *It must be sensitive to initial conditions (the "butterfly effect")*: The data points in a chaotic system are arbitrarily in close approximation to each other with significantly different future paths.
  - *It must be topologically mixing*: The topological transitivity or topological mixing relates to the evolution of the system over time such that any given region may eventually overlap with another region.
  - *It must have dense periodic orbits*: Every point in the space is approached arbitrarily closely by periodic orbits.

  To sum up, chaos theory as defined by Kellert is "the qualitative study of unstable aperiodic behavior in deterministic nonlinear systems" (Kellert 1993, p. 2). As understood, a chaotic system is nonlinear and sensitive to initial conditions. There is also no periodic behavior in such systems, and the motion remains random. Considering these characteristics, a few applications based on chaos theory include observation of weather patterns, stock market predictions, algorithmic trading, bird migration patterns, observation of social phenomena, robotics, and study of brain waves.

- **Evidential reasoning:** Evidential reasoning (ER) is a recent approach that has been developed mainly on the basis of AI, decision theory, statistical analysis, and computer technology. In decision theory, ER approach is a generic evidence-based multi criteria decision analysis (MCDA) approach and can deal with problems having uncertainties that include randomness and ignorance. ER supports assessments, decision analysis, and evaluation activities. For instance, ER contributes to the environmental impact assessment for developing a proposal or a project related to the environment.

  The ER approach constitutes the modeling framework of multi-criteria decision-making (MCDM) problems using the following concepts:

o **Belief structures:** The belief structure is used to represent the performance of an alternative assessed against a criterion.
o **Belief decision matrix:** A belief decision matrix is a list of values stored in rows and columns in which each element is a belief structure and is used to identify, analyze, and rate the performance of relationships between sets of values.
o **ER algorithms:** This algorithm is mainly governed by using four basic steps: generation of basic probability masses, combining basic probability masses, generation of combined degrees of belief, and generation of utility interval.
o **Rule- and utility-based information transformation techniques:** It involves both qualitative and quantitative data for decision-making to transform various sets of assessment grades to a common framework of discernment.

As soft computing is tolerant of uncertainty, imprecision, and approximation, it allows researchers to carry out various experiments to solve real-world complex problems. As discussed at the beginning of this chapter, the three core components of soft computing include the fuzzy logic-based computing, neurocomputing, and GA. All these techniques contribute greatly to develop probable solutions to a problem rather than a precise fixed solution. Hence, soft computing is a boon to the computing world for solving problems that are not possible to be solved by traditional computational models.

Exercises

A) Choose the correct answer from among the alternatives given:
  a) The truth values of fuzzy logic can be:
    i) Either 0 or 1
    ii) Less than 0 or greater than 1
    iii) Between 0 and 1
    iv) Between −1 and 1
  b) Which among the following is not a part of a neuron?
    i) Dendrite
    ii) Axon
    iii) Soma
    iv) Spinase
  c) Which among the following is not a regression technique?
    i) Polynomial regression
    ii) Associative regression
    iii) Lasso regression
    iv) Ridge regression

d) Each iteration of the genetic algorithm is called:
  i) Generation
  ii) Run
  iii) Itemset
  iv) Mutation

e) The probability P(A|B) in Bayes theorem can be expressed as:
  i) $P(A|B) = \frac{P(A,B)P(B)}{P(A)}$
  ii) $P(A|B) = \frac{P(B|A)P(A)}{P(B)}$
  iii) $P(A|B) = \frac{P(B|A)P(B)}{P(A)}$
  iv) $P(A|B) = \frac{P(A,B)P(A)}{P(B)}$

f) In association analysis, *confidence* _____
  i) Determines the total number of itemsets in a dataset
  ii) Determines how frequently itemsets appear in a dataset
  iii) Indicates how often a rule has been found to be true
  iv) Indicates how many itemsets are purchased on an average per transaction

g) Each connection link in ANN is linked with _____ that contains statics about the input signal.
  i) Activation function
  ii) Bias
  iii) Weights
  iv) Neurons

h) Where can the Bayes rule be used?
  i) For answering probabilistic queries
  ii) For dealing with training and testing data
  iii) For building a decision tree
  iv) For creating clusters of nodes

B) Answer the following questions:
  1) Define soft computing. Explain, in brief, the various components of soft computing.
  2) Who is the founder of fuzzy logic? How is a membership function defined in fuzzy logic?
  3) Explain the following machine learning techniques:
     a) Association analysis
     b) Clustering
     c) Reinforcement learning
  4) Differentiate between:
     a) Soft computing and hard computing
     b) Crisp logic and fuzzy logic

c) Supervised learning and unsupervised learning
d) Classification and regression
e) Probabilistic reasoning (PR) and evidential reasoning

5) What is an artificial neuron? List some commercial practical applications of ANNs.

6) Define the terms chromosome and crossover as used in genetic algorithms. Explain, in detail, all the various phases of genetic algorithms.

7) State the importance of semi-supervised learning. List some commercial practical applications of machine learning.

8) Explain the various types of machine learning. What are the applications of supervised machine learning in modern businesses?

2

Fuzzy Computing

The Father of fuzzy lozic, Lotfi. A. Zadeh, proposed the idea of fuzzy computing in the year 1965, but the popularity of fuzzy computing was mainly gained during the 1990s. Some solutions of real-life problems can generate crisp results, like *"Yes"* or *"No,"* *"True"* or *"false,"* *"0"* or *"1."* That means, an element can either belong to or do not belong to the set of Universe Ú. Now, if the element belongs to the set of Universe Ú, it is considered 1, else 0. This set of elements having precise output is known as the *"crisp set,"* which can be represented with the help of a membership function to represent the output. Figure 2.1 illustrates the difference between a crisp set and a fuzzy set. While the crisp set displays binary output, fuzzy set displays a more realistic, varying output.

If we consider an element y and a set S, the membership function can be denoted as given in Eq. (2.1). A membership function (μ) represents the relationship between the values of elements in a set and their degree of membership in the set. Here, in Eq. (2.1), the output can be either 1 (y belongs to the set S) or 0 (y does not belong to the set S), based on the given membership function.

$$\mu_S(y) = \begin{cases} 1, & \text{if } y \in S \\ 0, & \text{if } y \notin S \end{cases} \tag{2.1}$$

However, in real-life problems, solutions may not be always attained in crisp form. This is where the role of fuzzy logic comes into play. Each element of a fuzzy set can partially belong to one set and can also partially belong to other sets. Hence, fuzziness indicates vagueness and uncertainty, as there is no finite output for each given element. To understand this, let us take a simple example. A male person is considered tall if he is equal or above 5.5 ft, else he is considered short. This is an example of a crisp logic, as illustrated in Figure 2.2(a) where, 0 indicates short, and 1 indicates tall.

In real-life circumstances, it is not always possible to consider a person as either tall or short based on a precise value (5.5 ft in this example). In Figure 2.2(a), if a person's height is 5.49 ft, he will be considered as short. This is so because, as

Principles of Soft Computing Using Python Programming: Learn How to Deploy Soft Computing Models in Real World Applications, First Edition. Gypsy Nandi.
© 2024 The Institute of Electrical and Electronics Engineers, Inc. Published 2024 by John Wiley & Sons, Inc.

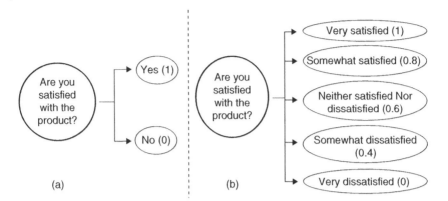

Figure 2.1 (a) Crisp set of values (b) Fuzzy set of values.

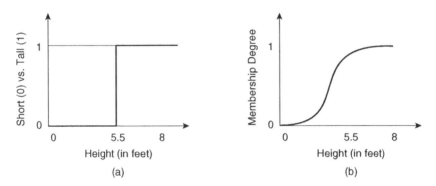

Figure 2.2 (a) Crisp logic; (b) fuzzy logic.

per the condition, a person can be considered tall if he is having the minimum 5.5 ft of height. However, the person has fallen short of only 0.05 ft so as to be considered tall.

Figure 2.2(b) illustrates another case in which varying levels of height measurement is considered, such as, very short (here, $\mu_U(x) = 0.2$), short (here, $\mu_U(x) = 0.4$), average (here, $\mu_U(x) = 0.5$), tall (here, $\mu_U(x) = 0.8$), and very tall (here, $\mu_U(x) = 1$). That is, in case of fuzzy logic example, we considered the varying degrees of height and can be quantified as *very short*, *short*, *average*, *tall*, and *very tall*. This degree of association can be technically coined as membership value. Mathematically, it can be formulated as shown in Eq. (2.2).

$$\mu_U(x) = [0, 1] \tag{2.2}$$

Based on the value of height of a male person, we can estimate the degree of his tallness. In this case, the output is not crisp or precise – tall or not tall (i.e., short).

Rather, the output can be very short, very tall, or even average, considering the varying value of height. It is a better approach in this case, as one is estimating the varying possible output by associating it with the degree of tallness. Let μ_S: y indicate the degree of membership of y to set S. A minimum degree value of 0 indicates that y is least bound to set S, and a value of 1 indicates that y is strongly bound to set S. Any other value between 0 and 1 indicates the varying degree of strength by which y is bound to set S.

2.1 Fuzzy Sets

The word fuzzy indicates *"ambiguity"* or *"vagueness."* Unlike crisp values, fuzzy values include membership values anywhere between the range 0 and 1, i.e., there is no clear or crisp boundary. A fuzzy set is any set that contains an ordered pair, in which the first element represents the element belonging to a set, and the second element represents the degree of membership of the element to the set. Let us now understand the mathematical representation of a fuzzy set. If U is a universe of discourse, and x is a particular element of U, then a fuzzy set S defined on U can be written as a collection of ordered pairs. Mathematically, the fuzzy set can be represented as in Eq. (2.3).

Here, $\mu_S(x)$ is the membership function of set S.

$$S = \{x, \mu_S(x) \mid x \in U\} \tag{2.3}$$

Let $U = \{s1, s2, s3, s4\}$ be the reference set of fruits. Let S be the fuzzy set of *"sweet"* fruits, where *"sweet"* is a fuzzy term. $S = \{(s1, 0.25)\ (s2, 0.75)\ (s3, 0.9)\ (s4, 0.5)\}$. Here S indicates that the sweetness of $s1$ is 0.25, $s2$ is 0.75, and so on.

The membership function fully defines a fuzzy set and can be graphically represented in any shapes, such as triangular, z-shape, trapezoidal, sigmoidal, or Gaussian. The shape of the membership function is dependent on the chosen problem domain and the kind of standard function being used. This function can be any user-defined function, sigmoid function, piecewise linear function, Gaussian function, and many more. Let us consider an example of a membership function for creating a fuzzy set having real numbers near the zero (0) value. The membership function can be defined as given in Eq. (2.4).

$$\mu_S(x) = \frac{1}{1 + x^2} \tag{2.4}$$

Considering Eq. (2.4), let us now tabulate few values of $\mu_S(x)$ with respect to x and also plot the corresponding graph for the membership function.

As can be seen from Table 2.1 and from Figure 2.3, when "x" value is 0, the membership function value is exactly 1; it is so as the membership function is based on finding numbers close to 0. For 1 and −1, the membership function value is

Table 2.1 The x value and the corresponding membership function value.

X	$\mu_S(x)$
−3	0.1
−2	0.2
−1	0.5
0	1
1	0.5
2	0.2
3	0.1

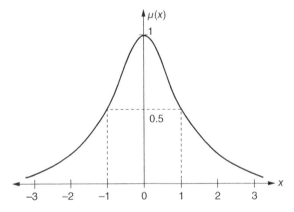

Figure 2.3 Membership function of fuzzy set having real number close to 0.

0.5 (close to 1). For the remaining values (such as −3, −2, 2, and 3), the membership function values vary between 0 and 1. The membership degree is close to 1 if the x value is close to 0. As the x value moves far away from 0, the membership function value accordingly moves far away from 1.

2.1.1 Features of Fuzzy Membership Functions

(a) **Support**: The support of fuzzy set A is a crisp set that contains all elements $\mathbf{x} \in X$ such that $\mu_A(x) > 0$, i.e., the membership value of the elements is greater than 0.

$$\text{support}(A) = \{\mathbf{x}: \mu_A(x) > 0 \, \forall \, \mathbf{x} \in X\}$$

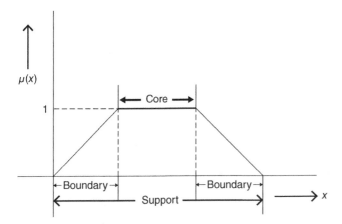

Figure 2.4 Support, core, and boundary of fuzzy membership function.

If support is finite, it is called as *compact support*. If the support returns a single element, it is called as *fuzzy singleton*.

(b) **Core**: The core of a fuzzy set A is a crisp set that contains elements for which the membership value is 1.

$$\text{core}(A) = \{x: \mu_A(x) = 1 \,\forall\, x \in X\}$$

Figure 2.4 illustrates the support and core of a fuzzy set in a graph form that contains elements x along the x-axis and the membership function $\mu(x)$ along the y-axis. As can be examined, support and core maintain a boundary in which the membership value of core is always 1 and of support is always greater than 0. Boundaries of fuzzy sets comprise of only that part of elements x whose membership value is given by $\mu_A(x) \in [0, 1]$.

```
If A = {1/p, 0.4/q, 0.7/r, 0/s, 0.9/t}, then,
    Support(A)  = {p, q, r, t}
    Core(A)     = {p}
```

(c) **Height**: The height of a fuzzy set A is the maximum value of the membership function. If the height value is 1, it is considered as a normal fuzzy set. However, if the height value is less than 1, it is considered as a subnormal fuzzy set. The height of a fuzzy set is represented as:

$$\text{Height}(A) = \text{Max}\{\mu_A(x)\} \,\forall\, x \in X$$

(d) **Normal fuzzy set**: A fuzzy set whose membership function has at least one value equal to 1. In such a case, the core of a fuzzy set is nonempty,

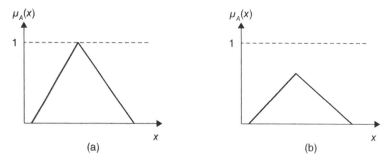

Figure 2.5   (a) Normal fuzzy set; (b) subnormal fuzzy set.

and its height is equal to 1. Also, for a fuzzy set having one and only one element whose membership value is equal to one, such an element is typically referred to as the *prototypical element*. Contrary to the normal fuzzy set is the subnormal fuzzy set whose height value will be always less than 1. Figure 2.5 illustrates the difference between a normal fuzzy set and a subnormal fuzzy set.

(e) **Convex fuzzy set**: Here the membership function is either strictly monotonically increasing, strictly monotonically decreasing, or strictly monotonically increasing and then strictly monotonically decreasing for increasing value of the element in the universe of discourse. A fuzzy set A is convex if:

$$\text{for } a, b, c \in A \text{ and } a < b < c, \mu_A(b) >= \min\left[\mu_A(a), \mu_A(c)\right]$$

Figure 2.6 illustrates the difference between a convex fuzzy set and a nonconvex fuzzy set. As can be understood from the figure, in Case (a) the membership function is initially strictly monotonically increasing and then strictly monotonically decreasing for increasing value of the element in the universe of discourse. Hence, it is a case of convex fuzzy set, which is not so in case of Case (b).

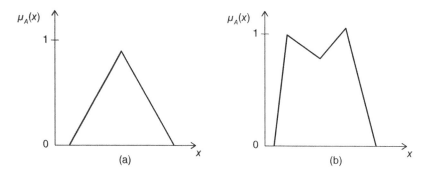

Figure 2.6   (a) Convex fuzzy set; (b) nonconvex fuzzy set.

2.2   Fuzzy Set Operations

There are basically three standard fuzzy set operations. To understand this, let us consider two fuzzy sets A and B for which the following operations hold true:

Fuzzy Union/Fuzzy OR $\mu_{A \cup B}(x) = \mu_A(x) \vee \mu_B(x) = \max\{\mu_A(x), \mu_B(x)\}$
Fuzzy Intersection/Fuzzy AND $\mu_{A \cap B}(x) = \mu_A(x) \wedge \mu_B(x) = \min\{\mu_A(x), \mu_B(x)\}$
Fuzzy Complement/Fuzzy NOT $\mu_{\neg A}(x) = 1 - \mu_A(x)$

Figure 2.7 illustrates the three standard fuzzy set operations – (a) fuzzy union ($\mu_{A \cup B}(x)$), (b) fuzzy intersection ($\mu_{A \cap B}(x)$), and (c) fuzzy complement ($\mu_{\neg A}(x)$). These operations are highlighted in grey color. For the union operation in the fuzzy sets A and B, the result obtained is the maximum value of the membership function, and for the intersection operation, the result is the minimum of both. In case of fuzzy complement, the result generated for fuzzy set A includes all elements in the Universal set that are not in A.

Let us try to find fuzzy union, fuzzy intersection, and fuzzy complement for two fuzzy sets X and Y, as given in Program 2.1. This is a Python program that initially creates two fuzzy sets X and Y having four elements each – set X contains the values 0.3, 0.5, 0.6, and 0.7, and set Y contains the values 0.4, 0.8, 0.2, and 0.6. The `dict ()` function in Python is used in the program to create a dictionary of values. Also, sets U, I, and C are used to create sets for fuzzy union, fuzzy intersection, and fuzzy complement of X and Y.

Program 2.1   *Fuzzy Set Operations*

```
X = dict ()
Y = dict ()
U = dict ()        #for fuzzy union
I = dict ()        #for fuzzy intersection
C = dict ()        #for fuzzy complement
```

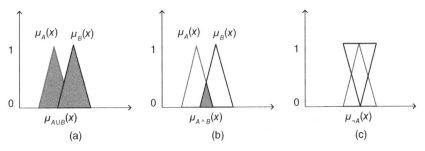

Figure 2.7   Fuzzy set operations: (a) Fuzzy union; (b) fuzzy intersection; and (c) fuzzy complement.

```
X = {"x1": 0.3, "x2": 0.5, "x3": 0.6, "x4": 0.7}        #first fuzzy
                                                          set
Y = {"x1": 0.4, "x2": 0.8, "x3": 0.2, "x4": 0.6}        #second fuzzy
                                                          set

print('Fuzzy Set #1 :', X)
print('Fuzzy Set #2 :', Y)

#Finding fuzzy union
or X_val, Y_val in zip(X, Y):
        X_values = X[X_val]
        Y_values = Y[Y_val]
        if X_values > Y_values:
            U[X_val] = X_values
        else:
            U[Y_val] = Y_values

#Finding fuzzy complement
for X_val, Y_val in zip(X, Y):
        X_values = X[X_val]
        Y_values = Y[Y_val]
        if X_values < Y_values:
            I[X_val] = X_values
        else:
            I[Y_val] = Y_values

#Finding fuzzy complement for first fuzzy set
for X_val in X:
   C[X_val]= 1 - X[X_val]

print('Fuzzy Set Union : ', U)
print('Fuzzy Set Intersection : ', I)
print('Fuzzy Set Complement : ', C)
```

The output of the Program 2.1 is given next. The output prints both the fuzzy sets, and also displays the union and intersection of these two sets. Finally, the complement of the first set is also displayed in the output.

Fuzzy Set #1 : {'x1': 0.3, 'x2': 0.5, 'x3': 0.6, 'x4': 0.7}
Fuzzy Set #2 : {'x1': 0.4, 'x2': 0.8, 'x3': 0.2, 'x4': 0.6}
Fuzzy Set Union : {'x1': 0.4, 'x2': 0.8, 'x3': 0.6, 'x4': 0.7}
Fuzzy Set Intersection : {'x1': 0.3, 'x2': 0.5, 'x3': 0.2, 'x4': 0.6}
Fuzzy Set Complement : {'x1': 0.7, 'x2': 0.5, 'x3': 0.4, 'x4': 0.3}

2.3   Fuzzy Set Properties

Most of the properties of crisp set also holds true for fuzzy set. Considering X and Y as two fuzzy sets, some of the main fuzzy set properties are discussed below:

(a) **Involution**: The involution property states that the complement of complement of a set is the set itself.

$$(X')' = X$$

(b) **Commutativity**: The commutative property for any two fuzzy sets (X and Y) states that when applying union or intersection operations, the order of operands does not alter the result.

$$(X \cup Y) = (Y \cup X)$$

$$(X \cap Y) = (Y \cap X)$$

(c) **Associativity**: The associative property for any three fuzzy sets (X, Y, and Z) states that it can be applied on any two operands followed by the third operand when applying union or intersection operations. However, the relative order of operands should not be changed.

$$(X \cup Y) \cup Z = Z \cup (Y \cup Z)$$

$$(X \cap Y) \cap Z = Z \cap (Y \cap Z)$$

(d) **Distributivity**: The distributive property for any three fuzzy sets (X, Y, and Z) is explained as given in equations below:

$$X \cup (Y \cap Z) = (X \cup Y) \cap (X \cup Z)$$

$$X \cap (Y \cup Z) = (X \cap Y) \cup (X \cap Z)$$

(e) **Idempotency**: For any fuzzy set X, the idempotent property is stated below:

$$X \cup X = X$$

$$X \cap X = X$$

(f) **Identity**: If ϕ is considered as the null set and U as the Universal set, the following identity property for a fuzzy set X is given as follow:

$$X \cup \phi = X$$

$$X \cap \phi = \phi$$

$$X \cup U = U$$

$$X \cap U = X$$

Here, the union or intersection of a fuzzy set X with the null set ϕ will result in the fuzzy set X. Also, the union of a fuzzy set X with the Universal set U will result in the fuzzy set X, while the intersection of a fuzzy set X with the Universal set U will result in the Universal set U.

(g) **Transitivity**: The transitive property for any three fuzzy sets (X, Y, and Z) states that if X is a subset of Y and Y is a subset of Z, then X is a subset of Z. This is mathematically explained as:

$$\text{if } X \subseteq Y \text{ and } Y \subseteq Z \text{ then } X \subseteq Z$$

(h) **Absorption**: The absorption property produces the fuzzy set X after it applies the union and intersection operations in the below given order for any two fuzzy sets X and Y.

$$X \cup (X \cap Y) = X$$

$$X \cap (X \cup Y) = X$$

(i) **De Morgan's Law**: The De Morgan's law for fuzzy sets can be stated as:
   a. The complement of a union is the intersection of the complement of individual sets

$$(X \cup Y)' = X' \cap Y'$$

   b. The complement of an intersection is the union of the complement of individual sets

$$(X \cap Y)' = X' \cup Y'$$

(j) **Fuzzy relation**: A fuzzy relation is the Cartesian product of two sets X and Y, in which X and Y are fed as input, and the fuzzy relation is calculated by finding the Cartesian product of the two sets. Mathematically, the relation can be stated as follows:

   If X' is a fuzzy set defined on a set of Universe say X, and Y' is a fuzzy set defined on the set of Universe say Y, then the Cartesian product can be defined as follows:

$$X' \, X \, Y' = R' \subset X \, x \, Y$$

Let us try to understand how Cartesian product is applied on fuzzy sets with the help an example. Let the membership function values for X' and Y' be as follows:

$$X' = \{0.2/x_1 + 0.3/x_2 + 1.0/x_3\}$$

$$Y' = \{0.4/y_1 + 0.9/y_2 + 0.1/y_3\}$$

Now, to find the relation R' over $X' \times Y'$, let us calculate the Cartesian product by plotting the fuzzy relation matrix. To find R', we need to follow the following rule:

$$\mu_{R'}(X, Y) = \mu_{X' \, x \, Y'}(X, Y) = \min(\mu_{X'}(X), \mu_{Y'}(Y))$$

$$R' = X' \times Y' = \begin{array}{c} \\ x_1 \\ x_2 \\ x_3 \end{array} \begin{array}{ccc} y_1 & y_2 & y_3 \\ \left[\begin{array}{ccc} 0.2 & 0.2 & 0.1 \\ 0.3 & 03 & 0.1 \\ 0.4 & 0.9 & 0.1 \end{array}\right] \end{array} \begin{array}{l} \text{min}(\mu_{X'}(x_1), \mu_{Y'}(y_1)) \\ \\ \\ \text{min}(\mu_{X'}(x_3), \mu_{Y'}(y_2)) \end{array}$$

Cartesian product: $X' \times Y'$

As fuzzy relation describes interaction among elements, it is an important concept used in case of fuzzy computing. It is important to note that the Cartesian product operation is not commutative, i.e., $X' \times Y' \neq Y' \times X'$. Only if $X' = Y'$, that is, the two sets are equal, then the commutative property will hold true.

2.4 Binary Fuzzy Relation

A binary fuzzy relation is a relation that connects two sets X and Y, usually denoted by $R(X, Y)$. When the sets X and Y are not the same, i.e., $X \neq Y$, it is referred to as bipartite graphs. On the contrary, if $X = Y$, then it is referred to as directed graph or digraph. In fact, as $X = Y$, the relation can also be written as $R(X, X)$ or $R(X^2)$.

If we consider $X = \{x_1, x_2, x_3, \ldots, x_n\}$ and $Y = \{y_1, y_2, y_3, \ldots, y_m\}$, the fuzzy relation can be expressed as a $n \times m$ matrix called the fuzzy matrix. The matrix can be denoted as $R(X, Y)$, as shown below:

$$R(x, y) = \begin{bmatrix} \mu_R(x_1, y_1) & \mu_R(x_1, y_2) & \cdots & \mu_R(x_1, y_m) \\ \mu_R(x_2, y_1) & \mu_R(x_2, y_2) & \cdots & \mu_R(x_2, y_m) \\ \vdots & & \cdots & \vdots \\ \mu_R(x_n, y_1) & \mu_R(x_n, y_2) & \cdots & \mu_R(x_n, y_m) \end{bmatrix}$$

For a binary fuzzy relation $R(X, Y)$, its domain is the fuzzy set dom $R(X, Y)$ whose membership function is:

$$\mu_{\text{dom } R}(X) = \max_{y \in Y} \mu_R(x, y) \text{ for each } x \in X$$

Also, for a fuzzy relation $R(X, Y)$, its range is the a fuzzy set ran $R(X, Y)$ whose functions are defined by:

$$\mu_{\text{ran } R}(Y) = \max_{x \in X} \mu_R(x, y) \text{ for each } y \in Y$$

In addition, the height of a fuzzy binary relation $R(X, Y)$ is a number $h(R)$, which is the largest membership grade attained by any pair (x, y) and is defined as:

$$h(R) = \max_{y \in Y} \max_{x \in X} R(x, y)$$

To understand further, let us first of all consider a simple example. Given $X = \{x_1, x_2, x_3\}$ and $Y = \{y_1, y_2\}$, the cartesian product of the two sets X and Y results in a fuzzy relation R that can be expressed as $R = X \times Y$. Let the relation R expressed in a matrix format be having fuzzy membership values as given in Eq. (2.5):

$$R = X \times Y = \begin{bmatrix} 0.6 & 1.0 \\ 0.5 & 0.8 \\ 0.9 & 0.3 \end{bmatrix} \qquad (2.5)$$

Now, the domain of relation R (considering the maximum value per row) can be defined as:

$$\text{Dom } R = \{1.0, 0.8, 0.8\}$$

Next, the range of relation R (considering the maximum value per column) can be defined as:

$$\text{Ran } R = \{0.9, 1.0\}$$

Lastly, the height of relation R (considering the largest membership grade) is:

$$h(R) = \{1.0\}$$

2.5 Fuzzy Membership Functions

A membership function for a fuzzy set A on the Universe of disclosure X is defined as $\mu_A(x) \to [0, 1]$, where each element of X is mapped to a value between 0 and 1. This value is called membership value or degree of membership of the element in X to the fuzzy set A. There are various types of membership functions. When plotted in a graph, they all adapt to different shapes. Each shape of a membership function indicates how the membership value is going to vary in certain defined limits.

Let us now study the various commonly used membership function types:

i. **Singleton membership function**: Singleton membership function assigns a membership value of 1 to particular value of x (say, when $x = a$), and assigns value 0 to rest of all. Figure 2.8 illustrates a case of singleton membership function, and Eq. (2.6) gives the general mathematical notation of the formulation of this function.

Mathematically, a singleton membership function is formulated as:

$$\mu(x) = \begin{cases} 1, & \text{if } x = a \\ 0, & \text{otherwise} \end{cases} \qquad (2.6)$$

ii. **Triangular membership function**: Triangular membership function is a very commonly used membership function and is mostly used in fuzzy

Figure 2.8 Singleton membership function.

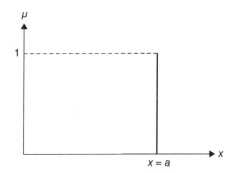

Figure 2.9 Triangular membership function.

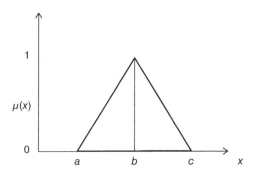

controller designs. This function is defined by three parameters: a, b, and c – "a" defines the lower boundary value, "b" defines the height of the triangle, and "c" defines the upper boundary value. Figure 2.9 illustrates a case of triangular membership function and Eq. (2.7) gives the general mathematical notation of the formulation of this function.

Mathematically, a triangular membership function is formulated as:

$$\mu(x) = \begin{cases} 0, & x \leq a \\ \dfrac{x-a}{b-a}, & a \leq x \leq b \\ \dfrac{c-x}{c-b}, & b \leq x \leq c \\ 0, & x \geq c \end{cases} \tag{2.7}$$

If the value of x is less than "a," then the membership value is 0. If the value of x is less than "b" but greater than "a," then the membership value is in $[0, 1]$, i.e., between 0 and 1. If input x is equal to "b," then it is having full membership for the given set. If the value of x is greater than "b" but less than "c," then the membership value is in the interval $[1, 0]$, i.e., between 1 and 0. For any other values of "x" greater than "c," the membership value is 0.

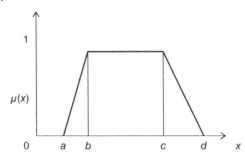

Figure 2.10 Trapezoidal membership function.

iii. **Trapezoidal membership function:** Trapezoidal membership function is constrained by four parameters – a, b, c, and d. The values from b to c represent the highest membership value that the element can take. If x is between a and b or between c and d, it will have membership value between 0 and 1. Figure 2.10 illustrates a case of trapezoidal membership function, and Eq. (2.8) gives the general mathematical notation of the formulation of this function.

Mathematically, a trapezoidal membership function is formulated as:

$$\mu(x) = \begin{cases} 0, & x \leq a \\ \dfrac{x-a}{b-a}, & a \leq x \leq b \\ 1, & b \leq x \leq c \\ \dfrac{d-x}{d-c}, & c \leq x \leq d \\ 0, & d \leq x \end{cases} \tag{2.8}$$

iv. **Gaussian membership function:** The Gaussian membership function is defined by two parameters – mean $(\overline{x})$ and standard deviation (σ). The mean $(\overline{x})$ represents the center of the Gaussian curve, and the standard deviation (σ) represents the spread of the curve. Different values of these parameters control the shape of the curve. The smaller the value of σ is, the narrower the bell of the curve is. Figure 2.11 illustrates a case of Gaussian membership function, and Eq. (2.9) gives the general mathematical notation of the formulation of this function.

Mathematically, a gaussian membership function is formulated as (2.9)

$$\mu(x) = e^{\left[-\frac{1}{2}\left(\frac{\overline{x}-f}{\sigma}\right)^2\right]} \tag{2.9}$$

v. **Sigmoidal membership function:** The sigmoidal membership function has a characteristic of being S-shaped. It is one of the most commonly used functions in fuzzy set theory as well as in machine learning. It provides a gradual variation from nonmembership (i.e., 0) to complete membership

Figure 2.11 Gaussian membership function.

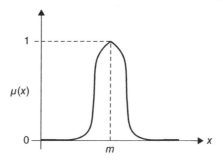

Figure 2.12 Sigmoidal membership function.

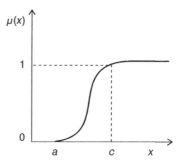

(i.e., 1). The sigmoidal membership function is mainly controlled by two parameters – "*a*" and "*c*." The membership function value is 0 for value of "*x*" less than "*a*" and equal to 1 for any value of "*x*" greater than "*c*." Other fuzzy membership values lie between 0 and 1. Figure 2.12 illustrates a case of sigmoidal membership function, and Eq. (2.10) gives the general mathematical notation of the formulation of this function.

Mathematically, a sigmoidal membership function is formulated as (2.10)

$$\mu(x) = \frac{1}{1 + e^{-a(x-b)}} \tag{2.10}$$

There are few other graphical forms to represent membership functions, but the important standard ones have been discussed in this section.

2.6 Methods of Membership Value Assignments

Since the membership function basically represents all fuzziness for a particular fuzzy set, its description is the essence of a fuzzy property or operation. There are many ways to assign membership values of functions to fuzzy variables. Some of the standard methods of assigning membership values are discussed below:

i. **Intuition**: In case of intuition method, the skills and expertise together with the intuition of a person in a given context is mostly used to design

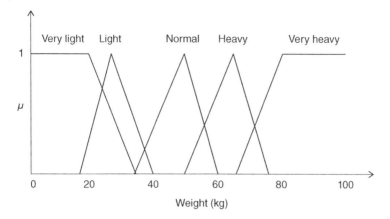

Figure 2.13 Membership function for the fuzzy variable "weight".

the behavioral change of the degree of fuzziness with respect to a domain. Intuitions comprise of contextual and semantic knowledge about a subject; it may also involve linguistic truth values about this knowledge. In Figure 2.13, the membership function corresponding to the varying weight of persons with respect to the measuring weight (in kg) is shown. The figure shows the various shapes on the universe of weight as measured in kilogram. Each curve is a membership function corresponding to various fuzzy variables, such as very light, light, normal, heavy, and very heavy. However, the curves considered are based on intuition of the analyst based on his perception and expertise.

ii. **Inference**: Here knowledge base is used for deductive reasoning. Given a set of facts and a database of knowledge, a conclusion is inferred or deduced. From the given knowledge and the set of facts, rules can be framed, and finally the degree of membership can be inferred. Let us try to understand this with the help of an interpretation of a geometric figure. Our knowledge base and facts are given as follows.

   (a) For angles A, B, C of a triangle, the sum total of all the angles is 180°. i.e., $A + B + C = 180°$.

   (b) $A \geq B \geq C \geq 0$

   Now we need to predict "*In what category of – right-angled, isosceles, obtuse, or acute angled triangle, the diagram shown in Figure* 2.14 *is going to fall?*"

   The different fuzzy membership function design for different types of triangles could be as follows:

   Isosceles: $\mu_I(A, B, C) = 1 - 1/180 * \min(A–B, B–C)$. In this case if $A = B$ or $B = C$, then $\min(A - B, B - C, C - A)$ is going to return 0 and $\mu_I(A, B, C) = 1$ is going to be an isosceles (base angles are equal). For all other cases, the triangle is not going to be an isosceles. The division by 180 is done in order to bring the value to an interval $[0, 1]$.

Figure 2.14 Triangle for prediction to a category.

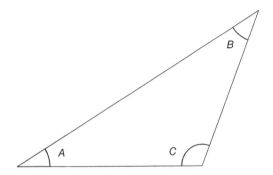

Equilateral: $\mu_E(A, B, C) = 1 - 1/180^* \min(A - B, B - C, C - A)$. In this case, if $A = B = C$, then $\min(A - B, B - C, C - A)$ is going to return 0 and $\mu_I(A, B, C) = 1$ is going to be an equilateral triangle. The division by 180 is done in order to bring the value to an interval $[0, 1]$.

Obtuse: $\mu_O(A, B, C) = 1 - 1/180^* \min\{(A - (B + C), B - (A + C), C - (A + B)\}$. Here, whichever angle is greater than $90°$ is assumed to have values greater than sum total of the other two angles.

The resultant probability of the triangle falling to any of the above class from our consideration would be

$$\mu_{OIE}(A, B, C) = \min \{\mu_O(A, B, C), \mu_E(A, B, C), \mu_I(A, B, C)\}$$

Considering Figure 2.14, if the values of angles $A = 120°$, $B = 40°$ and $C = 20°$ is assumed, then

$$\mu_I(A, B, C) = 0.88$$
$$\mu_E(A, B, C) = 0.80, \mu_O(A, B, C) = 0.66, \text{and,}$$
$$\mu_{OIE}(A, B, C) = \min (0.88, 0.8, 0.66) = 0.66.$$

Therefore, based on the above considerations, the triangle shown in Figure 2.14 is an obtuse triangle.

Rank ordering: Here the membership function is developed based on the rank order of comparative parameters between a pair of variables. The preferences can be assessed by individuals, a group or committee, a public poll, or any other standard similar methods that can be used to assign membership values to a fuzzy variable. The preference is calculated by making a pairwise comparisons of one variable with another, and later determines the ordering of the membership (such as, 1st, 2nd, and 3rd).

Let us consider the Table 2.2 for understanding the concept of rank ordering. In this example, it is considered that 100 persons from America are surveyed for the preference of breakfast items among four items – *sandwich*, *pancakes*, *sausages*, and *cereal*.

Table 2.2 Paired comparison for breakfast item preference.

	Cereal	Sandwich	Pancakes	Sausages
Cereal	—	65	32	20
Sandwich	40	—	38	42
Pancakes	45	50	—	70
Sausages	80	20	98	—
Total	165	135	168	132
Percentage	27.5%	22.5%	28%	22%
Rank order	2nd	3rd	1st	4th

Based on the survey, it is found that 65 people prefer *sandwich* over cereal, 32 people prefer *pancakes* over *cereal,* and 20 people prefer *sausage* over *cereal*. Once the entire comparisons are filled pairwise, it is found that the item *pancakes* get the first preference, as it has been voted the highest, when compared to the rest of the three items. *Cereal, sandwich,* and *sausages* are ranked as second, third, and fourth, respectively.

Based on the percentage value obtained in Table 2.2, the corresponding membership function can be drawn by following the inference method, as given in Figure 2.15.

As can be seen in this example, there are four items – *sandwich, pancakes, sausages,* and *cereal*. Hence the total number of items (n) is 4. Therefore, the number of judgments or comparisons to be made (N) can be calculated using the Eq. (2.11):

$$N = (n^*(n - 1))/2 \tag{2.11}$$

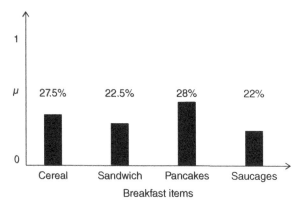

Figure 2.15 Membership functions based on rank ordering of items.

In the given example, the number of judgments $(N) = ((4*(4-1))/2 = 6$. This means, one person has to provide 6 pairwise compared judgements. Comparing the total number of preferences, for each of the four proposals, we can conclude that *pancakes* are the most preferred, followed by *cereal*, *sandwich*, and *sausages*, respectively.

iii. **Angular fuzzy sets**: Angular fuzzy sets (AFS) are defined on a universe of angles, and the sets are of repeating shapes for every 2π cycles. AFS are used in the quantitative description of the linguistic variables, popularly known as *"truth values."* This method depends only on the value of angle and is easy to interpret. The linguistic variables vary by a value of θ, and the corresponding membership function is defined by using Eq. (2.12). Here, in the equation, "*t*" is considered as the horizontal projection of the radial vector.

$$\mu_\theta = t \tan \theta \qquad (2.12)$$

Angular fuzzy models having rotational characteristics have been developed by Hadipriono and Sun. In this model, the linguistic variables are represented with angles, in which each value of the variable is denoted by an angle. Often the angular model is represented by a semi-circle, in which the angle rotates between $-\pi/2$ and $\pi/2$. The unresolved or neutral linguistic value is represented by a horizontal line with the angle $\theta = 0$. Correspondingly, the angle of $\theta = \pi/2$ represents an absolutely positive (or no risk) linguistic value, and the angle of $\theta = -\pi/2$ represents an absolutely negative linguistic value. Figure 2.16 illustrates this concept of linguistic variables and their associated angles.

Let us now form AFSs with an example based on profit or loss of a company. If the company has witnessed neither a profit nor a loss for a particular year, we can consider it as neutral (i.e., $\theta = 0$). If a little profit was witnessed by the company, it can be considered as label "Fairly Positive" with a value of $\theta = \pi/8$. Similarly, if a little loss was witnessed by the company, it can be considered as label "Fairly Negative" with a value of $\theta = -\pi/8$. By using these linguistic labels for varying percentage of profits and losses, the model of the AFS is shown in Figure 2.17.

Correspondingly, Figure 2.18 displays the angular fuzzy membership function for the company's earnings. Based on the profit or loss of the company, the labels are assigned as – neutral (N), very little profit (VLP), average profit (AP), very high profit (VHP), absolute profit (ABP), very little loss (VLL), average loss (AL), very high loss (VHL), and absolute loss (AL).

iv. **Neural networks**: Neural networks also help in finding the fuzzy membership values. To understand this, let us consider several data points scattered over the space. The task is to classify these data points into three groups or classes ($C1$, $C2$, and $C3$). For this, the membership value to a class with respect to a given input is determined. The available set of values is divided into two

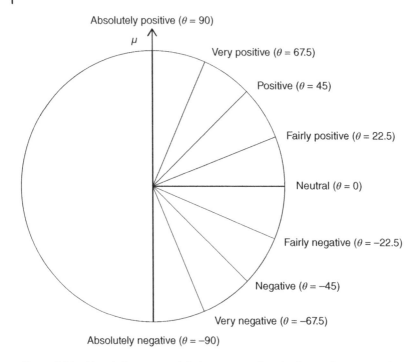

Figure 2.16 Linguistic terms and their corresponding θ values using angular fuzzy model.

parts – *training* and *testing*. The training set is used to converge the neural network, and the testing part is used to validate the neural network.

As seen in Figure 2.19(a), the neural network considers two inputs $X1$ and $X2$, which can be considered as the coordinate values of a data point. The training is carried out, and the output is displayed to determine the input $(X1, X2)$ belongs to which of the three classes among $C1$, $C2$, and $C3$. Table 2.3 shows the set of two coordinate input values that should belong to any one of the three classes – $C1$, $C2$, or $C3$. Whichever point $(P1, P2, P3, \text{or } P4)$ falls to a given class $(C1, C2, \text{or } C3)$ gets membership value 1 to that class and a membership value of 0 to other classes. The final result is displayed in a graphical format in Figure 2.19(b). With more and more appropriate training instances, the classification behavior of the neural network can be made more appropriate.

While applying the neural network for the testing set, the result that will be generated for each data point will be fuzzy in nature. For example, a data point $X(x1, x2)$ may belong to class $C1$ with a fuzzy value of 0.2, $C2$ with a fuzzy value of 0.7, and $C3$ with a fuzzy value of 0.1. This clearly indicates that the data point "X" belongs to class $C2$ with the highest fuzzy value of 0.7.

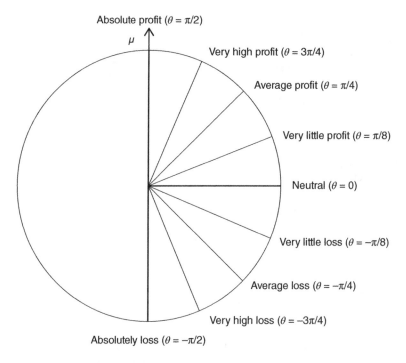

Figure 2.17 An example of company's earnings for a year using angular fuzzy model.

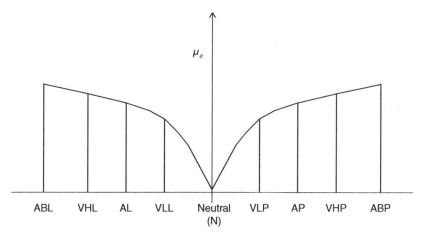

Figure 2.18 Angular fuzzy membership function.

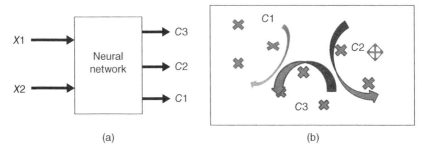

(a)   (b)

Figure 2.19 (a) ANN with two input and three class output (b) Graphical result of the Classified Output.

Table 2.3 Input vector set to the neural network.

	P1	P2	P3	P4
$x1$	2.3	4.5	4.8	3.5
$x2$	3.4	6.7	9.4	8

v. **Genetic algorithm**: Genetic algorithms (GA) are used to determine the fuzzy membership functions by mapping a set of input values to corresponding output degree of a membership function. In GA, the membership functions are coded into bit strings that are connected. Next, an evaluation function is used to evaluate the fitness of each set of membership functions.

Let us consider an example to understand the concept of GA in determining fuzzy membership functions. Consider the input and output fuzzy membership function, as shown in Figure 2.20. The linguistic rules can be as follows:

Rule 1: If x is slow, then y is easy

Rule 2: If x is fast, then y is difficult

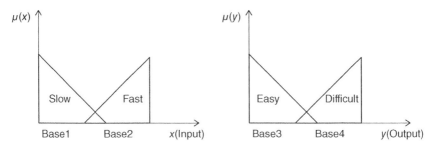

Figure 2.20 Input and output membership function of a fuzzy system.

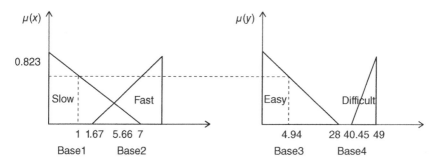

Figure 2.21 Solution of first chromosome in population.

The problem of applying Genetic Algorithm (GA) here is to find appropriate output base lengths. Each chromosome could be of 64-bit length, i.e., sum of total length of each base of all the four right-angled triangles (base1, base2, base3, and base4), assuming length of each base is 6 bits.

As seen from Figure 2.21, the grade of membership (not detailed) is 0.823 for input value $x = 1$. If y is a direct defuzzification of x, then y for *"easy"* membership function corresponding to *"slow"* membership function of x is 4.94. The real output is actually 1. The error value can be thereby framed as:

$$(\text{Actual} - \text{Observed})^2 \text{ i.e., } (1 - 4.94)^2 = 15.52$$

vi. **Inductive reasoning**: An automatic generation of membership functions can be accommodated by using the essential characteristic of the inductive reasoning. The induction is performed by the entropy minimization principle, which clusters most optimally the parameter corresponding to the output classes. The method generates memberships functions based solely on data provided. The method of inductive reasoning works best for complex systems where the data are abundant and static. This method may not be suitable for situations where the data are dynamic, as the corresponding membership functions will continually change with time.

There are standard laws of induction, which are summarized here:

- Given a set of irreducible outcomes of an experiment, the induced probabilities are those probabilities consistent with all available information that maximize the entropy of the set.
- The induced probability of a set of independent observations is proportional to the probability density of the induced probability of a single observation.
- The induced rule is that rule consistent with all available information of which the entropy is minimum.

Among these three laws above, the third one is appropriate for membership function development.

Figure 2.22 The fuzzification and defuzzification processes.

2.7 Fuzzification vs. Defuzzification

Fuzzification is the process of converting crisp input values to fuzzy values. That is, it converts precise data into imprecise data. There can be many standard methods used for carry out the process of fuzzification, such as, intuition method, inference method, AFS, neural network, genetic algorithm, and inductive reasoning. All these methods have been elaborately discussed in the previous section. The fuzzification process permits the system inputs and outputs to be expressed in *linguistic terms* so as to apply rules that can satisfy a complex system.

Defuzzification, on the other hand, is the process of converting fuzzy set into a crisp set. In fact, defuzzification is the exact opposite process of fuzzification. It converts imprecise data into precise data. The importance of defuzzification is to make decision making easy in real-world scenario so as to make a concrete choice or conclusion. The entire process of fuzzification and defuzzication can be easily understood from the Figure 2.22.

Defuzzification is a comparatively complex process and may be carried out using several standard methods as discussed below:

i. **Max-Membership principle**: This defuzzification method, also known as the height method, is limited to peak output functions. The method is applicable only when the value of height is unique. This means that the highest peak value should not repeat and occur only once. This method of defuzzification can be illustrated with an example given in Figure 2.23.

The algebraic expression used to carry out the height method for finding the crisp value (z^*) is given in Eq. (2.13).

$$\mu(z^*) >= \mu(z) \text{ for all } z \in Z \tag{2.13}$$

Let us consider an example of a fuzzy set for an adult, which is defined as follows:

$$\text{Adult} = \{(15, 0.3), (20, 0.5), (35, 0.9), (50, 0.5), (55, 0.2)\}$$

Now, using the height method, it can be considered that the crisp value for an adult is 35. Therefore, a person of 35 years can be considered as an adult.

Figure 2.23 An example of max-membership principle of defuzzification.

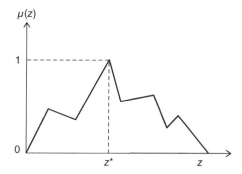

Figure 2.24 An example of mean-max membership method of defuzzification.

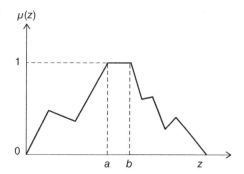

ii. **Mean-Max membership**: The mean-max membership method is similar to the max-**membership** method, except that the locations of the maximum membership need not be unique. This method of defuzzification can be illustrated with an example given in Figure 2.24. In this Figure, it can be noticed that more than one point (say, a and b) is having the highest membership value (peak value). The mean of these two values (a and b) are calculated to find the crisp value.

The algebraic expression used to carry out the mean-max membership method for finding the crisp value (z^*) is given in Eq. (2.14).

$$z^* = \frac{\sum_{i=1}^{n} \overline{z_i}}{n} \tag{2.14}$$

Let us again consider the example of a fuzzy set for an adult, which is defined as follows:

$$\text{Adult} = \{(20, 0.3), (25, 0.5), (30, 0.9), (40, \ 0.9), (45, 0.4), (50, 0.2)\}$$

Now, using the mean-max membership method, it can be considered that the crisp value for an adult is $(30 + 40)/2 = 35$. Therefore, a person of 35 years can be considered as an adult.

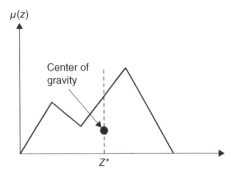

$\mu(z)$

Center of
gravity

z^*

Figure 2.25 An example of center of mass method of defuzzification.

iii. **Centroid method**: This method, also known as the center of mass, center of area, **or** center of gravity, is the most commonly used defuzzification method. The basic principle in this method is to find the point z^* where a vertical line would slide the aggregate into two equal masses. To find the center of gravity, the entire area is divided into subregions (such as, triangle, trapezoidal, rectangle, etc.). The centroid is found by dividing the aggregated output into the regular structures and finding the area under the curve of each regular structure. The sum of the center of gravity of each of these subareas is then used to determine the defuzzified value for a fuzzy set.

This centroid method of defuzzification can be illustrated with an example given in Figure 2.25.

For a continuous set, the defuzzified output z^* is given by the algebraic equation shown in Eq. (2.15):

$$z^* = \frac{\int \mu(z). \ z\,dz}{\int \mu(z)\,dz} \tag{2.15}$$

Here, $\int \mu(z)\,dz$ denotes the area of the region bounded by the curve z.

For a discrete set, the defuzzified output z^* is given by the algebraic equation shown in Eq. (2.16):

$$z^* = \frac{\sum_{i=1}^{n} x_i \mu(x_i)}{\sum_{i=1}^{n} \mu(x_i)} \tag{2.16}$$

Here, n indicates the number of subareas, x_i is the center of gravity of a subarea (i), and $\mu(x_i)$ represents the area of the subarea.

Let us consider a fuzzy set consisting of four subareas, as shown in Table 2.4, and their corresponding area value and centroid value.

Hence, the defuzzified value is:

$$z^* = \frac{(1.15 + 1.02 + 0.27 + 1.02)}{(0.5 + 0.3 + 0.15 + 0.3)} = \frac{3.46}{1.25} = 2.77$$

Table 2.4 Subareas and their properties.

Subarea no.	Area ($\mu(x_i)$)	Center of gravity (x_i)	$x_i\mu(x_i)$
1	0.5	2.3	1.15
2	0.3	3.4	1.02
3	0.15	1.8	0.27
4	0.3	3.4	1.02

Figure 2.26 An example of weighted average method of defuzzification.

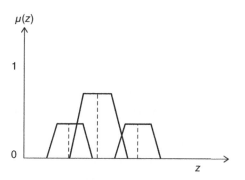

iv. **Weighted average method**: This method is applicable only for **symmetrical** output membership functions. Each membership function is weighted by its respective maximum membership value. This method can be illustrated with the help of the Figure 2.26.

In weighted average method, the defuzzified output z^* is given by the algebraic equation shown in Eq. (2.17):

$$z^* = \frac{\sum \mu(z).z}{\sum \mu(z)} \tag{2.17}$$

Here, z' is the maximum value of the membership function, $\sum$ denotes the algebraic summation, and z is the element with maximum membership function.

Let us consider an example consisting of a fuzzy set Z that consists of elements along with corresponding maximum membership values, as shown below:

$$Z = \{(60, 0.6), (70, 0.4), (80, 0.2), (90, 0.2)\}$$

Now the defuzzified value z^* for the given set Z will be:

$$Z^* \frac{(0.6 * 60) + (0.4 * 70) + (0.2 * 80) + (0.2 * 90)}{0.6 + 0.4 + 0.2 + 0.2} = \frac{98}{1.4} = 0.71$$

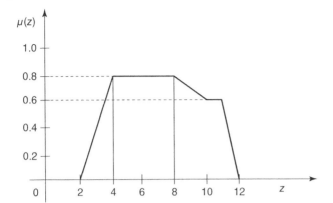

Figure 2.27 Fuzzy membership plot.

Now, using the weighted average method, it can be considered that the crisp value for the given dataset Z is 71.

v. **Maxima methods**: The maxima methods consider values with the maximum membership. There are different maxima methods found, which are discussed below:

(a) ***First of maxima method (FOM)***: Here the smallest value from a domain with maximum membership value is considered. From the illustration shown in Figure 2.17, the defuzzified value z^* of the fuzzy set is 4.

(b) ***Last of maxima method (LOM)***: Here the largest value from a domain with maximum membership value is considered. From the illustration shown in Figure 2.17, the defuzzified value z^* of the fuzzy set is 8.

(c) ***Mean of maxima method (MOM)***: Here the element with the highest membership value is considered. If there are more than one such element, the mean value of the maxima is considered. From the Figure 2.27, the values of z are 4, 6, and 8 that have the maximum membership value and hence cardinality (n) is 3. The defuzzification value z^* is given by $z^* = (4+6+8)/3 = 6$.

2.8 Fuzzy c-Means

The fuzzy c-means is an efficient technique applied on a dataset for grouping the data points into a number of clusters. The specialty of this technique is that each data point is considered to belong to more than one cluster by a certain degree. This technique is very different from the popular K-means clustering technique. K-means clustering is a hard clustering technique, as each data point can strictly belong to only one cluster. However, in fuzzy c-means clustering, which is considered as a soft clutering technique, a data point may belong to more than one cluster.

Definitely, fuzzy c-means takes more time to generate results than the traditional K-means, as it requires a greater number of steps as explained below.

Let us now understand how the fuzzy c-means algorithm work. The main task is to group a set of "n" data points into "c" clusters. The algorithm initially requires the selection of the membership values of each data point for each cluster taken at random. Also, it requires selection of centroid value of each cluster based on the random assignment of membership values. The entire algorithm can be divided into the following steps:

Step 1: Randomly assign the fuzzy membership values in the matrix

Let us consider a set of four data points – (1, 5), (2, 7), (3, 4), and (4, 6). Also, let us consider two clusters – cluster 1 and cluster 2. This step involves randomly assigning fuzzy membership values (γ) for each data point to decide its probability of belonging to either of the cluster. This is depicted in the Table 2.5, which demonstrates the fuzzy membership matrix. As can be seen from the Table, the data point (1, 5) belongs to Cluster 1 with a probability (membership value) of 0.8 and to Cluster 2 with a probability (membership value) of 0.2. Similarly, the data point (2, 7) belongs to Cluster 1 with a probability (membership value) of 0.4 and to Cluster 2 with a probability (membership value) of 0.6. For the next two data points too, membership values have been randomly assigned as shown in Table 2.5.

Step 2: Calculate and find the centroid of each cluster

The second step is to find the value of centroid for both the clusters using the Eq. (2.18).

$$v_{ij} = \frac{\sum_{k=1}^{n} \gamma_{ik}^{m} \cdot x_{ki}}{\sum_{k=1}^{n} \gamma_{ik}^{m}} \tag{2.18}$$

Here, "γ" is the membership value, and "m" is the fuzziness parameter (generally $1.25 \leq m \leq 2$). Often the value of "m" is considered as 2. Also, γ_{ik} means the membership value of the kth data point in the ith cluster.

Table 2.5 Fuzzy Membership Matrix.

		Data points			
		(1, 5)	**(2, 7)**	**(3, 4)**	**(4, 6)**
Cluster	1	0.80	0.40	0.90	0.30
	2	0.20	0.60	0.10	0.70

Considering the Table 2.5, the centroid for Cluster 1 is calculated as:

$$v_{11} = \frac{0.8^2 * 1 + 0.4^2 * 2 + 0.9^2 * 3 + 0.3^2 * 4}{0.8^2 + 0.4^2 + 0.9^2 + 0.3^2} = \frac{3.75}{1.7} = 2.20$$

$$v_{12} = \frac{0.8^2 * 5 + 0.4^2 * 7 + 0.9^2 * 4 + 0.3^2 * 6}{0.8^2 + 0.4^2 + 0.9^2 + 0.3^2} = \frac{8.1}{1.7} = 4.76$$

Similarly, the centroid for Cluster 2 is calculated as:

$$v_{21} = \frac{0.2^2 * 1 + 0.6^2 * 2 + 0.1^2 * 3 + 0.7^2 * 4}{0.2^2 + 0.6^2 + 0.1^2 + 0.7^2} = \frac{2.75}{0.9} = 3.06$$

$$v_{22} = \frac{0.2^2 * 5 + 0.6^2 * 7 + 0.1^2 * 4 + 0.7^2 * 6}{0.2^2 + 0.6^2 + 0.1^2 + 0.7^2} = \frac{5.7}{0.9} = 6.33$$

Therefore, the centroids for Cluster 1 and Cluster 2 are (2.20, 4.76) and (3.06, 6.33), respectively.

Step 3: Find out the distance of each data point from the centroid of each cluster.

The first data point considered in our example is (1, 5). Using the Eucledian distance measure, the distance is measured from this data point to the centroid values (2.20, 4.76) and (3.06, 6.33).

For the data point (1, 5), distance D_{11} from the centroid value (2.20, 4.76) is:

$$D_{11} = ((1{-}2.20)^2 + (5 - 4.76)^2)^{0.5} = 1.22$$

Again, for the data point (1, 5), distance D_{12} from the centroid value (3.06, 6.33) is:

$$D_{12} = ((1{-}3.06)^2 + (5{-}6.33)^2)^{0.5} = 2.45$$

Let us also find the distances of the second data point (2, 7), the centroid values (2.20, 4.76), and (3.06, 6.33).

For the data point (2, 7), distance D_{21} from the centroid value (2.20, 4.76) is:

$$D_{21} = ((2{-}2.20)^2 + (7 - 4.76)^2)^{0.5} = 2.25$$

Again, for the data point (2, 7), distance D_{22} from the centroid value (3.06, 6.33) is:

$$D_{22} = ((2{-}3.06)^2 + (7{-}6.33)^2)^{0.5} = 1.25$$

Similarly, the distances of all the remaining two data points (3, 4) and (4, 6) from the centroids are to be calculated. The final calculation is given in the Table 2.6 for all the data points.

Step 4: Update the membership values of each data point

Based on the distance calculation, the membership values are now required to be updated in the membership matrix, as given in the Table 2.5.

Table 2.6 Data point distance to a given cluster.

Cluster 1		Cluster 2	
Datapoint	**Distance**	**Datapoint**	**Distance**
$(1, 5)$	1.22	$(1, 5)$	2.45
$(2, 7)$	2.25	$(2, 7)$	1.25
$(3, 4)$	1.10	$(3, 4)$	2.33
$(4, 6)$	2.19	$(4, 6)$	1.00

The membership values are to be calculated using the Eq. (2.19).

$$\gamma_{ij} = \left[\sum_{1}^{n} \left(d_{ki}^2 / d_{kj}^2 \right)^{1/m-1} \right]^{-1} \tag{2.19}$$

For the first data point, distances calculated in the previous steps are $D_{11} = 1.22$ and $D_{12} = 2.45$. Therefore, the updated membership values can be obtained as:

$$\gamma_{11} = [\{[(1.22)^2/(1.22)^2] + [(1.22)^2/(2.45)^2]\} \wedge \{(1/(2-1))\}]^{-1} = 0.80$$
$$\gamma_{12} = [\{[(2.45)^2/(2.45)^2] + [(2.45)^2/(1.22)^2]\} \wedge \{(1/(2-1))\}]^{-1} = 0.20$$

As can be seen,

$$\gamma_{12} = 1 - \gamma_{11} = 0.20$$

In this case, the updated membership values γ_{11} and γ_{12} are 0.80 and 0.20, respectively. However, it is found to be exactly of the same value as the originally randomly assigned membership values, as can be seen in the Table 2.5.

Let us again calculate the new membership values for the seconds data point $(2, 7)$. For this first data point, distances calculated in the previous steps are $D_{21} = 2.25$ and $D_{22} = 1.25$. Therefore, the updated membership values can be obtained as:

$$\gamma_{11} = [\{[(2.25)^2/(2.25)^2] + [(2.25)^2/(1.25)^2]\} \wedge \{(1/(2-1))\}]^{-1} = 0.24$$
$$\gamma_{12} = [\{[(1.25)^2/(1.25)^2] + [(1.25)^2/(2.25)^2]\} \wedge \{(1/(2-1))\}]^{-1} = 0.76$$

Likewise, compute all other membership values for both the clusters and accordingly update the membership matrix. The final result is displayed in the Table 2.7.

Step 5: Steps 2–4 are to be repeated until:
- the constant values are obtained for the membership values, or,
- the difference is less than the tolerance value (a small value up to which the alteration in values of the previous two consequent updation is acceptable).

Table 2.7 Updated Fuzzy Membership Matrix.

		Data points			
		(1, 5)	(2, 7)	(3, 4)	(4, 6)
Cluster	1	0.8	0.24	0.82	0.17
	2	0.2	0.76	0.18	0.83

Step 6: Lastly, if required, defuzzify the obtained membership values by converting the fuzzy values into crisp values (based on the finally obtained membership values) to let the data points fall into one cluster.

Let us try to implement Fuzzy c-Means clustering as given in Program 2.2. This is a Python program contributed by a programmer in gihub. It uses the famous *iris* dataset available in the Kaggle website. At first, the dataset (filename: *iris.csv*) is loaded, and the several parameters are defined. For this, the fuzziness parameter (m) is considered as 2 in the program, the number of clusters (k) is considered as 3, the number of data points (n) is found out from the dataset using the *len()* function. Also, instead of a two-dimensional data, this program considers data of a higher dimension (d), which is 4. The entire steps are repeated, and the maximum number of iterations considered is 12.

Next, in the program, the membership function values (or weights) are randomly assigned to each data point, and accordingly the centroid of the three clusters is obtained. Next, for each of the three clusters, the distance is accordingly calculated for all of the data points. Also, accordingly, the weights are updated for each data point. The updating of membership function values (weights) is carried out for the maximum of 12 iterations, and the final centroid value of each cluster is obtained. Finally, the data visualization graph for all the clusters are displayed to visualize the three clusters formed for all the data points of the *iris* dataset.

Program 2.2 *Fuzzy c-Means (FCM) Clustering*

```
#Source Code Credit: github
#Importing packages
import pandas as pd
import numpy as np
import random
import operator
import math
import matplotlib.pyplot as plt
```

```
from scipy.stats import multivariate_normal
from sklearn.datasets import load_iris

#Load Dataset
"""
from google.colab import files
uploaded = files.upload()
df_full = pd.read_csv('Iris.csv')
df = df_full.drop(columns=['Id'])
df.shape
df.head()
df = df.drop(columns=['Species'])
df.head()
"""
iris = load_iris()
df = pd.DataFrame(iris.data)
echo "Loading the First Five Records"
df.head()

#Number of data
n = len(df)
#Number of clusters
k = 3
#Dimension of data
d = 4
# m parameter
m = 2
#Number of iterations
MAX_ITERS = 12

#Initializing membership functions
def initializeMembershipWeights():
  """
  membership_mat = []
  for i in range(n):
    wts = []
    sum=0;
    for j in range(k):
      weight = np.random.random_integers(1,10)
      wts.append(weight)
      sum = sum + weight
    weights = [w/sum for w in wts]
    membership_mat.append(weights)
    print(membership_mat)

  """
  weight = np.random.dirichlet(np.ones(k),n)
  weight_arr = np.array(weight)
  return weight_arr
```

```
#Calculating Centroids of Clusters
def computeCentroids(weight_arr):
  C = []
  for i in range(k):
    weight_sum = np.power(weight_arr[:,i],m).sum()
    Cj = []
    for x in range(d):
      numerator = ( df.iloc[:,x].values * np.power(weight_
                    arr[:,i],m)).sum()
      c_val = numerator/weight_sum;
      Cj.append(c_val)
    C.append(Cj)
  return C

#Updating Membership Values
def updateWeights(weight_arr,C):
  denom = np.zeros(n)
  for i in range(k):
    dist = (df.iloc[:,:].values - C[i])**2
    dist = np.sum(dist, axis=1)
    dist = np.sqrt(dist)
    denom = denom + np.power(1/dist,1/(m-1))

  for i in range(k):
    dist = (df.iloc[:,:].values - C[i])**2
    dist = np.sum(dist, axis=1)
    dist = np.sqrt(dist)
    weight_arr[:,i] = np.divide(np.power(1/dist,1/(m-1)),denom)
  return weight_arr

#Running the algorithm
def FuzzyMeansAlgorithm():
  weight_arr = initializeMembershipWeights()
for z in range(MAX_ITERS):
    C = computeCentroids(weight_arr)
    updateWeights(weight_arr,C)
 return (weight_arr,C)
final_weights,Centers = FuzzyMeansAlgorithm()

#Visualizing the Clusters
X = np.zeros((n,1))
plt.figure(0,figsize=(8,8))
plt.axis('equal')
#scatter plot of sepal length vs sepal width
plt.xlabel('Sepal Length', fontsize=16)
plt.ylabel('Sepal Width', fontsize=16)
plt.title('Sepal Plot', fontsize=25,color='b')
plt.grid()
```

```
for center in Centers:
  plt.scatter(center[0],center[1], marker='D',color='r')
clr = 'b'
for i in range(n):
    cNumber = np.where(final_weights[i] == np.amax(final_
            weights[i]))
    if cNumber[0][0]==0:
      clr = 'y'
    elif cNumber[0][0]==1:
      clr = 'g'
    elif cNumber[0][0]==2:
      clr = 'm'
    plt.scatter(list(df_sepal.iloc[i:i+1,0]),
        list(df_sepal.iloc[i:i+1,1]), alpha=0.25,s=100,color=clr)
plt.show()

#scatter plot of petal length vs petal width
X = np.zeros((n,1))
plt.figure(0,figsize=(8,8))
plt.axis('equal')
plt.xlabel('Petal Length', fontsize=16)
plt.ylabel('Petal Width', fontsize=16)
plt.title('Petal Plot', fontsize=25,color='b')
plt.grid()
for center in Centers:
  plt.scatter(center[2],center[3], marker='D',color='r')
clr = 'b'
for i in range(n):
    cNumber = np.where(final_weights[i] == np.amax(final_
            weights[i]))
    if cNumber[0][0]==0:
      clr = 'y'
    elif cNumber[0][0]==1:
      clr = 'g'
    elif cNumber[0][0]==2:
      clr = 'm'
    plt.scatter(list(df_petal.iloc[i:i+1,0]),
        list(df_petal.iloc[i:i+1,1]), alpha=0.25, s=100, color=clr)
plt.show()
```

The output for the Program 2.2 is displayed using visualization graphs. Figure 2.28 shows the scatter plot diagram for (a) the sepal length versus the sepal width, and (b) the petal length versus the petal width. The three red diamond-shaped markers indicate the final centroid values for the three different clusters. The colors of the data points indicate to which cluster it belongs to.

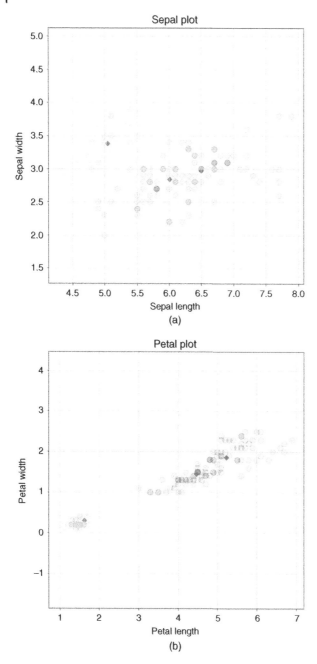

Figure 2.28 Scatter plot for (a) Sepal length versus sepal width, and (b) Petal length versus petal width.

Loading the First Five Records

	0	1	2	3
0	5.1	3.5	1.4	0.2
1	4.9	3.0	1.4	0.2
2	4.7	3.2	1.3	0.2
3	4.6	3.1	1.5	0.2
4	5.0	3.6	1.4	0.2

The Fuzzy c-means is a widely used algorithm for clustering data points that may belong to more than one cluster. While Program 2.2 imports the standard Python libraries to implement the Fuzzy c-means algorithm, the *skfuzzy* (*scikit-fuzzy*) library can also be used to implement the same algorithm, as it has a rich in-built predefined functions specifically dedicated for fuzzy operations. The easiest way of fuzzy implementation in Python is by using Scikit package. In Linux platform, the package can be installed by using pip.

```
pip install-U scikit-fuzzy
```

Fuzzy logic has a wide extended application in many industrial appliances as well as home appliances, starting from the smooth transition of a building elevator, washing machines, air conditioner, vacuum cleaner, etc. Most of the recent fuzzy-based control systems are adaptive, i.e., the membership function shape and scaling factors are changed during the course of operation based on constrained and environmental influence of input variables.

Exercises

A) Choose the correct answer from among the alternatives given:
   a) Fuzzy logic is based on:
      i) Crisp set logic
      ii) Fixed-valued logic
      iii) Multivalued logic
      iv) Binary set logic
   b) A fuzzy set whose membership function has at least one value equal to 1 is called _____
      i) Normal fuzzy set
      ii) Convex fuzzy set
      iii) Support fuzzy set
      iv) Membership fuzzy set

c) If $A = \{0.6/p,\ 0/q,\ 1/r,\ 0/s,\ 0.7/t\}$, then, support($A$) and core($A$) are _____ and _____, respectively.
   i) $\{q, s\}, \{p, r, t\}$
   ii) $\{q, s\}, \{r\}$
   iii) $\{q, r, s\}, \{p, t\}$
   iv) $\{p, r, t\}, \{r\}$

d) The _____ property states that the complement of a set is the set itself.
   i) associative
   ii) involution
   iii) commutative
   iv) transitivity

e) The Gaussian membership function is defined by two parameters, namely _____ and _____.
   i) Mean, standard deviation
   ii) Mean, fuzzification factor
   iii) Standard deviation, fuzzification factor
   iv) Lower boundary value, height

f) A sigmoidal membership function is formulated as:

$$\mu(x) = \frac{1}{1 + e^{-a(x-b)}}$$

$$\mu(x) = e^{\left[-\frac{1}{2}\left(\frac{x-f}{\sigma} \right)^2 \right]}$$

$$\mu_\theta = t \tan \theta$$

$$\mu_S(x) = \frac{1}{1 + x^2}$$

g) The region of universe that is characterized by complete membership in the set is called
   i) Core
   ii) Support
   iii) Boundary
   iv) Fuzzy

h) Which among the following is not a method of defuzzification?
   i) Max-membership principle
   ii) Mean-max membership
   iii) Convex-max membership
   iv) Weighted average method

i) In genetic algorithm, the membership functions are coded into _____.
   i) Bit strings

    ii) Support values

    iii) Boundary values

    iv) Probabilistic values

  j) In case of fuzzy c-means clustering, which value(s) is/are constantly updated until a certain iteration is reached?

    i) Membership values of data points belonging to clusters

    ii) Centroid values of clusters

    iii) Either (a) or (b)

    iv) Both (a) and (b)

B) Answer the following questions:

  1) What is a fuzzy set? What is a membership function of a fuzzy set?

  2) Can a fuzzy membership be True and False at the same time? Justify your answer.

  3) What is the purpose of defuzzyfication? Explain any two standard methods used for defuzzyfication.

  4) Determine the intersection and unions of the following fuzzy sets

$$A = \{(3, 0.1), (4, 0.3), (5, 0.6), (7, 0.8), (8, 0.6), (11, 0.4), (12, 0.9), (6, 0.3)\}$$

$$B = \{(3, 0.1), (6, 0.2), (7, 0.4), (8, 0.6), (8, 0.6)\}$$

  5) State the De Morgan's law. Also prove the De Morgan's law by considering the two fuzzy sets A and B given in Question 4.

  6) Explain any two standard ways by which membership values can be assigned to fuzzy variables.

  7) Given a binary fuzzy relation $R(X, Y)$ such that:

$$R = X \times Y = \begin{bmatrix} 0.6 & 0.9 & 1.0 \\ 0.8 & 0.7 & 0.3 \\ 0.4 & 0.4 & 0 \end{bmatrix}$$

    vi. What is the height of R?

    vii. Find the domain and range of R.

    viii. Find the inverse of R.

  8) Show that the function

$t(x) = \max\{\min(x - a/b - a, \ c - x/c - b), \ 0\}$ gives the triangular set determined by the points $(a, 0), (b, 1), (c, 0)$ for $a < b < c$.

Consider the linguistic variable "Age". Let the term "old" be defined by

$$\mu_{old}(x) = \begin{cases} 0 & \text{if } x \in [0, 40] \\ (1 + \{(x - 40)/5\}^{-2})^{-1} & \text{if } x \in (40, 100] \end{cases}$$

Determine the membership function of the terms "very old," "not very old," and "more or less old."

9) Consider a fuzzy set for *optimum number of hours of sleep per day (SPD)* defined as follows:

$$SPD = \{(5, 0.3), (6, 0.5), (8, 0.9), (12, 0.5), (14, 0.2)\}$$

Find the crisp value for *Optimum Sleeping Hours per Day* using:
   i) The height method
   ii) The mean-max membership method
   iii) The centroid method
   iv) The weighted-average method

3

Artificial Neural Network

Human brain is a collection of many billions of interconnected neurons. A neuron is a cell in a neural network system of a human body, and it uses biochemical reactions to obtain data for processing and transmitting information. It primarily consists of four parts – dendrite, soma, axon, and synapse. Dendrites are tree-like structures that act as the receptors that receive signals from the other neurons. Once the signals are received, the soma is the main cell body that sums up all these incoming signals to create input. The axon is the area through which neuron signals travel to other neurons when a neuron is fired. The end of axon of one neuron makes a contact to the dendrite of the other neuron through synapse (terminals). A neuron gets fired only if certain conditions are met.

As can be seen in Figure 3.1, the dendrites gather data from neighboring neurons and deliver it to the soma. The processing of data takes place in the soma ("the brain of the cell") and passes through axon. Axons are like the wires and are insulated with a substance called myelin, which help in sending electrical signals in right direction. The signals finally reach to synapses, which are typically connected to the dendrites of other neurons.

A neuron remains at resting potential until it receives enough electrical signals, based on which it gets ready to fire its action potential. A postsynaptic neuron that transmits the signal away from the synapse can have many excitatory or inhibitory presynaptic neurons. An impulse can be stimulated based on the summation value of all neurotransmitters received. The excitatory signals exceed the inhibitory signals by a certain quantified value called the threshold value. Once this threshold is exceeded, the neuron gets fired. A certain positive weight is assigned to incoming excitatory signals, and negative weight is assigned to inhibitory signals. A weight value technically indicates the amount of impact of a signal on excitation of the neuron. Finally, a cumulative value is obtained by multiplying the signals with the weight of all the incoming synapses. A neuron gets excited and fires only if the cumulative value exceeds a certain threshold value.

Principles of Soft Computing Using Python Programming: Learn How to Deploy Soft Computing Models in Real World Applications, First Edition. Gypsy Nandi.
© 2024 The Institute of Electrical and Electronics Engineers, Inc. Published 2024 by John Wiley & Sons, Inc.

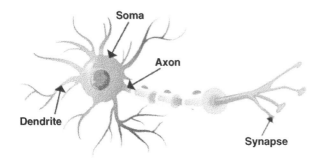

Figure 3.1 Main parts of a neuron.

3.1 Fundamentals of Artificial Neural Network (ANN)

Artificial neural networks (ANNs) have been a major area of research in various fields of study, such as medical science, engineering, economics, and forecasting. ANNs are widely used in solving problems whose solutions require knowledge that is quite difficult to stipulate but have adequate data to find an optimal solution. It is a mathematical formulation in its simplest form that performs similar to the complex biological neural network system.

ANN assumes that information processing takes place at neurons, and signals are passed between neurons (or nodes) over connection links. A neuron is a processing unit that has some inputs and only one output. ANN requires a minimum of one input layer and one output layer. In between, there can be zero to any number of hidden layers. The input to the neurons of the input layer of the network is fed as input vector. There may be a number of layers of neurons and a number of neurons in each layer. Each neuron in a layer is connected to all the neurons of the subsequent higher layer. Also, each connection link has an associated weight that is multiplied to the transmitted signal. Finally, an activation function is applied to the cumulative value (sum of all weighted signals) to obtain the output.

As can be seen in Figure 3.2, each input of a neuron (x_i) is weighted by a factor (w_i), and the summation of all "n" inputs is calculated using Equation (3.1):

$$\sum_{i=1}^{n} x_i w_i = a \tag{3.1}$$

Next, a standard activation function f is applied to the result (a) to determine at what extent the signal should progress further through the network to affect the final outcome. The output is the result obtained as $f(a)$, as shown in Equation (3.2).

$$\text{Output} = f(a) = \text{activation\_function} \left(\sum_{i=1}^{n} x_i w_i \right) \tag{3.2}$$

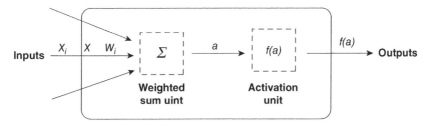

Figure 3.2 Working of a neuron.

The tunable parameters of this entire network are the weights (w_i) that are applied with each input. When input is combined with weights by a node, it either amplifies or dampens the input, thereby conveying implication to inputs with regard to the task the algorithm is trying to learn. If the signal passes through, the neuron is said to be "*activated.*"

There are standard mathematical procedures, often called as *training* or *learning*, for tuning the weight values. Tuning the weights in a neural network is a crucial step in the training process. The goal of weight tuning is to find the optimal set of weights and biases that allow the network to make accurate predictions or classifications. This process is essential for achieving high performance in various machine learning tasks. Some of the important goals of weight tuning include:

(a) **Minimizing Loss Function:** The primary goal of weight tuning is to minimize the loss function, which quantifies the difference between the network's predictions and the actual target values. Lower loss indicates better alignment between predictions and targets.

(b) **Increasing Accuracy:** Weight tuning aims to increase the accuracy of the network's predictions or classifications on both the training data and new, unseen data.

(c) **Avoiding Overfitting:** Weight tuning helps prevent overfitting, where the network memorizes the training data instead of learning the underlying patterns. Overfitting can lead to poor performance on new data.

(d) **Achieving Convergence:** Properly tuned weights contribute to faster convergence during training. This means the network reaches a satisfactory level of performance in fewer training iterations.

(e) **Ensuring Stable Learning:** Well-tuned weights promote stable learning dynamics and prevent issues like vanishing gradients, which can hinder the training process in deep networks.

This process of weight tuning is typically achieved through optimization algorithms that iteratively update the network's parameters. The mathematical procedures involved in this training process is described next:

(a) **Forward Pass:** During each iteration of training, a set of input data (often called a training sample) is fed into the neural network. Each neuron in the network receives inputs from the previous layer, computes a weighted sum of those inputs, adds a bias term, and applies an activation function to produce an output.

(b) **Compute Loss:** The output of the neural network is compared to the actual target output for that input using a loss function (also known as a cost function). The loss function quantifies how far off the network's predictions are from the desired outputs. Common loss functions include mean squared error for regression tasks and cross-entropy for classification tasks.

(c) **Backpropagation:** Backpropagation is the core of the training process. It calculates the gradients of the loss with respect to the weights and biases of the network. These gradients indicate how much each weight and bias contribute to the overall error. The gradients are calculated using the chain rule of calculus. The process starts from the output layer and propagates backward through the layers.

(d) **Weight Update:** With the gradients calculated, optimization algorithms are used to update the weights and biases. These algorithms adjust the parameters in a way that reduces the loss function. One common optimization algorithm is gradient descent. It involves subtracting a fraction (learning rate) of the gradient from each weight. The direction of the update is determined by the gradient's sign.

(e) **Batch and Epochs:** Instead of updating weights after every single input (stochastic gradient descent), optimization often involves using batches of inputs. The gradient is averaged over the batch, and a weight update is applied. Training is typically organized into epochs, where the entire training dataset is processed. The network goes through multiple epochs to iteratively improve its performance.

(f) **Regularization:** To prevent overfitting, regularization techniques are often applied during training. Regularization adds a penalty term to the loss function based on the magnitudes of the weights. L1 and L2 regularization are common approaches.

(g) **Hyperparameters:** Learning rate, regularization strength, batch size, and more are hyperparameters that need to be tuned. They impact the training process, and can affect convergence and generalization.

(h) **Termination:** Training continues for a predefined number of epochs or until a termination criterion is met (e.g., loss drops below a threshold, performance stabilizes).

The training process is iterative, with each iteration aiming to adjust the weights and biases in a way that improves the network's performance. This process continues until the network's performance reaches a satisfactory level or plateaus. While the explanation provided here is a simplified overview, the actual calculations can be complex, especially in deep networks with multiple layers and connections. Let's consider a network with the architecture:

- **Input Layer:** 2 neurons
- **Hidden Layer:** 3 neurons
- **Output Layer:** 1 neuron

Step 1: Forward Pass

Given an input $(x1, x2) = (0.5, 0.7)$, the network's weights and biases are as follows:

Hidden Layer: weights (w_h) and biases (b_h)
Output Layer: weights (w_o) and bias (b_o)

During the forward pass, the weighted sum of inputs is calculated for each neuron in the hidden layer as follows:

```
z_h1 = w_h1 * x1 + w_h2 * x2 + b_h1
z_h2 = w_h3 * x1 + w_h4 * x2 + b_h2
z_h3 = w_h5 * x1 + w_h6 * x2 + b_h3
```

Next, an activation function (e.g., sigmoid) is applied to the hidden layer's outputs. This can be done using Python code as follows:

```
a_h1 = sigmoid(z_h1)
a_h2 = sigmoid(z_h2)
a_h3 = sigmoid(z_h3)
```

Next, the weighted sum of inputs is calculated for the output neuron as follows:

```
z_o = w_o1 * a_h1 + w_o2 * a_h2 + w_o3 * a_h3 + b_o
```

Finally, an activation function is applied to the output neuron's output (e.g., linear for regression or sigmoid for binary classification):

```
a_o = sigmoid(z_o)
```

Step 2: Compute Loss

Assuming the target output y_target = 0.9, the loss function (mean squared error) is calculated as:

```
loss = 0.5 * (y_target - a_o)^2
```

Step 3: Backpropagation

Now, let us calculate the gradients of the loss with respect to the weights and biases in reverse order:

(a) **Output Layer:**

Gradient of loss with respect to output activation:

- Calculate the gradient of the loss with respect to the output activation (d_loss/da_o):

```
d_loss/da_o = a_o - y_target
```

- Calculate the gradient of the output activation with respect to the weighted sum (d_a_o/dz_o):

```
d_a_o/dz_o = sigmoid_derivative(z_o) = sigmoid(z_o)
      * (1 - sigmoid(z_o))
```

- Calculate the gradients of the weighted sum with respect to the output layer weights and bias (d_z_o/dw_o1, d_z_o/dw_o2, d_z_o/dw_o3, and d_z_o/db_o):

```
d_z_o/dw_o1 = a_h1
d_z_o/dw_o2 = a_h2
d_z_o/dw_o3 = a_h3
d_z_o/db_o = 1
```

(b) **Hidden Layer:**

- Use the chain rule to calculate the gradient of the loss with respect to the hidden layer activations (d_loss/da_h1, d_loss/da_h2, d_loss/da_h3):

```
d_loss/da_h1 = (d_loss/da_o) * (d_a_o/dz_o) * w_o1
d_loss/da_h2 = (d_loss/da_o) * (d_a_o/dz_o) * w_o2
d_loss/da_h3 = (d_loss/da_o) * (d_a_o/dz_o) * w_o3
```

- Calculate the gradient of the activation function with respect to the weighted sum (d_a_h1/dz_h1, d_a_h2/dz_h2, d_a_h3/dz_h3):

```
d_a_h1/dz_h1 = sigmoid_derivative(z_h1)
d_a_h2/dz_h2 = sigmoid_derivative(z_h2)
d_a_h3/dz_h3 = sigmoid_derivative(z_h3)
```

- Calculate the gradients of the weighted sum with respect to the hidden layer weights and bias (d_z_h1/dw_h1, d_z_h1/dw_h2, d_z_h1/db_h1, d_z_h2/dw_h3, d_z_h2/dw_h4, d_z_h2/db_h2, d_z_h3/dw_h5, d_z_h3/dw_h6, d_z_h3/db_h3):

```
d_z_h1/dw_h1 = x1
d_z_h1/dw_h2 = x2
d_z_h1/db_h1 = 1
```

```
d_z_h2/dw_h3 = x1
d_z_h2/dw_h4 = x2
d_z_h2/db_h2 = 1

d_z_h3/dw_h5 = x1
d_z_h3/dw_h6 = x2
d_z_h3/db_h3 = 1
```

Step 4: Weight Update:
Using the calculated gradients, the weights and biases in the network are adjusted using an optimization algorithm like gradient descent. The goal is to update the parameters in a way that reduces the loss. This process of calculating gradients and updating weights is performed iteratively over multiple epochs until the loss converges to a satisfactory level or the training process is completed.

Backpropagation is a fundamental concept that allows neural networks to learn from data by adjusting their parameters to minimize prediction errors. While the example provided is simplified, the actual calculations can be more complex, especially in deeper networks with more layers and connections.

3.2 Standard Activation Functions in Neural Networks

An activation function, as mentioned in Section 3.1 of this chapter, is used to determine the output of a neural network by comparing the obtained result with a threshold value. It is also at times called as transfer function. It basically maps the resulting values within a fixed range such as 0 to 1, or −1 to +1, depending upon the function applied. The activation function basically adds nonlinearity into the output of a neuron.

Let us discuss the various standard activation functions used in neural networks in this section. All activation functions can be categorized as binary step function, linear function, and the various nonlinear functions (such as sigmoid and Rectified Linear Unit [ReLU]). It is the various nonlinear activation functions that are most often used in generating output in case of neural networks.

3.2.1 Binary Step Activation Function

This function uses the threshold value to decide whether a neuron should be activated or not. That is, the input fed to the activation function is at first compared to a threshold value, and the final output is obtained accordingly as either 0 or 1. In this case, if the input is greater than the threshold value, the neuron is activated; else, it is deactivated.

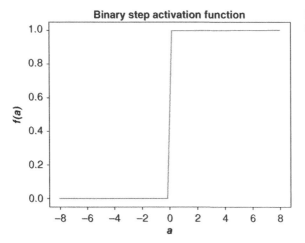

Figure 3.3 Binary step activation function.

Figure 3.3 shows a case of binary step function that can result in either of the two output –0 or 1. The x-axis denotes the value of "a" that is within the integer range −8 to +8. When the value of "a" is greater than or equal to 0, the output $f(a)$ results in 1 (as can be seen from the figure), and the output $f(a)$ results in 0 when the value of "a" is less than 0. Mathematically, the binary step function for Figure 3.3 can be represented as given in Equation (3.3):

$$f(a) = \begin{cases} 0 \text{ for } a < 0 \\ 1 \text{ for } a \geq 0 \end{cases} \tag{3.3}$$

To plot the graph as shown in Figure 3.3, the corresponding Python code is provided in Program 3.1. The plotted graph displays the binary step function based on the value of "a." The output generated can be either 0 or 1, based on the condition given in the program.

Program 3.1 *Python Code to Display Binary Step Activation Function*

```
import numpy as np
import matplotlib.pyplot as plt

def binaryStep(a):
    return np.heaviside(a,1)

a = np.linspace(-8, 8)
plt.plot(a, binaryStep(a))
```

```
plt.title('Binary Step Activation Function',
          fontweight='bold')
plt.xlabel("a", fontweight='bold')
plt.ylabel("f(a)", fontweight='bold')
plt.show()
```

Binary step function suffers from a major limitation, as it cannot provide multivalue outputs. As a result, it cannot be used in several tasks such as multiclass classification. Also, in case of binary step function, the gradient of the step function is zero, which causes a difficulty in the process of backpropagation (to be discussed later).

3.2.2 Linear Activation Function

The linear activation function, also called as identity activation function, results in an output that remains proportional to the input. Mathematically, the linear activation function can be represented as given in Equation (3.4):

$$f(a) = a \tag{3.4}$$

Figure 3.4 shows a case of linear activation function that results in the same value of "a" for $f(a)$.

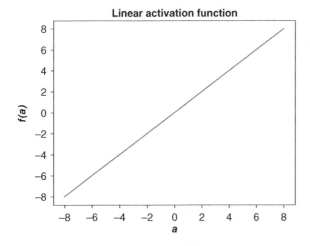

Figure 3.4 Linear activation function.

To plot the graph as shown in Figure 3.4, the corresponding Python code is provided in Program 3.2. The plotted graph displays the linear function based on the value of "*a*." The output generated is proportional to the value of "*a*," as given in the condition of the program.

Program 3.2 *Python Code to Display Linear Activation Function*

```
import numpy as np
import matplotlib.pyplot as plt

def linear(a):
    return (a)

a = np.linspace(-8, 8)
plt.plot(a, linear(a))
plt.title('Linear Activation Function', fontweight
        ='bold')
plt.xlabel("a", fontweight='bold')
plt.ylabel("f(a)", fontweight='bold')
plt.show()
```

The linear activation function suffers from a major limitation in neural network, as it is not possible to use backpropagation to find how the neural weights should change based on the errors found.

3.2.3 Sigmoid/Logistic Activation Function

This function, which is plotted as an "S"-shaped graph, guarantees to provide an output in the range of 0–1. Because of this, sigmoid function is often used for probability prediction, which demands an output to be between 0 and 1. Mathematically, the sigmoid activation function can be represented as given in Equation (3.5):

$$f(a) = \frac{1}{1 + e^{-a}} \tag{3.5}$$

Figure 3.5 shows a case of sigmoid activation function that displays an S-shape graph. The result obtained is within the range of 0–1.

To plot the graph as shown in Figure 3.5, the corresponding Python code is provided in Program 3.3. The plotted graph displays the sigmoid activation function based on the value of "*a*." The output generated is between 0 and 1 based on the condition given in the program.

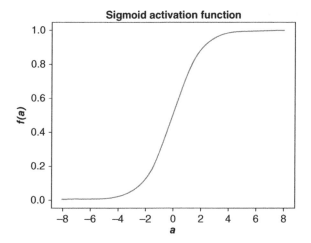

Figure 3.5 Sigmoid activation function.

Program 3.3 *Python Code to Display Sigmoid Activation Function*

```python
import numpy as np
import matplotlib.pyplot as plt

def sigmoid(a):
    return 1/(1+np.exp(-a))

a = np.linspace(-8, 8)
plt.plot(a, sigmoid(a))
plt.title('Sigmoid Activation Function',
          fontweight='bold')
plt.xlabel("a", fontweight='bold')
plt.ylabel("f(a)", fontweight='bold')
plt.show()
```

The sigmoid function suffers from a major problem called as the vanishing gradient problem, which happens because even a large input of data is finally converted to an output having a small range of 0–1. Therefore, their derivatives become much smaller, and it does not always give satisfactory output.

3.2.4 ReLU Activation Function

ReLU is the most commonly used activation function in neural networks. It is a nonlinear function that displays its output the same as the value of input if the

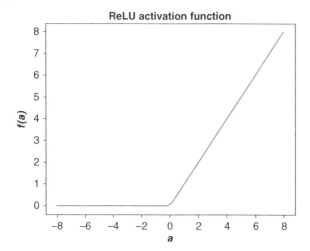

Figure 3.6 ReLU activation function.

input is positive; otherwise, it displays the output as zero (0). Mathematically, the ReLU activation function can be represented as given in Equation (3.6):

$$f(a) = \max(0, a) \tag{3.6}$$

Figure 3.6 shows a case of ReLU activation function that displays the output as 0 if the input is less than or equal to zero; otherwise it displays the same value as input "a." Thus, the result obtained is within the range of 0–a.

To plot the graph as shown in Figure 3.6, the corresponding Python code is provided in Program 3.4. A simple if–else statement is used to handle the condition and display the output accordingly for the given input, which is in the range of −8 to +8.

Program 3.4 *Python Code to Display ReLU Activation Function*

```
import numpy as np
import matplotlib.pyplot as plt

def relu(a):
    z=[]
    for i in a:
        if i<0:
            z.append(0)
        else:
            z.append(i)
    return z
```

```
a = np.linspace(-8, 8)
plt.plot(a, relu(a))
plt.title('ReLU Activation Function', fontweight='bold')
plt.xlabel("a", fontweight='bold')
plt.ylabel("f(a)", fontweight='bold')
plt.show()
```

The ReLU function helps resolve the vanishing gradient problem, which is found in case of the sigmoid activation function. Also, the ReLU function takes lesser time for the model and minimize the errors. However, one issue that may occur while using the ReLU function is that it will constantly provide the output as 0 if the neurons get stuck with the negative values. As a result, "dead neurons" are created that can never recover.

3.2.5 Tanh Activation Function

The tanh activation function is similar to the sigmoid function, as both form an S-shape with the main difference in that the range of the tanh function is from −1 to +1, whereas the range is from 0 to 1 for sigmoid function. Mathematically, the tanh activation function can be represented as given in Equation (3.7):

$$f(a) = \frac{e^a - e^{-a}}{e^a + e^{-a}} \tag{3.7}$$

Figure 3.7 shows a case of tanh activation function that displays the output, which is zero-centered (i.e., -1 <= output <= 1). This function can be used

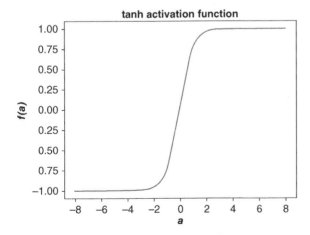

Figure 3.7 tanh activation function.

for hidden layers of a neural network, as it allows centering of data by bringing the mean value close to 0.

To plot the graph as shown in Figure 3.7, the corresponding Python code is provided in Program 3.5. In this program, the simple *tanh()* function is used to take the value of "*a*" as input and display the corresponding output. The input "*a*" is expected to be in the range of −8 to +8.

Program 3.5 *Python Code to Display Tanh Activation Function*

```
import numpy as np
import matplotlib.pyplot as plt

def tanh(a):
    return np.tanh(a)

a = np.linspace(-8, 8)
plt.plot(a, tanh(a))
plt.title('tanh Activation Function', fontweight='bold')
plt.xlabel("a", fontweight='bold')
plt.ylabel("f(a)", fontweight='bold')
plt.show()
```

Like the sigmoid function, the tanh function is often used for binary classification. However, tanh also suffers from the vanishing gradient problem near the boundaries just as in case of the sigmoid activation function.

3.2.6 Leaky ReLU Activation Function

The leaky ReLU is a variation of the ReLU activation function that mainly tries to solve the issue of the dying ReLU problem that creates "dead neurons." It is considered as an improved version of the ReLU function as in case of ReLU, the gradient is 0 for all the values of inputs that are less than zero. In case of leaky ReLU, this problem is addressed by considering the output of input value of "*a*" as an extremely small linear component of "*a*."

Mathematically, the leaky ReLU activation function can be represented as given in Equation (3.8):

$$f(a) = \max(z * a, a) \tag{3.8}$$

Here, z is a constant value having a small magnitude (e.g., 0.01, 0.03, 0.05, etc.).

Figure 3.8 shows a case of leaky ReLU activation function that displays similar output as the ReLU activation function for a>=0. However, if a<0, unlike the

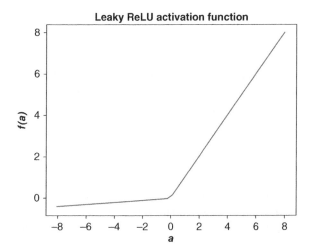

Figure 3.8 Leaky ReLU activation function.

ReLU function (where, $f(a) = 0$), the output is not exactly zero but nearby a zero value.

To plot the graph as shown in Figure 3.8, the corresponding Python code is provided in Program 3.6. Here, in this program, the constant factor considered for multiplying when input a is less than 0 is 0.05.

Program 3.6 *Python Code to Display Leaky ReLU Activation Function*

```python
import numpy as np
import matplotlib.pyplot as plt

def lkrelu(a):
    z=[]
    for I in a:
        if i<0:
            z.append(0.05 * i)
        else:
            z.append(i)
    return z

a = np.linspace(-8, 8)
plt.plot(a, lkrelu(a))
plt.title('Leaky ReLU Activation Function',
          fontweight='bold')
plt.xlabel("a", fontweight='bold')
```

```
plt.ylabel("f(a)", fontweight='bold')
plt.show()
```

The leaky ReLU activation function is hardly used in cases where the ReLU provides an optimal output. However, to avoid the *"dying ReLU"* problem, leaky ReLU is often considered as a better choice, as it performs better and produces better results.

3.2.7   SoftMax Activation Function

This is a multidimensional activation function that is often used in neural network to decide upon the output in case of multiclass classification. The function mainly calculates the probabilities distribution of an event over "*n*" different events. Let us consider "*a*" as the series of values from the neurons of the output layer; the SoftMax function can be calculated as given in Equation (3.9):

$$f(a)_i = \frac{e^{a_i}}{\sum_{j=1}^{n} e^{a_i}} \tag{3.9}$$

Figure 3.9 shows a case of SoftMax activation function that considers the input range between −8 and +8. If the number of classes is only two, the SoftMax function produces the same output as the sigmoid function.

To plot the graph as shown in Figure 3.9, the corresponding Python code is provided in Program 3.7. The SoftMax function uses the exponential that acts as the nonlinear function.

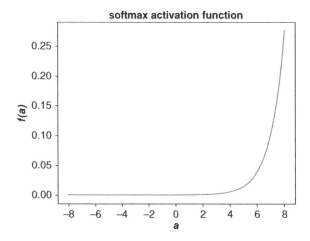

Figure 3.9   SoftMax activation function.

Program 3.7 *Python Code to Display SoftMax Activation Function*

```python
import numpy as np
import matplotlib.pyplot as plt

def softmax(a):
    return np.exp(a) / np.sum(np.exp(a), axis=0)

a = np.linspace(-8, 8)
plt.plot(a, softmax(a))
plt.title('softmax Activation Function',
          fontweight='bold')
plt.xlabel("a", fontweight='bold')
plt.ylabel("f(a)", fontweight='bold')
plt.show()
```

Usually, the ReLU activation function is used in hidden layer to avoid the vanishing gradient problem and better computation performance, and the SoftMax function is used in last output layer for generating the final output.

Table 3.1 summarizes the list of all the standard activation functions covered in this section, and provides each of their corresponding equations and plot.

Now, the main query that may arise in one's mind is which activation function is the best choice to be used. Well, it all depends on the nature of task to be solved. One basic and easy rule for choosing the appropriate activation function for the output layer is:

- For *linear regression* – choose the linear activation function
- For *probability prediction* – choose the logistic activation function
- For *binary classification* – choose the logistic or tanh activation function
- For *multiclass classification* – choose the SoftMax activation function
- For *multilabel classification* – choose the sigmoid activation function
- For *neural network* – choose the ReLU and SoftMax activation functions

In the next section, we will learn about the two main types of ANN – feed-forward neural network and feed-backward neural network. To begin with, the simplest neural feed-forward network model, namely the *Perceptron*, is discussed followed by the more complex models that are often used in many applications.

3.3 Basic Learning Rules in ANN

As ANN models are adaptive in nature, learning rules help ANN to adapt to change itself with change in environment. Basically, the learning rules are applied in ANN

Table 3.1 List of standard activation functions.

Activation function	Equation	Plot
Binary step	$f(a) = \begin{cases} 0 \text{ for } a < 0 \\ 1 \text{ for } a \geq 0 \end{cases}$	
Linear	$f(a) = a$	
Sigmoid or Logistic	$f(a) = \dfrac{1}{1 + e^{-a}}$	
ReLU	$f(a) = \max(0, a)$	
Tanh	$f(a) = \dfrac{e^a - e^{-a}}{e^a + e^{-a}}$	
Leaky ReLU	$f(a) = \max(z * a, a)$	
SoftMax	$f(a)_i = \dfrac{e^{a_i}}{\sum_{j=1}^{n} e^{a_i}}$	

models to improve the performance of the model. It is an iterative process used for learning from the existing condition of the network and accordingly enhance the ANN's performance. It is a mathematical method that updates the weights and bias levels of a neural network during its training process.

All learning rules fall under either of the three categories – supervised learning rule, unsupervised learning rule, and reinforcement learning rule. In case of supervised learning rule, the desired output is compared with the actual output, and accordingly the weights are adjusted. Unsupervised learning rule combines the input vectors of similar type to form clusters. There is no direct feedback provided from the environment with regard to the desired output. Reinforcement learning rule function by receiving some feedback from the environment based on which the network performs adjustments of the weights to get better critic information in future.

Discussed below are the six standard learning rules used in ANNs. While Hebbian learning rule and competitive learning rule are unsupervised in nature, Perceptron learning rule, delta learning rule, correlation learning rule, and Outstar learning rule is supervised in nature.

3.3.1 Hebbian Learning Rule

The Hebbian learning rule, proposed by Donald Hebb, is one of the simplest unsupervised learning rules used in neural networks. This learning rule is often applied in logic gates, as it is very suitable for bipolar data. The method of weight updating is based on the correlation adjustment of weights. Prior to any learning, the values of all weights (w_{ji}) are set to zero (0), and also the bias value is assigned to zero (0). According to the rule's assumptions, if two neighboring neurons operate in the same phase, the weight between them increases. Oppositely, if two neighboring neurons operate in different phase, the weight between them decreases.

The mathematical formula used in the Hebbian learning rule is given in Equation (3.10):

$$\delta W_{ij}(t) = \alpha x_i(t) \cdot y_j(t) \tag{3.10}$$

Here, $\delta W_{ij}(t)$ is the change in weight value at time step t, α is the positive and constant learning rate that vary between 0 and 1, $x_i(t)$ is the input value from presynaptic neuron at time step t, and $y_j(t)$ is the output value of presynaptic neuron at time step t. In this case, based on the learning rule, if the cross product of input and output, or correlation term ($x_i(t) \cdot y_j(t)$) is positive, an increase of weight $W_{ij}(t)$ occurs; otherwise, the weight decreases.

3.3.2 Perceptron Learning Rule

The Perceptron learning rule was introduced by Rosenblatt. In this learning rule, prior to any learning, random values are assigned to all weights (w). Being supervised in nature, the learning occurs by comparing the desired output with the actual output. A change is made to the weights of the connection based on the weights difference. The learning stops when the actual output is equal to the obtained output.

Perceptron is a function that computes the function $f(x)$ by multiplying its input (x) with the learned weight coefficient. The output value $f(x)$ is generated as shown in Equation (3.11).

$$f(x) = \begin{cases} 1 & \text{if } \sum_{i=1}^{n} w_i x_i \geq \theta \\ 0 & \text{if } \sum_{i=1}^{n} w_i x_i < \theta \end{cases} \tag{3.11}$$

Here, "w" is the vector of real-valued weights, "θ" is the threshold value, and "x" is the vector of input values.

In the Perceptron learning rule, the predicted output is compared with the actual/known output. If both these values do not match, an error is propagated backward, and weight adjustment occurs until there is no difference in both the desired and actual outputs. This can be explained using two cases as follows:

The weight in the Perceptron learning rule (W_i) is modified during the training process according to the rule given in Equation (3.12):

$$W_i = W_i + \delta W_i \tag{3.12}$$

where,

$$\delta W_i = \alpha \, (t - o)x_i$$

Here, δW_i is the change of value of weight (W_i). It can be either a positive or negative value. α is the positive and constant learning rate that is usually a small value that keeps a control so that an aggressive change does not occur during the training of the model. t is the ground truth label (actual output) for the training set, o is the derived output of the model, and x_i is the ith dimension of the input. The learning of the model stops when $o = t$, i.e., the model is able to classify or predict correctly.

3.3.3 Delta Learning Rule

Delta rule was introduced by Bernard Widrow and Marcian Hoff, and is also called as least mean square rule. Like any other learning rule, the main objective of the delta learning rule is to minimize the error in every iteration. Here, the modification of the weight of a node is equal to the product of the error and the input, where the error is the difference between the desired and actual output.

The mathematical formula used in the Delta learning rule is given in Equation (3.13):

$$\delta W_i = \alpha \cdot x_i \cdot e_j \tag{3.13}$$

Here, δW_i is the change in weight in the ith iteration. α is the positive and constant learning rate that is usually a small value that keeps a control so that an aggressive change does not occur during the training of the model. x_i is the ith dimension of the input, and e_j is the difference between the obtained output (t) and the actual output (y), i.e., $e_j = t - y$.

The new weight value (W_{new}) in every iterative step is calculated by considering the previous/old weight value (W_{old}), which is added to the change in weight value as shown in Equation (3.13). That is, $W_{new} = W_{old} + \delta W_i$.

3.3.4 Correlation Learning Rule

The correlation learning rule almost adapts the same principle as that of the Hebbian learning rule. Like the Hebbian learning rule, it considers that if the connection between neurons is similar, then the weights between them increases; otherwise, if the connection shows a negative relationship, then the weight between them decreases. However, the main difference between Hebbian learning rule and Correlation learning rule is that correlation learning rule is supervised in nature, while the former is an unsupervised learning rule.

The mathematical representation of the Correlation learning rule is given in Equation (3.14):

$$\delta W_i = \alpha \cdot x_i \cdot d_j \tag{3.14}$$

Here, δW_i is the change in weight in the ith iteration. α is the positive and constant learning rate that is usually a small value that keeps a control so that an aggressive change does not occur during the training of the model. x_i is the ith dimension of the input, and d_j is the desired output.

3.3.5 Competitive Learning Rule

The competitive learning rule is also called as *Winner-takes-All* learning rule and is a form of unsupervised learning. This rule uses a strategy in which the winner is chosen based on the neuron that gives the highest total inputs. Only one output neuron per group is declared the winner ("ON"), and rest of the output neurons are considered "OFF." As only the winning neuron is updated, and rest of the neurons are not marked for any change, hence the name is given as `Winner-takes-All` learning rule.

Suppose an output neuron (y_j) wants to be the winner, the condition is set by the mathematical formula as given in Equation (3.15):

$$y_j = \begin{cases} 1 & \text{if } x_j > x_k, \text{for all } k, j \neq k \\ 0 & \text{otherwise} \end{cases} \tag{3.15}$$

Here, x_j is the largest among all the other group of neurons in the network. Hence, the corresponding output neuron y_j is declared the winner.

Once the winning output neuron is found, the change in the corresponding weight value occurs using the formula given in Equation (3.16):

$$\delta W_{jk} = \begin{cases} \alpha(x_k - W_{jk}), & \text{if neuron } j \text{ wins} \\ 0, & \text{if neuron } j \text{ losses} \end{cases} \tag{3.16}$$

Here, $W_{jk} = (W_{j1}, W_{j2}, W_{j3}, ..., W_{jn})$ is moved toward the input vector. The basic idea in competitive learning is to converge the weight vectors toward local input clusters.

3.3.6 Outstar Learning Rule

The Outstar learning rule was introduced by Grossberg and is hence often called as Grossberg learning rule. This rule is supervised in nature, as the desired outputs are known in advance. The nodes are assumed to be arranged in layers, and the change in weight is calculated using the mathematical formula as given in Equation (3.17):

$$\delta W_{ij} = \alpha(d_j - w_i) \tag{3.17}$$

Here, δW_i is the change in weight in the ith iteration. α is the positive and constant learning rate that is usually a small value that keeps a control so that an aggressive change does not occur during the training of the model. d_j is the jth dimension of the desired output, and w_i is the weight of the presynaptic neuron.

3.4 McCulloch–Pitts ANN Model

The most primitive model of ANN was introduced in the year 1943 by McCulloch and Walter Pitts, and it is popularly known as the *McCulloch–Pitts* neuron model. In this highly simplified model, the neuron has a set of inputs (input vector) and one output. All the neurons on a neural network are connected by synapse. The synaptic strength between two neurons is indicated by a value in the interval [0, 1] termed as the weight value. The model only accepts binary input and also produces a binary output (0 or 1), which is determined by a threshold value. The diagrammatic representation of the *McCulloch–Pitts* neuron model is shown in Figure 3.10. Here, x_i is the ith input to the neural network, and w_i is the weight associated with the synapse of the ith input. The weights associated with each input can be either excitatory (positive) or inhibitory (negative). The same positive weight value (+w1) is assigned for all the excitatory connections entering into particular neuron. Similarly, the same negative weight value (−w2) is assigned for

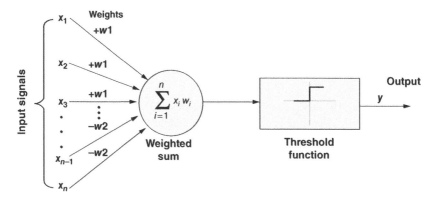

Figure 3.10 *McCulloch–Pitts* neuron model.

all the inhibitory connections entering into particular neuron. The weighted sum $g(x)$ is calculated as given in Equation (3.18):

$$g(x) = \sum_{i=1}^{n} x_i w_i \tag{3.18}$$

Finally, the threshold function is used to compute the output in binary form. Considering the threshold value as "θ," the output (y) is derived as either 0 or 1. Here, $y = 1$ if $f(g(x)) \geq \theta$; else $y = 0$ if $f(g(x)) < \theta$. The mathematical representation for deriving the output of the *McCulloch–Pitts* neuron model is given in Equation (3.19).

$$y = f(g(x)) = \begin{cases} 1, & f(g(x)) \geq \theta \\ 0, & f(g(x)) < \theta \end{cases} \tag{3.19}$$

Program 3.8 illustrates the Python code used to generate the *McCulloch–Pitts* neuron model. Here, four random binary input values are generated along with their corresponding weights. Next, the dot product is computed between the vector of inputs and weights. Finally, the output is generated by comparing the dot product value (dot) with the threshold value (T). If the dot value is greater than or equal to T, the neuron fires; otherwise, it does not fire.

Program 3.8 *Python Code for the McCulloch-Pitts Neuron Model*

```python
import numpy as np
np.random.seed(seed=0)

# generate random input vector I, sampling from {0,1}
X = np.random.choice([0,1], 4)

# generate random weight vector W, sampling from {-1,1}
W = np.random.choice([-1,1], 4)
print(f'Input vector:{X}')
print(f'Weight vector:{W}')

'computing the dot product between the vector of inputs
    and weights'
dot = X @ W
print(f'Dot product: {dot}')

'Comparing Weighted Input with Threshold Value'
def func(dot: int, T: float) -> int:
    if dot >= T:
        return 1
```

```
else:
    return 0

'Compute output based on threshold value'
T = 1
output = func(dot, T)
print(f'Output: {output}')
```

The corresponding sample output for Program 3.8 is given below:

```
Input vector:[0 1 1 0]
Weight vector:[1 1 1 1]
Dot product: 2
Output: 1
```

For the above case, if the threshold value is considered as 3 or more than 3, the final output would have been 0.

The McCulloch–Pitts neuron model is a primitive model that formed the base for understanding and applying the concept of neural network. As this model allows only binary inputs and output, it has limited applications. With time, several complex and advanced ANN models have been developed to solve the purpose of real-time applications. Some of these types of ANN models are covered in the next section of this chapter.

3.5 Feed-Forward Neural Network

ANN is used in diverse applications, and its complexity and working depend on the type of the ANN model being used. ANNs are mainly classified into the *feed-forward neural network* and the *feed-backward neural network*. There are many variations of both the cases of ANN, which is illustrated in Figure 3.11. As can be seen in figure, the main variations of feed-forward neural network are the single-layer perceptron, the multilayer perceptron, and the radial basis function network. The main variations of feed backward neural network are the self-organizing map (SOM), Bayesian regularized neural network, Hopfield network, and competitive network. Each of these varied types of ANNs are discussed in detail next.

The information in feed-forward neural network always moves in forward direction (and never in backward direction). Here, the connections between nodes do not form any cycle or loop. Here, data is fed through input nodes, and output is generated through output nodes. In between the input layer and the output layer,

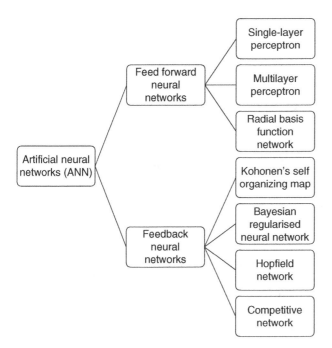

Figure 3.11 Types of artificial neural network (ANN).

there can be zero to any number of hidden layers. Each neuron in the network receives input from the neurons in the previous layer, computes a weighted sum of the inputs, and applies an activation function to produce an output. The weights and biases of the neurons are typically initialized randomly, and then adjusted during the training process to minimize the difference between the predicted output and the actual output.

Feedforward neural networks are commonly used in many applications, such as regression, image classification, and natural language processing. They also prove effective at modeling complex relationships between inputs and outputs. Three of the standard commonly used feed-forward ANNs are discussed next:

3.5.1 Single-Layer Perceptron

Frank Rosenblatt in 1950 proposed an enhanced version of McCulloch–Pitts (M–P) neuron model. Rosenblatt integrated the concept of McCulloch and Hebbian learning rule of weight adjustment. This model of neuron was called Perceptron. Here, the neuron is considered as linear threshold unit (LTU). Similar to the M–P model, the function calculates the weighted sum and produces a binary output based on the threshold value.

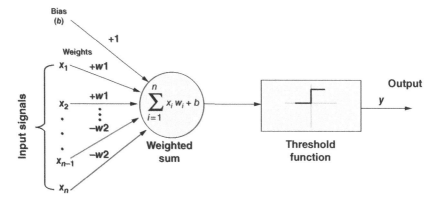

Figure 3.12 Single-layer *Perceptron* model of neural network.

A single Perceptron is also used to implement linearly separable functions, just like the M–P model. However, unlike the M–P model, an extra unit called "bias" is used in Perceptron model. The role of the bias is to smooth the neural network classifier and improve the performance of the model. The diagrammatic representation of a simple, single-neuron *Perceptron* model is shown in Figure 3.12. The neuron consists of multiple input signals along with their corresponding synaptic weights and also the bias (a constant) value.

The weighted sum $g(x)$ for the Perceptron model is calculated as given in Equation (3.20). It differs from the M–P neuron model (given in Equation (3.18)) for the addition of the bias value.

$$g(x) = \sum_{i=1}^{n} x_i w_i + b \tag{3.20}$$

Here, in Equation (3.20), "b" is the bias (an adjustable value), which has a significant role to play in the equation. Suppose all the input to the network is zero (0), then the weighted sum $g(x)$ is also going to be zero (0) in absence of the bias value "b." Now, as the weighted output is "0," it can never be greater than a positive threshold. Hence, the neuron will never be triggered. We can overcome this issue by the introduction of the bias variable. Now, if the linear threshold value is assumed to be "+1," then a bias value of "+1" could still make the neuron active with the input vector value as "0." In certain cases, for the same reason the bias can also be assumed as "−1."

To understand the role of bias, let us consider Figure 3.13. If the activation function (also known as transfer function) in this case is assumed as $f(x)=x$ (x is the input), then the output is multiplication factor of weight with "x," i.e., input (wx). Here, the ANN indicates a linear line.

Figure 3.13   A one-unit neural network model.

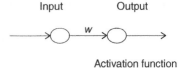

Figure 3.14   ANN output representation corresponding to Figure 3.11.

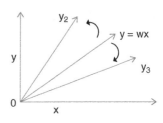

Figure 3.15   ANN output representation corresponding to Figure 3.14 after inclusion of bias.

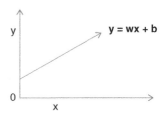

Figure 3.14 represents the ANN output corresponding to the neural structure shown in Figure 3.13. If the weight (w) is changed, then the line may shift either to a position in the direction of y_3 or y_2. But it would still pass through origin, and we cannot shift the line to intercept y-axis. This may not be optimal in approach to solving many problems.

By adding a constant "b," the intercept could be formed or the activation function could be shifted toward right or left. Figure 3.15 shows the output of the ANN after bias inclusion.

Next, the threshold function is used to compute the output of the Perceptron model in binary form. Considering the threshold value as "θ," the output (y) is derived as either 0 or 1. Here, $y = 1$ if $f(g(x)) \geq \theta$; else $y = 0$ if $f(g(x)) < \theta$. The mathematical representation for deriving the output of the Perceptron model is the same as in the *McCulloch–Pitts* neuron model. The mathematical representation for deriving the output of the *Perceptron* model is same as given in Equation (3.21).

$$y = \begin{cases} 1, & \text{if } f(g(x)) \geq \theta \\ 0, & \text{if } f(g(x)) < \theta \end{cases} \tag{3.21}$$

Now, to sum up the entire process, the single-perceptron takes inputs from the input layer, multiplies each input with its corresponding weight, sums up all the product of inputs and weights, and finally passes the weighted sum to the nonlinear function to produce the output.

Program 3.9 creates a function that sets desired inputs and epoch value of 10. The weights are updated for 10 epochs and iterated through the entire training set. The bias value is inserted into the input while performing the weight update. Accordingly, the error is computed, and the update rule is performed.

Program 3.9 *Single-Layer Perceptron*

```python
import numpy as np

class Perceptron(object):
    #Implements a perceptron network
    def __init__(self, input_size, lr=1, epochs=10):
        self.W = np.zeros(input_size+1)
        # add one for bias
        self.epochs = epochs
        self.lr = lr

    #Implement activation function - return 1 if
      input >= 0, 0 otherwise
    def activation_fn(self, x):
        #return (x >= 0).astype(np.float32)
        return 1 if x >= 0 else 0

    #Compute inner product and apply activation function
    def predict(self, x):
        z = self.W.T.dot(x)
        a = self.activation_fn(z)
        return a

    def fit(self, X, d):
        for _ in range(self.epochs):
            for i in range(d.shape[0]):
                x = np.insert(X[i], 0, 1)
                y = self.predict(x)
                e = d[i] - y
                self.W = self.W + self.lr * e * x

#provide training data (input)
if __name__ == '__main__':
    X = np.array([
        [0, 0],
```

```
        [0, 1],
        [1, 0],
        [1, 1]
    ])

#Output based on AND gate
d = np.array([0, 0, 0, 1])

perceptron = Perceptron(input_size=2)
perceptron.fit(X, d)
#Print the weight vector
print("Result: ")
print(perceptron.W)
```

The output of Program 3.9 is displayed next:

```
Result:
[-3, 2, 1]
```

The output displays the weight vector that uses the AND gate data as its input. Here, in the output, -3 indicates the bias value and 2 and 1 are the values of weights. The pre-activation is calculated as: $-3 + 0*2 + 0*1 = -3$, considering 0 as both the input values. Now, if we apply activation function, it will be 0 (for $x < 0$), which is the result of 0 AND 0. Similarly, if we consider the input values as 1 and 1, the pre-activation is calculated as: $-3 + 1*2 + 1*1 = 0$. If we apply activation function, it will be 1 (for $x >= 0$), which is the result of 1 AND 1.

3.5.2 Multilayer Perceptron

A multilayer Perceptron (MLP) has the same structure of a single-layer Perceptron with one or more hidden layers. MLP is a fully connected model that is categorized under the feedforward ANN model. It typically consists of three layers – the input layer, the hidden layer(s), and the output layer. As the network is fully connected, each node in one layer connects with a certain weight (w_{ij}) to every node in the subsequent layer. In case of MLP, the sigmoid activation function is used that takes real values as input, and converts them to numbers between 0 and 1 using the sigmoid formula. MLP uses backpropagation as the learning mechanism that iteratively adjusts the weights in the network and minimizes the cost function.

Figure 3.16 shows a multilayer connected neural network architecture. In Figure 3.16, there are "n" input nodes and three output nodes. The nodes in the input layer forwards their output to each of the "n" nodes in the hidden layer,

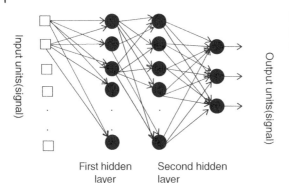

Figure 3.16 Multilayer Perceptron (all neuron connections are not shown).

and, in the same way, the hidden layer processes the information and passes it to the output layer.

The basic characteristics of a multilayer neuron are as follows:

i. Each neuron in the network has a nonlinear activation function and is also differentiable.
ii. Network contains one or more number of hidden layers (i.e., hidden from both input and output)
iii. There network exhibits high degree of connectivity.

The single-layer Perceptron cannot solve the XOR problem (XOR truth table validation by the network); however, adding additional layer to the Perceptron model can actually solve the XOR problem. Figure 3.17 shows a multilayer Perceptron model that successfully solves the XOR problem.

Considering an input $(1,0)$ (A is 1 and B is 0), the input on C would be $-1 * 0.5 + 1*1 + 0*1 = -0.5 + 1 = 0.5$. This value exceeds threshold value 0, and therefore C fires giving output 1. For D, the input would be $-1*1 + 1*1 + 0*1 = -1 + 1 = 0$, and, therefore D does not fire, giving output 0. The input on E would be $-1*0.5 + 1*1 + 0*-1 = 0.5$ and therefore E fires. It can also be proved that E would not be fired for same input $(1,1)$ or $(0,0)$.

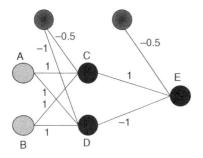

Figure 3.17 Multilayer Perceptron that solves the XOR problem (balanced weights mentioned).

The intermediate layers that are added in between the model to enhance the computation are termed as hidden layers. One may ask why they are termed as hidden. It is because the activation function in all those units and the associated weight are not known. If the output for a given input is not as same as the target, then one will not know that the misclassification is because of the wrong weight in the input to next layer or other layers (neurons).

The plain algorithmic representation of the MLP is mentioned as the following steps (assuming one hidden layer).

i. Input nodes are fed with an input vector.
ii. Inputs are feed forward through the network
    (a) Inputs and the associated first layer weights decides whether the hidden nodes fire or not. The activation function considered $g(.)$ is the sigmoid function.
    (b) The output of the hidden layer neurons and the second layer weights decides which output neurons will be fired or not.
iii. Error is computed as the sum of squared difference between the target output and the actual output of the network.
iv. Error is fed backward
    (a) First the second layer weight is updated and, then,
    (b) First layer weight is updated.

Program 3.10 applies the concept of multilayer Perceptron to predict employee churn using the "HR_comma_sep.csv" dataset available in the Kaggle website. Initially, the dataset is loaded, and preprocessing of data is done using label encoding. The data is encoded to map each value to a number. Label encoding is applied for the "salary" and "Department" columns. Next, the dataset is split into training set and testing set to assess the performance of the model.

The employee churn prediction model is built by using the MLPClassifier to predict employee churn. For this, the MLP Classifier object is created using the MLPClassifier() function. Then, the model is fit on the training set using fit(), and prediction is performed on the testing set using predict(). Finally, the accuracy score is found and displayed to analyze the performance of the model.

Program 3.10 *Multi-Layer Perceptron*

```
import numpy as np
import pandas as pd
from sklearn import preprocessing
from sklearn.model_selection import train_test_split
from sklearn.metrics import accuracy_score
from sklearn.neural_network import MLPClassifier
```

```
# Load data
data=pd.read_csv(' HR_comma_sep.csv')
print("Displaying First Few Records of Dataset")
print(data.head())

# Creating labelEncoder
le = preprocessing.LabelEncoder()

# Converting string labels into numbers.
data['salary']=le.fit_transform(data['salary'])
data['Department']=le.fit_transform(data['Department'])

# Spliting data
X=data[['satisfaction_level', 'last_evaluation',
     'number_project', 'average_montly_hours',
     'time_spend_company', 'Work_accident',
     'promotion_last_5years', 'Department', 'salary']]
y=data['left']

# Split dataset into training set and test set - 70%
     training and 30% test
X_train, X_test, y_train, y_test = train_test_split(X,
     y, test_size=0.3, random_state=42)

print("Applying MLPClassifier...")
clf = MLPClassifier(hidden_layer_sizes=(6,5),
random_state=5,verbose=True, learning_rate_init=0.02)

# Fit data onto the model
clf.fit(X_train,y_train)

# Make prediction on test dataset
ypred=clf.predict(X_test)
# Calcuate accuracy
print("Accuracy Score : " , round(accuracy_score(y_test,
     ypred),2))
```

The output of Program 3.10 is displayed next:

```
Displaying First Few Records of Dataset
```

```
Applying MLPClassifier...
Accuracy Score:   0.95
```

The function `MLPClassifier()` uses the *hidden_layer_sizes* parameter to set the number of layers and the number of nodes we wish to have in the Neural Network. It also uses the *random_state* parameter to set a seed for reproducing the same results. The *activation* parameter in not mentioned in the given program; hence, the default ReLu activation function is used to train the model. At the end of the program, the accuracy score is calculated and found to be 95% using the test samples of the given dataset.

3.5.3   Radial Basis Function Network

Radial basis function (RBF) network is a popular feedforward network that consists of an input layer, a single hidden layer, and an output layer. The input layer receives the input data and feeds it into the hidden layer of the RBF network. There is no computation performed in the input layer and is just used to feed the input forward to the single hidden layer.

The hidden layer contains a variable number of neurons. Each neuron comprises of a radial basis function centered on a point. The pattern of input received by the hidden layer may not be linearly separable; it accordingly transforms the input into a new space that is linearly separable. For this transformation, the hidden layer requires a higher dimensionality than the input layer. This is so because the pattern (input) that is not linearly separable requires to be transformed into higher dimensional space to be more linearly separable.

The output layer uses a linear activation function, which is calculated as a linear combination between the input vector and the weight vector. The computation in the output layer can be mathematically denoted as given in Equation (3.22):

$$y = \sum_{i=1}^{n} \varphi_i w_i \tag{3.22}$$

Here, y is the predicted result, φ_i is the ith neuron's output from the hidden layer, and w_i is the weight connection.

Figure 3.18 shows the radial basis function neural network architecture that consists of mainly three layers – the input layer, the hidden layer, and the output layer. As can be understood from the figure, the input layer receives the inputs $(X_1, X_2, \ldots, X_N)$ to the network and pass it to the hidden layer. The hidden layer uses radial basis functions $\varphi_1, \varphi_2, \ldots, \varphi_N$ (usually the Gaussian functions) to

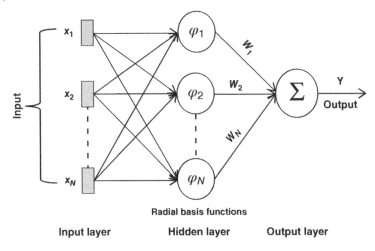

Figure 3.18 Radial basis function neural network architecture.

transform the inputs into a set of nonlinear features. Finally, the output layer takes these features and produces the final output of the network.

The RBF networks usually uses the Gaussian functions as the radial basis functions. Each node in the hidden layer corresponds to a particular Gaussian function, and the weights associated with each node determine the shape and position of the corresponding Gaussian. During training, the weights of the RBF network are adjusted by minimizing the difference between the predicted outputs and the actual outputs for a given set of inputs.

Considering the radial distance as $||x - \mu||$, the Gaussian function in RBF network is calculated using Equation (3.23):

$$\varphi(x) = \exp\left(\frac{||x - \mu||^2}{2\sigma^2}\right) \tag{3.23}$$

Here, in Equation (3.23), x is the input to the function (a vector), μ is the center of the Gaussian function (another vector), and σ is a scaling factor that determines the width of the Gaussian function ($\sigma > 0$). The || || notation denotes the Euclidean distance between the two vectors.

The output of each node is simply the value of the Gaussian function evaluated at the input to the node. Each output is passed on to the output layer, which are then combined to produce the final output of the network.

Program 3.11 illustrates the radial basis neural network that uses the `iris` dataset. The Iris dataset is a well-known dataset in the field of machine learning, and is commonly used for classification and pattern recognition tasks. It was introduced by the British biologist and statistician Ronald A. Fisher in 1936. The dataset contains measurements of four features (`sepal length`, `sepal` *width*, *petal length*, and *petal width*) measured in centimeters for three different species (*setosa*, *versicolor*, and *virginica*) of iris flowers. It is widely used as a beginner's dataset to demonstrate various machine learning concepts and algorithms. In Python, you can find the Iris dataset in libraries like *Scikit-learn* and *Seaborn*.

The dataset is initially split into training set and testing set. Next, the *RBF-Sampler()* function is used that performs random Fourier approximation of the radial basis function (RBF) kernel. The K-means clustering is used for obtaining the centers, and then the distance between each data point and the centers are computed using the *pairwise_distances_argmin_min()* function. After training the RBF model using Ridge regression, the model is finally evaluated using the test dataset, and the accuracy score is obtained to assess the performance of the model.

Program 3.11   *Radial Basis Neural Network*

```
from sklearn.datasets import load_iris
from sklearn.model_selection import train_test_split
from sklearn.metrics import accuracy_score
from sklearn.pipeline import make_pipeline
from sklearn.preprocessing import StandardScaler
from sklearn.cluster import KMeans
from sklearn.linear_model import Ridge
from sklearn.kernel_approximation import RBFSampler
from sklearn.metrics import pairwise_distances_argmin_min

# Loading the Iris dataset
iris = load_iris()
X, y = iris.data, iris.target
print("Displaying First 5 Records of the Iris Dataset")
print(iris.data[:5:])

# Split the data into training and testing sets
X_train, X_test, y_train, y_test = train_test_split(X,
    y, test_size=0.3, random_state=42)

# Create an RBF kernel approximation object
rbf_feature = RBFSampler(gamma=1, random_state=42)

# Cluster the data using KMeans to obtain the centers
kmeans = KMeans(n_clusters=10, random_state=42).fit
    (X_train)
```

```
centers = kmeans.cluster_centers_
# Compute the distances between each data point and the
    centers
distances = pairwise_distances_argmin_min(X_train,
    centers)

# Use the distances as features for training and testing
X_train_rbf = rbf_feature.fit_transform(distances[0].
    reshape(-1, 1))
X_test_rbf = rbf_feature.transform(pairwise_distances_
    argmin_min(X_test, centers)[0].reshape(-1, 1))

# Scale the data using StandardScaler
scaler = StandardScaler()
X_train_rbf = scaler.fit_transform(X_train_rbf)
X_test_rbf = scaler.transform(X_test_rbf)

# Train the RBF model using Ridge regression
rbf_model = make_pipeline(Ridge(alpha=0.1, random_
    state=42))
rbf_model.fit(X_train_rbf, y_train)

# Evaluate the model on the test set
y_pred = rbf_model.predict(X_test_rbf)
accuracy = accuracy_score(y_test, y_pred.round())
print(f"Accuracy Score: {round(accuracy,2)}")
```

The output of Program 3.11 is displayed next. The first five records of the Iris dataset is displayed, and finally the accuracy score of 98% is calculated and displayed.

```
Displaying First 5 Records of the Iris Dataset
[[5.1 3.5 1.4 0.2]
 [4.9 3.  1.4 0.2]
 [4.7 3.2 1.3 0.2]
 [4.6 3.1 1.5 0.2]
 [5.  3.6 1.4 0.2]]
Accuracy Score: 0.98
```

Multilayer Perceptron (MLP) and Radial Basis Function (RBF) are both popular feedforward neural network architectures. However, the major difference between MLP and RBF is that MLP consists of one or several hidden layers, while RBF consists of just one hidden layer. Also, RBF network has a faster learning speed compared to MLP.

3.6 Feedback Neural Network

A feedback neural network is a type of ANN in which the output from one or more neurons is fed back into the network as input to one or more previous neurons, creating what is called as a *"feedback loop."* Each neuron of the feedback neural network has a `"memory"` of its previous state, which helps in producing accurate predictions. Feedback neural networks are used in a wide variety of applications, such as signal processing, time series prediction, natural language processing, and speech recognition. Four of the commonly used feedback ANNs are: The Kohonen's SOM, the Bayesian regularised neural network, the Hopfield network, and the competitive network. Two of these models, namely, the SOM and the Hopfield neural network are discussed next:

3.6.1 Self-Organizing Map (SOM)

SOM is a special type of ANN that is based on competitive learning. For a given input all the neurons compete among themselves to claim this input. Claiming input means computing Euclidean distance of the input to all the neurons. Whichever distance is lesser from a neuron to the input becomes the winning neuron (also termed as the best matching unit). The synaptic strength (weight) connected to this neuron from the input is strengthened. Before we explore more through SOM, it is important to understand some facts of the working of natural human brain.

i. The neurons in human brain are interconnected by synapse in a very complex form.
ii. Neurons recognizing similar type of information are grouped closed together and connected by short synaptic connections.
iii. Contextual maps are understood in terms of decision-reducing mappings from higher dimensional parameter spaces onto the cortical surface.

The interest of SOM lies in building artificial topographic structure from the biological neural organizational structure with the ability to self-organize, as it eventually learns with every input. Hebbian learning is the most popular form of unsupervised learning. Mathematically Hebbian learning is formulated as given in Equation (3.24):

$$\frac{\delta w_{ij}(t)}{\delta t} = \alpha x_i(t) y_i(t) \tag{3.24}$$

Here, α is a positive learning rate ($0 < \alpha < 1$), and x is the input, and y is the output, respectively. However, with the above rule, the entire weight space may be saturated. To overcome this problem a forgetting term can be added. The modified equation is shown in Equation (3.25).

$$w_i(t+1) = \frac{w_i(t) + \alpha x_i(t)y(t)}{\left\{ \sum_{j=1}^{n} \left[w_j(t) + \alpha x_j(t)y(t) \right]^2 \right\}^{1/2}}$$

$$\cong w_i(t) + \alpha(t)\left[x_i(t) - y(t)w_i(t)\right] + O(\alpha^2) \tag{3.25}$$

If α is very small, then $O(\alpha^2)$ can be ignored.

Willshaw and Von Der Malsburg developed a self-organization retinotopic model in which the external stimuli are received by different sensors (visual, auditory, etc.), and then processed by the neural network and presented through the axons to the cerebral cortex. Different part of the cerebral cortex maps to different sensory inputs. Von der Malsburg and Willshaw and Willshaw are the first persons to give a mathematical form of the topographical mapping from the presynaptic to postsynaptic sheet.

As seen in Figure 3.19, all of the neurons in the presynaptic sheet are connected to each of the neuron in the postsynaptic sheet. In Figure 3.19, out of all the highlighted neurons in the postsynaptic sheet, the central neuron is the winning neuron, and the neighboring highlighted neurons are the excitatory neurons. This excitation signal originates in the winning neuron and traverses in symmetrical form until it is inhibited and dies off the effect.

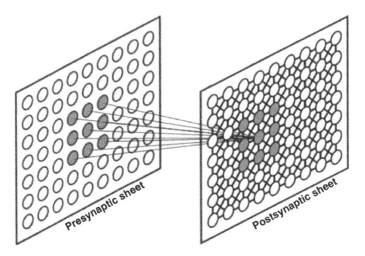

Figure 3.19 Von Der Malsburg and Willshaw Model of SOM.

The postsynaptic activities at time t,

$$\frac{\delta y_i(t)}{\delta t} + cy_i(t) = \sum_j w_{ij}(t)x_i(t) + \sum_k e_{ik}y_k^*(t) - \sum_{k'} b_{ik}y_{k'}^*(t) \tag{3.26}$$

As shown in Equation (3.26), c is a membrane constant, and w_{ij} in the equation indicates the synaptic weight between "I" and "j" cells in the presynaptic and postsynaptic sheet, respectively. X_i indicates the state of the presynaptic sheet, and is 1 if it is active and 0 otherwise. E_{kj} is the short-range excitation, and b_{kj} is the long-range inhibition constant. $Y_j^*(t)$ is the active cell in the postsynaptic sheet in time "t." The postsynaptic cell fires, provided a condition (as given in Equation (3.27)) is satisfied.

$$y_i^*(t) = \begin{cases} y_j^*(t) - \theta, & \text{if } y_j^*(t) > \theta \\ 0, & \text{otherwise} \end{cases} \tag{3.27}$$

The modifiable synaptic weight can be represented as given in Equation (3.28):

$$\frac{\delta w_{ij}(t)}{\delta t} = \alpha x_i(t)y_j^*(t), \text{ subject to } 1/N_x \sum w_{ij} = \text{constant} \tag{3.28}$$

where, α is the learning rate.

Kohonen, however, proposed a much simpler representation of the SOM model. In his proposal, a sigmoid type of nonlinear function was applied to Equation (3.25) that resulted in Equation (3.29).

$$y_j(t+1) = \varphi \left[w_j^T x(t) + \sum_i h_{ij} y_i(t) \right] \tag{3.29}$$

Whenever an input is presented, a spatially bounded cluster (bubble) is formed in the postsynaptic sheet that indicates the influence propagation of the activated neuron on the postsynaptic sheet.

$$y_j(t+1) = \begin{cases} 1 & \text{if neuron } j \text{ is inside the bubble} \\ 0 & \text{otherwise} \end{cases} \tag{3.30}$$

The shape of the cluster $\eta(t)$ is dependent on the inhibition and excitation, respectively. From not confining to the problem of weight exhaust, a forgetting term $\beta y_j(t)w_{ij}(t)$ is added. Assuming $\alpha = \beta$ and applying to Equation (3.30), the synaptic learning rule can be formulated as given in Equation (3.31):

$$\frac{\delta w_{ij}(t)}{\delta t} = \alpha y_j(t)x_i(t) - \beta y_j(t)w_{ij}(t) = \alpha[x_i(t) - w_{ij}(t)]y_j(t)$$

$$= \begin{cases} \alpha[x_i(t) - w_{ij}(t)], & \text{if } j \in (t) \\ 0, & \text{if } j(t) \end{cases} \tag{3.31}$$

Figure 3.20 shows Kohonen's self-organizing model (SOM). As can be seen from the figure, the input is connected to every unit of the postsynaptic sheet.

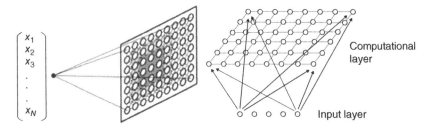

Figure 3.20 Kohonen's self-organizing model.

Whenever an input is presented to the SOM, the distance of the input to every neuron in the postsynaptic layer is computed. This distance measured is Euclidean distance of the input from the neurons of the postsynaptic layer. The distance of the input to whichever neuron is the smallest becomes the winning neuron. This neuron is also sometimes called as best matching unit (BMU). The weight updates of the winning unit occur together with the neighborhood neurons as defined. The neighborhood indicates the area of influence around the winning unit. This neighborhood function is a monotonically decreasing function.

Program 3.12 illustrates the Python code used for a SOM using the MiniSom library. Initially, the input data is randomly generated having 500 data points and 8 unique features. Next, we initialize the SOM using the MiniSom class from the MiniSom library. Here, we create a SOM with an 8 × 8 grid of neurons, each with 8 input features. After initializing the SOM, the training of the input data is done by using 500 iterations. Finally, the SOM is visualized by creating a figure with a size of 8 × 8 inches and then plot the SOM using the *pcolor* function. The *distance_map* method of the SOM returns a 2D numpy array representing the distance between each neuron in the SOM and its neighbors. Also, the *bone_r* colormap is used to visualize it as a heatmap.

Program 3.12 *Self-Organizing Map*

```
from minisom import MiniSom
import numpy as np

# create input data
data = np.random.rand(500, 8)

# initialize the SOM
som = MiniSom(8, 8, 8, sigma=1.0, learning_rate=0.5)

# train the SOM
som.train(data, 500)
```

```
# visualize the results
import matplotlib.pyplot as plt

plt.figure(figsize=(8, 8))
plt.pcolor(som.distance_map().T, cmap='bone_r')
plt.colorbar()

# plot the data points on the SOM
for I, x in enumerate(data):
    print(i)
    w = som.winner(x)
    plt.plot(w[0] + 0.5, w[1] + 0.5, 'o',
      markerfacecolor='None', markeredgecolor='red',
      markersize=10, markeredgewidth=2)
plt.show()
```

The output of Program 3.12 is given next, which basically displays a figure to plot the SOM with the given data inputs having 500 records and 8 features (Figure 3.21).

SOMs are used for a wide range of applications in various fields such as feature extraction, anomaly detection, clustering, data visualization, and dimensionality reduction. SOM is a powerful tool often used by researchers for data analysis. As SOM is computationally efficient, it can be trained on large datasets in a

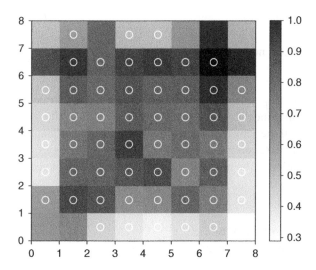

Figure 3.21 A self-organizing model (SOM) having 500 data points and 8 features.

reasonable amount of time. Also, SOMs can handle missing values or outliers in the input data, and are robust to incomplete or noisy data.

3.6.2 Hopfield Neural Network (HNN)

The Hopfield Neural Network is a type of ANN developed by Dr John J. Hopfield in 1982. It is a recurrent neural network that consists of one layer of "n" fully connected recurrent neurons. Each neuron in the network can be either "on" or "off", indicating that the state of the neuron can be represented by a binary value of either 0 to 1, or bipolar value of 0 or −1. The network is trained using an unsupervised learning – the Hebbian learning – that aims to strengthen the connections between neurons when they are activated together.

The weight updates for a set of binary input pattern $S(p)$ [$p = 1$ to P] and $S(p) = S_1(p) \dots S_i(p) \dots S_n(p)$ is given by Equation (3.32):

$$w_{ij} = \sum_{p=1}^{P} [2s_i(p) - 1][2s_j(p) - 1], \text{ for } i \neq j \tag{3.32}$$

Here, w_{ij} represents the weight matrix, which is calculated during the training process of the model. w_{ij} indicates the weight associated with the connection between the ith and the jth neuron, P is the number of patterns to be stored, and $s_i(p)$ and $s_j(p)$ are the ith element and the jth element of the pth pattern, respectively.

In case of bipolar inputs, the weight updates for the input pattern $S(p)$ [$p = 1$ to P] and $S(p) = S_1(p) \dots S_i(p) \dots S_n(p)$ is given by Equation (3.33):

$$w_{ij} = \sum_{p=1}^{P} [s_i(p)][s_j(p)], \text{ for } i \neq j \tag{3.33}$$

The algorithm of the Hopfield neural network is given as follows:

HNN Algorithm

Step 1: Initialize weights (w_{ij}) to store patterns obtained from the training algorithm using the Hebbian principle.

Step 2: Perform steps 3–9, if the activations of the network is not consolidated.

Step 3: For each input vector X, perform steps 4–8.

Step 4: Make initial activation of the network equal to the external input vector X as follows:

$$y_i = x_i \text{ for } i = 1 \text{ to } n$$

Step 5: For each unit y_i, perform steps 6–9.

Step 6: Calculate the total input of the network y_{in} as follows:

$$y_{in} = x_i + \sum_j y_j w_{ji}$$

Step 7: For a threshold value θ_i, apply the activation as follows over the total input to calculate the output as follows:

$$y_i = \begin{cases} 1 & \text{if } y_{in} > \theta_i \\ y_i & \text{if } y_{in} = \theta_i \\ 0 & \text{if } y_{in} < \theta_i \end{cases} \tag{3.34}$$

Step 8: The output y_i is broadcasted to all the other units. Accordingly, the activation vectors are updated.

Step 9: Finally, test the network for convergence.

Program 3.13 illustrates the Python code used for a Hopfield neural network. The program defines a *HFNW* class having two methods – `train()` and `predict()`. The weight matrix is updated based on the patterns. Finally, the `predict()` method takes in the input pattern and iteratively updates the neurons. The update is stopped either if the maximum iteration is reached or until convergence. The program chooses binary patterns (consisting of 0's and 1's) and finally displays a binary output.

Program 3.13 *Hopfield Neural Network*

```python
import numpy as np
class HFNW:
    def __init__(self, n):
        self.n = n
        self.weights = np.zeros((n, n))

    def train(self, patterns):
        self.weights = np.zeros((self.n, self.n))
        for p in patterns:
            self.weights += np.outer(p, p)
        np.fill_diagonal(self.weights, 0)

    def predict(self, input_pattern, max_iter=50):
        output = input_pattern.copy()
        for i in range(max_iter):
            new_output = np.sign(np.dot(self.weights,
                output))
            if np.array_equal(new_output, output):
                return new_output
            output = new_output
        return output
```

```
# Example usage
patterns = np.array([[0, 1, 0, 1], [1, 0, 1, 0], [1, 1,
                      0, 1]])
hn = HFNW(4)
hn.train(patterns)
input_pattern = np.array([0, 0, 1, 0])
predicted_pattern = hn.predict(input_pattern)
print("Input pattern:", input_pattern)
print("Predicted pattern:", predicted_pattern)
```

The output of Program 3.13 is given below. Here, the input pattern [0, 0, 1, 0] is closest to the pattern [1, 1, 1, 1], which is the pattern that the Hopfield network predicts.

```
Input pattern: [0 0 1 0]
Predicted pattern: [1. 1. 1. 1.]
```

The input received by the model can be a noisy or incomplete input binary pattern. The Hamming distance is used on the training pattern to calculate the number of bits that are different between two binary patterns. The network is trained until it reaches to a stable state, after which the output pattern is generated that resembles the closest stored pattern to the input pattern. Hopfield neural network are used in a variety of applications such as associative memory, image recognition, and optimization problem. However, one major limitation of this neural network is that it is sensitive to spurious patterns that gets retrieved instead of the pattern that is anticipated.

A real-life example of a Hopfield Neural Network is the use of these networks in content-addressable memory systems, also known as associative memory or pattern recognition. Hopfield Neural Networks are particularly well-suited for tasks involving pattern completion and pattern recall. Imagine a scenario where one wants to store and retrieve patterns in a memory system. A simple example of pattern recall in image denoising is demonstrated next:

Let's say there is an image that has been corrupted by adding noise to some of its pixels. If someone wants to restore the original image by removing the noise, Hopfield Neural Network can be used as an associative memory to help with this task.

Storage Phase: One can store the clean version of the image as a pattern in the Hopfield network. Each pixel's value is treated as a neuron state (either +1 or −1). The connections between neurons are adjusted based on the stored patterns to create an energy landscape that represents attractors for each pattern.

Pattern Recall Phase: The noisy version of the image can be input into the network. The noisy pixels can be represented as their noisy values (−1 or +1).

The network dynamics evolve based on the interactions between neurons and the energy landscape. Due to the attractors created during the storage phase, the network tends to settle into one of the stored patterns, which corresponds to a denoised version of the image.

In this example, the Hopfield Neural Network is acting as an associative memory that can recall the stored patterns based on partial or noisy inputs. It demonstrates the network's ability to complete patterns and retrieve information even when the input is incomplete or degraded. Keep in mind that while Hopfield Neural Networks have certain useful properties like pattern recall, they also have limitations, such as their capacity to store patterns and convergence properties. For more complex tasks, modern neural network architectures, such as deep learning models, are often preferred due to their ability to learn more intricate patterns and features from data.

Exercises

A) Choose the correct answer from among the alternatives given:
  a) What is the purpose of the activation function in a neural network?
    i) To assign random input values to the network.
    ii) To introduce nonlinearity into the network
    iii) To calculate the weights of the network
    iv) To assign a bias value for the network
  b) What is the purpose of the bias value in a neural network?
    i) To introduce nonlinearity into the network
    ii) To decide the input values for the network
    iii) To add a constant offset to the output of each neuron
    iv) To minimize the error between the predicted output and the actual output
  c) A 4-input neuron has weights 1, 2, 3, and 4. The transfer function is linear with the constant of proportionality being equal to 2. The inputs are 4, 10, 5, and 20, respectively. The output will be
    i) 48
    ii) 238
    iii) 76
    iv) 116
  d) Which activation function is commonly used for the hidden layers of a multilayer perceptron?
    i) ReLU
    ii) Linear
    iii) Tanh
    iv) Sigmoid

    e) Which layer has feedback weights in competitive neural networks?
       i) Input layer
       ii) Second layer
       iii) Both input and second layer
       iv) None of the mentioned

    f) In Hebbian learning initial weights are set _____
       i) To random values
       ii) To zero
       iii) Near to target value
       iv) Any of the above

    g) What is the purpose of the hidden layers in a multilayer perceptron?
       i) To perform classification or regression tasks
       ii) To adjust the weight and bias values
       iii) To transform the input into a form that can be more easily mapped to the output
       iv) To reduce the number of input features

    h) What is backpropagation in an ANN?
       i) The process of normalizing the input data to improve the performance of the network
       ii) The process of updating the weights of the network based on the error between the predicted and actual output
       iii) The process of training the network using a genetic algorithm
       iv) The process of selecting the optimal hyperparameters for the network

B) Answer the following questions:
    1) Explain, in detail, the structure of an artificial neural network (ANN).
    2) What is the difference between a Perceptron and a multilayer perceptron?
    3) Explain the role of the following in a neural network:
       a) Bias
       b) Weight
       c) Activation function
       d) Backpropagation
    4) Explain any four popular activation functions used in artificial neural networks (ANNs). Give an example for each case in which the activation function is best suited for solving a task.
    5) What is a single-layer perceptron? Mention any two applications of single-layer perceptron. Also, mention one major limitation of using a single-layer perceptron.
    6) A hospital manager wants to predict how many beds will be needed in the geriatric ward. He asks to design a neural network method for making this prediction. He has data for the last five years that cover

a) The number of people in the geriatric ward each week.

b) The weather (average day and night temperatures)

c) The season of the year (spring, summer autumn, winter)

d) Whether or not there was an epidemic (use a binary variable "yes" or "no")

Design a suitable MLP for this problem considering the decision to choose the number of hidden neurons, the inputs and the preprocessing, and whether or not the system would work.

7) What is a learning rule in ANN? Explain any two commonly used learning rules in ANN. How are learning rules chosen for a particular problem?

8) What is a radial basis neural network (RBNN)? Mention any one advantage and any one limitation of using RBNN.

9) How does a SOM work? Mention any two advantages of using the SOM model.

10) How are Hopfield neural networks different from other types of neural networks? Mention any two applications of Hopfield neural networks.

11) How do the learning algorithms differ between feedforward and feedback neural networks? Mention the common types of feedforward and feedback neural networks used in solving applications.

12) Consider a feedforward neural network with one input layer of three neurons, one hidden layer of four neurons, and one output layer of two neurons. How many total weights are there in the network, assuming no biases?

13) You have an input of 0.5 that goes through a sigmoid activation function. What is the output of the activation function?

14) You have a neural network with an input layer of four neurons, a hidden layer of three neurons, and an output layer of two neurons. How many bias neurons are there in the network?

4

Deep Learning

Traditional machine learning is a well-known, conventional approach used for solving simpler tasks that have limited data, while deep learning is a recent, advanced approach used for solving complex tasks involving large amounts of data. Some of the common examples of machine learning techniques include support vector machines, decision trees, random forests, linear regression, and logistic regression. Deep learning is a subset of machine learning that uses artificial neural networks (discussed in previous chapter) to learn from given dataset and make predictions to obtain result. Some of the common applications of deep learning involve speech recognition, image recognition, and natural language processing. This chapter will focus in depth about deep learning and its prominent techniques.

4.1 Introduction to Deep Learning

Deep learning models are built using layers of interconnected nodes (or neurons) that process and transform input data to generate output predictions. Each layer of neuron is involved in processing of input data and passing it on to the next layer, to gradually and finally make predictions with high accuracy. The entire model is designed to automatically learn and extract complex features from raw data that can be in the form of text, images, or audio. The main advantage of deep learning is that it can automatically learn complex features from raw data, without the need for manual feature engineering. However, such models are computationally intensive as they typically involve processing large amounts of data to train effectively. Figure 4.1 illustrates how deep learning outperforms the traditional machine learning in terms of accuracy and performance when the dataset size becomes large. Also, in deep learning, the feature vector extraction is not manually determined unlike traditional machine learning.

Principles of Soft Computing Using Python Programming: Learn How to Deploy Soft Computing Models in Real World Applications, First Edition. Gypsy Nandi.
© 2024 The Institute of Electrical and Electronics Engineers, Inc. Published 2024 by John Wiley & Sons, Inc.

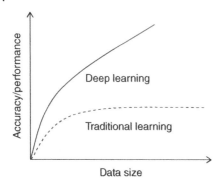

Figure 4.1 Deep learning performance.

To explore further the differences between traditional machine learning and deep learning, Figure 4.2(a) shows how the presence of a human expert is important in traditional machine learning to decide the proper feature vector for training the learning model in a given problem domain. The learning can be improved with the proper selection of features. However, in this example, there is a high chance that the strawberry object will be predicted but not the leaf (or, just the leaf will be predicted). On the other hand, in case of deep learning, the feature extraction and classification are accomplished by the deep network itself, as can be seen in Figure 4.2(b). The output of the classifier could be different

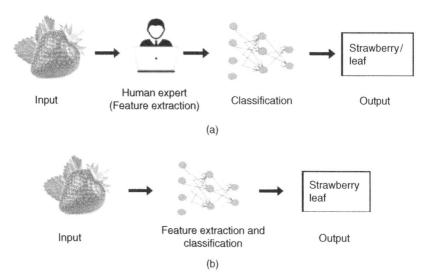

Figure 4.2 (a) Traditional machine learning (b) Deep learning.

objects present in the input space, such as strawberry as well as leaf, which can be predicted by the model itself.

Deep learning models are flexible and can be applied for a wide range of tasks that also include real-time applications. It can be trained on large datasets and generate output having high prediction accuracy. Also, as no human intervention is required to train the model, it reduces the need for manual feature engineering. Thus, deep learning has revolutionized today's world in many sectors, be it healthcare or industries, research or agricultural sectors, and so on.

4.2 Classification of Deep Learning Techniques

Deep learning neural networks are distinguished from simple neural networks on the basis of the number of hidden layers. While deep learning models have higher accuracy than a simple neural network, it however takes more time to train the deep learning model than the basic neural networks. Some of the standard deep learning models used in various applications are mentioned in Figure 4.3. These are the common deep learning models used in recent years. However, with more and more research and development, new deep learning models are evolving at a rapid rate.

Some deep learning models such as convolutional neural networks (CNNs), recurrent neural networks (RNNs), transformers, and autoencoders can be categorized as either supervised or unsupervised, depending on the type of learning task they are designed to solve. Generative adversarial networks (GANs) and deep reinforcement learning (Deep RL) falls under the category of unsupervised learning.

Four of the standard deep learning models (as mentioned in Figure 4.3), namely CNN, RNN, GAN, and autoencoders, are discussed in the next subsections.

4.2.1 Convolutional Neural Networks

A convolutional neural network (CNN), also known as *ConvNet*, is a type of deep learning neural network often used for image recognition and computer vision tasks. It works similar to the way a human brain processes visual information by automatically learning and extracting features from images. CNNs are mainly built using multiple layers, which mainly includes convolutional layers, pooling layers, and fully connected layers. Each of these layers have a major role to play for image, object or video recognition, and classification. CNNs are well-proven standard techniques for tasks that require understanding and analyzing visual information, and has recently gained huge popularity for its high accuracy of results.

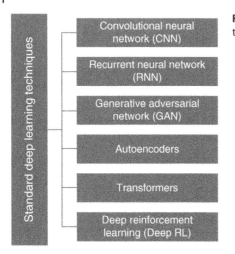

Figure 4.3 Standard deep learning techniques.

The convolutional layer is an essential component of the CNN architecture that applies the convolution operation for feature identification. It is the first layer of the network that uses filters (also known as kernels) to scan the input image. The filters help in identifying prominent features such as edges and textures. For this, the filters consider a subset of the input data and apply linear multiplication of weights with the input to obtain the desired output. Each filter is applied to a small area of the image called a *receptive field* and slides over the entire image to create a feature map.

Figure 4.4 shows an example of a convolutional filter (kernel) of 5×5, which is a small-sized matrix used to extract features from the input data. It slides over the input image in a systematic way, performing elementwise multiplication and summation operations. Common filter sizes are 3×3, 5×5, or 7×7. The filter can have a single channel (grayscale) or multiple channels (corresponding to different color channels). In Figure 4.4, the 32×32 colored image consists of three color

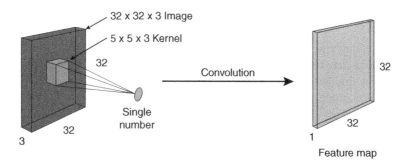

Figure 4.4 An example of feature map.

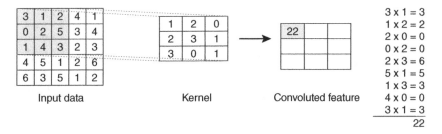

Figure 4.5 The first step of convolution operation.

channels (RGB) to which the kernel of 3×3 matrix is applied to the three color channels. The first step of convolution operation is shown in Figure 4.5 in which a filter (kernel) of 3×3 matrix slides over the input image of 5×5 matrix to produce a partial output feature map.

The convolution operation involves two main steps: elementwise multiplication and summation. The output in Figure 4.4 of each filter results in a feature map of $32 \times 32 \times 1$. This entire process of convolution allows recognizing low-level features such as edges and textures that allow detecting complex features such as shapes and patterns. The convolution operation requires the following two operations to be applied:

a) **Elementwise multiplication**: The filter is initially placed at the top-left corner of the input image, and an elementwise multiplication is performed between the filter and the corresponding pixels in the input image. The result is obtained by summing up these elementwise multiplications.

b) **Summation**: The sum of the elementwise multiplication is computed, and the result is assigned to a single pixel in the output feature map. This process is repeated for all possible positions (pixels) in the input image by sliding the filter over the image.

We know that every image is considered as a matrix of pixel values. These pixel values of an image are used for the process of convolution. To illustrate further, let us consider a grayscale image of $5 \times 5 \times 1$ input data. Here, the input image dimension is a 5 (height) $\times$ 5 (width) image having only one color dimension, as it is a grayscale image. A filter (kernel) of 3×3 is applied to the input data to produce a 3×3 feature map.

The above process is repeated by applying a particular stride value that determines the step-size with which the convolutional filter moves over the input image. If a stride value of 1 is applied, the input data now moves pixel by pixel, whereas a stride value of 2 moves the filter two pixels at a time. Stride affects the size of the output feature map. Figure 4.6 shows the next step of filter application for a stride value of 1, to obtain the next value of the convoluted feature.

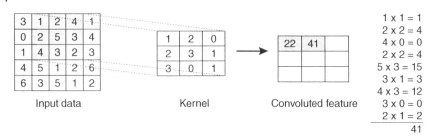

Figure 4.6 The second step of convolution operation.

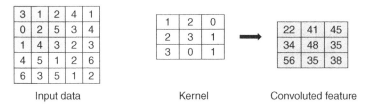

Figure 4.7 The convoluted feature after applying the convolution operation.

Moving on, the convolution process hops down from the left to the right and then top to bottom of the image with the same stride value, and repeats the process until the entire image is traversed. Continuing the above process of applying a stride value of 1, the final convoluted feature is calculated to obtain a complete matrix as illustrated in Figure 4.7. Smaller strides preserve more spatial information but may increase the computational cost.

After the convolution operation, an activation function is usually applied elementwise to the output feature map. This introduces nonlinearity and enables the network to learn complex relationships between features. Common activation functions used in CNNs include ReLU (Rectified Linear Unit), which sets negative values to zero and keeps positive values unchanged, and variants like Leaky ReLU and Parametric ReLU.

CNNs typically employ multiple filters in each layer. Each filter detects a specific feature or pattern in the input image. These filters are stacked together to form the depth dimension of the output feature map. For example, if a layer uses eight filters, the resulting output feature map will have a depth of 32, indicating that it captures eight different features.

The next step in CNN is the process of pooling that are applied to reduce the size of images and decrease the computational power required to process the data through dimensionality reduction. Pooling operates on individual feature maps independently, and helps to extract and retain the most important features while discarding unnecessary details. The pooling window slides over the feature map with a predefined stride, just like in convolutional operations. The stride determines how much the window shifts after each pooling operation. Common stride values are 1 or 2.

The two common and famous pooling methods are the max pooling and the average pooling, out of which the most common one is the max pooling method.

- **Max Pooling**: This pooling method returns the maximum value from the portion of the image covered by the kernel. It helps capture the most prominent features within the window and discard less important details.
- **Average Pooling:** This pooling method returns the average of all the values from the portion of the image covered by the kernel. It helps in reducing the spatial dimensions while providing a smoothed-down representation of the features.

Figure 4.8 illustrates the method of applying both max pooling and average pooling to obtain the result. In this example, a 2×2 filter is applied for pooling with a stride value of 2. Pooling enables CNNs to effectively process high-dimensional data, such as images, while extracting and retaining essential features. The output of the pooling operation is a downsampled feature map with reduced spatial dimensions. The size of the output feature map depends on the size of the pooling window, the stride, and the padding (if applied).

The pooled feature map is flattened to convert the resultant two-dimensional matrix into a single long continuous linear vector. Now, if consider the resultant matrix of Figure 4.8, which is obtained after applying max pooling, the flattened linear vector will be formed as shown in Figure 4.9.

Finally, the flattened linear vector from the pooling layer is fed as input to the fully connected layer to classify images. The fully connected (FC) layer, also known as the Dense layer, is a fundamental component of CNN that comes after the convolutional and pooling layers. It plays a critical role in capturing high-level

Figure 4.8 Max pooling vs Average pooling.

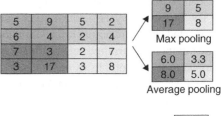

Figure 4.9 Flattening of pooled feature map.

Pooled feature map   Linear vector

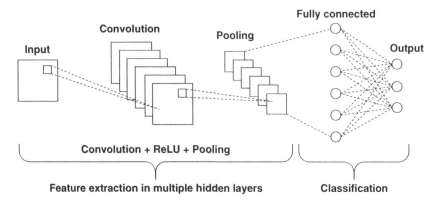

Figure 4.10 Basic CNN architecture.

features and making predictions based on the learned representations. It helps to transform the learned representations from earlier layers into a form suitable for the specific task at hand, such as classification or regression. FC layers are typically followed by a *softmax* activation function, which converts the output into probabilities.

Figure 4.10 shows the basic CNN architecture that contains the convolution layer, the activation layers (ReLU), the pooling layers, the fully connected layers, and finally the output layer. The output layer of a CNN is responsible for producing the final predictions or regression outputs. In classification tasks, the output layer typically uses *softmax* activation to generate class probabilities for multiclass classification. In regression tasks, the output layer can consist of a single neuron or multiple neurons, depending on the number of output units required.

The architectural representation of CNN is shown in Figure 4.11. Every component of the CNN network that has been discussed in this section are put together as a block diagram for visual perception.

The five main layers – convolution layer, activation layer, pooling layer, fully connected layer, and output layer – form the basic structure of a CNN architecture. The number and arrangement of these layers can vary depending on the specific problem and the complexity of the data. More advanced CNN architectures, such as *VGGNet*, *ResNet*, or *InceptionNet*, may incorporate additional specialized layers, skip connections, or other architectural innovations to improve performance on specific tasks or datasets. Some of the most well-known CNN architectures include the following:

a) **LeNet**: This was one of the first CNN architectures developed for handwritten digit recognition and contains two convolutional layers, two pooling layers, and three fully connected layers

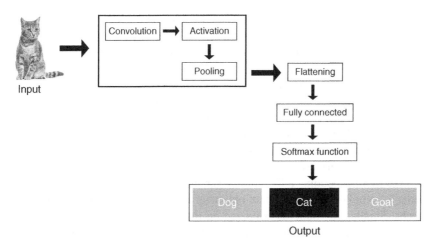

Output

Figure 4.11 Block diagram of CNN architecture. Source: Eric Isselée/Adobe Stock .

b) **AlexNet**: This architecture won the ImageNet Large Scale Visual Recognition Challenge in 2012 and consists of five convolutional layers, three fully connected layers, and uses ReLU activation functions.

c) **VGGNet**: This architecture uses small convolutional filters (3 × 3) with many layers (up to 19 layers) and has achieved top performance on the ImageNet dataset.

d) **GoogLeNet (Inception)**: This architecture uses a network-in-network approach, with multiple convolutional layers stacked on top of each other in parallel, and has achieved high accuracy on ImageNet while using fewer parameters than other networks.

e) **ResNet (Residual Network)**: This architecture introduced the concept of residual connections, which allow for training of very deep networks (up to hundreds of layers) without the problem of vanishing gradients.

f) **DenseNet**: This architecture connects each layer to every other layer in a feed-forward fashion, resulting in a densely connected network that improves feature reuse and reduces the number of parameters.

g) **EfficientNet**: This architecture uses a compound scaling method to scale the depth, width, and resolution of the network in a balanced way, resulting in a more efficient and accurate network.

These are just a few examples of prominent CNN architectures, and there are many other variations and extensions of these architectures as well. Many other architectures, such as *Xception*, *ResNeXt*, and *Inception-ResNet*, have also made significant contributions to the field of computer vision. Each architecture has its own design choices and optimizations, making them suitable for specific tasks or constraints.

Program 4.1 uses the CIFAR-10 dataset, which consists of 50,000 training images and 10,000 testing images, each belonging to one of the ten classes. The list of the ten classes include – *airplane, automobile, bird, cat, deer, dog, frog, horse, ship,* and *truck*. Initially, the code loads the dataset using the cifar10 module from *keras* and performs preprocessing steps such as normalizing the pixel values and converting the labels to one-hot encoded vectors. Here, the input shape mentioned is (32, 32, 3) to match the dimensions of the CIFAR-10 images.

Next, the program uses a simple CNN architecture with two convolutional layers followed by max pooling, a flattening layer, and two fully connected layers. The model is compiled with the Adam optimizer and trained for a fixed number of epochs. Finally, the model is evaluated on the test dataset, and predictions are made on unseen data. Here is an overview of the layers added in the code snippet:

- **Conv2D layer**: Performs 2D convolution on the input image.
- **MaxPooling2D layer**: Performs downsampling by taking the maximum value within a defined window.
- **Flatten layer**: Reshapes the multidimensional output from the previous layer into a 1D vector.
- **Dense layer**: Represents a fully connected layer that connects all neurons from the previous layer to the current layer

Overall, the sequential model provides a convenient way to define and organize the layers of a CNN in a sequential manner.

Program 4.1 *Convolutional Neural Network (CNN) to Predict Images*

```python
import numpy as np
from keras.datasets import cifar10
from keras.models import Sequential
from keras.layers import Conv2D, MaxPooling2D, Flatten, Dense
from keras.utils import to_categorical
import matplotlib.pyplot as plt

# Set the random seed for reproducibility
np.random.seed(42)

# Load the CIFAR-10 dataset
(X_train, y_train), (X_test, y_test) = cifar10.load_data()

# Normalize the pixel values to the range [0, 1]
X_train = X_train.astype('float32') / 255
X_test = X_test.astype('float32') / 255

# Convert the labels to one-hot encoded vectors
num_classes = 10
```

```
y_train = to_categorical(y_train, num_classes)
y_test = to_categorical(y_test, num_classes)

# Define the model architecture
model = Sequential()

# Add a 2D convolutional layer with 32 filters, a 3x3 kernel, and
    'relu' activation
model.add(Conv2D(32, (3, 3), activation='relu', input_shape=(32,
    32, 3)))

# Add a max pooling layer with a 2x2 pool size
model.add(MaxPooling2D(pool_size=(2, 2)))

# Add another 2D convolutional layer with 64 filters and 'relu'
    activation
model.add(Conv2D(64, (3, 3), activation='relu'))

# Add a max pooling layer with a 2x2 pool size
model.add(MaxPooling2D(pool_size=(2, 2)))

# Flatten the feature maps
model.add(Flatten())

# Add a fully connected layer with 128 neurons and 'relu'
    activation
model.add(Dense(128, activation='relu'))

# Add an output layer with 10 units and 'softmax' activation
model.add(Dense(num_classes, activation='softmax'))

# Compile the model
model.compile(loss='categorical_crossentropy', optimizer='adam',
    metrics=['accuracy'])

# Train the model
history = model.fit(X_train, y_train, batch_size=32, epochs=10,
    validation_data=(X_test, y_test), verbose=1)

# Evaluate the model
score = model.evaluate(X_test, y_test, verbose=0)
print('Test loss:', score[0])
print('Test accuracy:', score[1])

# Make predictions
predictions = model.predict(X_test)

# Visualize training and test loss
plt.plot(history.history['loss'], label='Training Loss')
plt.plot(history.history['val_loss'], label='Test Loss')
plt.xlabel('Epoch')
```

```
plt.ylabel('Loss')
plt.title('Training and Test Loss')
plt.legend()
plt.show()

# Visualize training and test accuracy
plt.plot(history.history['accuracy'], label='Training Accuracy')
plt.plot(history.history['val_accuracy'], label='Test Accuracy')
plt.xlabel('Epoch')
plt.ylabel('Accuracy')
plt.title('Training and Test Accuracy')
plt.legend()
plt.show()
```

During training, the CNN adjusts its internal parameters (weights and biases) based on the computed loss. The goal is to minimize the loss, which means reducing the discrepancy between predicted outputs and true outputs. This optimization process is achieved through techniques like backpropagation and gradient descent, where the gradients of the loss function with respect to the model parameters are used to update the parameters in a way that decreases the loss.

The "epoch" is a term used to represent a complete pass through the entire training dataset during the training process. In other words, an epoch is completed when the CNN has processed each training sample once and adjusted

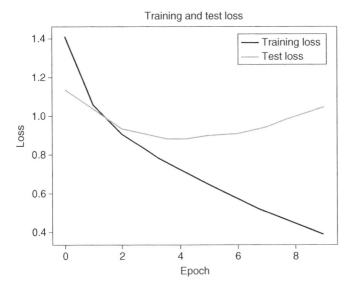

Figure 4.12 Training and test loss.

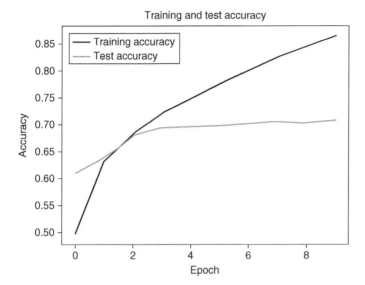

Figure 4.13 Training and test accuracy.

its parameters accordingly. During each epoch, the CNN makes predictions on the training data, compares them with the true labels, computes the loss, and updates the model's parameters based on the gradients.

Typically, training a CNN involves multiple epochs. By going through multiple epochs, the model has the opportunity to learn from the data and improve its performance iteratively. It can refine its internal representations, adapt its parameters, and hopefully converge to a state where the loss is minimized, and the model achieves better accuracy or performance on the given task.

The output of Program 4.1 is displayed below. The output also displays visualization graphs for training and test loss (as shown in Figure 4.12) and training and test accuracy (as shown in Figure 4.13).

```
Epoch 1/10
Epoch 1/10
1563/1563 [==============================] - 83s 52ms/step - loss:
1.4081 - accuracy: 0.4971 - val_loss: 1.1328 - val_accuracy: 0.6090
Epoch 2/10
1563/1563 [==============================] - 78s 50ms/step - loss:
1.0545 - accuracy: 0.6317 - val_loss: 1.0284 - val_accuracy: 0.6380
Epoch 3/10
1563/1563 [==============================] - 79s 51ms/step - loss:
0.9115 - accuracy: 0.6824 - val_loss: 0.9327 - val_accuracy: 0.6781
Epoch 4/10
1563/1563 [==============================] - 78s 50ms/step - loss:
0.8053 - accuracy: 0.7203 - val_loss: 0.8951 - val_accuracy: 0.6941
```

```
Epoch 5/10
1563/1563 [==============================] - 78s 50ms/step - loss:
0.7197 - accuracy: 0.7478 - val_loss: 0.8762 - val_accuracy: 0.6948
Epoch 6/10
1563/1563 [==============================] - 77s 49ms/step - loss:
0.6433 - accuracy: 0.7752 - val_loss: 0.8989 - val_accuracy: 0.6975
Epoch 7/10
1563/1563 [==============================] - 80s 51ms/step - loss:
0.5735 - accuracy: 0.8008 - val_loss: 0.9075 - val_accuracy: 0.7020
Epoch 8/10
1563/1563 [==============================] - 78s 50ms/step - loss:
0.5015 - accuracy: 0.8253 - val_loss: 0.9424 - val_accuracy: 0.7054
Epoch 9/10
1563/1563 [==============================] - 77s 50ms/step - loss:
0.4431 - accuracy: 0.8439 - val_loss: 0.9992 - val_accuracy: 0.7022
Epoch 10/10
1563/1563 [==============================] - 81s 52ms/step - loss:
0.3869 - accuracy: 0.8643 - val_loss: 1.0448 - val_accuracy: 0.7071
Test loss: 1.0448317527770996
Test accuracy: 0.707099974155426
```

In a convolutional neural network (CNN), "test loss" and "test accuracy" are performance metrics used to evaluate the effectiveness of the trained model on unseen or test data.

- **Test Loss**: The test loss is a measurement of how well the trained CNN model performs on the test dataset. It quantifies the error between the predicted outputs and the true outputs for the test samples. The test loss is typically calculated using a loss function, such as categorical cross-entropy for classification tasks or mean squared error for regression tasks. The lower the test loss, the better the model's predictions align with the true outputs.
- **Test Accuracy**: The test accuracy is a metric that indicates the proportion of correctly classified samples in the test dataset. It represents the percentage of test samples that the model correctly predicts the class label for. A higher test accuracy signifies better performance. The test accuracy is usually computed by comparing the predicted class labels with the true class labels and calculating the accuracy as the ratio of correctly classified samples to the total number of test samples

By visualizing the training and test loss as well as training and test accuracy, one can gain insights into how the model is learning and generalizing. These visualizations help in identifying potential issues such as overfitting or underfitting, and they can guide adjustments to the model or training process if necessary.

4.2.2 Recurrent Neural Network (RNN)

A recurrent neural network (RNN) is a deep learning technique that is designed to handle sequential data, such as time series or natural language. It is specifically suited for tasks that involve processing data with a temporal aspect or where the order of the data points matters. RNNs have recurrent connections that allow them to persist information, and pass it along to future time steps or elements in a sequence.

The key characteristic of RNN is its ability to capture and utilize temporal dependencies in the data. It achieves this by introducing loops or feedback connections in the network, which enables it to maintain an internal memory or hidden state. This hidden state allows the network to remember past information and use it to influence the computation at subsequent time steps. Figure 4.14 illustrates the simple working of RNN in which the information cycles through a loop in the middle, hidden layer. The left side of Figure 4.14 shows a notation of an RNN, while the RNN is being *unfolded* into a three-layer neural network on the right side.

The basic unit of an RNN is the recurrent neuron, which takes an input vector and combines it with the previous hidden state to produce an output and update the hidden state for the next time step. The output of the current time step can also be used as input for the next time step, creating a dynamic feedback loop. This recursive nature of RNNs enables them to model sequences of arbitrary lengths.

A single-layer RNN consists of the following components and computations:

(a) **Input and Output:**
   - At each time step t, the RNN takes an input vector $x(t)$.
   - It produces an output vector $y(t)$ at each time step.

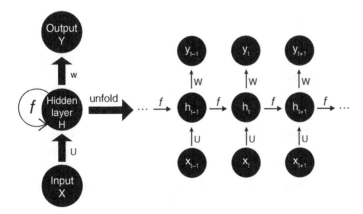

Figure 4.14 Working of RNN.

- The input and output vectors can have different dimensions based on the specific task.

(b) **Hidden State:**
- The RNN maintains a hidden state vector $h(t)$ at each time step, which serves as the memory of the network.
- The hidden state captures information from previous time steps and influences the current prediction.
- Initially, the hidden state is set to zero or a small random vector.

(c) **Recurrent Connections:**
- The hidden state at each time step is calculated based on the current input and the previous hidden state.
- The calculation of the hidden state involves two sets of weights: U (for the previous hidden state) and W (for the current input).
- The hidden state is updated using an activation function, typically a nonlinear function like tanh or ReLU.
- The update equation for the hidden state can be expressed as:

$$h(t) = f(W * h(t-1) + U * x(t)).$$

(d) **Output Calculations:**
- Once the hidden state is updated, the output at each time step is computed based on the hidden state.
- The output can be calculated using a set of weights W that connects the hidden state to the output.
- The output at time step t is obtained as:

$$y(t) = W * h(t)$$

(e) **Training:**
- During training, the RNN is typically trained using gradient-based optimization methods like backpropagation through time (BPTT).
- The objective is to minimize a loss function that measures the discrepancy between the predicted output and the target output.
- Gradients are calculated with respect to the various weights of each state, and updated using gradient descent or its variants.

One popular variant of RNNs is the long short-term memory (LSTM) network, which addresses the vanishing gradient problem by introducing specialized memory cells and gating mechanisms. LSTMs are capable of capturing long-term dependencies and have been widely used in tasks such as speech recognition, machine translation, and sentiment analysis. The LSTM network is discussed in detail next.

Another variant is the gated recurrent unit (GRU), which simplifies the architecture of LSTMs by combining the memory and hidden state into a single update gate. GRUs offer similar capabilities to LSTMs but with fewer parameters, making them more computationally efficient in certain scenarios.

Overall, RNNs have proven to be powerful tools for modeling and predicting sequential data. They excel in tasks that involve time series forecasting, language modeling, speech recognition, and machine translation, among others. Their ability to capture temporal dependencies makes them well-suited for tasks that require understanding and generating sequential information.

Long Short-Term Memory (LSTM) Network: LSTM is a type of RNN architecture that is specifically designed to address the vanishing gradient problem and capture long-term dependencies in sequential data. LSTMs are particularly effective in tasks involving long sequences, in which preserving and updating memory over long-time intervals is crucial. The working of an LSTM can be explained through its key components, and the flow of information during training and inference:

(a) **Cell State:**
- The LSTM network introduces a cell state (often called the "memory") that runs linearly throughout the sequence, allowing information to be stored and carried over long distances.
- The cell state can selectively retain or forget information, which makes it well-suited for capturing long-term dependencies.
- At each time step, the LSTM can read from and write to the cell state, which is regulated by gates.

(b) **Gates:**
- LSTMs use three main types of gates to control the flow of information: forget gate, input gate, and output gate.
- Each gate is composed of a sigmoid activation function, which outputs values between 0 and 1, representing the degree of information flow.

(c) **Forget Gate:**
- The forget gate determines which information from the previous cell state should be discarded.
- It takes the previous hidden state $h(t-1)$ and the current input $x(t)$ as inputs, passes them through a sigmoid activation function, and produces an output between 0 and 1 for each element of the cell state.
- An output of 0 indicates that the corresponding information should be forgotten, while an output of 1 means that the information should be retained.

(d) **Input Gate:**
- The input gate determines which new information from the current input should be stored in the cell state.
- It consists of two parts: an input gate that controls which values should be updated and a `tanh` layer that creates a vector of new candidate values.

- The input gate takes the previous hidden state `h(t−1)` and the current input `x(t)` as inputs, and passes them through sigmoid and tanh activation functions, respectively.
- The sigmoid output determines which values will be updated, while the tanh output creates the candidate vector of new values.

(e) **Updating the Cell State:**
- The cell state is updated based on the outputs of the forget gate and the input gate.
- The forget gate output f_t and the previous cell state $c(t−1)$ are multiplied elementwise to forget the irrelevant information.
- The input gate output it and the candidate vector are multiplied elementwise and added to the result of the forget gate operation, updating the cell state.
- The updated cell state $c(t)$ is given by: $c(t) = f_t * c(t−1) + i_t * tanh$ (candidate vector).

(f) **Output Gate and Hidden State:**
- The output gate determines the information that will be outputted from the LSTM cell.
- It takes the previous hidden state $h(t−1)$ and the current input $x(t)$ as inputs, passes them through a sigmoid activation function, and produces an output between 0 and 1.
- The updated cell state $c(t)$ is passed through a *tanh* activation function to squash the values between −1 and 1.
- The output gate output o_t and the squashed cell state $tanh(c(t))$ are multiplied elementwise to produce the current hidden state $h(t)$.
- The hidden state carries the relevant information from the cell state, and is passed to the next time step and also used for generating the output prediction.

(g) **Training and Inference:**
- During training, LSTMs are typically trained using gradient-based optimization methods like BPTT.
- The objective is to minimize a loss function that measures the discrepancy between the predicted output and the target output.
- Gradients are calculated with respect to the LSTM's parameters and updated using gradient descent or its variants.
- During inference or testing, the LSTM can be used to generate predictions for new input sequences by feeding the inputs one step at a time and updating the hidden state accordingly.

LSTMs have proven to be highly effective in a wide range of tasks involving sequential data, such as speech recognition, language translation, sentiment analysis, and time series prediction, among others. They have enabled the modeling of complex dependencies over long sequences and have become a cornerstone in the field of deep learning for sequential data processing.

To further understand the concept of LSTM in RNN, a simple example to predict the next odd number in a numerical sequence is considered. Suppose there is a sequence of odd numbers: [1, 3, 5, 7, 9, 11, 13, 15, 17, 19], the goal is to train an LSTM to predict the next odd number in the sequence. For input preparation, the sequence is divided into input (X) and output (Y) pairs. Now, if the sequence length is set to 3, the input and output will be:

$$X : [1, 3, 5], [3, 5, 7], [5, 7, 9], \dots, [13, 15, 17]$$

$$Y : 7, 9, 11, \dots, 19$$

Next, the LSTM model is to be created using a deep learning framework like Keras or PyTorch. The LSTM model will have an input shape matching the sequence length (e.g., 3) and the number of features (e.g., 1 in this case). The model will also have one or more LSTM layers followed by one or more fully connected (dense) layers for prediction. The LSTM model is trained using the prepared input and output pairs (X and Y). During training, the LSTM learns to capture the patterns and dependencies in the sequence data. The model optimizes its internal parameters through the backpropagation algorithm to minimize the prediction error (e.g., mean squared error).

After training, the LSTM model can be used to make predictions on new sequences. To predict the next odd number in the sequence, the last three elements are provided as input to the trained LSTM model. The LSTM processes the input sequence, updates its internal state, and generates the predicted output. For example, if the input sequence is [15, 17, 19], the LSTM should predict the next number, which is 21. By training an LSTM on sequential data, it can learn to recognize patterns and dependencies specific to the given task. In this case, the LSTM learns the pattern of incrementing odd numbers and can make accurate predictions based on that pattern.

Program 4.2 uses an RNN (specifically an LSTM) for sentiment classification of text data. A small set of sample text is used having corresponding sentiment labels: positive (1) and negative (0). The goal is to train the RNN to predict the sentiment of new text data. At first, the text data is tokenized using the *Tokenizer* class from *keras*. The tokenizer assigns a unique index to each word in the vocabulary. Then, the text data is converted to sequences of integers using *texts_to_sequences* function. To ensure equal-length input sequences, the sequences are padded using *pad_sequences* function. The length of the longest sequence determines the maximum sequence length, and all other sequences are padded or truncated accordingly.

The RNN model is created using the sequential API in `keras`. It consists of an embedding layer, an LSTM layer, and a Dense output layer with a sigmoid activation function for binary classification. The model is compiled with the Adam optimizer and binary cross-entropy loss. It is then trained on the padded sequences and corresponding labels using the fit function. For testing, new text data is provided in the `test_texts` list. The same preprocessing steps (tokenization and padding) are applied to the test data. The model then predicts the sentiment for each test sample using predict function, and the predicted labels are determined by applying a threshold of 0.5. Finally, the predicted sentiment labels are printed for each test text.

Program 4.2   *Recurrent Neural Network (RNN) for Sentiment Analysis*

```
import numpy as np
from keras.models import Sequential
from keras.layers import Embedding, LSTM, Dense
from keras.preprocessing.text import Tokenizer
from keras.preprocessing.sequence import pad_sequences

# Sample text data
texts = [
    "I love this movie!",
    "This film is fantastic.",
    "Such a great film!",
    "This movie is terrible.",
    "I don't like this at all."
]

# Corresponding sentiment labels (1 for positive, 0 for negative)
labels = np.array([1, 1, 1, 0, 0])

# Tokenize the text data
tokenizer = Tokenizer()
tokenizer.fit_on_texts(texts)
word_index = tokenizer.word_index
vocab_size = len(word_index) + 1

# Convert text data to sequences of integers
sequences = tokenizer.texts_to_sequences(texts)

# Pad sequences to ensure equal length
max_sequence_length = max([len(seq) for seq in sequences])
padded_sequences = pad_sequences(sequences, maxlen=max_sequence_
    length)

# Create the RNN model
model = Sequential()
model.add(Embedding(vocab_size, 10, input_length=max_sequence_
    length))
```

```
model.add(LSTM(10))
model.add(Dense(1, activation='sigmoid'))

# Compile the model
model.compile(optimizer='adam', loss='binary_crossentropy',
    metrics=['accuracy'])

# Train the model
model.fit(padded_sequences, labels, epochs=10, verbose=1)

# Test the model with new input
test_texts = [
    "This is a great movie!",
    "I dislike it.",
    "It's amazing!"
]
test_sequences = tokenizer.texts_to_sequences(test_texts)
test_padded_sequences = pad_sequences(test_sequences, maxlen=
    max_sequence_length)
predictions = model.predict(test_padded_sequences)
predicted_labels = [1 if pred >= 0.5 else 0 for pred in
    predictions]

# Print the predictions
for i in range(len(test_texts)):
    print("Text:", test_texts[i])
    print("Sentiment Prediction:", predicted_labels[i])
    print()
```

The output of Program 4.2 is given next that displays the testing texts and their corresponding sentiment prediction. A sentiment label of 1 indicates positive sentiment, whereas a sentiment label of 0 indicates negative sentiment.

```
Text: This is a great movie!
Sentiment Prediction: 1

Text: I dislike it.
Sentiment Prediction: 0

Text: It's amazing!
Sentiment Prediction: 1
```

According to the output, the program predicts a positive sentiment for the text "This is a great movie!" and "It's amazing!". On the other hand, it predicts a negative sentiment for the text "I dislike it.". These predictions are based on the training of the RNN model using the provided sample texts and their corresponding sentiment labels.

4.2.3   Generative Adversarial Network (GAN)

A generative adversarial network (GAN) is a deep learning model that consists of two neural networks: a generator and a discriminator. The concept behind GANs was introduced by Ian Goodfellow and his colleagues in 2014. The generator network takes random noise as input and tries to generate synthetic data, such as images, text, or sound, that resembles the training data it was trained on. The goal of the generator is to produce outputs that are convincing and indistinguishable from real data.

The discriminator network, on the other hand, is trained to differentiate between real data and the synthetic data generated by the generator. It acts as a binary classifier, trying to determine whether a given input is real or fake. The discriminator is trained using a combination of real data from the training set and the synthetic data generated by the generator. During training, the generator and discriminator networks are trained simultaneously in a competitive setting. The generator aims to produce increasingly realistic samples to fool the discriminator, while the discriminator gets better at distinguishing between real and fake samples. This process creates a feedback loop where both networks improve over time.

The training of GANs typically involves an adversarial loss function, such as the minimax loss. The generator seeks to minimize this loss, while the discriminator seeks to maximize it. This adversarial training process drives both networks to improve their performance until the generator produces high-quality outputs that can successfully fool the discriminator.

GANs have been successfully applied in various domains, including image synthesis, text generation, video generation, and even generating realistic human faces. They have also been used for tasks such as data augmentation, style transfer, and anomaly detection. To learn about how GAN works, it is important to understand the steps involved in implementing GAN, including the setup and environment under which GAN does work.

a) **Architecture Setup**: The GAN consists of two neural networks: the generator and the discriminator. The generator takes random noise as input and produces synthetic data, while the discriminator takes both real and synthetic data as input, and tries to classify them as either real or fake.

b) **Training Data**: The GAN is trained on a dataset consisting of real data samples, such as images, text, or audio that represents the target distribution.

c) **Training Process:**
 - *Initialization:* The generator and discriminator networks are initialized with random weights.
 - *Iterative Training:* The training process alternates between two main steps:

Step 1: Generator Update

o The generator generates a batch of synthetic data by taking random noise as input.

o The generated data is passed to the discriminator, and the discriminator's output is obtained.

o The generator's parameters are updated based on the discriminator's feedback, aiming to produce synthetic data that the discriminator classifies as real.

Step 2: Discriminator Update

o The discriminator is presented with a batch of real data samples from the training dataset and a batch of synthetic data generated by the generator.

o The discriminator's parameters are updated based on its ability to correctly classify the real and synthetic samples.

o The generator is not updated during this step to keep the generator–discriminator competition intact.

d) **Loss Functions:**

- *Generator Loss:* The generator aims to minimize the discriminator's ability to distinguish between real and synthetic data. This is typically achieved by using an adversarial loss function, such as the minimax loss, which encourages the generator to generate realistic data that fools the discriminator.

- *Discriminator Loss:* The discriminator aims to correctly classify real and synthetic samples. It is trained using a binary classification loss function, such as binary cross-entropy, to maximize its ability to distinguish between real and fake data.

- *Iterative Improvement:* The generator and discriminator continue to update their parameters in an iterative manner, each trying to outperform the other. This competition drives the GAN toward generating increasingly realistic synthetic data.

- *Convergence:* The GAN training process is considered to have converged when the generator produces synthetic data that is indistinguishable from real data, and the discriminator performs at chance level in distinguishing between real and synthetic samples.

One of the key advantages of GANs is their ability to learn and generate complex, high-dimensional data distributions. GANs can also be used to augment training datasets by generating additional synthetic samples. This helps in improving the robustness and generalization of machine learning models. GAN-generated data can introduce diversity, balance class distributions, and fill gaps in the training data, leading to better model performance. GANs are also used for unsupervised learning tasks, as this model is fit to learn from unlabeled data. Without the need for explicit labels, GANs can capture and model the underlying structure of the data distribution, enabling unsupervised feature learning and clustering.

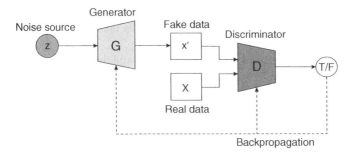

Figure 4.15 Use of GAN to generate synthetic images.

Program 4.3 shows how the GAN model is used to generate synthetic images that resemble the real images from the CIFAR-10 dataset. The generator network takes random noise as input and learns to generate realistic images. The discriminator network aims to distinguish between real images from the dataset and fake images generated by the generator. The pictorial demonstration of the program is given in Figure 4.15.

Initially, in Program 4.3, the dataset is loaded and the training images (`x_train`) are preprocessed by scaling the pixel values between −1 and 1. For defining the generator network, an input layer (`generator_input`) is defined with a shape of (100,), representing a random noise vector. The noise vector is passed through a Dense layer with ReLU activation, followed by a reshape layer to transform it into a 4D tensor. Convolutional transpose layers are added to upsample the tensor gradually, creating a generator output tensor of shape (32, 32, 3). Finally, a generator model (generator) is created using the Model class, with the input and output layers.

Next, for defining the discriminator network, an input layer (`discrimi-nator_input`) is defined with a shape of (32, 32, 3), representing an image. Convolutional layers are added to downsample the input tensor, extracting features. The tensor is then flattened, followed by a Dense layer with sigmoid activation, giving the discriminator's output. A discriminator model (discriminator) is created using the Model class, with the input and output layers. The discriminator model is compiled using binary cross-entropy loss, and the Adam optimizer with a learning rate of 0.0002 and beta1 value of 0.5. Also, the discriminator's trainable parameter is set to False, freezing its weights during GAN training.

Now, the GAN model is defined by using an input layer (`gan_input`) defined with a shape of (100), representing the random noise vector. The generator model is called with the input layer to get the generator output. The discriminator model is called with the generator output to get the GAN output. A GAN model (`gan`) is created using the Model class, with the input layer and GAN output. The

GAN model is compiled using binary cross-entropy loss, and the Adam optimizer with a learning rate of 0.0002 and beta1 value of 0.5.

Finally, the code proceeds to the training loop, where the GAN model is trained for a specified number of epochs. In each epoch, the code iterates over batches of real and generated images. For each batch, random noise is generated as input for the generator. The generator generates fake images using the random noise input. Real images are randomly selected from the CIFAR-10 dataset. Real and fake images are concatenated along with their corresponding labels. The discriminator is trained on this batch of real and fake images, using the concatenated data and labels. New random noise is generated as input for the generator. Labels for the generator are set to ones, aiming to maximize the discriminator's error. The GAN is trained by updating the generator's weights using the random noise and labels. The losses of the discriminator and GAN are printed for each epoch.

Program 4.3 *Generative Adversarial Network (GAN) for Generating Synthetic Images*

```python
import numpy as np
import tensorflow as tf
from tensorflow.keras.datasets import cifar10
from tensorflow.keras.layers import Dense, Reshape, Conv2D,
    Conv2DTranspose, Flatten, Input
from tensorflow.keras.models import Model
from tensorflow.keras.optimizers import Adam

# Load and preprocess the CIFAR-10 dataset
(x_train, _), (_, _) = cifar10.load_data()
x_train = (x_train.astype('float32') - 127.5) / 127.5

# Define the generator network
generator_input = Input(shape=(100,))
x = Dense(4 * 4 * 256, activation='relu')(generator_input)
x = Reshape((4, 4, 256))(x)
x = Conv2DTranspose(128, kernel_size=4, strides=2, padding='same',
    activation='relu')(x)
x = Conv2DTranspose(64, kernel_size=4, strides=2, padding='same',
    activation='relu')(x)
x = Conv2DTranspose(3, kernel_size=3, strides=1, padding='same',
    activation='tanh')(x)
generator_output = tf.image.resize(x, (32, 32))
generator = Model(generator_input, generator_output)

# Define the discriminator network
discriminator_input = Input(shape=(32, 32, 3))
x = Conv2D(64, kernel_size=3, strides=2, padding='same',
    activation='relu') (discriminator_input)
x = Conv2D(128, kernel_size=3, strides=2, padding='same',
    activation='relu')(x)
```

```
x = Conv2D(256, kernel_size=3, strides=2, padding='same',
    activation='relu')(x)
x = Flatten()(x)
discriminator_output = Dense(1, activation='sigmoid')(x)
discriminator = Model(discriminator_input, discriminator_output)

# Compile the discriminator network
discriminator.compile(loss='binary_crossentropy', optimizer=
    Adam(lr=0.0002, beta_1=0.5), metrics=['accuracy'])

# Freeze the discriminator weights during GAN training
discriminator.trainable = False

# Define the GAN model
gan_input = Input(shape=(100,))
gan_output = discriminator(generator(gan_input))
gan = Model(gan_input, gan_output)

# Compile the GAN model
gan.compile(loss='binary_crossentropy', optimizer=Adam(lr=0.0002,
    beta_1=0.5))

# Training loop
epochs = 100
batch_size = 128
steps_per_epoch = len(x_train) // batch_size

for epoch in range(epochs):
    for step in range(steps_per_epoch):

        # Generate random noise as input for the generator
        noise = np.random.normal(0, 1, size=(batch_size, 100))

        # Generate fake images using the generator
        generated_images = generator.predict(noise)

        # Select a random batch of real images from the dataset
        real_images = x_train[np.random.randint(0, x_train.shape[0],
            size=batch_size)]

        # Concatenate real and fake images
        x = np.concatenate((real_images, generated_images))

        # Create labels for real and fake images
        labels = np.concatenate((np.ones((batch_size, 1)), np.zeros
            ((batch_size, 1))))

        # Train the discriminator on real and fake images
        discriminator_loss = discriminator.train_on_batch(x,
            labels)
```

```
# Generate new random noise for the generator
noise = np.random.normal(0, 1, size=(batch_size, 100))

# Create labels for the generator to maximize the
  discriminator's error
y = np.ones((batch_size, 1))

# Train the GAN by updating the generator's weights
gan_loss = gan.train_on_batch(noise, y)

# Print the losses for each epoch
  print(f"Epoch: {epoch+1}, Discriminator Loss:
  {discriminator_loss[0]}, GAN Loss: {gan_loss}")
```

The output of Program 4.3 will show the discriminator loss and GAN loss for each epoch during the training process. Additionally, the generated output will be printed for each epoch. Here's an example of how the output might look like:

```
Epoch: 1, Discriminator Loss: 0.6522918949127197,
  GAN Loss: 0.9615811114311218
Epoch: 2, Discriminator Loss: 0.5419158930778503,
  GAN Loss: 1.1447433233261108
Epoch: 3, Discriminator Loss: 0.4025923316478729,
  GAN Loss: 1.3756206035614014
...
Epoch: 100, Discriminator Loss: 0.1257862150669098,
  GAN Loss: 3.3319873809814453
```

The goal of this training process is for the generator to improve its ability to generate more realistic images over time, while the discriminator becomes better at distinguishing between real and fake images. Through this adversarial process, the generator and discriminator networks learn to improve iteratively, leading to the generation of higher-quality synthetic images.

The discriminator loss and GAN loss values will vary depending on the dataset, model architecture, hyperparameters, and the progress of the training process. The goal is typically to see a decrease in the discriminator loss and an increase in the GAN loss over the epochs. It is important to note that since the generator network is generating images, the program does not explicitly display the generated images in the provided code snippet. However, the code can be modified to save or display the generated images during or after the training loop if desired.

4.2.4 Autoencoders

Autoencoders are a class of artificial neural networks used in unsupervised learning and deep learning. They are designed to learn efficient representations of input data by compressing it into a lower dimensional latent space and then reconstructing the original data from this compressed representation. The goal of an autoencoder is to replicate its input at the output layer while minimizing the reconstruction error.

The architecture of an autoencoder typically consists of two main components: an encoder and a decoder. The encoder takes the input data and maps it to a lower dimensional latent representation, which captures the essential features of the data. The decoder then takes this latent representation and reconstructs the original input data. The encoder and decoder components are usually symmetrical, and the middle layer represents the compressed latent space.

Figure 4.16 shows an example of an autoencoder that takes in a noisy input and learns to create a compressed representation of the input data to reconstruct the original data from that representation. This autoencoder is designed for denoising images by using the encoder and the decoder. The encoder reduces the dimensionality of the input image to capture its essential features, while the decoder reconstructs the clean image from the compressed representation. During the training process, the noisy images are passed through the autoencoder's encoder to obtain the compressed latent representations. The loss is calculated between the noisy input images and the reconstructed clean images. The loss function can be mean squared error (MSE) or any other suitable image similarity metric. The loss is then backpropagated through the decoder, and the model's parameters are updated using an optimization algorithm like stochastic gradient descent (SGD) or Adam. The steps – forward pass, loss calculation, and backpropagation – are repeated for multiple epochs, iterating over the training sets.

The performance of the trained denoising autoencoder is evaluated on a separate test set. The image quality metrics, such as peak signal-to-noise ratio (PSNR) or structural similarity index (SSIM), is measured to assess the denoising effectiveness. Once the autoencoder is trained and evaluated, one can apply it to remove noise from new images. Given a noisy image, pass it through the trained autoencoder's encoder to obtain the compressed representation and then pass it through the decoder to reconstruct the denoised image.

The training of an autoencoder involves minimizing the difference between the input data and its reconstruction, typically using a loss function such as mean

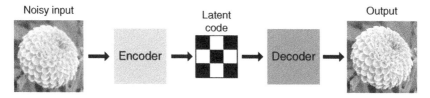

Figure 4.16 An Autoencoder used for denoising images. Source: Alina Yudina/Adobe Stock .

squared error (MSE). This loss function measures the discrepancy between the original input and the reconstructed output. By optimizing this loss function, the autoencoder learns to capture the most important features of the data in the latent representation. Autoencoders follow a series of steps for obtaining its output, which is explained in detail next.

a) **Data Preparation**: First, you need to prepare your input data. This involves collecting a dataset of examples that represent the data you want the autoencoder to learn from. The data can be in various forms such as images, text, or numerical data.

b) **Architecture Design**: Decide on the architecture of the autoencoder. Typically, an autoencoder consists of an encoder and a decoder. The encoder takes the input data and maps it to a lower dimensional latent representation, and the decoder reconstructs the original input from the latent representation. The encoder and decoder can be designed using various types of neural network layers, such as fully connected layers, convolutional layers, or recurrent layers, depending on the nature of the input data.

c) **Training Data Split**: Split the dataset into a training set and a validation set. The training set will be used to train the autoencoder, while the validation set will be used to monitor the model's performance during training and tune hyperparameters.

d) **Training Process:**
   - *Forward Pass*: Pass the training examples through the autoencoder's encoder to obtain the compressed latent representations.
   - *Loss Calculation:* Calculate the loss between the input data and the reconstructed output. Common loss functions used in autoencoders include mean squared error (MSE) or binary cross-entropy, depending on the type of data.
   - *Backpropagation:* Propagate the loss backward through the decoder to update the model's parameters. This is done using gradient descent optimization algorithms such as stochastic gradient descent (SGD) or Adam.
   - *Repeat:* Repeat the forward pass, loss calculation, and backpropagation steps for multiple epochs, iterating over the training set. During each epoch, the model gradually learns to reconstruct the input data more accurately.

e) **Hyperparameter Tuning**: Adjust the hyperparameters of the autoencoder, such as learning rate, batch size, or the number of hidden layers, based on the performance on the validation set. This step helps improve the model's generalization ability and avoid overfitting.

f) **Evaluation**: Once training is complete, evaluate the performance of the trained autoencoder using a separate test set. Calculate metrics such as reconstruction loss, accuracy, or any other relevant evaluation metric based on the specific task or domain.

g) **Application of Autoencoder**: After training and evaluation, you can use the trained autoencoder for various purposes. For example, if an image autoencoder is trained, new images can be encoded into the latent space to obtain their compressed representations or generate new images by sampling from the learned latent space.

The above steps provide a general overview of how autoencoders work. There are different types of autoencoders, such as sparse autoencoders, denoising autoencoders, and variational autoencoders, which have additional steps or modifications in their working process to achieve specific objectives or address particular challenges.

Program 4.4 shows how the autoencoder model is used to denoise images using the MNIST dataset that is available online. Initially, the dataset is divided into training and testing sets, containing image data and corresponding labels. The pixel values of the images are normalized between 0 and 1, by dividing them by 255.0. The images are reshaped from (28, 28) to a flattened vector of size 784 ($28 \times 28 = 784$).

The autoencoder architecture is defined by setting the input dimension to 784, corresponding to the flattened image vector size. The encoding dimension is set to 32, which determines the size of the compressed latent space. An input layer is created using input with the shape equal to the input dimension. A hidden layer (encoder) is created using Dense with the encoding dimension and ReLU activation. An output layer (decoder) is created using Dense with the input dimension and sigmoid activation. The model is created, taking the input layer and the output layer as arguments.

Next, the autoencoder model is compiled with the Adam optimizer and the binary cross-entropy loss function. The fit method is used to train the autoencoder on the training data. The training is performed for a specified number of epochs (50) with a batch size of 256. The autoencoder learns to minimize the reconstruction loss between the input and output.

Finally, after training, a subset of test images (10 examples) is encoded and reconstructed using the trained autoencoder. The autoencoder's prediction method is used to reconstruct the selected test images. The original and reconstructed images are then displayed using matplotlib. The images are displayed using imshow with the "gray" colormap.

Program 4.4 *Autoencoder for Denoising Images*

```
import numpy as np
import matplotlib.pyplot as plt
from keras.layers import Input, Dense
from keras.models import Model
from keras.datasets import mnist
```

```
# Load the MNIST dataset
(train_data, _), (test_data, _) = mnist.load_data()

# Preprocess and normalize the pixel values between 0 and 1
train_data = train_data.astype('float32') / 255.0
test_data = test_data.astype('float32') / 255.0

# Reshape the data into flattened vectors
train_data = train_data.reshape((len(train_data), np.prod
    (train_data.shape[1:])))
test_data = test_data.reshape((len(test_data), np.prod(test_
    data.shape[1:])))

# Define the autoencoder architecture
input_dim = train_data.shape[1]
encoding_dim = 32
input_img = Input(shape=(input_dim,))
encoded = Dense(encoding_dim, activation='relu')(input_img)
decoded = Dense(input_dim, activation='sigmoid')(encoded)
autoencoder = Model(input_img, decoded)

# Compile the autoencoder model
autoencoder.compile(optimizer='adam', loss='binary_crossentropy')

# Train the autoencoder
epochs = 50
batch_size = 256
autoencoder.fit(train_data, train_data,
                epochs=epochs,
                batch_size=batch_size,
                shuffle=True,
                validation_data=(test_data, test_data))

# Use the trained autoencoder to reconstruct test images
num_examples = 10
encoded_imgs = autoencoder.predict(test_data[:num_examples])

# Display the original and reconstructed images
plt.figure(figsize=(20, 4))
for i in range(num_examples):
    # Display original images
    ax = plt.subplot(2, num_examples, i + 1)
    plt.imshow(test_data[i].reshape(28, 28), cmap='gray')
    ax.get_xaxis().set_visible(False)
    ax.get_yaxis().set_visible(False)

    # Display reconstructed images
    ax = plt.subplot(2, num_examples, i + 1 + num_examples)
    plt.imshow(encoded_imgs[i].reshape(28, 28), cmap='gray')
    ax.get_xaxis().set_visible(False)
```

```
ax.get_yaxis().set_visible(False)
    plt.show()
```

The autoencoder model aims to learn a compressed representation of the input images in the hidden layer (encoder) and then reconstruct the original images from this compressed representation in the output layer (decoder). The model is trained to minimize the difference between the input and output images, thereby learning to capture the essential features of the data in a compressed latent space. By displaying the original and reconstructed images, one can visually assess the performance of the autoencoder in capturing and reconstructing the handwritten digit images.

The partial output of Program 4.4 is given next. The training is performed for a specified number of epochs (50) with a batch size of 256. Epochs 1, 2, 49, and 50 are shown in the output along with the ten reconstructed test images. By displaying the original and reconstructed images, one can visually assess the performance of the autoencoder in capturing and reconstructing the handwritten digit images.

```
Epoch 1/50
235/235 [==============================] - 4s 12ms/step - loss:
0.2761 - val_loss: 0.1916
Epoch 2/50
235/235 [==============================] - 3s 12ms/step - loss:
0.1713 - val_loss: 0.1543
... ...
... ...
Epoch 49/50
235/235 [==============================] - 3s 11ms/step - loss:
0.0927 - val_loss: 0.0915
Epoch 50/50
235/235 [==============================] - 3s 11ms/step - loss:
0.0927 - val_loss: 0.0915
1/1 [==============================] - 0s 87ms/step
```

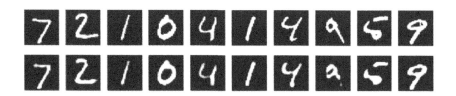

Program 4.4 can be modified to experiment with different architectures, hyperparameters, and datasets. Additionally, you can explore other variations of autoencoders, such as convolutional autoencoders or variational autoencoders, for different types of data and tasks.

Autoencoders, like any other machine learning model, have their own advantages and disadvantages. Autoencoders can learn from unlabeled data without requiring explicit class labels and are, therefore, used for unsupervised learning. Autoencoders can also learn compact representations of high-dimensional data by compressing it into a lower dimensional latent space. This makes them useful for feature extraction and dimensionality reduction tasks, where the learned representations can capture the most important features of the data. As seen in the previous program, this model can also be used for image denoising. Lastly, autoencoders can be used for anomaly detection, where they are trained on normal data and are capable of identifying unusual or anomalous patterns during the reconstruction phase.

Exercises

A) Choose the correct answer from among the alternatives given:
   a) In which of the following applications can we use deep learning to solve the problem?
      i) Protein structure prediction
      ii) Prediction of chemical reaction
      iii) Detection of exotic particles
      iv) All of these
   b) Identify the true statements for a 1×1 convolutions in a convolutional neural network (CNN).
      i) Help in dimensionality reduction
      ii) Used for feature pooling
      iii) Due to small kernel size less overfitting
      iv) All of the above
   c) If the number of nodes in the input layer is 10 and in the hidden layer is 5, the maximum number of connections from the input layer to the hidden layer would be
      i) 50
      ii) Less than 50
      iii) More than 50
      iv) Any value can be derived
   d) An input image is transformed into a size of 28×28 and a filter of size 7×7 with a stride of 1 is used. What is the size of the convoluted matrix?
      i) 22×22
      ii) 21×21
      iii) 28×28
      iv) 7×7

e) Which of the following layers in a convolutional neural network (CNN) is responsible for reducing the spatial dimensions of the input?
   i) Convolutional layer
   ii) Pooling layer
   iii) Fully connected layer
   iv) Activation layer

f) Which activation function is commonly used in convolutional neural networks (CNNs) for introducing nonlinearity?
   i) Linear activation
   ii) Sigmoid activation
   iii) ReLU activation
   iv) Tanh activation

g) In a convolutional neural network (CNN), what does the term "kernel" refers to?
   i) The entire set of weights in a convolutional layer
   ii) The output of a convolutional layer
   iii) The filter or feature detector applied to the input
   iv) The pooling operation applied to the feature maps

h) Which of the following statements about convolutional neural network (CNN) architectures is true?
   i) CNNs are always deeper than fully connected neural networks.
   ii) CNNs can have both convolutional and fully connected layers.
   iii) CNNs can only be applied to image data, not other types of data.
   iv) CNNs do not have any pooling layers.

i) What is the purpose of the *softmax* activation function in the output layer of a CNN for multiclass classification?
   i) To introduce nonlinearity to the output predictions.
   ii) To normalize the output probabilities, ensuring they sum up to 1.
   iii) To reduce the dimensionality of the output feature maps.
   iv) To speed up the training process of the CNN.

j) If a convolutional neural network (CNN) is trained on an object recognition dataset (ImageNet) and then fed with a completely white image as input, will the output probabilities for this input image be same for all the class?
   i) Yes
   ii) No
   iii) Cannot answer

k) What is the primary advantage of using RNNs compared to traditional feed-forward neural networks?
   i) RNNs can handle variable-length input sequences.

  ii) RNNs are faster in training and inference.

  iii) RNNs have a higher accuracy for image classification tasks.

  iv) RNNs require fewer computational resources.

l) Which of the following layers is specifically designed for handling sequential data in an RNN?

  i) Convolutional layer

  ii) Pooling layer

  iii) Recurrent layer

  iv) Fully connected layer

m) What are the primary components of a generative adversarial networks (GANs) architecture?

  i) Generator and discriminator

  ii) Encoder and decoder

  iii) Convolutional layers and pooling layers

  iv) Input data and output data

n) Which of the following best describes the training process of a generative adversarial network (GAN)?

  i) The generator and discriminator are trained simultaneously in an adversarial manner.

  ii) The generator is trained first, followed by the training of the discriminator.

  iii) The discriminator is trained first, followed by the training of the generator.

  iv) The generator and discriminator are trained separately and combined during inference.

o) Which part of an autoencoder is responsible for encoding the input data into a lower-dimensional representation?

  i) Encoder

  ii) Decoder

  iii) Fully connected layer

  iv) Activation function

p) How is the quality of the reconstructed output measured in autoencoders?

  i) Mean squared error (MSE)

  ii) Cross-entropy loss

  iii) Accuracy

  iv) F1 score

B) Answer the following questions:

1) Identify the value in place of "?" in the following considerations:

INPUT

1	1	1	0	0
0	1	1	1	0
0	0	1	1	1
0	0	1	1	0
0	1	1	0	0

FILTER

1	0	1
0	1	0
1	0	1

CONVOLVED FEATURE

?		

2) Describe the concept of pooling in convolutional neural networks (CNNs). What is its purpose, and how does it help in reducing spatial dimensions?

3) Differentiate RNN from CNN. Compare and contrast the best uses of each of them with respect to given problem.

4) Elaborate on the vanishing gradient problem in RNNs. What causes it, and how does it affect the training process and the ability of RNNs to capture long-term dependencies?

5) Explain the role of the hidden state in an RNN. What information does it store, and how is it updated during each time step?

6) Describe the architecture of an long short-term memory (LSTM) network. What are the key components of an LSTM cell, and how do they help in capturing long-term dependencies in sequential data?

7) For the below given input matrix of size 7×7, compute the output on applying a max pooling of size 3×3 with stride value $= 2$.

1	2	4	1	4	0	1
0	0	1	6	1	5	5
1	4	4	5	1	4	1
4	1	5	1	6	5	0
1	0	6	5	1	1	8
2	3	1	8	5	8	1
0	9	1	2	3	1	4

8) Discuss the training process of a Generative adversarial network (GAN). How does the adversarial training objective lead to the improvement of both the generator and discriminator over time?

9) Explain the architecture of an autoencoder, including the encoder and decoder components. How do these components work together to compress and reconstruct the input data?

5

Probabilistic Reasoning

Soft computing techniques often utilize probabilistic reasoning alongside other methods to handle uncertainty and complex real-world problems. In probabilistic reasoning, uncertain information is represented using probability distributions. These distributions capture the likelihood or belief in different outcomes or states of a system. By combining known evidence or observations with prior knowledge and assumptions, probabilistic reasoning allows for the estimation of probabilities of events and the calculation of conditional probabilities. This chapter will focus in depth about probabilistic reasoning, and its key components and techniques.

5.1   Introduction to Probabilistic Reasoning

Probabilistic reasoning is a framework used to make inferences and decisions under uncertainty. It is based on the principles of probability theory, and provides a systematic way to reason about uncertain information and estimate probabilities of different events or outcomes. Probabilistic reasoning finds applications in various domains, including machine learning, artificial intelligence, decision making, natural language processing, and robotics. It enables reasoning under uncertainty, and provides a principled approach to handle complex problems where uncertainty and incomplete information are present.

To understand probabilistic reasoning, it is important to first understand what probability and the core terms associated with it mean. Probability is the chance of the occurrence of some events, tasks, or phenomena. Knowledge of probability is an important measure to deal with uncertainty and randomness that often occur in many aspects of our daily life. It is numerically quantified as a value between 0 and 1. The value 0 for probability indicates impossibility, and the value 1 for probability indicates certainty. The other core terms related to probability are discussed next:

Principles of Soft Computing Using Python Programming: Learn How to Deploy Soft Computing Models in Real World Applications, First Edition. Gypsy Nandi.
© 2024 The Institute of Electrical and Electronics Engineers, Inc. Published 2024 by John Wiley & Sons, Inc.

Table 5.1 Random experiments and possible outcomes.

Random experiment	Possible outcome
Tossing coin	Head (H), tail (T)
Rolling a dice	Dice numbers: 1, 2, 3, 4, 5, 6
Result of a game	Win (W), loss (L)
Choosing a vowel	Outcome: a, e, i, o, u

5.1.1 Random Experiment

A random experiment is a process or activity that leads to uncertain outcomes. In other words, it is an experiment or event where the outcome cannot be precisely predicted with certainty beforehand. It involves the element of chance or randomness. For example, flipping a coin is a classic random experiment. The outcome of the experiment can result in either heads or tails, and the probability of each outcome is either 0.5% or 50% for a fair coin. Table 5.1 cites some examples of an experiment and its possible outcomes. For a random experiment, the list of possible outcomes is exhaustive and mutually exclusive.

When an experiment is carried out on probabilities, it can be found that the sum of probabilities of all possible outcomes is equal to 1. If an experiment consists of three possible outcomes – U, V, and W, then $P(U) + P(V) + P(W) = 1$. For an event E, the probability can be calculated as:

$$P(E) = n(E)/n(T)$$

Here, $n(E)$ indicates the number of ways an event can occur, and $n(T)$ indicates the total number of outcomes.

Let us consider an example of a six-sided dice, which consists of six different values from 1 to 6. To find the probability of rolling a specific outcome on a six-sided dice, one needs to divide the number of favorable outcomes by the total number of possible outcomes. Here, the total number of outcomes $n(T)$ is 6. For a particular number to be displayed per throw of the dice, there is only one possible way, i.e., $n(E) = 1$. Therefore, the probability of a particular number to be displayed per throw is $P(E) = 1/6 = 0.1667$, i.e., 16.67%.

5.1.2 Random Variables

In probability theory, a random variable is a variable that takes on different numerical values based on the outcome of a random experiment or event. It assigns a numerical value to each possible outcome of the experiment. Random variables can be categorized as either discrete or continuous:

- **Discrete Random Variables:** A discrete random variable takes on a countable set of distinct values. For example, the number of heads obtained in multiple coin flips or the outcome of rolling a fair six-sided dice are examples of discrete random variables. The values of a discrete random variable are usually represented by integers or a finite set of numbers.
- **Continuous Random Variables:** A continuous random variable takes on an uncountable set of values within a specific range or interval. It can represent measurements or quantities that can take on any value within a given range. Examples include the height or weight of a person, or the time it takes for an event to occur. The values of a continuous random variable can take on any real number within a defined range.

Let us consider two dices that will be considered to be a win when thrown together, if the sum of the two values of the two dices is found to be 10. The set of possible values a random variable X can have by throwing the two dices are:

$$Y = (2, 3, 4, 5, 6, 7, 8, 9, 10, 11, 12)$$

Thus, a random variable can be defined based on the outcome of a process. The probability of a random variable's value will not be equally the same. For instance, if the sum of the two values of the two dices thrown has to be 2, then there is only one possibility – sum 2{(1, 1)}. However, if the sum of the two values of the two dices thrown has to be 10, then there are three possibilities – sum 10{(4, 6)}, sum 10{(5, 5), and sum 10{(6, 4)}}.

5.1.3 Independence

In probability theory, two or more variables are statistically independent if the occurrence of one variable does not affect the occurrence of the other variable(s) to occur. Two random variables X and Y are said to be independent if either of the following statements are true:

$P(X|Y) = P(X)$, for all values of X and Y

$P(X \cap Y) = P(X)^* P(Y)$, for all values of X and Y

Here, the two conditions are equivalent, and so, if one condition is met, the other condition will also be met. If any one condition is not met, then the variables X and Y are said to be dependent. The first statement discusses the conditional probability $P(X|Y)$ and states that "*the probability of X, given Y, is X.*" The second statement, also sometimes called as the product rule, discusses the probability of intersection of X and Y, and is found to be equal to the product of the probability of X and probability of Y.

5.1.4 Sample Space

In probability theory, the sample space refers to the set of all possible outcomes of a random experiment or event. It is denoted by the symbol Ω (uppercase omega), and is a fundamental concept for understanding and analyzing probabilities. The sample space represents the complete set of all possible outcomes that can occur when conducting an experiment. Each outcome within the sample space is unique and exhaustive, meaning that one and only one of these outcomes will occur. If the outcomes are denoted by $O_1, O_2, O_3, \ldots$, then for a sample space Ω, it can be denoted by:

$$\Omega = \{O_1, O_2, O_3, \ldots\}$$

For example, if a coin is tossed three times in sequence, the number of outcomes in the sample space will be eight (H-H-H, T-H-H, H-T-H, H-H-T, T-H-T, T-T-H, H-T-T, and T-T-T). These eight possible outcomes consisting of the various possibilities of heads and tails are called the sample space. An event E is the subset of a sample space, and the probability of the event E occurring is a number between 0 and 1 (inclusive), i.e., $0 \leq P(E) \leq 1$. Here, $P(\varphi) = 0$, where φ refers to a null event and $P(\Omega) = 1$.

Understanding the sample space is crucial in probability theory as it forms the foundation for further analysis of probabilities, such as defining probability distributions, calculating probabilities of events, and making predictions based on observed outcomes.

5.1.5 Odds and Risks

In probability, odds and risks are two concepts that relate to the likelihood or probability of an event occurring. While they both provide information about the chance of an event happening, they are used in slightly different contexts and have distinct interpretations.

- **Odds**: Odds can be defined as the probability that an event will occur divided by the probability that the event will not occur. Hence, if the probability of an event to occur is X, then the probability of the event not occurring is $1 - X$. In such a case, the odds of an event can be expressed as:

  Odd of event $E = X/(1 - X)$

  For example, if the probability of an event E to occur is 60%, then the value of odds will be:

  Odd of event $E = 0.60/(1 - 0.60) = 1.5$

  The range of odds is between 0 and positive infinity. A probability of 0 indicates that the event is impossible. In such a case, odd of the event is also 0.

- **Risks**: Risks, on the other hand, refer to the potential harm or negative consequences associated with an event. It refers to the probability of occurrence of an event or outcome. The range of risk is a decimal number between 0 and 1. It is interesting to note that odds can be converted to risks, and risks can be converted to odds using the following formulae:

$$\text{Risks} = \frac{\text{Odds}}{1 + \text{Odds}}$$

$$\text{Odds} = \frac{\text{Risks}}{1 - \text{Risks}}$$

While odds focus on the relative likelihood of an event happening compared to not happening, risks focus on the potential negative outcomes or consequences associated with the event. Both odds and risks are important considerations in decision making, risk assessment, and understanding uncertainty. They are commonly used in various fields, including gambling, finance, insurance, and healthcare, to evaluate probabilities and make informed choices based on the potential outcomes and associated risks.

Program 5.1 illustrates a simple Python code to define a sample space, which is a standard 52 deck of cards in this case. User-defined functions are used to calculate the odds and risks based on a given event and the sample space. The odds are calculated as the ratio of favorable outcomes to the total number of outcomes. The risk is calculated as one minus the sum of event probabilities. Finally, the results are printed, which provide insights into the odds and risks associated with drawing a heart or a face card from the deck.

Program 5.1 *Odds and Risks in Probability Estimations*

```
import random

# Sample Space (deck of cards)
suits = ['Hearts', 'Diamonds', 'Clubs', 'Spades']
ranks = ['Ace', '2', '3', '4', '5', '6', '7', '8', '9', '10',
         'Jack', 'Queen', 'King']
deck = [(rank, suit) for suit in suits for rank in ranks]

# Odds Calculation
def calculate_odds(event, sample_space):
    favorable_outcomes = len(event)
    total_outcomes = len(sample_space)
    odds = favorable_outcomes / (total_outcomes - favorable_outcomes)
    return odds

# Risk Calculation
def calculate_risk(event_probabilities):
    risk = 1 - sum(event_probabilities)
    return risk
```

```
# Selecting a random card
random_card = random.choice(deck)
print("Randomly selected card:", random_card)

# Event of drawing a heart
hearts = [card for card in deck if card[1] == 'Hearts']
heart_odds = calculate_odds(hearts, deck)
heart_risk = calculate_risk([1 / len(deck) for _ in range
            (len(hearts))])

# Event of drawing a face card (Jack, Queen, or King)
face_cards = [card for card in deck if card[0] in ['Jack', 'Queen',
            'King']]
face_card_odds = calculate_odds(face_cards, deck)
face_card_risk = calculate_risk([1 / len(deck) for _ in range
        (len(face_cards))])

print("Odds of drawing a heart:", heart_odds)
print("Risk of drawing a heart:", heart_risk)
print("Odds of drawing a face card:", face_card_odds)
print("Risk of drawing a face card:", face_card_risk)
```

The output of Program 5.1 is displayed below. The output of the program will vary, since it involves random card selection. The program randomly selects a card from the deck. In this example, the selected card is the 4 of diamonds. Then, both the odds and risks are calculated for the event of drawing a heart. The output 0.33 indicates that the probability of drawing a heart from the deck is 33%, and the output 0.75 indicates that the risk associated with drawing a heart is 75%.

Also, the odds and risks are calculated for the event of drawing a face card (Jack, Queen, or King). The output 0.3 indicates that the probability of drawing a face card is 0.3. This means that there is approximately 30% chance of selecting a face card from the deck. Lastly, the output 0.769 indicates that the risk associated with drawing a face card is 0.769. This means that there is approximately a 76.9% chance of not selecting a face card from the deck.

```
Randomly selected card: ('4', 'Diamonds')
Odds of drawing a heart: 0.3333333333333333
Risk of drawing a heart: 0.75
Odds of drawing a face card: 0.3
Risk of drawing a face card: 0.7692307692307693
```

The output provides insights into the likelihood (odds) and potential negative outcomes (risk) associated with the events of drawing a heart or a face card from the deck of cards. Knowledge about probability helps us in making decisions on what is likely to occur based on an estimate or on the previous real-time collected data. A data analyst often uses probability distributions of data for various statistical analyses.

5.1.6 Expected Values

In probability theory, the expected value (or expectation) is a measure of the average or long-term value of a random variable. It represents the theoretical average outcome we would expect to observe over repeated trials or a large number of occurrences of an event. The expected value of a discrete random variable X is denoted as $E[X]$ or μ. It is calculated by summing the products of each possible value of X with its corresponding probability.

Mathematically, the expected value is defined as:

$$E[X] = \mu = \sum(x^* P(X))$$

where x represents the values that X can take, and $P(X)$ represents the corresponding probability.

For example, consider rolling a fair six-sided dice. The random variable X represents the outcome of a single roll. The possible values of X are 1, 2, 3, 4, 5, and 6, each with a probability of 1/6. To calculate the expected value of X, we sum the products of each value with its probability:

$$E[X] = (1 * 1/6) + (2 * 1/6) + (3 * 1/6) + (4 * 1/6) + (5 * 1/6) + (6 * 1/6) = 3.5$$

Therefore, the expected value of rolling a fair six-sided dice is 3.5. This means that over a large number of rolls, the average outcome will tend to be very close to 3.5.

The expected value is a fundamental concept in probability theory and has various applications. It provides a way to summarize the central tendency or average behavior of a random variable. It helps in decision making, risk assessment, and estimating long-term outcomes. The expected value also serves as the basis for other statistical measures, such as variance and covariance.

5.2 Four Perspectives on Probability

There are four commonly recognized perspectives on probability, each providing a different interpretation and approach to understanding the concept of probability. These perspectives include the classical approach, the empirical approach, the subjective approach, and the axiomatic approach. Each of these approaches are discussed next:

5.2.1 The Classical Approach

The classical approach to probability, often called a priori approach, is considered to be the simplest and the oldest approach. The assumption made in the classical approach is that the outcomes of a random experiment are equally likely to occur. According to this perspective, the probability of an event is determined by the ratio of favorable outcomes to the total number of equally likely outcomes. The simple formula used in this approach is as shown below:

$$P(E) = \frac{\text{Number of favorable outcomes}}{\text{Number of possible outcomes}}$$

This perspective is commonly applied in situations where all possible outcomes are known and equally likely to occur. The most common example of the classical approach to probability is the toss of a coin, which has only two possible outcomes – head and tail, and each of the outcome has an equal chance to occur. Another example of classical probability is the dice having six values from 1 to 6, and it rolls to display in the upward direction a single value as the outcome when the dice is thrown. Each of the values between 1 and 6 for a rolling dice has an equal chance to occur.

Let us consider a lucky draw contest in which one is asked to pick up one chit out of 10 chits. The 10 chits contain numbers from 1 to 10 each. If the condition of win is by picking up an even-numbered chit, then the probability of win will be $5/10 = 0.5$. This is so as the number of even-numbered chits is 5, and the total number of chits is 10. The classical approach is a very simple method to calculate probability. However, real-life situations may not allow each outcome to have an equal chance to occur. In such a case, the classical approach may fail to work for finding the probability of an outcome.

5.2.2 The Empirical Approach

The empirical approach, also called as the frequentist approach, to probability relies on experiments to find the probability value. For instance, while carrying out an experiment, if a particular process is conducted b number of times, and a particular outcome O1 occurs a number of times, then the frequency ratio is a/b.

Empirical probability relies on the performance of repeated trials of an experiment. As this approach is based on the law of large numbers, more experiments are needed to be conducted to achieve more accuracy in the result. One advantage of empirical probability compared to the classical approach is that the method is relatively free of any assumptions, as the experiments are repeated many a number of times.

The empirical approach to probability is found using the formula as shown below:

$$P(E) = \frac{\text{Number of times event occurs}}{\text{Total number of times experiment performed}}$$

Let us consider that a coin is thrown 50 times, out of which head appears 15 times. So, the total number of times the experiment is conducted is 50, and the total number of times head occurred is 15. The experimental probability of getting the head is then $15/50 = 0.3$.

5.2.3 The Subjective Approach

The subjective approach to probability is based on one's beliefs. It views probability as a subjective assessment based on an individual's knowledge, information, and personal judgment. According to this perspective, probabilities can vary between individuals depending on their subjective assessments and available information. The subjective perspective is often employed in decision theory, Bayesian inference, and personal probability assessments.

In this approach, no extra experiment is conducted, and it is strictly based on one's personal opinion and experience. However, as only an individual's personal beliefs or experiences are involved, there is a high chance of biasness. For example, one may be of the opinion that there are 70% chances that the person will win the match of chess, considering the past experiences played with the same opponent.

5.2.4 The Axiomatic Approach

The axiomatic approach to probability contains a set of predefined axioms (or rules) to be followed. This approach to probability was first established by the Russian mathematician Andrey Nikolaevich Kolmogorov. His approach is based on three well-defined axioms that are often applied to decide the probability of any event. These three sets of axioms are stated below:

Axiom 1: The first axiom states that the probability of an event is a nonnegative real number. This can be expressed as $P(E) \geq 0$, where $P(E)$ refers to the probability of an event E. Here, 0 represents an event that will never happen.

Axiom 2: The second axiom states that the probability of sample space is 1. This can be expressed as the set of all possible outcomes denoted by $P(S) = 1$.

Axiom 3: If X and Y are mutually exclusive outcomes, then $P(X \cup Y) = P(X) + P(Y)$. This indicates that if X and Y are mutually exclusive outcomes, then the probability of either X or Y happening is the sum of the probabilities of X happening and Y happening.

The axiomatic approach to probability has provided a logically seamless structure of the modern theory of probability and has facilitated the enhanced probability requirements of modern natural science.

5.3   The Principles of Bayesian Inference

Bayesian inference is a framework for reasoning and making decisions under uncertainty, based on Bayes' theorem. It combines prior knowledge or beliefs with observed data to update and revise our understanding of the probability of different events or hypotheses. It is widely used in various fields, including statistics, machine learning, decision analysis, and artificial intelligence, for modeling uncertainty, parameter estimation, hypothesis testing, and decision making under uncertainty. It utilizes Bayes' theorem as a foundational tool. To gain a deep understanding of Bayesian inference principles, let's now thoroughly explore Bayes' theorem.

Bayes' Theorem – Bayes' theorem is the core principle of Bayesian inference. It mathematically expresses the relationship between the prior probability, the likelihood, and the posterior probability. It states that the posterior probability of a hypothesis or parameter value, given the observed data, is proportional to the product of the prior probability and the likelihood.

$$P(H|D) = \frac{P(D|H) * P(H)}{P(D)}$$

where:

- $P(H|D)$ is the posterior probability of hypothesis H, given data D.
- $P(D|H)$ is the likelihood of observing data D, given hypothesis H.
- $P(H)$ is the prior probability of hypothesis H.
- $P(D)$ is the probability of observing data D (the normalizing constant).

The Bayes' rule of probability is pictorially depicted in Figure 5.1. In the equation of Bayes' theorem, the probability $P(D|H)$ is called the *likelihood function*, which assesses the probability of the observed data that arises from hypothesis H. The likelihood function is a known value, as it states one's knowledge of how one expects the data to look, considering the hypothesis H to be true. The probability $P(H)$ is called the *prior*, which analyses one's prior knowledge before the data are considered. It is basically the strength of one's belief in the fairness of the outcome.

The probability $P(D)$ is called the *evidence*, which is determined by summing all possible values of H and weighted by how strongly one believes in each value of H. The probability $P(H|D)$ is called the *posterior*, which reflects the probability of the hypothesis after consideration of the data.

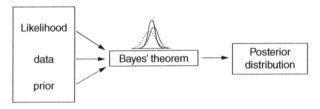

Figure 5.1   Schematic representation of Bayes' theorem.

Bayesian inference is an iterative process. After obtaining the posterior probability from one round of analysis, it can serve as the prior probability for the next round, incorporating new data and refining our understanding further. This iterative updating allows for continual learning and revision of beliefs, as more evidence becomes available.

Now, let us consider a simple example of *P*(dengue), which means how often dengue in patients occur, and *P*(headache) means how often headache occurs in patients. In such a case:

- *P*(dengue|headache) means how often dengue is found in patients when we can find that patients are suffering from headache.
- *P*(headache|dengue) means how often we can find patients suffer from headache when the patient is suffering from dengue.

This indicates that the Bayesian formula helps in predicting "*forward*" when the details are known about "*backward.*"

Now, if occurrence of dengue in patients is rare (5%), but headache is fairly common (12%) in several patients, and 70% of patients suffer from headache when the patient is suffering from dengue, then:

$$P(\text{dengue}|\text{headache}) = \frac{P(\text{headache}|\text{dengue}) * P(\text{dengue})}{P(\text{headache})}$$

$$= (70^* 5)/12 = 29.167$$

Thus, the results indicate that the probability of dengue to be found in patients when the latter is suffering from headache is 29.17%.

Program 4.12 illustrates the Python code to describe a coin flipping scenario where to estimate the posterior probabilities of the coin landing heads after observing a series of coin flips. We assume a prior belief of a fair coin (50% probability of heads) and a likelihood of observing heads given a fair coin (60% probability). The code simulates a series of coin flips using *np.random.choice()* and stores the results in the *observed_data* array.

Initially, the prior probabilities and the likelihoods are defined. As a fair coin is assumed, so the prior probability of the coin landing heads is set to 0.5, and the prior probability of tails is calculated as 1 minus the probability of heads. The likelihood of observing heads given a fair coin is set to 0.6, and the likelihood of tails is calculated as 1 minus the likelihood of heads. Next, the coin flip is simulated using *np.random.choice()*. The code generates 10 number of coin flips and stores the results in the *observed_data* array. In this example, as it is a fair coin, it is assumed to generate output with equal probabilities of heads (*"H"*) and tails (*"T"*).

The Bayesian inference is then performed using a loop that iterates through each observed coin flip. In the Bayesian inference section, an array *posterior_heads* is initialized to store the posterior probabilities of the coin landing heads. The length of the array is set to *num_flips+1* to account for the prior probability as the first element. The posterior probabilities of the coin landing heads are updated based on Bayes' theorem, taking into account the prior probability and the observed data. Finally, the code displays the observed data and the posterior probabilities of the coin landing heads at each step of the Bayesian inference process.

Program 5.2 *Applying Bayesian Inference for Coin Flipping*

```
import numpy as np

# Define prior probabilities
prior_heads = 0.5  # Prior belief of the coin landing heads
    (fair coin)
prior_tails = 1 - prior_heads  # Prior belief of the coin
    landing tails

# Define likelihoods
likelihood_heads = 0.6  # Likelihood of observing heads (given a
    fair coin)
likelihood_tails = 1 - likelihood_heads  # Likelihood of
    observing tails (given a fair coin)

# Simulate data (coin flips)
num_flips = 10
# Assuming a fair coin
observed_data = np.random.choice(["H", "T"], size=num_flips,
            p=[0.5, 0.5])

# Bayesian Inference
posterior_heads = np.zeros(num_flips+1)  # Posterior
    probabilities of the coin landing heads
posterior_heads[0] = prior_heads  # Assign prior probability as the
    first element

for i in range(num_flips):
    if observed_data[i] == "H":
        # Update posterior probability based on Bayes' theorem
        posterior_heads[i+1] = (likelihood_heads *
```

```
posterior_heads[i]) / \
            ((likelihood_heads * posterior_heads[i]) +
(likelihood_tails * (1 - posterior_heads[i])))
    else:
        posterior_heads[i+1] = (likelihood_tails *
posterior_heads[i]) / \
            ((likelihood_heads * (1 - posterior_heads[i])) +
(likelihood_tails * posterior_heads[i]))

# Display the results
print("Observed data:", observed_data)
print("Posterior probabilities of the coin landing heads:")
print(posterior_heads)
```

The output of Program 5.2 is displayed below. When the code is run, the output will vary each time due to the random nature of the coin flips. It will display the observed data and the calculated posterior probabilities of the coin landing heads at each step of the Bayesian inference process. This code showcases the principles of Bayesian inference by updating prior probabilities based on observed data, allowing us to make probabilistic estimations and revise our beliefs over time.

```
Observed data:['H' 'T' 'H' 'H' 'T' 'H' 'H' 'H' 'H' 'T']
Posterior probabilities of the coin landing heads:
[0.5          0.6          0.5          0.6          0.69230769 0.6
 0.69230769   0.77142857   0.83505155   0.88363636 0.83505155]
```

5.4   Belief Network and Markovian Network

Belief network and Markovian network are both graphical models used in probabilistic modeling and reasoning. While they share some similarities, they have distinct characteristics and are applied in different contexts. Belief networks utilize directed acyclic graphs (DAGs) to capture causal dependencies, while Markovian network use undirected graphs to represent conditional independence. Belief network excel in tasks involving Bayesian inference and decision making, while Markovian network are well-suited for modeling spatial or temporal dependencies in tasks, such as image analysis and pattern recognition. The two network models are discussed next:

- **Belief Network:** Belief networks, also known as Bayesian networks, are graphical models that represent probabilistic relationships among a set of variables. They are based on the principles of Bayesian inference and utilize DAGs to depict the dependencies between variables.

- **Markovian Network (Markov Random Field):** Markovian networks, also known as Markov random fields or undirected graphical models, are graphical models that represent the dependencies between variables in a probabilistic system. Unlike belief networks, they utilize undirected graphs to capture the relationships between variables.

5.4.1 Syntax and Semantics

5.4.1.1 Belief Network

In a Belief network, nodes represent random variables or events, and directed edges indicate the probabilistic dependencies between variables. Each node represents a variable, and the edges indicate the direct influence or causal relationships between them. The edges in the graph are typically annotated with conditional probability distributions (CPDs) that capture the likelihood of a variable given its parent variables.

Each node in a Belief network is associated with a CPD, which describes the probability of the node, given its parent nodes. The CPDs quantify the probabilistic relationships between variables. The semantics of a Belief network involve computing marginal probabilities (probabilities of individual variables) and conditional probabilities (probabilities of variables, given other variables) based on the network structure and the associated CPDs.

5.4.1.2 Markovian Network

In a Markovian network, nodes represent variables, and the absence of directed edges signifies that the variables are conditionally independent, given their neighbors. The connections between nodes indicate the dependencies between variables. Markovian networks are often used to model spatial or temporal dependencies, where variables interact with their neighboring variables. A clique in a Markovian network refers to a fully connected subgraph, where every node in the subgraph is connected to every other node. Cliques help capture the conditional dependencies between variables.

The semantics of a Markovian network lie in the representation of the joint probability distribution of the variables. The potential functions associated with each clique capture the probabilistic relationships between variables and determine the overall probability distribution. The absence of a direct edge between two variables in the graph indicates their conditional independence, given the remaining variables in the network.

5.4.2 Conditional Independence

Conditional independence plays a crucial role in both Belief networks and Markovian networks. It refers to the concept that the probability distribution of a set of

Figure 5.2 (a) Belief network where A and C are conditionally independent, given B and D, but not vice versa (b) Markovian network where A and C are conditionally independent, given B and D, and vice versa.

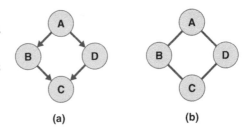

(a)　　　　　　(b)

variables can be factorized based on the conditional independence relationships between them. Figure 5.2 cites an example of both Belief networks and Markovian networks. The figure demonstrates the conditional independence with the help of an example of a graph.

In Belief networks, conditional independence is represented by the absence of direct edges between certain nodes in the graph. If two variables A and C are conditionally independent, given variables B and D (Figure 5.2(a)), it means that knowing the values of B and D provides enough information to explain the relationship between A and C, and the direct connection between A and C is unnecessary.

In Markovian networks, conditional independence is represented by the notion of separation between sets of variables. If two sets of variables A and C are separated by a third set of variables B and D in the network graph (Figure 5.2(b)), it implies that A and C are conditionally independent, given B and D, and also vice versa.

The Markov property states that each variable in the Markovian network is conditionally independent of all other variables, given its neighbors in the graph. The concept of conditional independence in Markovian networks allows for efficient computation and modeling of complex systems by exploiting the local dependencies between variables. It helps factorize the joint probability distribution into manageable components.

Program 5.3 illustrates the creation of a simple Belief Network and a Markovian network. In the code, two classes are defined: `BeliefNetwork` and `MarkovianNetwork`. The `BeliefNetwork` class represents a simple belief network with two nodes: A and B. The `add_node` method is used to add nodes to the network, along with their parents and conditional probability tables. The `compute_probability` method calculates the probability of a given node based on the evidence provided.

The `MarkovianNetwork` class represents a simple Markovian network with two states: A and B. The `add_transition` method is used to add transitions between states, along with their next states and transition probabilities. The `compute_probability` method calculates the probability of transitioning from a given state to a next state. In the code, instances of both networks are created and tested by calculating probabilities based on evidence and transitions.

Program 5.3 *Creating Belief Network and Markovian Network*

```python
# Import required libraries
import numpy as np
import networkx as nx
import matplotlib.pyplot as plt

# Define a simple belief network
class BeliefNetwork:
    def __init__(self):
        self.nodes = {}

    def add_node(self, node_name, parents, probabilities):
        self.nodes[node_name] = {"parents": parents,
    "probabilities": probabilities}

    def compute_probability(self, node_name, evidence):
        node = self.nodes[node_name]
        parents = node["parents"]
        probabilities = node["probabilities"]

        parent_values = tuple([evidence[parent] for parent in
        parents])
        prob_index = np.where(np.all(probabilities[..., :-1] ==
        parent_values, axis=-1))
        probability = probabilities[prob_index][0, -1]
        return probability

    def visualize_network(self):
        G = nx.DiGraph()
        for node_name, node in self.nodes.items():
            G.add_node(node_name)
            for parent in node["parents"]:
                G.add_edge(parent, node_name)

    pos = nx.spring_layout(G, seed=42)
    nx.draw(G, pos, with_labels=True, node_color='skyblue',
    node_size=1000, font_size=12, edge_color='gray', arrows=True)
    plt.title('Belief Network')
    plt.show()

# Define a simple Markovian network
class MarkovianNetwork:
    def __init__(self):
        self.transitions = {}

    def add_transition(self, state, next_states, probabilities):
        self.transitions[state] = {"next_states": next_states,
        "probabilities": probabilities}

    def compute_probability(self, state, next_state):
        transition = self.transitions[state]
```

```python
        next_states = transition["next_states"]
        probabilities = transition["probabilities"]

        index = next_states.index(next_state)
        return probabilities[index]

    def visualize_network(self):
        G = nx.DiGraph()
        for state, transition in self.transitions.items():
            G.add_node(state)
            for next_state in transition["next_states"]:
                G.add_edge(state, next_state)

        pos = nx.spring_layout(G, seed=42)
    nx.draw(G, pos, with_labels=True, node_color='skyblue',
    node_size=1000, font_size=12, edge_color='gray', arrows=True)
        plt.title('Markovian Network')
        plt.show()

# Create an instance of the belief network
belief_net = BeliefNetwork()
belief_net.add_node("A", [], np.array([[0, 0.5], [1, 0.5]]))
belief_net.add_node("B", ["A"], np.array([[0, 0.7], [1, 0.3]]))

# Create an instance of the Markovian network
markov_net = MarkovianNetwork()
markov_net.add_transition("A", ["A", "B"], np.array([0.7, 0.3]))
markov_net.add_transition("B", ["A", "B"], np.array([0.2, 0.8]))

# Test the belief network
evidence = {}
evidence["A"] = 0  # Node A is false
prob_A = belief_net.compute_probability("A", evidence)
print("Probability of A:", prob_A)

evidence["B"] = 0  # Node B is false
prob_B_given_A = belief_net.compute_probability("B", evidence)
print("Probability of B given A:", prob_B_given_A)

# Visualize the belief network
belief_net.visualize_network()

# Test the Markovian network
state = "A"
next_state = "B"
prob_transition = markov_net.compute_probability(state, next_state)
print("Transition probability from", state, "to", next_state, ":",
prob_transition)

# Visualize the Markovian network
markov_net.visualize_network()
```

The output of Program 5.3 is given next. In this code, the probability of node "A" is computed based on the evidence given as **evidence["A"]** = 0 (Node A is false.) by calling the *compute_probability* method of the *belief_net* object. The result is stored in the *prob_A* variable, and it is displayed as output. Similarly, the probability of node "B" is computed based on the evidence given as **evidence["B"]** = 0 (Node B is false). The result is stored in the *prob_B_given_A* variable, and it is displayed as output. By executing this code, you should see the probabilities of nodes "A" and "B" printed based on the given evidence in the belief network.

```
Probability of A: 0.5
Probability of B given A: 0.7
```

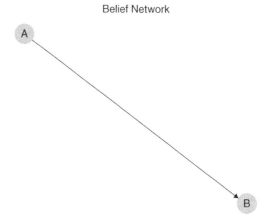

Belief Network

```
Transition probability from A to B : 0.3
```

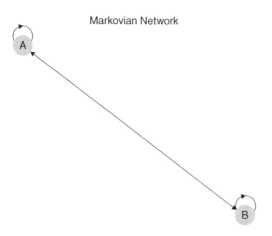

Markovian Network

The above output also displays the graphical representation of the belief network and Markovian network using network graphs. For this, a new method `visualize_network` is added to both the `BeliefNetwork` and `MarkovianNetwork` classes. These methods use the `networkx` library to create a directed graph of the network and the matplotlib library to visualize the graph.

5.4.3 Learning Methods of the Networks

Learning methods for Markovian networks and Belief networks differ due to the distinct characteristics and underlying assumptions of these graphical models. It is important to explore the learning methods for each network type:

(i) **Learning Methods for Markovian Networks:** The following are some standard learning methods for Markovian Networks:

   (a) **Maximum Likelihood Estimation (MLE):** MLE is a commonly used method for learning Markovian networks. It involves estimating the parameters (potential functions) of the model that maximize the likelihood of the observed data. MLE aims to find the parameter values that make the observed data most probable under the Markovian network.

   (b) **Conditional Random Field (CRF) Learning:** Conditional random fields are a specific type of Markovian network used for structured prediction tasks. Learning CRFs involves optimizing the model parameters to maximize the conditional likelihood of the observed outputs, given the inputs. Various optimization algorithms, such as gradient descent or convex optimization, can be used for CRF learning.

   (c) **Expectation–Maximization (EM) Algorithm:** The EM algorithm is an iterative optimization method used for learning Markovian networks. It involves alternating between an expectation step (E-step) and a maximization step (M-step). The E-step computes the expected values of the latent variables, while the M-step updates the model parameters based on these expectations.

   (d) **Contrastive Divergence:** Contrastive divergence is a learning algorithm used specifically for training restricted Boltzmann machines (RBMs), which are a type of Markovian network. It involves approximating the gradient of the log-likelihood function using Gibbs sampling and stochastic approximation techniques.

(ii) **Learning Methods for Belief Networks:** The following are some standard learning methods for Belief Networks:

   (a) **Parameter Learning:** Parameter learning in Belief networks aims to estimate the CPDs associated with each node. This involves using observed data to infer the parameters of the CPDs. Various methods can be employed, including maximum likelihood estimation (MLE), Bayesian estimation, and Bayesian structure learning.

(b) **Bayesian Structure Learning:** Bayesian structure learning involves inferring the structure of the Belief network, including the directed edges between nodes. This learning method integrates prior knowledge, such as expert opinions or domain-specific constraints, with observed data to estimate the most likely network structure. Techniques such as score-based methods (e.g., Bayesian scoring) and search-and-score algorithms (e.g., Markov Chain Monte Carlo) can be employed for Bayesian structure learning.

(c) **Constraint-Based Methods:** Constraint-based methods learn the network structure by applying statistical independence tests to identify conditional independence relationships between variables. These methods use independence-based criteria, such as the PC algorithm or the Grow–Shrink algorithm, to construct a network structure that is consistent with the observed data.

(d) **Hybrid Methods:** Hybrid learning methods combine different approaches, such as parameter learning and structure learning, to simultaneously estimate the parameters and infer the structure of Belief networks. These methods leverage both data-driven approaches and domain knowledge to learn accurate and interpretable network models.

Overall, learning methods for Markovian networks focus on estimating the parameters or potential functions, while learning methods for Belief networks involve parameter learning and structure learning to determine the CPDs and network structure. The choice of learning method depends on the specific characteristics of the network, the available data, and the learning objectives.

5.5 Hidden Markov Model

The hidden Markov model (HMM) is a probabilistic model that captures temporal dependencies in sequential data, where the underlying states or processes are not directly observable. HMMs are widely used in various fields, including speech recognition, natural language processing, bioinformatics, and more. In an HMM, the system is modeled as a Markov process with hidden states that generate observed outputs. The model assumes that the observed outputs are influenced by the underlying hidden states, but the hidden states themselves are not directly observed. Instead, we observe a sequence of outputs that provide partial information about the hidden states.

The key components of a HMM include the following:

(a) **Hidden States:** The hidden states represent the unobservable, underlying processes or states of the system. Each hidden state corresponds to a specific condition or behavior.

(b) **Observations:** The observations represent the data that we have access to. Each observation is generated by the hidden state at a particular time step.

(c) **State Transition Probabilities:** These probabilities define the likelihood of transitioning from one hidden state to another at each time step. The state transition probabilities are typically represented by a transition matrix, where each entry indicates the probability of transitioning from one state to another.

(d) **Emission Probabilities:** These probabilities define the likelihood of observing a particular output, given the current hidden state. The emission probabilities are usually represented by an emission matrix or probability distribution, where each entry represents the probability of generating a specific output, given a hidden state.

(e) **Initial State Distribution:** This distribution represents the probabilities of starting the sequence in each possible hidden state. It defines the initial probabilities of the hidden states.

To understand the components of the Hidden Markov Model, let us consider a simple example. If a weather model with two states: `"Sunny"` and `"Rainy"` is considered, the weather conditions can be modeled based on the observations of people's activities. The possible observations are `"Happy"` and `"Sad"`. Here, the two states in the example are:

- "Sunny": Represents a sunny weather condition
- "Rainy": Represents a rainy weather condition

The initial probabilities represent the probability of starting in each state. For example, $P(\text{"Sunny"}) = 0.6$, $P(\text{"Rainy"}) = 0.4$. This means that the weather is initially sunny with a probability of 0.6 and rainy with a probability of 0.4.

The transition probabilities represent the probability of transitioning between states. For example: $P(\text{"Sunny"} \rightarrow \text{"Sunny"}) = 0.7$, $P(\text{"Sunny"} \rightarrow \text{"Rainy"}) = 0.3$, $P(\text{"Rainy"} \rightarrow \text{"Sunny"}) = 0.4$, $P(\text{"Rainy"} \rightarrow \text{"Rainy"}) = 0.6$. This means that there is a 0.7 probability of staying in the sunny state, a 0.3 probability of transitioning from sunny to rainy, a 0.4 probability of transitioning from rainy to sunny, and a 0.6 probability of staying in the rainy state.

The emission probabilities represent the probability of observing a particular output (observation), given the current state. For example: $P(\text{"Happy"} \mid \text{"Sunny"}) = 0.8$, $P(\text{"Sad"} \mid \text{"Sunny"}) = 0.2$, $P(\text{"Happy"} \mid$

"Rainy") = 0.4, *P*("Sad" | "Rainy") = 0.6. This means that if the weather is sunny, there is a 0.8 probability of observing "Happy" and a 0.2 probability of observing "Sad". If the weather is rainy, there is a 0.4 probability of observing "Happy" and a 0.6 probability of observing "Sad".

All these components collectively define the Hidden Markov Model. The initial probabilities determine the starting state, the transition probabilities govern state transitions over time, and the emission probabilities link the hidden states to observable outputs. Using this model, sequences of observations can be generated based on the state transitions and emission probabilities.

HMMs are associated with three fundamental problems that are often encountered when working with these models:

(a) **Evaluation Problem:** Given a sequence of observations, the evaluation problem involves calculating the probability of the observed sequence, given the model. This is often solved using the forward–backward algorithm or the Viterbi algorithm.

(b) **Decoding Problem:** The decoding problem aims to find the most likely sequence of hidden states that generated the observed sequence of outputs. The Viterbi algorithm is commonly used to solve this problem.

(c) **Learning Problem:** The learning problem involves estimating the parameters of the HMM, namely the state transition probabilities, emission probabilities, and initial state distribution, from the observed data. This can be solved using methods like the Baum–Welch algorithm, which employs the expectation–maximization (EM) algorithm.

In Program 5.3, the Python code defines the *HiddenMarkovModel* class that represents a simple Hidden Markov Model. It has methods to add states, generate a sequence of observations, compute forward probabilities, compute backward probabilities, and compute state probabilities. Next, an instance of the *HiddenMarkovModel* class is created by the name *hmm*. States are added to the HMM using the *add_state* method. Each state is specified with its name, initial probability, transition probabilities, and emission probabilities.

In this example, there are two states, "Sunny" and "Rainy", with corresponding probabilities and emission probabilities. A sequence of observations is generated from the HMM using the *generate_sequence* method. The length of the sequence is specified as an argument. This sequence represents the observed data that we will use for further calculations. The observed sequence generated by the HMM is displayed as output.

Next, the forward probabilities are computed for the observed sequence using the *compute_forward_probabilities* method. The forward probabilities represent the probability of being in a particular state at each time step, given the observed sequence. The forward probabilities are also displayed as output.

Also, the backward probabilities are computed for the observed sequence using the *compute_backward_probabilities* method. The backward probabilities represent the probability of observing the remaining part of the sequence given being in a particular state at each time step. The backward probabilities are also displayed as output.

Finally, the state probabilities are computed for the observed sequence using the *compute_state_probabilities* method. The state probabilities represent the probability of being in each state at each time step, given the observed sequence. The state probabilities are also displayed as output.

Program 5.4 *Creating a Simple Hidden Markov Model*

```
# Import required libraries
import numpy as np
import networkx as nx
import matplotlib.pyplot as plt

# Define a simple Hidden Markov Model
class HiddenMarkovModel:
    def __init__(self):
        self.states = []
        self.initial_probabilities = {}
        self.transition_probabilities = {}
        self.emission_probabilities = {}

    def add_state(self, state_name, initial_prob, transition_probs,
    emission_probs):
        self.states.append(state_name)
        self.initial_probabilities[state_name] = initial_prob
        self.transition_probabilities[state_name] = transition_probs
        self.emission_probabilities[state_name] = emission_probs

    def generate_sequence(self, length):
        sequence = []
        state = np.random.choice(self.states, p=list
        (self.initial_probabilities.values()))
        sequence.append(state)

        for _ in range(length - 1):
            state=np.random.choice(self.states, p=list
            (self.transition_probabilities[state].values()))
        observation = np.random.choice(list(self.emission_
    probabilities[state].keys()), p = list(self.emission_
    probabilities[state].values()))
            sequence.append(observation)

        return sequence

    def compute_forward_probabilities(self, observations):
```

```python
        T = len(observations)
        alpha = np.zeros((T, len(self.states)))

        # Initialize the forward probabilities for the first
          observation
        for i, state in enumerate(self.states):
    alpha[0][i]=self.initial_probabilities[state] *
self.emission_probabilities[state].get(observations[0], 0)

        # Recursively compute forward probabilities for the
          remaining observations
        for t in range(1, T):
            for i, state in enumerate(self.states):
    alpha[t][i] = sum(alpha[t-1][j] * self.transition_
    probabilities[prev_state][state] * self.emission_
    probabilities [state].get(observations[t], 0)
     for j, prev_state in enumerate(self.states))

                # Handle division by zero
                if alpha[t][i] == 0:
                    alpha[t][i] = np.finfo(float).eps

        return alpha

    def compute_backward_probabilities(self, observations):
        T = len(observations)
        beta = np.zeros((T, len(self.states)))

        # Initialize the backward probabilities for the last
          observation
        for i, state in enumerate(self.states):
            beta[T-1][i] = 1

        # Recursively compute backward probabilities for the
          previous observations
        for t in range(T-2, -1, -1):
            for i, state in enumerate(self.states):
    beta[t][i] = sum(beta[t+1][j] * self.transition_
    probabilities[state][next_state] * self.emission_
    probabilities[next_state].get(observations[t+1], 0)
     for j, next_state in enumerate(self.states))

                # Handle division by zero
                if beta[t][i] == 0:
                    beta[t][i] = np.finfo(float).eps

        return beta

    def compute_state_probabilities(self, alpha, beta):
        T = len(alpha)
        state_probs = np.zeros((T, len(self.states)))
```

```
    # Compute the state probabilities for each observation
    for t in range(T):
        denominator = sum(alpha[t] * beta[t])

        # Handle division by zero
        if denominator == 0:
            state_probs[t] = np.zeros(len(self.states))
        else:
            state_probs[t] = alpha[t] * beta[t] / denominator

    return state_probs

#Generating HMM Graph
def visualize_hmm(self):
    G = nx.DiGraph()
    G.add_nodes_from(self.states)

    for state in self.states:
        for next_state, transition_prob in self.transition_
        probabilities[state].items():
            G.add_edge(state, next_state, weight=transition_
            prob)

    pos = nx.spring_layout(G)
    labels = {state: state for state in self.states}
    edge_labels = {(u, v): f"{prob:.2f}" for (u, v, prob) in
                   G.edges(data="weight")}
nx.draw_networkx(G, pos, with_labels=True, labels=labels,
node_color="skyblue", node_size=1000, font_size=12,
edge_color="gray", arrows=True)
    nx.draw_networkx_edge_labels(G, pos, edge_labels=edge_labels,
    font_size=10)

    plt.title("Hidden Markov Model")
    plt.show()

# Create an instance of the Hidden Markov Model
hmm = HiddenMarkovModel()

# Add states to the HMM
hmm.add_state("Sunny", 0.6, {"Sunny": 0.7, "Rainy": 0.3},
{"Happy": 0.8, "Sad": 0.2})
hmm.add_state("Rainy", 0.4, {"Sunny": 0.4, "Rainy": 0.6},
{"Happy": 0.4, "Sad": 0.6})

# Generate a sequence of observations from the HMM
observed_sequence = hmm.generate_sequence(10)
print("Observed sequence:", observed_sequence)

# Compute the forward probabilities for the observed sequence
```

```
forward_probabilities = hmm.compute_forward_probabilities
(observed_sequence)
print("Forward probabilities:\n", forward_probabilities)

# Compute the backward probabilities for the observed sequence
backward_probabilities = hmm.compute_backward_probabilities
(observed_sequence)
print("Backward probabilities:\n", backward_probabilities)

# Compute the state probabilities for the observed sequence
state_probabilities = hmm.compute_state_probabilities
(forward_probabilities, backward_probabilities)
print("State probabilities:\n", state_probabilities)

# Visualize the Hidden Markov Model as a graph
hmm.visualize_hmm()
```

The output of Program 5.3 is given below. In the output, the observed sequence is a list of length 10, generated randomly by the HMM. The forward probabilities represent the probability of being in each state at each time step, given the observed sequence. In this example, we have a 10×2 matrix, where each row represents the forward probabilities for each time step.

The output also prints the backward probabilities, which represent the probability of observing the remaining part of the sequence given, being in a particular state at each time step. It is also a 10×2 matrix, where each row represents the backward probabilities for each time step.

The state probabilities that are displayed at the end of the output represent the probability of being in each state at each time step, given the observed sequence. It is computed using the forward and backward probabilities. The result is a 10×2 matrix, where each row represents the state probabilities for each time step. By analyzing the state probabilities, one can observe how the HMM assigns probabilities to each state at each time step, based on the observed sequence.

The Python code uses the *visualize_hmm* method to the *HiddenMarkovModel* class that uses the *networkx* and *matplotlib* libraries to visualize the HMM as a graph. After computing the state probabilities, the *visualize_hmm* method is called to generate the graph representation of the HMM. The graph shows the states as nodes and the transition probabilities as weighted edges. The arrows indicate the direction of transitions.

```
Observed sequence: ['Rainy', 'Sad', 'Happy', 'Sad',
  'Sad', 'Happy', 'Happy', 'Happy', 'Happy', 'Sad']
Forward probabilities:
 [[0.00000000e+00  0.00000000e+00]
  [2.22044605e-16  2.22044605e-16]
  [1.95399252e-16  7.99360578e-17]
  [3.37507799e-17  6.39488462e-17]
```

```
[9.84101689e-18   2.90967250e-17]
[1.48219215e-17   8.16413603e-18]
[1.09127996e-17   3.73802322e-18]
[7.30733518e-18   2.20666152e-18]
[4.79823939e-18   1.40647899e-18]
[7.84271833e-19   1.37001553e-18]]
Backward probabilities:
[[0.00154341 0.00207201]
 [0.00507403  0.00462802]
 [0.00690004  0.01008337]
 [0.01858355  0.02387968]
 [0.06643712  0.05156864]
 [0.101632    0.07936   ]
 [0.15488     0.12416   ]
 [0.232       0.208     ]
 [0.32        0.44      ]
 [1.          1.        ]]
State probabilities:
[[0.          0.         ]
 [0.52298511 0.47701489]
 [0.62585086 0.37414914]
 [0.29114471 0.70885529]
 [0.30349193 0.69650807]
 [0.69924818 0.30075182]
 [0.78456311 0.21543689]
 [0.78694319 0.21305681]
 [0.71273528 0.28726472]
 [0.36405163 0.63594837]]
```

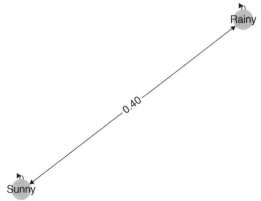

Hidden Markov Model

It is to be noted that the observed sequence generated by the HMM in the program will be different for each run of the code. The observed sequence is generated randomly based on the probabilities defined in the HMM. Hence, the program will display different output values at each run of the code.

HMMs find applications in various domains, such as speech recognition to model phonemes or words, natural language processing, bioinformatics for gene finding, protein structure prediction, and sequence alignment, finance for modeling stock prices, market trends, and trading strategies, and robotics. In summary, Hidden Markov Models are probabilistic models that capture temporal dependencies in sequential data with hidden states. They provide a powerful framework for modeling and analyzing sequential data, allowing for inference, decoding, and learning tasks.

5.6   Markov Decision Processes

Markov decision processes (MDPs) are mathematical models used to formalize sequential decision making problems in the field of artificial intelligence, reinforcement learning, and operations research. MDPs provide a framework for modeling situations where an agent interacts with an environment over a series of discrete time steps.

To solve an MDP, various algorithms and techniques can be employed, such as dynamic programming, Monte Carlo methods, and temporal difference learning. These methods aim to compute or approximate the optimal policy that maximizes the expected cumulative rewards. Value iteration and policy iteration are popular algorithms used for solving MDPs.

Figure 5.3 illustrates the role of agent that interacts with its environment by performing actions sequentially at each discrete time steps. As the agent interacts with the environment, the state of the environment gets changed, due to which the agent receives an award from the environment. By choosing the right action for each state, the MDP achieves its primary goal of agents maximizing the total long-term reward over time from its environment. The key components of an MDP are as follows:

(a) **State Space**: A finite set of states that the system can be in at any given time. States represent the complete description of the system at a particular time step.

(b) **Action Space**: A finite set of actions that the agent can take in each state. Actions represent the decisions or choices available to the agent.

(c) **Transition Probabilities**: For each state–action pair, the MDP defines the probabilities of transitioning to different states based on the action taken. These probabilities capture the dynamics of the environment.

Figure 5.3 Markov decision process.

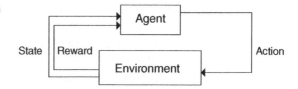

(d) **Reward Function:** A function that assigns a real value, known as a reward, to each state–action pair or state transition. The reward represents the immediate desirability or utility of being in a particular state or taking a specific action.

(e) **Discount Factor:** A value between 0 and 1 that determines the importance of future rewards relative to immediate rewards. It helps in balancing immediate rewards against long-term rewards, and influences the agent's preference for immediate gains or long-term planning.

If we consider a 3 × 3 grid navigation problem as a Markov Decision Process (MDP), then an agent can move in four directions: up, down, left, and right. The agent's goal is to reach a specific terminal state while maximizing its cumulative rewards. The MDP components are as follows:

- **State Space:** The agent can be in any of the nine grid cells, represented as S1, S2, ..., S9.
- **Action Space:** The agent can take four actions: up (U), down (D), left (L), and right (R).
- **Transition Probabilities:** When the agent takes an action, there is a 0.8 probability that it will move in the desired direction and a 0.1 probability of moving in each of the perpendicular directions. For example, if the agent chooses to move up from state S2, there is a 0.8 chance that it will end up in S1, 0.1 chance in S2 (staying in the same state), and 0.1 chance in S5 (moving left).
- **Reward Function:** The agent receives a reward of −1 for each step taken until it reaches the terminal state, which is the goal. The terminal state has a reward of +10.

Using a suitable algorithm, such as value iteration or policy iteration, we can find an optimal policy that maximizes the agent's expected cumulative rewards. The policy will provide the recommended action to take in each state to reach the terminal state while accumulating the most reward possible.

Program 5.4 illustrates the Python code to create a MDP. The code defines the grid world environment using a 2D NumPy array called grid. Each element in the array represents a cell in the grid, with the following meanings – *0: Empty cell*, *1: Goal state*, and *-1: Obstacle*. The MDP parameters are defined, including the number of states (*num_states*), number of actions (*num_actions*), and the discount factor (*gamma*). The transition probabilities are defined using a 3D NumPy array called `transition_probs`. The array's dimensions represent the current state, action, and next state, respectively. The transition probabilities are set based on the grid world environment.

The rewards are defined using a 2D NumPy array called `rewards`. The array's dimensions represent the current state and action, respectively. The rewards are set based on the grid world environment. Value iteration is performed to find the optimal value function. The code iteratively updates the values of each state by considering the maximum *Q*-value, which is the expected cumulative reward for each action. The process continues until the values converge within a certain threshold (`epsilon`).

The optimal policy is determined based on the calculated values. The code iterates over each state, calculates the *Q*-values for all actions, and selects the action with the highest *Q*-value as the optimal action for that state. The grid world, along with states and actions, is printed as output. The code creates two grids: `grid_with_states` and `grid_with_actions`. It maps the states to "S" followed by the state number and maps the actions based on the optimal policy. Obstacles are labeled as "X", and the goal state remains as "G". Finally, the grids are printed to display the states and corresponding actions in the grid world.

Program 5.5 *Creating a Simple Markov Decision Process*

```
import numpy as np

# Define the grid world environment
grid = np.array([
    [0, 0, 0, 1],
    [0, -1, 0, -1],
    [0, 0, 0, 0]
])

# Define the MDP parameters
num_states = np.size(grid)
num_actions = 4
gamma = 0.9  # Discount factor

# Define the transition probabilities
transition_probs = np.zeros((num_states, num_actions,
    num_states))
transition_probs[0, 0, 1] = 1.0
transition_probs[0, 1, 0] = 1.0
```

```
transition_probs[1, 0, 2] = 1.0
transition_probs[1, 1, 1] = 1.0
transition_probs[1, 2, 3] = 1.0
transition_probs[1, 3, 1] = 1.0

# Define the rewards
rewards = np.zeros((num_states, num_actions))
rewards[0, 0] = 0 # No reward for moving up from state 0
rewards[0, 1] = 0 # No reward for moving down from state 0
rewards[1, 0] = 0 # No reward for moving up from state 1
rewards[1, 1] = 0 # No reward for moving down from state 1
rewards[1, 2] = 0 # No reward for moving left from state 1
rewards[1, 3] = -1 # Reward of -1 for moving right from
    state 1
rewards[2, :] = 10 # Reward of 10 for all actions in
    state 2

# Perform value iteration to find the optimal value
    function
values = np.zeros(num_states)
epsilon = 0.0001  # Convergence threshold
while True:
    prev_values = np.copy(values)
    for s in range(num_states):
        max_q_value = float("-inf")
        for a in range(num_actions):
            q_value = rewards[s, a] + gamma * np.sum
    (transition_probs[s, a, :] * values)
            max_q_value = max(max_q_value, q_value)
        values[s] = max_q_value
    if np.max(np.abs(values - prev_values)) < epsilon:
        break

# Find the optimal policy
policy = np.zeros(num_states)
for s in range(num_states):
    max_q_value = float("-inf")
    for a in range(num_actions):
        q_value = rewards[s, a] + gamma * np.sum
    (transition_probs[s, a, :] * values)
        if q_value > max_q_value:
```

```
                max_q_value = q_value
                policy[s] = a

# Print the grid with states and actions
print("Grid with States and Actions:")
grid_with_states = np.copy(grid).astype(str)
grid_with_actions = np.copy(grid).astype(str)

states = np.arange(num_states).reshape(grid.shape)
for i in range(grid.shape[0]):
    for j in range(grid.shape[1]):
        if grid[i, j] == -1:
            grid_with_states[i, j] = "X"
            grid_with_actions[i, j] = "X"
        elif grid[i, j] == 1:
            grid_with_states[i, j] = "G"
            grid_with_actions[i, j] = "G"
        else:
            grid_with_states[i, j] = f"S{states[i, j]}"
            if policy[states[i, j]] == 0:
                grid_with_actions[i, j] = "U"
            elif policy[states[i, j]] == 1:
                grid_with_actions[i, j] = "D"
            elif policy[states[i, j]] == 2:
                grid_with_actions[i, j] = "L"
            elif policy[states[i, j]] == 3:
                grid_with_actions[i, j] = "R"

print("States:")
print(grid_with_states)
print("Actions:")
print(grid_with_actions)
```

The output of Program 5.4 is displayed next. The output consists of two parts: the grid representation with states (*grid_with_states*) and the grid representation with actions (*grid_with_actions*).

States: The original grid is displayed, where each state is labeled as "S" followed by its state number. Obstacles are labeled as "X", and the goal state is labeled as "G".

Actions: The grid is the same as the original grid, but each cell is labeled with the action to be taken from that state. Here, `"U"` represents moving Up, `"D"` represents moving Down, `"L"` represents moving Left, and `"R"` represents moving Right. Obstacles and the goal state remain the same.

The output displays the grid world environment along with the corresponding states and actions based on the optimal policy determined through value iteration.

5.7   Machine Learning and Probabilistic Models

Machine Learning (ML) and Probabilistic Models are two closely related concepts that play a significant role in modern data analysis and decision making. Here is an explanation of these concepts and how they intersect:

- **Machine Learning:** Machine learning is a field of artificial intelligence that focuses on the development of algorithms and models that allow computers to learn from data, and make predictions or decisions without being explicitly programmed. ML algorithms are designed to automatically identify patterns, relationships, and insights in the data, and use them to make predictions or take actions.
- **Probabilistic Models:** Probabilistic models are mathematical models that use probability theory to represent uncertainty or randomness in data or phenomena. These models capture the probabilistic dependencies and relationships among variables and enable reasoning under uncertainty. They provide a framework for understanding and quantifying uncertainty in the data, making predictions, and performing probabilistic inference.

Probabilistic models and machine learning intersect in several ways as discussed next:

(a) **Probabilistic Models as Learning Algorithms:** Many machine learning algorithms are based on probabilistic models. These models learn from labeled data by estimating the parameters of a probability distribution that represents the underlying data generation process. Examples of such models include Gaussian mixture models, naive Bayes classifiers, and hidden Markov models. These models use probability distributions to describe the data and make predictions based on statistical inference.

(b) **Bayesian Machine Learning:** Bayesian machine learning combines machine learning techniques with probabilistic models. It allows for the integration of prior knowledge or beliefs into the learning process. Bayesian methods use Bayes' theorem to update the prior beliefs based on observed data, resulting in posterior beliefs that reflect both prior knowledge and observed evidence. This approach provides a principled way to handle uncertainty and enables reasoning under limited or sparse data.

(c) **Probabilistic Inference in Machine Learning:** Probabilistic inference is a fundamental task in both probabilistic modeling and machine learning. It involves computing the posterior probability distribution over unobserved variables, given observed data. Machine learning algorithms often leverage probabilistic inference techniques, such as variational inference or Markov chain Monte Carlo (MCMC), to estimate the posterior distribution and make predictions or decisions.

(d) **Uncertainty Quantification:** Probabilistic models are valuable for quantifying uncertainty in machine learning predictions. They provide not only a point estimate but also a measure of uncertainty associated with each prediction. This uncertainty quantification is particularly important in decision making tasks where the consequences of incorrect predictions need to be considered. Probabilistic models can provide probabilistic forecasts, confidence intervals, or predictive distributions that capture the uncertainty in the predictions.

To further understand using of probabilistic models as learning algorithms, let us consider a simple example of email spam classification. Suppose one wants to build a spam email classifier that can automatically classify incoming emails as either "spam" or "not spam" based on their content. To accomplish this, one can leverage the intersection of machine learning and probabilistic models as follows:

- **Data Collection:** Collect a labeled dataset of emails where each email is labeled as either "spam" or "not spam". This dataset will be used for training the machine learning model.
- **Feature Extraction:** Convert each email into a set of features that can be used for classification. Examples of features could include the frequency of certain words or phrases, the presence of specific keywords, or the length of the email.
- **Model Training:** Choose a machine learning algorithm that utilizes probabilistic modeling. One common approach is to use Naive Bayes, a probabilistic classifier. Naive Bayes assumes that each feature is conditionally independent of other features given the class label. Train the Naive Bayes classifier on the labeled dataset.
- **Model Evaluation:** Assess the performance of the trained model using evaluation metrics such as accuracy, precision, recall, or F1-score. This step helps to understand how well the model is performing and identify areas for improvement.
- **Model Deployment:** Once the model has been trained and evaluated, it can be deployed to classify new, unseen emails. When a new email arrives, the model uses the extracted features to calculate the probabilities of it belonging to the

"spam" or "not spam" class. The email is then classified based on the higher probability.

The intersection of machine learning and probabilistic models in this example allows for the quantification of uncertainty through probability estimates. It enables the classifier to provide not only the predicted class label but also the probability or confidence associated with that prediction, indicating how certain or uncertain the model is about its decision.

Program 5.5 illustrates the Python code for email spam classification using Naïve Bayes classifier. The email classifier can automatically classify incoming emails as either "spam" or "not spam" based on their content. The *Spambase* dataset is loaded from the UCI Machine Learning Repository using the provided URL. The dataset is then split into training and testing sets using `train_test_split` from scikit-learn. Next, the Naive Bayes classifier (*MultinomialNB()*) is created and trained on the training set. Predictions are made on the test set, and accordingly the accuracy of the classifier is calculated. Finally, the accuracy score and confusion matrix are printed to assess the performance of spam classification model.

Program 5.6 *Email Spam Classification using Naïve Bayes Classifier*

```python
import pandas as pd
from sklearn.feature_extraction.text import CountVectorizer
from sklearn.model_selection import train_test_split
from sklearn.naive_bayes import MultinomialNB
from sklearn.metrics import accuracy_score, confusion_matrix
import urllib

# Load the Spambase dataset from the UCI Machine Learning
    Repository
url = "https://archive.ics.uci.edu/ml/machine-learning-databases/
    spambase/spambase.data"
data = pd.read_csv(urllib.request.urlopen(url), header=None)

# Split the dataset into features (X) and labels (y)
X = data.iloc[:, :-1]
y = data.iloc[:, -1]

# Split the dataset into training and testing sets
X_train, X_test, y_train, y_test = train_test_split(X, y,
test_size=0.2, random_state=42)

# Train the Naive Bayes classifier
naive_bayes = MultinomialNB()
naive_bayes.fit(X_train, y_train)

# Make predictions on the test set
y_pred = naive_bayes.predict(X_test)
```

```
# Calculate the accuracy of the classifier
accuracy = accuracy_score(y_test, y_pred)
print("Accuracy:", accuracy)

# Calculate and display the confusion matrix
confusion_mat = confusion_matrix(y_test, y_pred)
print("Confusion Matrix:")
print(confusion_mat)
```

The output of Program 5.5 is displayed next. The output consists of two parts: the accuracy and the confusion matrix. The accuracy represents the percentage of correctly classified instances (emails) out of the total instances in the test set. The confusion matrix provides a detailed breakdown of the predicted and actual labels, showing the true positives, true negatives, false positives, and false negatives in a tabular format. By examining the accuracy and the confusion matrix, you can gain a better understanding of how well the spam classification model is performing and analyze the model's predictions in more detail.

```
Accuracy: 0.7861020629750272
Confusion Matrix:
[[445  86]
 [111 279]]
```

In summary, probabilistic models and machine learning are intertwined concepts that leverage probability theory and statistical inference to learn from data, make predictions, and quantify uncertainty. Machine learning algorithms can be based on probabilistic models, and probabilistic models provide a principled framework for handling uncertainty and performing inference in machine learning tasks.

This Chapter provides a comprehensive foundation for understanding and applying probabilistic reasoning techniques in various domains. The chapter aims to equip readers with the necessary knowledge and tools to reason under uncertainty, model probabilistic relationships, and make informed decisions based on available evidence.

Exercises

A) Choose the correct answer from among the alternatives given:

    a) In a survey, it is found that 30% of respondents own a car, while 70% do not own a car. What is the odds of not owning a car?

    i) 0.3

    ii) 0.7

    iii) 0.43

    iv) 1.33

b) In the classical perspective, the probability of drawing a heart from a standard deck of 52 playing cards is:

    i) 1/4

    ii) 1/13

    iii) 4/13

    iv) 1/52

c) In Bayes' theorem, $P(A|B)$ represents:

    i) The prior probability of event A.

    ii) The prior probability of event B.

    iii) The conditional probability of event A, given event B.

    iv) The conditional probability of event B, given event A.

d) Bayes' theorem involves the multiplication of:

    i) The prior probabilities

    ii) The posterior probabilities

    iii) The prior and posterior probabilities

    iv) The conditional probabilities

e) In a Markov network, cliques represent:

    i) Random variables

    ii) Evidence or observations

    iii) Joint distributions

    iv) Maximal fully connected subsets of nodes

f) In a belief network, the probability of a variable is calculated based on:

    i) Its parents and their conditional probabilities

    ii) Its children and their conditional probabilities

    iii) Evidence or observations

    iv) Random sampling from the network

g) The main assumption in a HMM is:

    i) All hidden states are dependent on each other

    ii) The observations are independent of each other

    iii) The transition probabilities are constant over time

    iv) The hidden states satisfy the Markov property

h) In an HMM, the emission probabilities represent:

    i) The probabilities of transitioning between hidden states

    ii) The probabilities of observing the hidden states

    iii) The probabilities of transitioning between observable states

    iv) The probabilities of observing the observable states

   i) The goal of an agent in Markov decision process is to:
     i) Maximize the immediate rewards at each state
     ii) Minimize the number of steps required to reach the goal state
     iii) Maximize the long-term cumulative rewards over time
     iv) Randomly explore different states and actions
   j) The discount factor in Markov decision process determines:
     i) The probability of transitioning to a new state
     ii) The rate at which rewards are accumulated over time
     iii) The number of states in the MDP
     iv) The optimal policy for the agent

B) Answer the following questions:

1) Discuss the concept of sample space and random variables in probability theory.
2) In a study, the probability of an event A occurring is 0.3. Calculate the odds of event A occurring, and determine the corresponding risk.
3) Describe the classical and empirical approaches to probability, and discuss their differences in terms of their underlying assumptions and application domains.
4) In a population, 2% of people have a certain disease. A diagnostic test for the disease has a sensitivity of 95% (correctly identifies those with the disease) and a specificity of 90% (correctly identifies those without the disease). If a randomly selected person tests positive for the disease, what is the probability that they actually have the disease?
5) Explain the key components and concepts of a Markov decision process (MDP) and their role in modeling decision making problems under uncertainty.
6) Describe the key components and concepts of a HMM, and explain how they are used to model sequential data with hidden states.
7) Suppose you are a robot navigating in a grid-world environment. At each step, you can move either up, down, left, or right. However, there are some cells in the grid that are blocked and cannot be entered. Your goal is to reach a target cell while avoiding the blocked cells. Formulate this problem as an MDP, and find the optimal policy to reach the target.
8) Discuss the three fundamental problems that are often encountered when working the HMM.

6

Population-Based Algorithms

Population-based optimization techniques (PBOT) have been a hot area of research in the last two decades. In PBOT, the solution is a data point that is spread in the search space. Population-based algorithms are mainly metaheuristic algorithms that provide good performances in a wide range of domains. Two such significant population-based optimization algorithms are – evolutionary algorithms and swarm intelligence algorithms, as shown in Figure 6.1.

One of the most popular evolutionary algorithms is the genetic algorithm (GA), which is explained in detail in the next section. Also, two popular swarm intelligence algorithms include ant colony optimization (ACO) and particle swarm optimization (PSO), which are explained in the later sections of this chapter.

6.1 Introduction to Genetic Algorithms

Genetic algorithms (GAs) were invented by John Holland in the 1960s. Later, Holland along with his colleagues and students developed the concepts of GA at the University of Michigan in the 1960s and 1970s as well. A GA is a metaheuristic that is inspired by the Charles Darwin's theory of natural evolution. GA are a part of the larger class of evolutionary algorithms (EA), which focus on selecting the fittest individuals for reproduction in order to produce offspring. Since the offspring are supposed to inherit the characteristics of the parents, it is expected that the offspring will have better fitness than parents if the parents have good fitness and, in turn, will have a better chance of survival. If this process continues to repeat multiple times, at some point of time, a generation of the fittest individuals will be formed.

Principles of Soft Computing Using Python Programming: Learn How to Deploy Soft Computing Models in Real World Applications, First Edition. Gypsy Nandi.

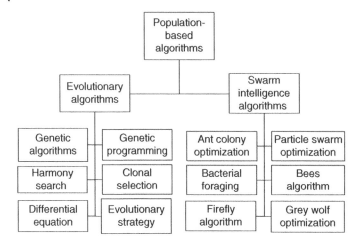

Figure 6.1 Standard population-based algorithms.

6.2 Five Phases of Genetic Algorithms

The GA consists of five main phases: population initialization, fitness function calculation, parent selection, crossover, and mutation. All these phases are diagrammatically illustrated with the help of a flowchart in Figure 6.2, which shows the step-wise flow of the phases. Each of the step-wise phases of the GA is explained next.

6.2.1 Population Initialization

The first phase of GA begins with the process of considering the initial population, which is a set of individuals that can provide solution to a given problem. Traditional GA store all the genetic information in a chromosome that is represented by using a bit array (string of "1's" and "0's"). Each individual possesses some characteristics, which are defined by a set of variables or parameters, also called as genes (individual bit). Thus, for an individual, a set of genes, represented using a string of bits, is combined together to form a chromosome, which brings in solution to a problem. Figure 6.3 illustrates a sample example of gene, chromosome, and population. The length of the string (i.e., the number of bits) is dependent on the problem to be solved.

Population initialization can be achieved in either of the following two ways:

- Random initialization – the initial population is populated with completely random solutions.
- Heuristic initialization – the initial population is populated using a known heuristic for the problem.

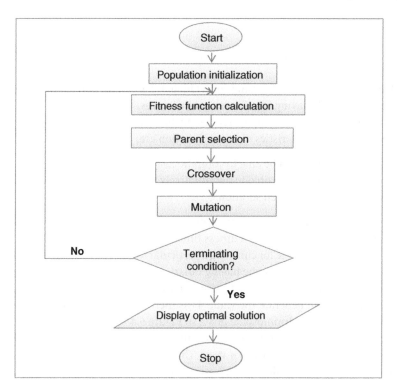

Figure 6.2 Flowchart of the phases of genetic algorithm.

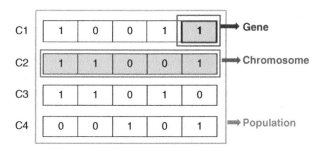

Figure 6.3 A Sample example of gene, chromosome, and population.

6.2.2 Fitness Function Calculation (Evaluation)

Fitness function or evaluation function in GA determines how fit a solution is. This is done by assigning a fitness score to each chromosome in the current population. The fitness value of a chromosome indicates how well or fit the chromosome

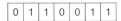

Figure 6.4 A chromosome consisting of seven genes.

is to solve a given problem. Choosing individuals for reproduction is based on selection of individuals having best fitness quality scores.

The calculation of fitness quality generates the fitness scores for every individual. Two important characteristics of fitness function are:

- The fitness function should be able to compute fast.
- The fitness function must be able to quantitatively measure the fitness value of individuals based on the given solution.

Each problem will have its own fitness function, as it depends on the nature of the given problem. Hence choosing a fitness function is a challenging task in GA, as there is no hard and fast rule for choosing a particular fitness function for a given problem. Usually, for a chromosome having binary information, the fitness value can be considered as the number of 1's present in the chromosome. For instance, the fitness function will generate the value 4 (as there are four 1's) based on the binary information of the chromosome given in Figure 6.4.

Let us consider another example of fitness function for the two variables p and q, the sum of which should be t, i.e., $p + q = t$. This equation can also be written as $p + q - t = 0$. The fitness function in this case can be the inverse of $|p + q - t|$, i.e.,

$$\text{Fitness Function} = 1/|p + q{-}t|$$

6.2.3 Parent Selection

In the selection phase a pair of the fittest individuals (parents) are chosen based on the fitness score. These two individuals pass their genes to the next generation. Also, the selection process reduces the population size by discarding those individuals having less than or equal to the average mean fitness score. Hence, in each iteration, the new population will be smaller than the existing population.

There are several parameters that guide the selection method for choosing the optimal chromosomes for a given population. Few such parameters are discussed below:

- **Selection pressure:** It is the degree to which better chromosomes are favored. The higher the selection pressure, the higher the chances of better chromosomes being favored.
- **Selection variance:** It is the expected variance of the fitness distribution of the population after applying the selection method to the normalised Gaussian distribution.

- **Selection intensity:** It is the expected average fitness value of the population after applying a selection method on population whose fitness is distributed according to unit normal distribution.
  There are several selection techniques for choosing the fittest individuals, such as fitness proportionate selection, tournament selection, rank-based selection, and truncation selection. Let us discuss, in brief, these common parent selection techniques.

- **Fitness proportionate selection:** This is one of the most popular ways of parent selection. In this selection method, every individual has a probability of becoming a parent based on its fitness value. The fitter individuals will, however, have a greater chance of mating to produce new offsprings, as the fittest individuals have the highest share of the wheel. The probability $p(x)$ of a chromosome "x" having fitness $f(x)$ to be selected among "n" individuals using the fitness proportion selection method is given by:

$$p(x) = \frac{f(x)}{\sum_{j=1}^{n} f(j)}$$

  The fitness proportionate selection can be implemented in many ways. Two such variations of the fitness proportionate selection method are – the Roulette wheel selection and the Stochastic Universal sampling.

- **The Roulette wheel selection:** In this method, a circular wheel is divided into "n" pies (i.e., "n" chromosomes), and a fixed point is initially placed at one of the pies. This is illustrated in Figure 6.4, which considers a total of five chromosomes – A1 to A5. The wheel is then rotated, and, once it stops, the fixed point is checked to find on which pie it stopped. The region of the pie that gets selected by considering the fixed point is then chosen as the parent chromosome (A1 in case of Figure 6.5). The process is repeated to choose the next parent chromosome. The idea behind using the concept of Roulette wheel is that greater size of the pie is owned by fitter individuals and therefore has a greater chance of being placed on the fixed point. Thus, each individual chromosome of the current population has the probability of being selected proportional to its fitness.

- **The Stochastic universal sampling (SUS):** This method is very similar to the Roulette wheel selection method discussed above, except that the rotating wheel possesses more than one fixed point instead of having just one fixed point. This is illustrated in Figure 6.6, which considers a total of five chromosomes – A1 to A5. In such a case, more than one parent gets selected by rotating the wheel just once (A1 and A3 in case of Figure 6.6). This method leads to selection of highly fit individuals at least once. SUS allows even the weaker members of the population a chance to get selected. However, it can perform badly when one of the members of the population has a significantly large fitness value compared to the rest of the members of chromosomes in the population.

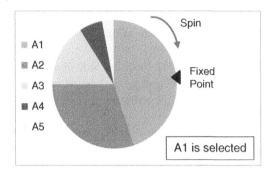

Figure 6.5 The Roulette wheel parent selection.

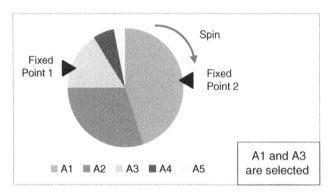

Figure 6.6 The Stochastic universal sampling parent selection.

- **Tournament selection:** This method carries out several tournaments among few randomly chosen chromosomes present in the current population. The winner of each tournament is selected based on the fitness value, which is then used for crossover. This selection method can be used for negative fitness values.

  For instance, for a population size on "n," "m" ($m < n$), individuals are randomly selected to become the target parent. This is illustrated in Figure 6.7 in which initially four chromosomes are randomly selected (B, F, G, and J) for the first tournament, and parent C gets finally selected in the first tournament out of these four chromosomes. Several such tournaments are carried out, and eventually the best solution will have to be selected more than once, and the worst solution will not be selected at all.

- **Rank-based Selection:** In this method, each individual chromosome is ranked according to its fitness value. For instance, rank "n" ("n" is the number of chromosomes) will be attained by the chromosome having the highest fitness value, rank "$n-1$" will be attained by the chromosome having the second highest fitness value, rank 1 will be attained by the chromosome having the

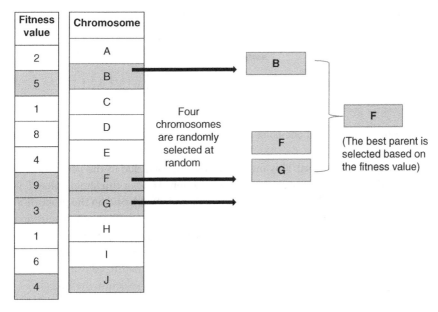

Figure 6.7   An example of tournament selection.

lowest fitness value, and so on. The probability $p(x)$ of a chromosome "x" being selected using the rank selection method is given by:

$$p(x) = \frac{\text{rank}(x)}{n\,(n-1)}$$

Figure 6.8 shows an example of five chromosomes being sorted and ranked according to their fitness value from rank 1 to rank 5.

The rank selection method will solely consider the rank values of the chromosomes rather than their absolute fitness. In turn, this method keeps up selection pressure when the fitness variance is low.

Chromosome	Fitness value
A1	22
A2	31
A3	18
A4	27
A5	34

Sort according to fitness values and accordingly assign ranks

Chromosome	Fitness value	Rank
A5	34	5
A2	31	4
A4	27	3
A1	22	2
A3	18	1

Figure 6.8   An example of rank-based selection.

Parent chromosomes
Offspring chromosomes

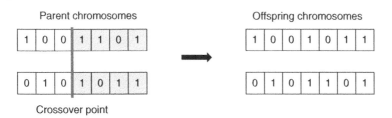

Crossover point

Figure 6.9 An example of one-point crossover.

- **Truncation selection:** This method is seldom used due to the generation of less optimum output for chromosome selection. Here, a threshold value T is considered usually between the range of 50% and 100% based on the proportion of the population to be selected as parent chromosomes. Truncation selection retains the fittest $T\%$ of the chromosomes, whereas the rest of the chromosomes are discarded. This method has the greatest advantage of rapid convergence and is easy to implement; however, it often results in premature convergence, and hence is not considered as one of the preferred parent selection methods.

6.2.4 Crossover

The most significant phase is the crossover, which can be carried out in several different ways. One way of mating of parents is by randomly choosing a crossover point from within the genes. A new offspring is created by exchanging the genes of parents up to the crossover point, which is then added to the population.

There are several crossover operators that can be chosen based on the nature of the problem dealt with. Four such standard crossover genetic operators are discussed next. By using any of these crossover operators, the basic idea is to combine the genetic information of parents to produce new offsprings.

- **One-point crossover:** This operator chooses a random crossover point, and then the tails of two of the parents are interchanged to get new offsprings. This operation is explained with the help of an example given in Figure 6.9.
- **Multi-point crossover:** This operator chooses more than one random crossover points, and then the data between the crossover points are interchanged to get new offsprings. The substrings between these two crossover points are called the mapping sections. This operation is explained with the help of an example given in Figure 6.10, which considers two-point crossover to generate offprings. In this example, three mappings are defined: $5 \leftrightarrow 3$, $2 \leftrightarrow 9$, and $7 \leftrightarrow 4$.
- **Uniform crossover:** This operator treats each gene separately and with a lottery method (say, flipping of a coin) decides whether a chromosome will be included

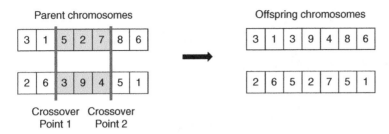

Figure 6.10 An example of two-point crossover.

Figure 6.11 An example of uniform crossover.

or not in the offspring. Hence, each bit of the parents is independently chosen from the parents to create offsprings rather than choosing a continuous segment of the bit array. This operation is explained with the help of an example given in Figure 6.11. The highlighted cells are the random cells chosen whose bit information is swapped to generate new offsprings.

- **Partially mapped crossover:** This operator initially follows a similar approach as the two-point crossover in which two random crossover points are chosen, and then the data between the crossover points are interchanged to get new offsprings. This operation is explained with the help of an example given in Figure 6.12, which initially considers two-point crossover and accordingly defines four mappings: $4 \leftrightarrow 1$, $5 \leftrightarrow 8$, $6 \leftrightarrow 7$, and $7 \leftrightarrow 6$.

The rest of the gene values (initially marked as "x" in Figure 6.12 to indicate currently unknown value) of the offsprings that do not fall between the crossover points are filled by partial mapping. In case of partial mapping, the additional gene values are filled from the original parent values for those "x" for which there is no conflict. Usually, conflict arises if the gene value matches with the values considered for mapping. (4, 1, 5, 8, 6, and 7).

6.2.5 Mutation

The mutation phase is mainly carried out to maintain diversity in the genetic population. After the generation of offsprings due to crossover, these offspring chromosomes can be mutated with an assigned mutation probability. For this, a randomly

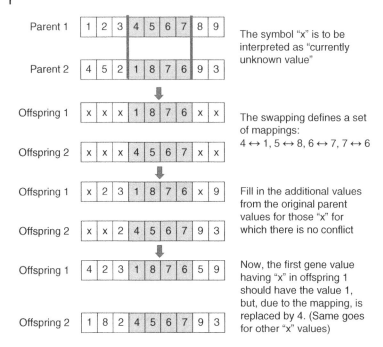

The symbol "x" is to be interpreted as "currently unknown value"

The swapping defines a set of mappings:
$4 \leftrightarrow 1, 5 \leftrightarrow 8, 6 \leftrightarrow 7, 7 \leftrightarrow 6$

Fill in the additional values from the original parent values for those "x" for which there is no conflict

Now, the first gene value having "x" in offspring 1 should have the value 1, but, due to the mapping, is replaced by 4. (Same goes for other "x" values)

Figure 6.12 An example of partially mapped crossover.

selected floating-point value is chosen, and the mutation process is carried out on the offspring if this value is found to be less than the mutation probability; otherwise, no mutation occurs. The following are the various mutation operators that can be chosen for performing GA implementation:

- **Bit flip mutation:** This operator selects one or more random bits and flips those bit values. This operation is mostly used for binary encoded GA. An example of bit flip mutation is given in Figure 6.13 in which the highlighted cells indicate the randomly selected bits in the bit array.
- **Random resetting:** This operator follows a similar principle as the bit flip mutation, with the only difference in that it works for integer representation. Random resetting operation selects one or more random integer values, and flips those values to any value within an acceptable range. An example of random resetting mutation is given in Figure 6.14 in which the highlighted cells indicate the randomly selected values in the integer array.

Figure 6.13 An example of bit flip mutation.

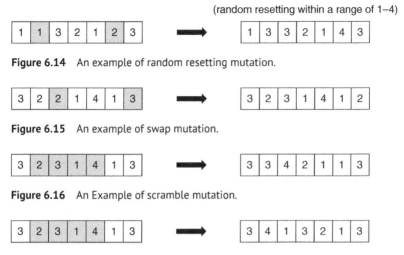

Figure 6.14 An example of random resetting mutation.

Figure 6.15 An example of swap mutation.

Figure 6.16 An Example of scramble mutation.

Figure 6.17 An example of inverse mutation.

- **Swap mutation:** This operator exactly chooses two gene values in a chromosome and swaps those two values. An example of swap mutation is given in Figure 6.15 in which the highlighted cells indicate the two chose gene values in the integer array.
- **Scramble mutation:** This operator follows a similar principle as the swap mutation except that a subset of gene values is chosen instead of swapping only two positions, and those values are randomly shuffled. An example of scramble mutation is given in Figure 6.16 in which the highlighted cells indicate the subset of gene values chosen for shuffling.
- **Inverse mutation:** This operator, like the scramble mutation, selects a set of genes but the entire values are inverted from right to left, instead of shuffling the gene values of the subset. An example of scramble mutation is given in Figure 6.17 in which the highlighted cells indicate the subset of gene values chosen for mutation operation. The four gene values selected are directly inverted from right to left: $(2, 3, 1, 4) \rightarrow (4, 1, 3, 2)$, and the rest of the gene values remain unaltered.

6.3 How Genetic Algorithm Works?

The original GA was invented by John Holland in the early 1970s. The GA was invented to imitate some of the procedures observed in natural evolution. The main idea of GA is to use the power of natural evolution to solve many optimization problems. When compared to several traditional optimization techniques, a GA has proved to provide significant benefits in searching a large state space, multimodal state space, or n-dimensional surface.

Given below in Algorithm 6.1 is the generic GA based on its various phases to solve a given problem. Each iteration of the GA algorithm is called as *generation*, and the entire set of *generations* is called as *run*. There are three input parameters to be supplied for the GA. Care should be taken to provide optimum values for all the three input parameters, as the success of GA relies a lot on the values of these input parameters. A brief description of these three input parameters is given below.

- **Size of the population (n):** It is the number of chromosomes considered for the population. If the "n" value is very high, the GA slows down, whereas if the "n" value is very low, there is a less probability of occurring of crossover. This indicates that a suitable population size has to be chosen for optimum result of a given problem.
- **Crossover probability (p_c):** It determines the amount of crossover to be performed. If the offspring generated is an exact replica of its parent chromosomes, then the crossover probability is 0. Now, if there are 10 chromosomes, and crossover probability is 0.6, in that case crossover will be performed for 6 chromosomes.
- **Mutation probability (p_m):** The mutation operator is applied to a new string of chromosome with a specific low mutation probability or mutation rate. This value of mutation rate is usually calculated as $1/n$ where "n" is the population size, or $1/t$, where, "t" is the length of each chromosome.

Algorithm 6.1   The Generic Genetic Algorithm

---

1. Start with a randomly generated population of chromosomes (candidate solutions of a problem).
2. Calculate the fitness value $f(x)$ for each chromosome x in the population.
3. Repeat the following steps until a terminating solution is met:
   a. Select a pair of parent chromosomes from the current population (using any standard parent selection method)
   b. With probability p_c (the "crossover probability"), perform the crossover (choose any standard crossover operator) to generate two new offsprings from each pair of parent
   c. Mutate the two offspring at each locus with probability p_m (the mutation probability), and place the resulting chromosomes in the new population.
4. Replace the current population with the new population
5. Go to Step 2.

As seen in the previous section, after the random generation of initial population, the GA evolves through the three main operators: selection (for equating survival of the fittest), crossover (for allowing mating between individuals), and mutation (for introducing random modifications).

The terminating condition for GA will decide when the algorithm will stop running. Initially, the GA produces faster results with better solutions in every iteration. But the generation of better results tends to saturate as the number of iterations becomes more, and negligible improvement in solution can be seen. The GA has to then end when the solution is close to optimal after a certain number of iterations. Any one among the various terminating conditions for GA can be chosen to derive an optimal result:

- When not much improvement is found in solution after certain number of iterations
- When a predetermined number of iterations (generations) has been carried out
- When the objective function value has reached a certain predefined value.

To understand the GA, let us consider the simple *"MAXONE"* problem, which considers tossing a coin and prefers to get the result as tail in each toss. The coin is tossed 60 times and is marked either 0 (when head is achieved) or 1 (when the desired tail is achieved). Let the tossing of coin of 60 times be divided into groups of six clusters, such that in each cluster 10 results of tossing are stored. The resultant output of this problem is to maximize the number of 1's by carrying out all the phases of GA in each iteration until an optimum solution is achieved. Let us consider the following tossing results for 6 clusters (C1 to C6), as shown in Table 6.1. Accordingly, the fitness value of each cluster is calculated based on the number of 1's per cluster.

Table 6.1 Initial population and the fitness values.

Cluster	Toss results (Head = 0/Tail = 1)	Fitness value
C1	1 1 0 0 1 0 0 0 1 0	$f(C1) = 4$
C2	0 1 0 1 0 0 1 1 1 0	$f(C2) = 5$
C3	1 1 1 0 0 1 1 0 1 1	$f(C3) = 7$
C4	0 1 0 0 0 1 0 0 1 1	$f(C4) = 4$
C5	1 1 0 1 1 0 1 1 1 1	$f(C5) = 8$
C6	1 0 1 0 0 1 0 0 0 0	$f(C6) = 3$
Total fitness value		**31**

Table 6.2 Clusters arranged for selection based on fitness values.

Cluster	Toss results	Alias cluster name
C3	1 1 1 0 0 1 1 0 1 1	C1'
C5	1 1 0 1 1 0 1 1 1 1	C2'
C2	0 1 0 1 0 0 1 1 1 0	C3'
C5	1 1 0 1 1 0 1 1 1 1	C4'
C3	1 1 1 0 0 1 1 0 1 1	C5'
C1	1 1 0 0 1 0 0 0 1 0	C6'

The total fitness of the entire population is 31. After the calculation of fitness values of the initial population, the next task is to carry out selection. For this, let us choose the Roulette wheel selection. Now, let us design the Roulette wheel based on the six fitness values calculated. Cluster C5 has the highest fitness value of 8 out of a total fitness value of 31, which is equal to approximately 26%. Similarly, for clusters C1 and C4, fitness percentage is 13% each. The fitness percentage is 15% for cluster C2, and it is 23% for cluster C3. Lastly, it is only 10% for cluster C6. As can be seen in Figure 6.18, the area of the pies of the wheel is proportionate to the fitness of the wheel.

The next task is to spin the Roulette wheel to perform selection. The chances of fitter individuals being selected are high, as those individuals cover major portions of the wheel. According to the spinning, let us consider that the selection operation has considered the following results in order: C3, C5, C2, C5, C3, and C1. This is tabulated in Table 6.2. The number of times of spinning is based on the number of individuals present in the population (6 in our example). The clusters are provided with an alias name for easy reference (C1' to C6').

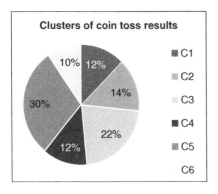

Figure 6.18 The Roulette wheel consisting of clusters of population.

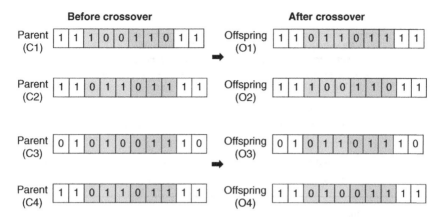

Figure 6.19 Crossover operations performed for two pairs of chromosomes.

The next task is to perform crossover between each couple based on a predefined crossover probability (say, $p_c = 0.6$). This indicates that for a population size of 6 (as in our example), any four individuals can be chosen for mating. Let us then consider mating of C1′ with C2′, and mating of C3′ with C4′, as shown in Figure 6.19. As discussed before, there are several crossover operations, and let us choose two-point crossover by considering the crossover point values of 2 and 8.

The final step is to now apply mutation with a predefined mutation probability based on the length of each bit string (say, $p_m = 1/t = 1/10 = 0.1$). Before applying mutation, the values of all the individuals are tabulated in Table 6.3. The bit flip mutation is applied to each individual (cluster) in which one bit chosen at random (as $p_m = 0.1$) is flipped for each individual. However, mutation is applied only to new offsprings and not to chromosomes that do not undergo crossover.

For this, let us consider that the first two clusters are randomly chosen to get flipped at their third locus, and the fifth and sixth clusters are again randomly chosen to get flipped at their sixth locus. Table 6.3 highlights those bit values that are randomly flipped. After the flipping phase is over, one iteration of GA can be considered to be complete, and the new population generated is now ready for the second iteration.

As can be seen from the above example of MAXONE problem, there has been a huge change in the fitness value after completion of the first iteration itself. The initial population had a fitness value of 31, and it got raised to 41 after the first generation of GA. Each of these phases is repeated many a times until a stopping criterion is met. Usually, a typical GA is run from 50 to 500 generations. Thus, the MAXONE problem can be easily addressed by using GA to raise the number of 1's in the final result.

Table 6.3 New population generated after mutation.

Cluster	Bit values after crossover (but before mutation)	Bit values after applying mutation	Fitness value
O1	1 1 0 1 1 0 1 1 1 1	1 1 1 1 1 0 1 1 1 1	$f(O1) = 9$
O2	1 1 1 0 0 1 1 0 1 1	1 1 0 0 0 1 1 0 1 1	$f(O2) = 6$
O3	0 1 0 1 1 0 1 1 1 0	0 1 0 1 1 0 1 1 1 0	$f(O3) = 6$
O4	1 1 0 1 0 0 1 1 1 1	1 1 0 1 0 0 1 1 1 1	$f(O4) = 7$
C5′	1 1 1 0 0 1 1 0 1 1	1 1 1 0 0 0 1 1 1 1	$f(C5') = 7$
C6′	1 1 0 0 1 0 0 0 1 0	1 1 0 0 1 1 0 1 1 0	$f(C6') = 6$
Total fitness value		41	

6.4 Application Areas of Genetic Algorithms

GAs can be applied in various fundamental and important application areas for solving optimization problems. Its relevance and prominence has been realized in various real-life applications. Two such application areas in which GA are frequently used are the travelling salesman problem and the vehicle routing problem, which are briefly discussed in this section.

6.4.1 Using GA in Travelling Salesman Problem

GAs have been widely used to solve the classic travelling salesman problem (TSP). TSP considers finding the shortest route between two nodes (start node and end node) of a complete weighted graph G having n nodes and $n(n - 1)$ edges, so that all other nodes are visited exactly once while travelling. Few practical applications of TSP include finding the shortest costumer servicing route, planning bus service routes, regular distribution of goods, etc. TSP is a NP-hard problem, and hence no exact algorithm can solve it in polynomial time. Several methods have been discussed to solve TSP, such as branch and bound method, cutting plane method, explicit enumeration, implicit enumeration, and dynamic programming.

Figure 6.20 shows an illustrative example of the TSP in which all capitals of eight north-eastern states of India have to be covered by a travelling salesman. If the salesman randomly starts from a point, say Dispur in Assam, the problem is to solve which capital should the salesman visit one-by-one to cover all the eight places by considering the shortest route of travel. Also, the salesman cannot visit any capital twice, and he/she needs to return back to the Dispur capital of Assam

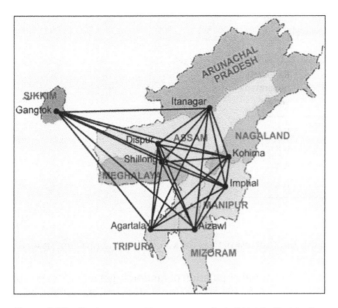

Figure 6.20 Routes connecting every capital of North-East India.

at the end. When the problem is stated, it looks like an easy problem to state, but not so easy to be solved, especially when there are many areas to be covered.

The first phase or task of GA is to represent individuals of the initial population, i.e. possible solutions or tours in this case. Now, in TSP, each city can be encoded as a $\lfloor log_2 (n) \rfloor$ long string, in which each individual of the population (a complete route) is a string of length $n \lfloor log_2 (n) \rfloor$. For simplicity, let us consider that only four cities are needed to be covered by the salesman, namely C1, C2, C3, and C4. Each city can be represented in 3-bit format, but only four values will be covered such as 000, 001, 010 and 011. The other bit patterns will not represent any city, and hence the offspring(s) generated may not lead to legal tours after performing a crossover. For such concerns, the binary representation of TSP is hardly used in practice.

It has been realized that the best way to represent a tour is by using path representation. So, if we again consider five cities to be travelled, namely C1, C2, C3, C4, and C5, the tour C1 → C3 → C5 → C4 → C2 → C1 can be represented as (135421), in which each decimal number represents a city. If city x is placed in yth position, this indicates that city x will be the yth city to be visited during the tour. The total number of tours possible considering "n" cities will be $(n - 1)!/2$. Thus, if five cities are considered, as in our example, the total number of tours is $4!/2 = 12$. For covering only five cities, the total number of tours is 12. Hence, as the value of "n" increases, the possible solutions are even more. Choosing of the

Table 6.4 A 2-D array of cities and their randomly generated weight values.

City	Randomly generated weight
C2	0.6
C3	0.8
C4	0.3
C5	0.5

best solution that decides the shortest path is thus a challenging problem that can be easily addressed by GAs.

Now, let us first of all set the initial population of randomly generated tours. For this, let us consider a two-dimensional array consisting of cities and randomly generated decimal numbers between 0 and 1 for representing the weights of each city. The array will consist of $(n - 1)$ city names (as one of the cities will be considered as the starting point, say city C1) and their associated weight values. An example is given in Table 6.4. Next, the weights can be arranged in ascending order to decide a tour path. Based on values provided in Table 6.4, it can be considered that the tour will be C1 → C4 → C5 → C2 → C3 → C1, which can be mentioned as (145231). This process will be repeated "n" number of times to store "n" individual tour information in the initial population, where "n" value has to be determined by the user as an input parameter.

Once the initial population has been set, the next phase of GA is fitness calculation for finding the fitness value of each individual (tour) in the given population. This can be easily done by summing up the costs of each pair of adjacent genes. Since TSP is a minimization problem (the lower the cost function, the better will be the possible solution), the fitness value will be calculated as:

$$f(z) = 1/f(z)$$

where, z is the total path length of the tour. For instance, for the ordering of tour (145231) mentioned above, the distance between each pair of genes (cities) will help in calculating the fitness value. Thus, the cities represented by "1" and "4" is first found and stored in a variable "sum"; then the distance between the cities represented by "4" and "5" is considered and added to the previous "sum" value, and so on. The tour's fitness value is ultimately set to the overall sum of all distances between 1 and 4, 4 and 5, 5 and 2, 2 and 3, and, lastly, 3 and 1.

It is obvious that the smaller the value of the sum (overall distance), the higher will be the fitness of the individual (tour). If one of the tours T1 covered have an overall distance value as 120 (km), and another tour T2 has an overall distance value as 180 (km), the fitness value of tours T1 and T2 will be 0.008 and 0.006, respectively. As the fitness value of tour T1 is higher than tour T2, the chances of crossover for T1 are higher than that of tour T2. After the calculation of fitness values of the initial population, the next task is to carry out selection. For this, let us choose the Roulette wheel selection, which considers fitness value of each tour and accordingly selects $n/2$ parents for a population size of "n."

After the selection process, the next task is the crossover operation. The main consideration to be made is that the new offspring generated should not result in visiting of a city more than once. For this, any classical crossover operator, such as one-point crossover or multipoint crossover, cannot be used to solve the TSP, as these crossover operators may often lead to a penalty of selecting the same city for a single tour. The better choice would be to create offsprings without repeating the gene (city) values. For instance, let us consider two parents chosen for crossover as given in Figure 6.21. By using this crossover operation, the offsprings generated do not result in duplication of city values.

Lastly, mutation needs to be carried out for completing one generation of TSP using GA. However again, a conventional mutation method that replaces a city (gene) value with another randomly chosen city value will result in duplication of city values, which is not permissible. To solve this issue, two random gene values of an individual are selected, and these two values are swapped to maintain unique city values per tour. An example of mutation for TSP is shown in Figure 6.22.

After the swapping in mutation phase is over, one iteration of GA can be considered to be complete, and the new population generated is now ready for the second iteration. Each of the phases of GA is repeated many a times until a stopping

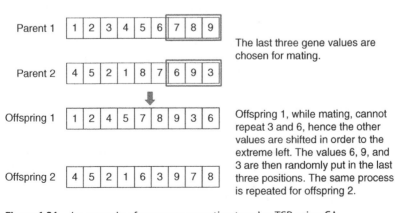

Figure 6.21 An example of crossover operation to solve TSP using GA.

Figure 6.22 An example of mutation to solve TSP using GA.

criterion is met. The final result is expected to find one of the best solutions for the classical TSP.

6.4.2 Using GA in Vehicle Routing Problem

The vehicle routing problem (VRP) generalizes the well-known travelling salesman problem (discussed in the previous subsection). The VRP was first proposed by Dantzig and Ramser in 1959. The basic idea of this problem is to consider one or more vehicles located in different depots that can deliver goods to several customers located at several places with the primary objective to minimize the total route cost. The VRP problem can be depicted by a graph in which the nodes are the depots and the several destinations where customers are expecting to receive their goods, whereas the edges are the connecting roads between two nodes. The edges may be either directed or undirected, depending on whether the connecting path between two nodes, say destinations A and B, allows one-way route (A → B) or two-way route (A ↔ B). Each edge has an associated cost, which is generally the distance between A and B, or the travelling time to reach from A to B, or vice versa.

When the VRP problem considers only one vehicle located at one depot that needs to cover few sets of routes with the least total distance, and there are no other additional constraints to be considered, the VRP problem reduces to a TSP and can be solved easily using the concept of GAs to solve the TSP problem. However, in a more realistic case, there may be more than one vehicle located at more than one depot and are ready to provide service of depositing goods by travelling each route only once to save cost and time. For instance, let us consider two depots Depot 1 and Depot 2, as illustrated in Figure 6.23. Using VRP, the optimum result has been found to solve as to how the two vehicles of two different depots should choose each of its route to cover all destinations exactly once. Vehicle from Depot 1 chooses the route 1 → 2 → 3, and the other vehicle from Depot 2 travels the route 4 → 6 → 5.

Also, in a more realistic case, a vehicle may provide the service of delivery by considering one or more of the following constraints as listed below:

- Each vehicle may have the maximum capacity (weight or volume) of goods to be carried. For instance, the tankers that carry petrol have a limitation on the amount of petrol to being carried.
- Each vehicle may have a time period within which it must leave the depot or return back after providing the delivery service.

Figure 6.23 An example of the vehicle routing problem.

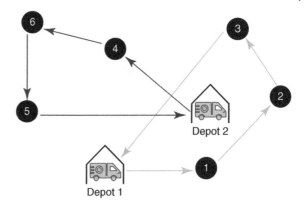

Depot 2

Depot 1

• The vehicles may follow working hours (for providing rest to drivers during the nonworking hours). Also, the departure and arrival timing of a vehicle from depot and back to depot is needed to be maintained

The complexity of VRP can be solved using the approach used in GAs. In case of VRP, each chromosome of the population represents a route, which can be a possible solution to the VRP problem. There can be several variations of the VRP. Let us consider one such variation called the *varying-capacity single central depot system* for the VRP in which there are a number of destination points to be covered by a fixed vehicle parked at a central depot. The vehicle has to follow the given objectives and constraints:

Objectives

• Minimizing the distance travelled by each vehicle (finding the shortest route)
• Minimizing the total number of vehicles to be used for covering all routes

Constraints

• A vehicle has to start its destination from the central depot and should come back to the central depot again after covering a route.
• Vehicle capacity constraint is taken into consideration.

The flowchart illustrating solution of VRP using GA is illustrated in Figure 6.24. The five important phases followed by any GA are also followed in VRP to derive an optimal solution for the same. Initially, "n" number of feasible routes is considered to build the initial population. Each destination point "x_i" is represented by a unique value (x_1, x_2, x_3, etc.), as illustrated in Figure 6.23. Each chromosome of the population is built by storing several values of "x_i" to represent a valid route to be served by one vehicle. The central depot "x_0" is considered as the starting

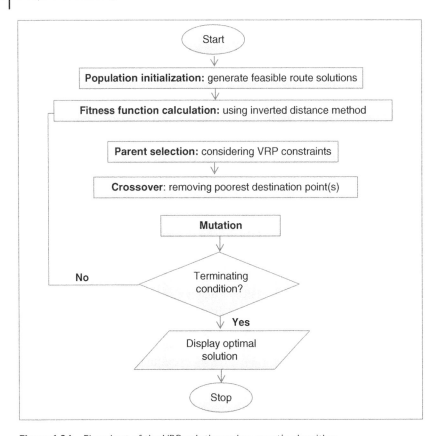

Figure 6.24 Flowchart of the VRP solution using genetic algorithm.

and ending points of each route. Care should be taken while building the initial population that every route must be feasible in terms of capacity constraint.

The various notations used for finding the solution of the problem are as follows:

x_i: the destination i to where good has to be delivered; x_0 represents the central supply depot

x_{ij}: value of x_{ij} can be either 0 or 1. When $x_{ij} = 1$, it means x_i and x_j are directly adjacent to each other; when $x_{ij} = 0$, it means means x_i and x_j are not directly adjacent.

(x_i, x_j): the connection or edge between x_i and x_j

v: the vehicle identification number

V: the total number of all vehicles

W: the storage capacity of each vehicle

y_k: value of y_k can be either 0 or 1. When $y_k = 1$, it means that the vehicle k will help in delivering of goods; when $y_k = 0$, it means the vehicle k will not be involved in delivering of goods.

y_{ijk}: the vehicle k passes through the edge (x_i, x_j)

d_{ij}: the distance covered by edge (x_i, x_j)

q_i: the requirement quantity of customer in destination point x_i

n_k: the number of destination points covered by the vehicle k

p_k: the total quantity of goods delivered by the vehicle k

c_m: the total cost of one solution

Now, the basic target of single central-depot varying capacity vehicles in the VRP is:

$$f(m) = \min(c_m)$$

where,

$$c_m = \sum_k y_k \sum_i^n \sum_j^n x_{ij} d_{ij} y_{ijk}$$

Also, the following constraints are to be followed:

- x_{ij} can be either 0 or 1
- y_{ij} also can be either 0 or 1
- values of k, w, and d_{ij} should be greater than 0
- $W > q_i > 0$
- $n \geq n_k > 0$
- $W > p_k > 0$

Generating initial population: To produce individuals, the finite automaton M can be used, which is equated as:

$$M = \left(Q, \sum, \delta, q_0, F\right)$$

Here,

- Q (collection of states) $= \{(q_{x_i,q})\}$
- $\sum = \{x_i\} \cup \{g(x_i, x_j)\}$,
- δ is the transition function
- q_0 (the initial state) $= \{(0, W)\}$
- F (the final state) $= \{(0, 0)\}$

When M starts, a vehicle can be considered to have departed from the state $(0, W)$. Again, when the vehicle returns to the state $(0, W)$, one full route is constructed and then another vehicle begins. When M stops, an individual chromosome is born and the vehicle returns to the state $(0, 0)$. This process is repeated to produce new individual chromosomes for the population.

For choosing the shortest route $g(x_i, x_j)$, the next destination point to be selected should be:

$$\text{next}(x_i) = \{x_j \mid x_{ij} = 1, q_j > 0\}$$

Fitness evaluation: To evaluate the fitness value of each chromosome, it will be measured as the total distance covered by the individual chromosome, the number of destination points covered by the chromosome, as well as the total quantity dispatched by the vehicle (which should be less than or equal to the vehicle capacity).

Selection: In a traditional GA approach, a pair of individual chromosomes is selected to reproduce offsprings. However, this traditional approach will fail to perform correctly in case of VRP, as each individual chromosome produces a complete solution. If fragments of chromosomes are interchanged, neither of the parent chromosomes will then probably cover all the destination points. Hence, a new approach has to be used for crossovers of two chromosomes by selecting one of the poorest quality chromosomes (based on quality evaluation function) and another randomly selected chromosome from the rest of the population.

Crossover: For the crossover to occur for the VRP solution, the typical crossover operators will fail to give a valid result, as it might not lead to a valid shortest route. Next, a destination point is randomly chosen from a chromosome having poorest fitness quality, and it is simply removed or destroyed from that chromosome. There can be two cases based on which either of the crossover will be performed. As mentioned before, $g(x_i, x_j)$ represents the shortest route between x_i and x_j. In the example considered in Figure 6.25, $g(x_4, x_1) = x_4 x_7 x_1$; $g(x_3, x_6) = x_3 x_6$; $g(x_1, x_4) = x_1 x_7 x_4$; $g(x_3, x_1) = x_3 x_6 x_1$.

Case I: If the removed destination point belongs to the collection of all destination points in the selected chromosome, it will be accepted. In this case, the destination point x_3 is picked as the poorest point that is making the chromosome weak. This crossover operation is explained in Figure 6.25(a).

Case II: If the *removed* destination point does not belong to the collection of all destination points in the selected chromosome, it will be randomly inserted into the selected chromosome using the shortest ways to smooth. In this case, the destination point x_1 is picked as the poorest point that is making the chromosome weak. This crossover operation is explained in Figure 6.25(b).

Mutation: The last step of GA is the mutation process. For this, the unlawful offsprings (that violates any given conditions of VRP) produced after crossover are split by the central depot. This results in production of new chromosomes. After mutation, a new population is generated, which is ready for the next iteration of GA.

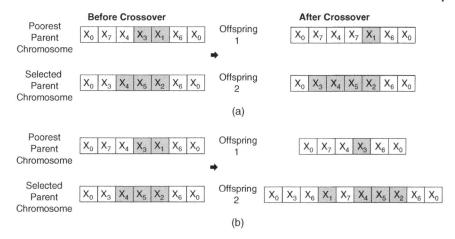

Figure 6.25 Crossover operation for VRP using Genetic Algorithm approach. (a). Case I for Crossover. (b). Case II for Crossover.

6.5 Python Code for Implementing a Simple Genetic Algorithm

Here we discuss one simple approach of GA that starts with a base population of randomly generated strings. The concept of natural selection is adapted, and a certain number of generations are iterated to find out the fittest string. While experimenting with this code, the parameters of the source code can be modified by choosing other optimal values for the global variables. For instance, GENERATIONS is the number of iterations that will be carried out before returning the fittest string.

```
#Python Code#
#This source code is available in github
import random
# Setup optimal string and GA input variables.
    OPTIMAL     = "Hello, World"
    DNA_SIZE    = len(OPTIMAL)
    POP_SIZE    = 20
    GENERATIONS = 5000
    # Helper functions
    # These are used as support, but aren't direct GA-specific
        functions.
    def weighted_choice(items):
    """
    Chooses a random element from items, where items is a list
    of tuples in the form (item, weight). weight determines
    the probability of choosing its respective item.
```

```
   Note: this function is borrowed from ActiveState Recipes.
   """
   weight_total = sum((item[1] for item in items))
   n = random.uniform(0, weight_total)
   for item, weight in items:
     if n < weight:
       return item
     n = n - weight
   return item

def random_char():
   """
   Return a random character between ASCII 32 and 126 (i.e. spaces,
   symbols,  letters, and digits). All characters returned will be
   nicely printable.
   """
   return chr(int(random.randrange(32, 126, 1)))

def random_population():
   """
   Return a list of POP_SIZE individuals, each randomly
   generated via iterating DNA_SIZE times to generate a string of
   random characters with random_char().
   """
   pop = []
   for i in range(POP_SIZE):
     dna = ""
     for c in range(DNA_SIZE):
       dna += random_char()
     pop.append(dna)
   return pop

# GA functions
# These make up the bulk of the actual GA algorithm.
def fitness(dna):
   """
   For each gene in the DNA, this function calculates the
   difference between it and the character in the same position in the
   OPTIMAL string. These values are summed and then returned.
   """
   fitness = 0
   for c in range(DNA_SIZE):
     fitness += abs(ord(dna[c]) - ord(OPTIMAL[c]))
   return fitness

def mutate(dna):
   """
```

For each gene in the DNA, there is a 1/mutation_chance chance that it will be switched out with a random character. This ensures diversity in the population, and ensures that is difficult to get stuck in local minima.

```
    """
    dna_out = ""
    mutation_chance = 100
    for c in range(DNA_SIZE):
        if int(random.random()*mutation_chance) == 1:
            dna_out += random_char()
        else:
            dna_out += dna[c]
    return dna_out

def crossover(dna1, dna2):
    """
    Slices both dna1 and dna2 into two parts at a random index within
    their length and merges them. Both keep their initial sublist up to
    the crossover index, but their ends are swapped.
    """
    pos = int(random.random()*DNA_SIZE)
    return (dna1[:pos]+dna2[pos:], dna2[:pos]+dna1[pos:])

# Main driver
# Generate a population and simulate GENERATIONS generations.

if __name__ == "__main__":
    # Generate initial population. This will create a list of
    #   POP_SIZE strings,
    # each initialized to a sequence of random characters.
    population = random_population()

    # Simulate all of the generations.
    for generation in range(GENERATIONS):
        if generation%1000==0:
            print("Fittest String After Generation %s : %s" %
                (generation, population[0]))
        weighted_population = []    weighted_population = []

        # Add individuals and their respective fitness levels to the
            weighted
        # population list. This will be used to pull out
            individuals via certain
        # probabilities during the selection phase. Then, reset the
            population list
        # so we can repopulate it after selection.
        for individual in population:
```

```
    fitness_val = fitness(individual)

    # Generate the (individual,fitness) pair, taking in account
      whether or
    # not we will accidently divide by zero.
    if fitness_val == 0:
      pair = (individual, 1.0)
    else:
      pair = (individual, 1.0/fitness_val)

    weighted_population.append(pair)

  population = []

  # Select two random individuals, based on their fitness
    probabilites, cross
  # their genes over at a random point, mutate them, and add them
    back to the
  # population for the next iteration.
  for _ in range(POP_SIZE//2):
    # Selection
    ind1 = weighted_choice(weighted_population)
    ind2 = weighted_choice(weighted_population)

    # Crossover
    ind1, ind2 = crossover(ind1, ind2)

    # Mutate and add back into the population.
    population.append(mutate(ind1))
    population.append(mutate(ind2))

# Display the highest-ranked string after all generations have
  been iterated
# over. This will be the closest string to the OPTIMAL string,
  meaning it
# will have the smallest fitness value. Finally, exit the
  program.
fittest_string = population[0]
minimum_fitness = fitness(population[0])

for individual in population:
  ind_fitness = fitness(individual)
  if ind_fitness <= minimum_fitness:
    fittest_string = individual
    minimum_fitness = ind_fitness

print("Fittest String: %s" % fittest_string)
exit(0)
```

The above Python code is run and tested to generate the fittest string after every 1000 iterations. and the output is generated as given in Figure 6.26.

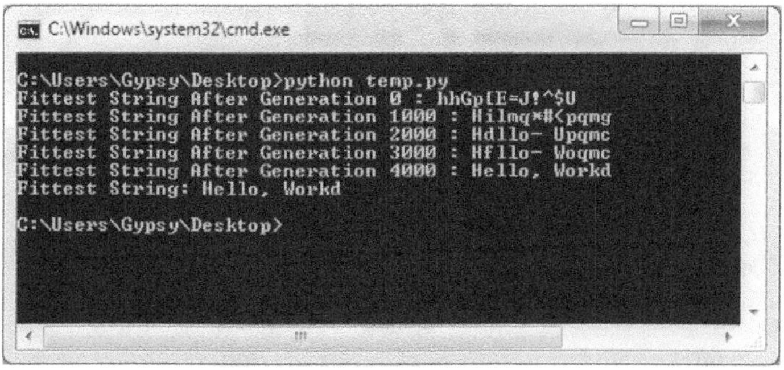

Figure 6.26   Output of the genetic algorithm code.

6.6   Introduction to Swarm Intelligence

A swarm is a dense group of homogenous agents that coordinates among themselves and the environment for an interesting, combined clustered behavior to emerge. The term swarm is mostly used in biological concepts to explain the coordinated behavior of a group of animals, fishes, or birds. For example, a crowd of birds flocking together or a colony of ants marching together are impressive examples of clustered behavior found in biological environment. Figure 6.27 cites few examples of social living beings that adapts to the swarm behavior for collective work.

Swarm behavior has been studied since ages, and it was first simulated on a computer by Craig Reynolds in 1986 with the help of a simulated program *"boids."* Early studies of swarm behavior emphasized on three basic rules:

- Follow the same direction as one's neighbour
- Maintain closeness with one's neighbour
- Avoid collisions with one's neighbour

"Boids"-simulated program followed the above three basic rules to evolve interesting behavioral effects. However, many subsequent and current models use variations of these three rules to develop stimulating behavioral outcomes. Each study of swarm behavior requires stimulation of mathematical model for a deeper understanding of the behavior model.

Many complex problems may not achieve an optimal solution. This requires a compromise between suboptimal solutions that can be achievable in a stipulated time. Swarm intelligence (SI), which is relatively a new integral branch of artificial intelligence, targets to solve such complex problems that require suboptimal solutions. The theory of SI is based on the concepts of biological system in which animals use strategies to move and work collectively for an easy survival.

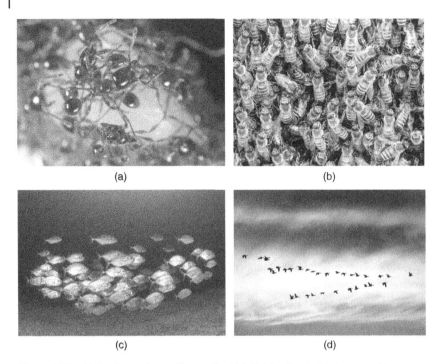

(a)

(b)

(c)

(d)

Figure 6.27 (a) A colony of ants. Source: Backiris/Adobe Stock. (b) A swam of honey bees. Source: garten-gg/Pixabay. (c) A school of fish. Source: Milos Prelevic/Unsplash. (d) A flock of birds. Source: Ethan/Adobe Stock.

This characteristic is found in many insects, animals, and birds such as, ants, bats, glow-worms, bees, monkeys, and lions. These agents (ants, bees, etc.) have limited unsophisticated individual capabilities, but the task gets simple and easy when they interact and cooperate together.

The social collaborations among the swarm agents can be of two types – direct or indirect. In case of direct interactions, agents interact with each other through chemical, audio, or visual contacts. For example, the waggle dance of honey bees that creates a loud buzzing sound for communication among each other while searching for food. On the other hand, if interactions among swarm agents are indirect, it is known as stigmergy. Indirect communications occur through the environment in which one individual agent may create a change in the environment, and the rest of the agents adapt to such changes for an easy problem solving or survival strategy. For example, termites coordinate among themselves through the process of stigmergy to build complex nests for themselves. To do so, a termite initially creates a small mud ball from its environment and then deposits pheromones on the mud-ball.

Figure 6.28 Nest built by termites. Source: Walter_D/Adobe Stock.

The pheromone produced by a termite acts as a scent that signals nesting to the other termites. The other termites, in turn, get attracted to the smell of pheromones, and in turn deposit their own mud-balls to create a bigger nest. The larger the mudded nest becomes, the more attractive it looks, and sometimes it leads to the construction of interesting shapes such as tunnels, arches, and pillars (Figure 6.28).

6.7 Few Important Aspects of Swarm Intelligence

Let us now examine some common aspects of swarm intelligence (Figure 6.29), which are adapted from the common swarm behavioral features of biological systems. These aspects are based on common behavioral characteristics of many

Figure 6.29 Few aspects of swarm intelligence.

animals, insects, and birds that are collectively managed for a stimulating task to reach completion.

6.7.1 Collective Sorting

Reorganization of resources is mainly found to be performed by ants and termites in which the agents move and collect resources or items from their environment, and then spatially sorting these items according to similar clusters. Both ants and termites are eusocial insects and perform various complex tasks together by efficient coordination. One such task is picking up of items such as corpses or broods, and keeping it in a place of similar items for store. Eusocial insects exhibit this common characteristic of picking up of items that are dissimilar to other items placed nearby and release it when it encounters items that are similar.

This common behavior of eusocial insects has led to the development of several proficient applications. One such application is partitioning of the nodes of a graph into similar clusters. Partitioning occurs with the help of virtual ants, which move randomly in a two-dimensional space. Once a virtual ant finds a node that is not much connected to those around it, it picks up the node and then starts walking until it finds an area similar to the node that it is carrying. The ant then drops the node to make a stronger connection of similar cluster. This ultimately results in nodes of a graph being separated into regions of good local connectivity.

6.7.2 Foraging Behavior

Foraging is the task of searching of food resources by animals and insects. The foraging pattern, however, differs among each biological species. For instance, honey bees select foraging targets by swarm intelligence. All honey bees target a nectar source not based on the distance factor but rather the quality of the nectar. For foraging of nectars, the bees divide the task among themselves. Some take the charge of being "forager bees" by collecting the nectar from the environment to be stored to the hive. Some bees, on the other hand, take the charge of being "receiver bees" for transporting the nectar load from the "forager bees" to the storage area of the hive. The two types of coworkers involved in this foraging task need to coordinate intelligently for completion of the task of nectar collection, and this is a perfect instance of swarm intelligence.

The quality of the food source can be assessed by the honey bees by considering a simple mathematical equation as shown below:

$$\text{food\_quality}_{\text{source}} = \frac{en_{\text{val}} - en_{\text{cost}}}{en_{\text{cost}}}$$

In the above equation, the variable en_{val} (measured in Joules) represents the energetic value of the collected nectar, and the variable en_{cost} (measured in Joules) represents the energetic costs of the foraging trip. The number of dancing rounds needed to be performed during this foraging trip is based on this quality value of the food source.

6.7.3 Stigmergy

Stigmergy is the mechanism adapted by agents or individuals to indirectly interact among themselves via the environment to achieve a particular task. The term "stigmergy" was originated in the year 1959 by a French biologist, Grasse, and was gradually adapted by the biological swarm intelligence researchers. The principle adapted by the agents in stigmergy is very simple. An agent usually leaves some traces in the environment by carrying out an action that stimulates the other agents to repeat similar action for completing the task.

Stigmergy is experienced in real-life mainly by social insects such as bees, ants, and termites. For instance, when ants move in colonies in search of food, they leave behind traces of pheromones on their way back once the food source is found. Initially, the ants move in random directions and lead to different paths of different distances between nest and food source. However, once the shorter path is realized, more of pheromones are dropped on the shortest route, allowing the rest of the ants to follow the shortest path having stronger pheromones. This example indicates that few tasks do not require explicit planning to be completed but rather are dependent more on the state of medium. The medium is hence one of the most important components of the process of stigmergy.

In general, the stigmergic algorithms use the information provided by the medium, and the behavior of the agents are accordingly managed. These non-intelligent agents use very simple algorithms to exhibit collective intelligence. The actions performed for completion of the task are repetitive, which enriches the medium with information to allow collective behavior to complete the task efficiently.

The concept of stigmergy has been adapted by swarm robots. One such instance is burying RFID (Radio Frequency Identification) tags under the floor in the form of grids, which act as stigmergic medium. The robots are installed with RFID readers to access the information of the stigmergic medium. By doing so, various interesting tasks can be completed by multiple robots. One such task is building and storing stigmergic maps with the help of multiple robot cooperation. Stigmergic maps are navigation maps that are stored in the environment through the stigmergic medium.

6.7.4 Division of Labor

Some tasks can be performed well by proper division of labor among individuals. For accomplishing the task, the agents are divided into specialized workers and general workers. Specialized workers are given special tasks, which will not be possible for the general workers to accomplish. A good example of division of labour is exhibited by ants that form colonies to divide the work among themselves. Ant colonies have to undergo several different tasks such as foraging of resources, maintaining nest, brood feeding, and defending the colony. Usually, the forager ants perform the task of searching of food, while the nurse ants perform the task of feeding and tending the brood. In this way, the entire colony of ants is divided to perform certain tasks to maintain equilibrium of work in the environment.

A similar strategy of division of labor is encountered in "job shop" problem. In this problem, the task is to complete a given number of jobs by a fixed number of machines, considering time as one of the factor for on-time completion. Algorithms for "job shop" problem allow each machine to bid for jobs by considering its internal threshold value. If a machine has a low threshold value, it is more likely to bid for a job compared to a busy machine having higher threshold value. The algorithm is set in such a way to maintain a balance for completion of the number of jobs among machines by keeping a check on the work load of each machine. However, there is no central controller to decide which machine can perform a particular job. It is solely managed by each machine itself by proper bidding system.

6.7.5 Collective Transport

Group prey retrieval or collective transport is another collective behavior found among biological species. A common example of collective transport is found in ants, which carry out the task in four main phases:

a. Search for locating a large piece of food item;
b. Recruit ample number of ants for transportation of food item
c. Organize the transportation with proper coordination so as to move in the right direction
d. Start the movement for transferring the food item from the source to the nest where ants live.

While carrying out this four-phased process, the decision on the number of ants required carrying out the task is dependent on the item's weight, which indicates that the ants' group size is determined from the item's characteristics. Recruitment of ants ceases as soon as the group of ants already allotted for the task can manage transporting the prey toward the right direction.

Collective transport has been applied since many years in case of multirobotic systems. For carrying out the task of transportation of objects, usually three different strategies are used by robots – pulling, pushing, and caging.

- **Pushing:** This task was initially experimented for robots by using a bottom-up approach to design the controller of a robot. Various issues were addressed to solve the pushing problem, such as motion coordination, shape of the object being pushed, and stagnation. One of the most common problems faced while pushing an object by robots toward the destination is the collision problem. In such cases, collision needs to be detected, and accordingly necessary actions are needed to be taken for smooth movement. If the relative angle between a robot and the object crosses a certain threshold (computed using odometry and omni-directional camera), the robot again aligns itself for a suitable position for the correct angle of movement.

- **Pulling:** This task involves physical mechanisms to firstly connect a number of robots to the object. The robots then pull the object toward the destination using appropriate amount of strength. A common robot built using this technology is the *S-bot*. *S-bots* are simple robots equipped with a number of sensors and motors that allow these robots to carry out collective tasks of movement of objects.

- **Caging:** It is a special case of pushing strategy in which several robots accumulate together in an organized matter to cage or trap the object within the robot formation. The complexity of this process depends on the characteristic features of the object and the number of robots available for the task.

6.7.6 Self-Organization

Self-organization (SO) can be defined as "*a process in which patterns at the global level of a system emerge solely from numerous interactions among the lower level components of the system.*" SO is based on four basic rules: positive feedback, negative feedback, randomness, and multiple interactions.

- **Positive feedback (amplification):** Positive feedback in self-organizing system results in recurrent influence, which amplifies the initial change. A simple example of positive feedback loop is the birth rate that increases a given population for a species, and yet more births lead to a greater population, as illustrated in Figure 6.30.

  It is clear from the above example that when a positive feedback loop takes place in nature, the product of a reaction causes an increase in that reaction.

Figure 6.30 The positive feedback loop for birth rate of a population.

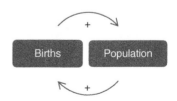

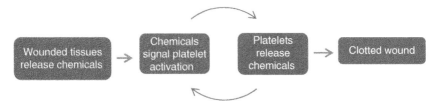

Figure 6.31 The positive feedback loop for clotting of wounded tissues.

In simple sense, a reaction **P** produces more of **Q**, which in turn produces more of **P**.

Another example of positive feedback is the clotting of blood, as shown in Figure 6.31. When tissues get injured, chemical signals gets released. These chemical signals activate platelets in the blood. The activated platelets, in turn, release more chemicals that activate more platelets. This rapid cascading process ultimately helps the wound to get clot.

- **Negative feedback:** Negative feedback results in reaction that is opposite to the initial action. It is a source of stability and creates a force against rapid dramatic change. For instance, the continuous growth of population of a certain species is controlled and stabilized by negative feedback by the number of death rates that occur for the same set of population (Figure 6.32).

  Homeostasis is another example of negative feedback in biological systems. Homeostasis is the state of control of the internal physical and chemical conditions of an organism required for its survival. For instance, the body temperature of an organism should be maintained near to 37 °C. However, if the body temperature of an organism exceeds 37 °C, the homeostasis process creates negative feedback by reducing the body temperature. This is done by reducing metabolic heat generation and increasing heat loss from the body (more blood supply to the skin and more sweating).

- **Randomness:** Self-organization is considered as a spontaneous process, as it does not require any control by an external force. It is rather triggered by random fluctuations where the local reaction is augmented by a positive feedback mechanism. The main advantage of randomness is that it enables continuous

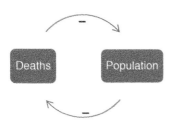

Figure 6.32 The negative feedback loop for death rate of a population.

exploration of several alternatives from which the best solution can be considered.

- **Multiple interactions:** In a self-organizing system, an organization is found to carry out multiple interactions among their components. Internal interactions among animal groups comprise of information transfers between individuals. Usually, information flows within groups via two distinct pathways – signals and cues. Signals are stimuli designed by natural selection to transfer information, whereas cues are stimuli that transfer information only incidentally. An example of stimuli is the chemicals deposited by ants while returning from a desirable food source to spread information to its group regarding the location of rich food sources. An example of cue, on the other hand, is the rutted trail made by deer walking through the woods, which is simply caused by animals walking along the same path.

6.8 Swarm Intelligence Techniques

Swarm intelligent (SI) techniques are heuristic search processes that can be applied in numerous domains such as fuzzy system, biomedicine, signal processing, image processing, data analysis, power systems, etc. In the last two decades, several SI techniques and their variations have been developed. In this section two of the most popular SI techniques – ACO and PSO – have been discussed that have been tested and applied in many standard applications.

6.8.1 Ant Colony Optimization

Ant colony optimization (ACO) is a population-based metaheuristic mainly used to find an approximate solution to a given challenging optimization problem. ACO uses a set of software agents called *artificial ants,* which help find good solutions to a given optimization problem. By applying ACO, an optimization problem is treated as finding the best path for a weighted graph. The process of movement of the artificial ants on the graph creates a pheromone model that consists of a set of parameters (nodes and/or edges) whose values are accordingly updated at runtime by the artificial ants.

6.8.1.1 How ACO Technique Works?

In biological systems, ants exhibit an interesting foraging behavior. At first, a worker ant comes out of its nest and randomly searches for food (Figure 6.33 (scene a)). Once it finds and reaches near a food source, it carries a little portion of the food as much as it is possible within its capacity. While returning back to its nest, chemical pheromone trail is deposited on the ground by the ant (Figure 6.33

(scene b)). An ant decides the quantity of pheromone to be deposited based on the quality and quantity of food discovered. The pheromone smell indicates the other worker ants about the presence of food in a nearby area. Thus, the main interesting fact about this entire process of pheromone deposition is that these pheromone trails help create an indirect communication between all the nearby ants, which help in finding the shortest path between the food source and the nest (Figure 6.33 (scene c)).

This process of foraging is repeated until the food source is exhausted. In such a case, the worker ants will stop marking with pheromones while returning on their way back. In this way eventually the previous pheromones will evaporate, and the path will no longer be used for food foraging. This is a case of negative feedback that stabilizes as well as counterbalances the ant network.

Another interesting case that has been studied in ant foraging is when worker ants meet a situation in which a path to a food source is branched. If both the paths are of the same length, the worker ants will eventually end up choosing only one path out of the two. Though initially each of the two paths may be equally randomly tested by the ants, the ants that follow a path more will leave more pheromones trails, which will eventually lead the other ants to follow the same path. This is again an instance of positive feedback, which helps ants in making a decision between two equally good paths of the same length. However, the scenario is not the same if the paths are of varying length. In such a case, the shortest path is found by the ants and accordingly used for food foraging.

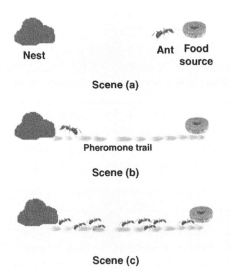

Figure 6.33 Ant foraging leaving pheromones trails.

Nest **Ant** **Food source**

Scene (a)

Pheromone trail

Scene (b)

Scene (c)

The shortest path is found easily, as few ants will reach the destination back faster, leaving stronger pheromone concentrations whereas the other ants will take more time to reach back the nest, and as a result the pheromone trail smell will evaporate faster than the shorter path. At each diverse path, ants will take a decision of choosing the shorter path by the smell of stronger pheromone concentrations, which will help ants to explore the shortest path between food source and nest in an optimized way. This principle of shortest path finding by ants has been adapted in many algorithms to solve the optimization problem.

6.8.1.2 Applying ACO to Optimization Problems
ACO was introduced in 1996 via an algorithm called "Ant System" (AS). ACO algorithms mirror aspects of the foraging behavior of ants quite realistically. To build a solution to an optimization problem, an artificial ant leaves some artificial pheromones along its path for helping the other artificial ants to follow the same path. This approach can be applied to bring a solution to many applications such as the travelling salesman problem, vehicle routing problem, quadratic assignment problem, job shop scheduling problem, and agent-based dynamic scheduling.

A clear example of applying this ACO technique is *reaching a city C2 by starting from city C1*. In this case, C1 is the start node, and C2 is the end node. The artificial ants are envisaged to have travelled across the network from start node C1 to end node C2 via many distinct nodes. Later when the other ants reach a junction, it intelligently choses an arc based on the stronger smell detected by the concentration level of pheromones. The stronger or better arcs will consist of remnants of trails created by prior ants that will, in turn, provide better solutions to path finding. Arcs with low pheromone levels indicate paths will lesser good solutions. As more and more artificial ants arrives at node C2, these ants also drop pheromones on the path and indirectly bring better solutions to path finding. If any other artificial ant tries following the previous ants, it tries to sense the updated better pheromone trail and accordingly follows the right shorter path.

The entire process of ACO technique is split into three main phases:

```
Initialization;
while not terminated do
    Construct solution using artificial ants;
    Local search (optional);
    Update pheromones;
End
```

- **Phase 1 – Solution construction:** The set of m artificial ants makes a random walk on the construction graph G(V, E).

- **Phase 2 – Local search:** For every individual problem, a local search can improve the constructed solution. However, it is an optional step, as it is highly variable according to problems.
- **Phase 3 – Pheromones update:** Values of pheromone level increase for promising solutions and decreases for undesired solutions due to pheromone evaporation.

6.8.1.3 Using ACO in Travelling Salesman Problem

In this section, the well-known travelling salesman problem (TSP) is discussed, which can be solved using the concept of ACO. TSP has also been discussed in this chapter before for solving the problem using GAs. TSP considers finding the shortest route between two nodes (start node and end node) of a complete weighted graph G having n nodes and $n(n-1)$ edges, so that all other nodes are visited exactly once while travelling. Few practical applications of TSP include finding the shortest costumer servicing route, planning bus service routes, regular distribution of goods, etc. TSP is a NP-hard problem, and hence no exact algorithm can solve it in polynomial time. Several methods have been discussed to solve TSP, such as branch and bound method, cutting plane method, explicit enumeration, implicit enumeration, and dynamic programming.

ACO is a metaheuristic method initially used in the early 1990s to solve the TSP problem. The basic idea of ACO is to simulate the real behavior of ants in nature. Figure 6.34 illustrates a list of 14 cities (circled green in color), and each city is connected to all the other cities to make a complete graph (light grey edges or lines). The TSP problem finds the shortest route to be travelled that covers all the cities (highlighted with black lines or edges in color).

The TSP can be defined as the problem of finding a special Hamiltonian cycle with the lowest cost in a complete weighted graph. Let $G = (N, E, W)$ be a complete weighted graph, where N is the set of nodes, E is the set of edges, and W is the set of costs or weights attached to each edge. Here, W is the cost matrix such that

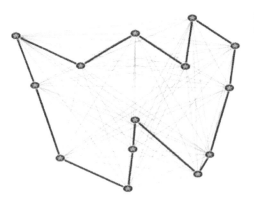

Figure 6.34 Travelling all the cities through the shortest path.

$W = (w_{ij})_{MxN}$. Therefore,

$$N = \{N_1, N_2, N_3, \ldots, N_n\} \text{ where } n \geq 3$$

$$E = \{e_{ij} \mid N_i, N_j \in N\}$$

$$W = \{w_{ij} \mid w_{ij} \geq 0 \text{ and } w_{ii} = 0 \, \forall \, i, \quad j \in \{1, 2, 3, \ldots, n\}\}$$

Now, considering an *n*-city TSP, the artificial ants are scattered randomly in these *n* cities. Each artificial ant will move forward based on the pheromone trail remained on the paths. One point to note is that, since the artificial ants have memory, the visited cities can be stored so as to not visit again. Moreover, as the artificial ants are not completely blind, they can estimate the distance between two cities. For doing so, the probability of a city *j* being selected by ant *k* after visiting city *i* can be equated as follows:

$$p_{ij}^k = \begin{cases} \dfrac{\varphi_{ij}^\alpha + \lambda_{ij}^\beta}{\sum_{s \, \in \, \text{unvisited}_k} \left(\varphi_{Nij}^\alpha + \omega_{Nij}^\beta\right)} & j \in \text{unvisited}_k \\ 0 & \text{otherwise} \end{cases} \tag{6.1}$$

where φ_{ij} is the intensity of pheromone trail between cities *i* and *j*, α is the parameter to regulate the influence of φ_{ij}. Again, λ_{ij} is the visibility of city *j* from city *i*, which is set as $1/d_{ij}$ (d_{ij} is the distance between city *i* and *j*), β is the parameter to regulate the influence of λ_{ij}, and unvisited$_k$ is the set of cities that have not been visited yet.

Initially a couple of *x* artificial ants are randomly placed in *n* cities. Each artificial ant then decides the next city to visit based on the probability p_{ij}^k, calculated as shown in Eq. (6.2). With "*n*" number of iterations, each ant makes a complete tour of all cities. While doing so, each ant leaves pheromones on its path. The pheromone trail levels are updated for a path that can be quantized as Q/L_k, where Q is a constant factor, and L_k is the length of the tour. However, with time, the pheromones get evaporated and the smell reduces. The updating rule for φ_{ij} is then calculated as given below:

$$\varphi_{ij}(c+1) = \rho \cdot \varphi_{ij}(c) + \Delta\varphi_{ij} \tag{6.2}$$

$$\Delta\varphi_{ij} = \sum_{k=1}^{x} \varphi_{ij}^k \tag{6.3}$$

$$\varphi_{ij}^k = \begin{cases} Q/L_k & \text{if ant } k \text{ travels on edge } (i,j) \\ 0 & \text{otherwise} \end{cases} \tag{6.4}$$

Here, *c* is the iteration counter and $\rho \in [0, 1]$ is the parameter to regulate the reduction of φ_{ij}. $\Delta\varphi_{ij}$ is the total increase of trail level on edge (*i,j*) and φ_{ij}^k is the increase of trail level on edge (*i,j*) caused by ant *k*.

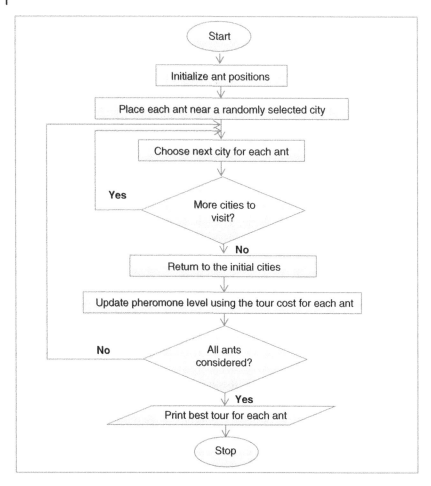

Figure 6.35 Flowchart of TSP using ACO.

A simple flowchart for the TSP using ACO is given in Figure 6.35. The pseudocode of the TSP algorithm is explained in Algorithm 6.2. In general, the "n" cities to be covered are divided into "m" groups. Each group visits a city only once. The two factors taken into consideration while computing the probability that a city j will be selected by an ant k after visiting city i are:

- The quantity of pheromone trails distributed on the path
- The visibility of city j from city i

The probability of a city j being selected by ant k after visiting city i is equated based on Eq. (6.1). Here, in the equation, unvisited$_k$ is the set of cities that are in the classes not yet visited by ant k. The updating rule for φ_{ij} per iteration is followed as given in Eqs. (6.2)–(6.4).

Algorithm 6.2   Pseudocode of ACO for TSP

```
begin
 Initialize ant positions
     For c=1 to iteration number do
     For k=1 to x do
           Repeat until ant k has completed a tour
               Select the city j to be visited next
               With probability p_ij given by Eq. (6.1)
                   Calculate L_k
               Update the trail levels according to
               Eqs. (6.3)-(6.5).
   end
```

The ACO algorithm uses a stopping criterion based on one or more of the following conditions:

- A predefined maximum number of iterations has been executed
- a specific level of solution quality has been reached
- the best solution has not changed over a certain number of iterations

It is interesting to realize how the pheromone levels play a major role in path finding. The interesting property of pheromone evaporation leads to stronger smell of pheromones on shorter edges and lighter smell of pheromones on longer edges. Based on these facts, many optimization problems have been easily solved by controlling the behavior of the virtual ants.

6.8.1.4   Python Code for Implementing ACO in TSP

The Python code given below can be used for implementing ACO for solving the travelling salesman problem. The following arguments are considered to find the shortest path after a certain number of iterations:

- **distances (2D numpy.array):** Square matrix of distances. Diagonal is assumed to be np.inf.
- **n_ants (int):** Number of ants running per iteration
- **n_best (int):** Number of best ants who deposit pheromone
- **n_iterations (int):** Number of iterations
- **decay (float):** Rate with which pheromone decays. The pheromone value is multiplied by decay, so 0.95 will lead to decay, 0.5 to much faster decay.
- **alpha (int or float):** exponent on pheromone, higher alpha gives pheromone more weight. Default = 1
- **beta (int or float):** exponent on distance, higher beta gives distance more weight. Default = 1

```python
#Python Code#
#This source code is available in github
import numpy as np
from numpy.random import choice as np_choice
class AntColony(object):
    def __init__(self, distances, n_ants, n_best, n_iterations,
                 decay, alpha=1, beta=1):
        self.distances  = distances
        self.pheromone = np.ones(self.distances.shape) /
                         len(distances)
        self.all_inds = range(len(distances))
        self.n_ants = n_ants
        self.n_best = n_best
        self.n_iterations = n_iterations
        self.decay = decay
        self.alpha = alpha
        self.beta = beta
    def run(self):
        shortest_path = None
        all_time_shortest_path = ("placeholder", np.inf)
        for i in range(self.n_iterations):
            all_paths = self.gen_all_paths()
            self.spread_pheronome(all_paths, self.n_best,
                           shortest_path=shortest_path)
            shortest_path = min(all_paths, key=lambda x: x[1])
if i % 10 == 0:
                    print ("Shortest Path - ", shortest_path)
            if shortest_path[1] < all_time_shortest_path[1]:
                all_time_shortest_path = shortest_path
            self.pheromone * self.decay
        return all_time_shortest_path
    def spread_pheronome(self, all_paths, n_best, shortest_path):
        sorted_paths = sorted(all_paths, key=lambda x: x[1])
        for path, dist in sorted_paths[:n_best]:
            for move in path:
                self.pheromone[move] += 1.0 / self.distances[move]
    def gen_path_dist(self, path):
        total_dist = 0
        for ele in path:
            total_dist += self.distances[ele]
        return total_dist
    def gen_all_paths(self):
        all_paths = []
        for i in range(self.n_ants):
            path = self.gen_path(0)
            all_paths.append((path, self.gen_path_dist(path)))
        return all_paths
    def gen_path(self, start):
        path = []
        visited = set()
        visited.add(start)
```

```
        prev = start
        for i in range(len(self.distances) - 1):
            move = self.pick_move(self.pheromone[prev],
                    self.distances[prev], visited)
            path.append((prev, move))
            prev = move
            visited.add(move)
        path.append((prev, start)) # going back to where we started
        return path
    def pick_move(self, pheromone, dist, visited):
        pheromone = np.copy(pheromone)
        pheromone[list(visited)] = 0
        row = pheromone ** self.alpha * (( 1.0 / dist) **
                self.beta)
        norm_row = row / row.sum()
        move = np_choice(self.all_inds, 1, p=norm_row)[0]
        return move
distances = np.array([[np.inf, 2, 2, 5, 7],
                [2, np.inf, 4, 8, 2],
                [2, 4, np.inf, 1, 3],
                [5, 8, 1, np.inf, 2],
                [7, 2, 3, 2, np.inf]])
ant_colony = AntColony(distances, 1, 1, 100, 0.95, alpha=1, beta=1)
shortest_path = ant_colony.run()
print()
print ("Final Shortest Path: {}".format(shortest_path))
```

The output of the above Python code is given in Figure 6.36.

6.8.2 Particle Swarm Optimization

Particle swarm optimization (PSO) is a nature-inspired population-based stochastic optimization technique developed by Kennedy and Eberhart in 1995.

```
Shortest Path -   ([(0, 2), (2, 3), (3, 4), (4, 1), (1, 0)], 9.0)
Shortest Path -   ([(0, 2), (2, 3), (3, 4), (4, 1), (1, 0)], 9.0)
Shortest Path -   ([(0, 2), (2, 3), (3, 4), (4, 1), (1, 0)], 9.0)
Shortest Path -   ([(0, 2), (2, 3), (3, 4), (4, 1), (1, 0)], 9.0)
Shortest Path -   ([(0, 1), (1, 4), (4, 2), (2, 3), (3, 0)], 13.0)
Shortest Path -   ([(0, 2), (2, 3), (3, 4), (4, 1), (1, 0)], 9.0)
Shortest Path -   ([(0, 2), (2, 3), (3, 4), (4, 1), (1, 0)], 9.0)
Shortest Path -   ([(0, 2), (2, 3), (3, 4), (4, 1), (1, 0)], 9.0)
Shortest Path -   ([(0, 1), (1, 4), (4, 2), (2, 3), (3, 0)], 13.0)
Shortest Path -   ([(0, 1), (1, 4), (4, 2), (2, 3), (3, 0)], 13.0)

Final Shortest Path: ([(0, 2), (2, 3), (3, 4), (4, 1), (1, 0)], 9.0)
```

Figure 6.36 Output of ant colony optimization.

PSO algorithms mimic the social behavior of fish schooling and bird flocking. The flocking behavior is commonly exhibited by flock of birds while foraging for food. This behavior is also commonly experienced by herd of animals, swarm of insects, or school of fishes. For instance, a flock of birds circle around an area when they discover a source of food. The birds closest to the food source chirp the loudest, so that the rest of the birds can proceed more toward that direction. In this way, the cluster gets tightened and more compact, until the food is shared and swallowed by all. The PSO approach can be applied to bring a solution to many applications such as the scheduling problem, sequential ordering problem, vehicle routing problem, combinatorial optimization problem, power system optimization problem, fuzzy neural networks, and signature verification.

6.8.2.1   How PSO Technique Works?

The PSO technique works on the same principle of foraging behavior of biological species. PSO initially considers a randomly distributed set of particles that move around the search space toward its own best experienced position. The simulated algorithm proceeds by advancing the position of each particle based on its velocity. The objective function is sampled after each position update. In due course of time, the particles cluster together around one or more optima with the help of a combination of exploration of good positions in the search space.

The four important components of PSO are the particle position vector p, the particle velocity vector v, the best solution of a particle p_i^{best}, and the best global solution p_{gBest}. Figure 6.37 illustrates how these components work in the general PSO algorithm. A brief description of these four components is given below:

- **Particle position vector p:** This vector stores the current location of each particle in the search domain. These values help in calculating the value of the objective function to solve the optimization problem.
- **Particle velocity vector v:** This vector determines the magnitude and direction of change in the position of each particle in the next iteration. This value of this vector becomes the deciding factor for the movement of particles in a specific direction around the search space.
- **Best solution of a particle p_i^{best}:** This value is the position of a particular particle i that has formed the lowest value of the objective function (i.e., the best solution with the lowest error).
- **Best global solution p_{gBest}:** This value determines the best single position found by all particles of the swarm (i.e., the best solution for all the swarm members.

An ordered triplet (p_i, v_i, p_i^{best}) corresponds to each particle in which p_i represents the current position of the particle, v_i represents the current speed of the particle, p_i^{best} is the best location of particle i. The group of particles move around the search space based on the influence of their own best past location as well as

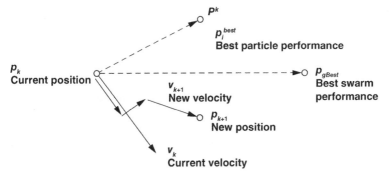

Figure 6.37 Velocity and position updates of particle in the PSO algorithm.

the best past location of the whole swarm of particles. In each iteration, a particle's velocity gets updated using the formula:

$$v_i(t+1) = v_i(t) + \left(c_1 x\ rand(\ ) \times \left(p_i^{best} - p_i(t)\right)\right)$$
$$+ (c_2 x\ rand(\ ) \times (p_{gBest} - p_i(t))) \tag{6.5}$$

Here,

- $v_i(t+1)$ is the new velocity of the ith particle
- c_1 and c_2 are positive constants, and represent the weighting coefficients for the personal best and global best positions, respectively
- $p_i(t)$ is the ith particle's position at time t
- p_i^{best} is the ith particle's best known position
- p_{gBest} is the best position known to the swarm
- $rand()$ is a function to generate a uniformly random variable between 0 and 1.

The values of c_1 and c_2 play a major role in deciding the search ability of the PSO approach. High values of c_1 and c_2 generate new positions that are in relatively distant regions of the search space. This makes the particles diverge to different directions and ultimately lead to a better global exploration. When the values of c_1 and c_2 are small, there is a lesser movement of particles that ultimately leads to a more refined local search. Also, when $c_1 > c_2$, the search behavior will be more prone to produce results based on particles' historically best experiences. Again, when $c_1 < c_2$, the search behavior will be more prone to produce results based on the swarm's globally best experience. A particle's position is accordingly updated using the formula:

$$p_i(t+1) = p_i(t) + v_i(t) \tag{6.6}$$

6.8.2.2 Applying PSO to Optimization Problems

The basic PSO algorithm considers three global variables:

- Target value or condition
- Global best (*gBest*) value indicating which particle's data is currently the closest to the target
- Stopping value indicating when the algorithm should stop if the target is not found

Also, the other main parameters to be considered in the PSO technique are the total number of particles, the total number of iterations, cognition and social behavior coefficients (c_1 and c_2), and inertia weight and/or constriction factor. In some cases, the total number of iterations is replaced with some termination criterion or a desired precision.

Algorithm 6.3   Pseudocode of the PSO Algorithm

```
For each particle
        {
                Initialize particle
        }

        Do until maximum iterations or minimum error criteria
        {
            For each particle
            {
                Calculate Data fitness value
                If the fitness value is better than pBest
                {
                        Set pBest = current fitness value
                }
                If pBest is better than gBest
                {
                    Set gBest = pBest
                }
        }
        For each particle
        {        Calculate particle Velocity
                Use gBest and Velocity to update particle Data
        }
```

According to the aforementioned Eqs. (6.5) and (6.6), the basic flow of the pseudocode of the PSO algorithm is explained in Algorithm 6.3. Also, the flowchart to demonstrate the PSO technique is given in Figure 6.38. The basic PSO algorithm consists of three main steps:

i. Evaluate fitness of each particle
ii. Update individual and global bests
iii. Update velocity and position of each particle

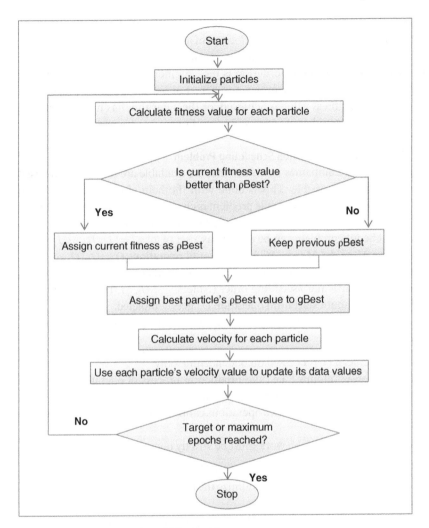

Figure 6.38 Flowchart of the PSO algorithm.

These steps are repeated until some stopping condition is met. The value of velocity is calculated based on how far an individual's data is from the target. The further it is, the larger is the value of velocity.

According to the pseudocode of the PSO algorithm, at the beginning the particles are initialized by randomly assigning each particle to an arbitrarily initial velocity and an arbitrary position in each dimension of the solution space. Next, the desired fitness function to be optimized is evaluated for each particle's position. Next, for each individual particle, update its historically best position based on the current fitness value. Also, update the swarm's globally best particle that has the swarm's best fitness value. The velocities of all particles are also equated using Eq. (6.5). Each particle is moved to its new position using Eq. (6.6). All these steps are repeated until a stopping criterion is met. As mentioned earlier, the criteria to stop could be that the maximum number of allowed iterations is reached; a sufficiently good fitness value is achieved; or the algorithm has not improved its performance for a number of consecutive iterations.

6.8.2.3 Using PSO in Job-Shop Scheduling Problem

In manufacturing companies machines that are available are required to be used as resourcefully as possible. This is done with the help of job shop scheduling problem (JSSP). In JSSP, a schedule problem is characterized as jobs sequence and allocation on machines during a time period so that the required fitness function is met. A schedule problem can be defined as a set of jobs $J = \{J_1, J_2, ..., J_n\}$, a set of machines $M = \{M_1, M_2, ..., M_m\}$, and a set of operations $O = \{O_1, O_2, ... , O_t\}$. A job J involves a sequence of t operations $O_{1t}, O_{2t}, ..., O_{it}, ... O_{kt}$, which must be processed in a particular ascending order (Note: $O_{it} < O_{i+1t}$). This indicates that operation O_{i+1t} cannot start until operation O_{it} gets completed.

For JSSP, the other following rules to be followed for processing operations on machines are:

- An operation can be processed on one machine only.
- An operation is "atomic," i.e., the production process of operation cannot be interrupted by an arrival of other operation
- In case of several processes, two operations cannot be processed on one machine simultaneously.
- The processing time of the work must be strictly obeyed.

The main aim of the scheduling problem is to find the best operation or jobs sequence on all machines so as to minimize the processing time and other essential parameters.

The PSO algorithm when applied to job shop scheduling problem is considered as an extended version of PSO algorithm to flow shop scheduling problem. The algorithmic steps for PSO applied to flow shop scheduling are as follows:

i. **Initialize:** Set $k = 0$, $r =$ twice the number of jobs. Also, randomly generate the position and velocity of each particle with respect to each job.
ii. **Apply SPV rule:** Find the permutations of jobs by SPV rule for each particle.
iii. **Machine sequence:** For each job, take different machine sequences as an input from input file for scheduling of jobs.

iv. **Make span evaluation:** Calculate make span for each permutation by using job-based representation (The particle having the least make span becomes the personal best for that iteration.).

v. **Job-based representation:** Construct a schedule according to the sequence of jobs.

vi. **Upgrade counter:** Upgrade the counter to next iteration ($k = k + 1$).

vii. **Upgrade inertia weight:** Upgrade the inertia weight by the formula $w^k = w^{k-1} \times \alpha$, ($\alpha$: decrement factor).

viii. **Update velocity value:** The velocity is updated as given in Eq. (6.5).

ix. **Update position:** The position is updated as given in Eq. (6.6).

x. **Change the sequence of jobs:** This is done based on the updated particle position.

xi. **Check new personal best value:** Find the new personal best and compare with the previous personal best (if value is low, update it as personal best value).

xii. **Find the global best:** The minimum value of personal best among all the personal best gives the global best, and the arrangement of jobs that give the global best will be adopted.

xiii. **Check stopping criteria:** Stop if the number of iterations exceeds the maximum number of iteration or exceeds the maximum CPU time.

PSO has many similarities when compared with evolutionary computation techniques such as GAs. However, unlike GA, the concept of PSO is simple, and does not deal with evolution operators such as crossover and mutation. In PSO, the main object considered is particles that fly through the problem space by following the current optimum particles. To conclude, PSO is easy to implement, as it requires adjustment of only few parameters. This is the reason as to why PSO has been successfully applied in many areas such as fuzzy system control, artificial neural network training, function optimization, and several other areas where GA can also be applied.

6.8.2.4 Python Code for Implementing PSO

The Python code given below can be used for implementing PSO by initializing particle's current position and velocity, and the best position and the best error values. A cost function `func1()` is used to solve the optimization problem. Each time, the current fitness value is evaluated and is compared with the previous best fitness value. If the current fitness value is better than the previous best, the current fitness value is then considered as the previous best. This process continues in each iteration, and accordingly the particle's position is updated based on new velocity updates.

#Python Code#

```
#This source code is available in github
from __future__ import division
import random
import math

#- COST FUNCTION ————————————+

# function we are attempting to optimize (minimize)
def func1(x):
    total=0
    for i in range(len(x)):
        total+=x[i]**2
    return total

#- MAIN ————————————+

class Particle:
    def __init__(self,x0):
        self.position_i=[]          # particle position
        self.velocity_i=[]          # particle velocity
        self.pos_best_i=[]          # best position individual
        self.err_best_i=-1          # best error individual
        self.err_i=-1               # error individual

        for i in range(0,num_dimensions):
            self.velocity_i.append(random.uniform(-1,1))
            self.position_i.append(x0[i])

    # evaluate current fitness
    def evaluate(self,costFunc):
        self.err_i=costFunc(self.position_i)

        # check to see if the current position is an
          individual best
        if self.err_i<self.err_best_i or self.err_best_i==-1:
            self.pos_best_i=self.position_i.copy()
            self.err_best_i=self.err_i

    # update new particle velocity
    def update_velocity(self,pos_best_g):
        w=0.5       # constant inertia weight (how much to weigh
                      the previous velocity)
        c1=1        # cognative constant
        c2=2        # social constant

        for i in range(0,num_dimensions):
            r1=random.random()
            r2=random.random()
```

```
            vel_cognitive=c1*r1*(self.pos_best_i[i]-self.
                            position_i[i])
            vel_social=c2*r2*(pos_best_g[i]-self.position_i[i])
            self.velocity_i[i]=w*self.velocity_i[i]+vel_cognitive+
                            vel_social

    # update the particle position based on new velocity updates
    def update_position(self,bounds):
        for i in range(0,num_dimensions):
            self.position_i[i]=self.position_i[i]+self.
                            velocity_i[i]

            # adjust maximum position if necessary
            if self.position_i[i]>bounds[i][1]:
                self.position_i[i]=bounds[i][1]

            # adjust minimum position if neseccary
            if self.position_i[i]<bounds[i][0]:
                self.position_i[i]=bounds[i][0]

class PSO():
    def __init__(self, costFunc, x0, bounds, num_particles,
                maxiter, verbose=False):
        global num_dimensions

        num_dimensions=len(x0)
        err_best_g=-1                   # best error for group
        pos_best_g=[]                   # best position for group

        # establish the swarm
        swarm=[]
        for i in range(0,num_particles):
            swarm.append(Particle(x0))

        # begin optimization loop
        i=0
        while i<maxiter:
            if verbose: print(f'iteration : {i+1:>4d}, best
                            solution: {err_best_g:10.6f}')
            # cycle through particles in swarm and evaluate fitness
            for j in range(0,num_particles):
                swarm[j].evaluate(costFunc)

                # determine if current particle is the best
                  (globally)
                if swarm[j].err_i<err_best_g or err_best_g==-1:
                    pos_best_g=list(swarm[j].position_i)
                    err_best_g=float(swarm[j].err_i)

            # cycle through swarm and update velocities and
              position
```

```
            for j in range(0,num_particles):
                swarm[j].update_velocity(pos_best_g)
                swarm[j].update_position(bounds)
            i+=1

        # print final results
        print('\nFINAL SOLUTION:')
        print(f' > {pos_best_g}')
        print(f' > {err_best_g}\n')

if __name__ == "__PSO__":
    main()


#- RUN ───────────────────────────-+
initial=[5,5]                    # initial starting location [x1,x2...]
bounds=[(-10,10),(-10,10)]   # input bounds [(x1_min,x1_max),
                                   (x2_min,x2_max)...]
        PSO(func1, initial, bounds, num_particles=15,
                   maxiter=30, verbose=True)
```

The above Python code is run and tested to generate the best solution for every iteration. The number of iterations considered for the output is 30, which can be altered by changing the parameter value. The snapshot of the output is displayed in Figure 6.39.

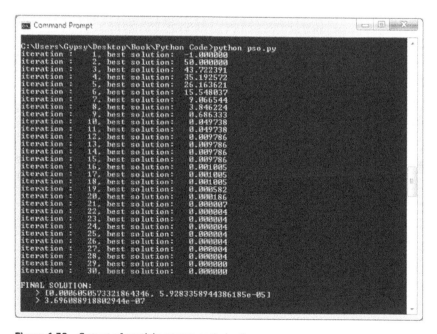

Figure 6.39   Output of particle swarm optimization.

Exercises

A) **Choose the correct answer from among the alternatives given:**

a) Which of the following is not found in Genetic Algorithms?
  i) selection
  ii) mutation
  iii) load balancing
  iv) crossover

b) A collection of genes form a/an _____
  i) chromosome
  ii) population
  iii) offspring
  iv) destination

c) The _____ phase is mainly carried out to maintain diversity in the genetic population
  i) selection
  ii) crossover
  iii) mutation
  iv) fitness calculation

d) In case of _____ mutation, a subset of gene values is chosen, and those values are randomly shuffled.
  i) bit-flip mutation
  ii) scramble
  iii) random resetting
  iv) inverse

e) Which among the following is not considered as an input parameter for the genetic algorithm?
  i) Size of population
  ii) Crossover probability
  iii) Mutation probability
  iv) Selection probability

f) _____ is a simulated program that exhibits swarm behavior.
  i) Ark
  ii) Boids
  iii) Swark
  iv) Crawl

g) _____ is the task of searching of food resources by animals and insects.
  i) Self-organization
  ii) Stigmergy
  iii) Foraging
  iv) Food scheduling

h) The _____ smell indicates the other worker ants about the presence of food in a nearby area.
    i) sweet
    ii) pungent
    iii) sour
    iv) pheromone
i) Homeostasis is another example of _____ feedback in biological systems.
    i) negative
    ii) positive
    iii) amplifying
    iv) neutral
j) Which among the following is not one of the main phases of the ACO technique?
    i) Edge construction
    ii) Solution construction
    iii) Local search
    iv) Pheromone updates
k) Which among the following is not one of the main steps of the particle swarm optimization algorithm?
    i) Evaluate fitness of each particle
    ii) Update individual and global bests
    iii) Evaluate the weight of each particle
    iv) Update velocity and position of each particle
l) The three different collective transport strategies used by swarm robots are:
    i) Pushing, pulling, and caging
    ii) Pushing, pulling, and grasping
    iii) Moving, pulling, and throwing
    iv) Pushing, throwing, and grasping

B) Answer the following questions:
  1) Discuss, in detail, all the five phases of the genetic algorithm.
  2) Explain any two types of:
  3) Crossover operator
  4) Mutation operator
  5) Selection operator
  6) What is the role of fitness function in genetic algorithm? Explain with an example.
  7) For the given two chromosomes, perform the:
     Chromosome 1: 6 5 4 1 3 8 9 7
     Chromosome 2: 3 7 1 9 4 8 2 5
  8) One-point crossover at the middle of the strings

9) Two-point crossover at 2nd and 6th positions
10) Uniform crossover at 2nd, 5th, and 7th positions
11) Partially mapped crossover from 3rd to 6th position
12) Implement a simple GA with fitness proportionate selection, Roulette wheel sampling, population size 100, single-point crossover rate $p_c = 0.7$, and bitwise mutation rate $p_m = 0.01$. Try it on the following fitness function: $f(x)$ = number of ones in x, where x is a chromosome of length 20. Perform 20 runs, and measure the average generation at which the string of all ones is discovered.
13) Define swarm intelligence. How does swarm intelligence work?
14) Explain the following terms related to biological species:
15) Stigmergy
16) Foraging behavior
17) Division of labor
18) Collective transport
19) Collective sorting
20) Self-organization
21) Differentiate between positive feedback and negative feedback in self-organization.
22) Explain any four common aspects of swarm intelligence with a proper example of each aspect.
23) How does ant colony optimization (ACO) technique work? Explain, in detail, the ACO algorithm.
24) Discuss the travelling salesman problem and how it can be solved using the ACO technique.
25) How does particle swarm optimization (PSO) technique work? Explain, in detail, the PSO algorithm.
26) Define the four important components of the PSO technique. How is a particle's velocity calculated and updated in each iteration of the PSO algorithm?
27) Discuss the job shop scheduling problem and how it can be solved using the PSO technique.

7

Rough Set Theory

Rough set theory, like the fuzzy logic theory, is a mathematical approach to deal with imperfect knowledge. The concepts of rough sets were introduced in the field of computer science in the year 1982 by a Polish mathematician and computer scientist, Zdzisław I. Pawlak. Applications of rough sets are varied and can be used in several areas such as machine learning, expert systems, pattern recognition, decision analysis, knowledge discovery from databases, image processing, voice recognition, and many more. Rough sets adapt a nonstatistical approach for data analysis and are used for analyzing and classifying imprecise, ambiguous, or inadequate information and knowledge. The fruitful applications of rough set theory in various domains of problems have rightly demonstrated its practicality and versatility.

Chapter 7 provides an expansive overview of rough set theory, its core principles, and its applicability in real-world scenarios. The chapter underscores the versatility of rough set theory in handling uncertainty and imprecision, making it a valuable tool for data analysis and decision support across various domains. By combining theoretical explanations, measures, and practical applications, the chapter equips readers with a comprehensive understanding of rough set theory and its significance. The fundamental concepts within the Pawlak rough set model, measures of approximation, decision rules, and various application areas where rough set theory proves valuable are also thoroughly covered in this chapter.

7.1   The Pawlak Rough Set Model

The Pawlak rough set model follows a mathematical approach to vagueness, which can be established by finding the boundary region (BR) of a set. If the BR of a set

Principles of Soft Computing Using Python Programming: Learn How to Deploy Soft Computing Models in Real World Applications, First Edition. Gypsy Nandi.
© 2024 The Institute of Electrical and Electronics Engineers, Inc. Published 2024 by John Wiley & Sons, Inc.

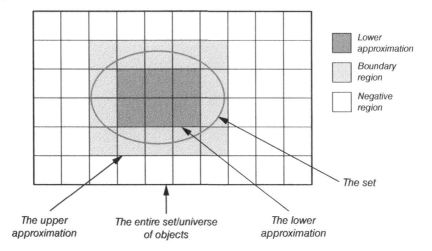

Figure 7.1 Basics of rough set theory.

S is found to be empty, it is called as a crisp set, and it is called as a rough set if the BR of a set S is nonempty. Rough sets are identified by approximations, namely the lower approximation and the upper approximation, as well as the BR (as illustrated in Figure 7.1). To understand the concept of approximations, let us understand few of the following basic terms connected with the rough set.

7.1.1 Basic Terms in Pawlak Rough Set Model

Let S and U be two sets such that $S \subseteq U$, in which U is the Universe set and S is the target S that we wish to represent using a set of attributes A.

(a) **Equivalence Relation**: An equivalence relation is a binary relation that captures the idea of indistinguishability or indiscernibility among objects with respect to certain attributes. In rough set theory, the equivalence relation defines the basis for grouping objects that share the same attribute values or characteristics, regardless of the class they belong to.
An equivalence relation should satisfy three properties:
- **Reflexivity**: Every object is equivalent to itself.
- **Symmetry**: If object A is equivalent to object B, then object B is equivalent to object A.
- **Transitivity**: If object A is equivalent to object B, and object B is equivalent to object C, then object A is equivalent to object C.
In rough set theory, an equivalence relation is often used to establish a partition of the universe into distinct equivalence classes.

(b) **Equivalence Class**: An equivalence class is a subset of the universe of objects that share the same equivalence relation with respect to certain attributes. In simpler terms, objects within an equivalence class are considered indiscernible based on the specified attributes. Each equivalence class represents a group of objects that are indistinguishable using only the available attribute information.

In the context of rough set theory, equivalence classes are used to simplify the analysis of data by grouping objects that are behaviorally similar. When you are dealing with an equivalence class, you are essentially treating all objects within that class as the same in terms of the considered attributes. This allows for a reduction in the complexity of the data, and helps in making generalizations and deriving decision rules.

(c) **Approximation space**: An approximation space is of the form (U, Z), where U is the nonempty Universe set and Z is an equivalence relation on U. Here, Z is an indiscernibility relation that partitions the Universe U into a collection of equivalence classes. This partition of the Universe is denoted by U/Z. The equivalence classes of Z can also be called as elementary sets or granules. In the approximation space, $[s]_Z \subseteq S$ denote the equivalence class containing $s \in S$.

(d) **Lower approximation:**

The lower approximation of a set S with respect to a set of attributes Z represents the elements that definitely belong to S based on the available information about Z. In other words, it contains the elements that can be confidently classified as part of set S, given the knowledge about set Z.

For a set S, its lower approximation with respect to relation Z is the set of all objects that are assured to be classified as S with respect to Z. The Z-lower approximation of set S, denoted by $\underline{Z}S$, is defined as:

$$Z\text{-lower} : \underline{Z}S = \{s \in U : [s]_Z \subseteq S\}$$

Few of the properties that the lower approximation satisfies for any two given subsets, S and T, such that $S, T \subseteq U$, are stated below:

$$\underline{Z}S\,(U) = U$$

$$\underline{Z}S(\emptyset) = \emptyset$$

$$\underline{Z}S(S) =\sim \underline{Z}S\,(\sim S)$$

$$\underline{Z}S\,(S \cup T) \supseteq \underline{Z}S(S) \cup \underline{Z}S(T)$$

$$\underline{Z}S(X \cap Y) = \underline{Z}S(S) \cap \underline{Z}S(T)$$

$$S \subseteq T \Rightarrow \underline{Z}S(S) \subseteq \underline{Z}S(T)$$

$$\underline{Z}S(S) \subseteq S$$

$$S \subseteq \underline{Z}S(\underline{Z}S(S))$$

$$\underline{Z}S(S) \subseteq \underline{Z}S(\underline{Z}S(S))$$

$$\underline{Z}S(S) \subseteq \underline{Z}S(\underline{Z}S(S))$$

(e) **Upper approximation**: The upper approximation of a set S with respect to a set of attributes Z includes the elements that may or may not belong to S, considering the uncertainty introduced by Z. It contains the elements for which there is insufficient evidence to definitively classify them as either in S or not in S.

For a set S, its upper approximation with respect to relation Z is the set of all objects that can be possibly classified as S with respect to Z. The Z-upper approximation of set S, denoted by $\overline{Z}S$, is defined as:

$$Z\text{-upper}: \quad \overline{Z}S = \{s \in U : [s]_Z \cap S \neq \emptyset\}$$

Few of the properties that the upper approximation satisfies for any two given subsets, S and T, such that $S, T \subseteq U$, are stated below:

$$\overline{Z}S(U) = U,$$

$$\overline{Z}S(\emptyset) = \emptyset$$

$$\overline{Z}S(X) = \sim \overline{Z}S(\sim S)$$

$$\overline{Z}S(S \cup T) = \overline{Z}S(S) \cup \overline{Z}S(T)$$

$$\overline{Z}S(S \cap T) \subseteq \overline{Z}S(S) \cap \overline{Z}S(T)$$

$$S \subseteq T \Rightarrow \overline{Z}S(S) \subseteq \overline{Z}S(T)$$

$$S \subseteq \overline{Z}S(S)$$

$$\overline{Z}S(\overline{Z}S(S)) \subseteq S$$

$$\overline{Z}S(\overline{Z}S(S)) \subseteq \overline{Z}S(S)$$

$$\overline{Z}S(\overline{Z}S(S)) \subseteq \overline{Z}S(S)$$

The lower and upper approximations provide a way to handle uncertainty when classifying elements into sets. Lower approximation provides a confident classification of elements, while upper approximation includes those elements that might still be considered for inclusion due to the uncertainty introduced by the given attributes. These concepts are fundamental in rough set theory for analyzing data when dealing with incomplete or uncertain information.

(f) **Boundary region (BR)**: The BR of a set S with respect to relation Z is the set of all objects, which can be categorized neither as S nor as not-S with respect to Z. It is basically the difference between the upper and the lower approximations.

$$BR(S) = \overline{Z}S - \underline{Z}S$$

If $\overline{Z}S = \underline{Z}S$, the boundary is empty. However, in general, $\overline{Z}S \neq \underline{Z}S$, and, in such a case, the BR consists of only those objects that can neither be ruled in nor ruled out as members of the target set S.

(g) **Positive region (PR):** The positive region (PR) is the same as the lower approximation of a set S and can be hence represented as:

$$PR = \{s \in U : [s]_Z \subseteq S\}$$

(h) **Negative region (NR):** The negative regions (NRs), denoted by Z-outside region of S, consist of those objects that are certainly not classified as belonging to set S. It can be calculated as:

$$NR = U - \overline{Z}S$$

(i) **Reduct:** Reduct is a set of attributes that can fully characterize knowledge in an information system. It can be formally defined as set of attributes R such that $R \subseteq B$ and $R = [s]_P$. This indicates that the equivalence classes induced by the minimal attribute set R are the same as the equivalence class structure induced by the attribute set B.

To understand the concept of reduct, let us consider an information table given in Table 7.1 having five attributes and ten objects. Here, attributes A1, A2, A3, and A4 are the conditional attributes, and A5 is the decision attribute. The various equivalence classes that can be formed by considering all the set of attributes $A = \{A1, A2, A3, A4, A5\}$ are:

{Ob1, Ob9}

{Ob2, Ob6, Ob10}

{Ob3}

{Ob4}

{Ob5}

{Ob7}, and

{Ob8}

Now, we have to find the reduct R for Table 7.1 with a set of minimal attributes that can yield the same combination of equivalence classes when all the attributes are considered. We shall not consider only one conditional attribute to find the reduct, as only one attribute in this example cannot contribute to finding decision attribute.

In such a case, considering two attributes, the reduct can be $R = \{A3, A4, A5\}$, as the set R will generate the equivalence classes also as {Ob1, Ob9}, {Ob2, Ob6, Ob10}, {Ob3}, {Ob4}, {Ob5}, {Ob7}, and {Ob8}. Note that there can also be more than one reduct in an information system. For instance, for Table 7.1, another set of reduct will be $R = \{A1, A2, A5\}$.

Table 7.1 An information table.

Object	A1	A2	A3	A4	A5
Ob1	B	C	A	B	Y
Ob2	C	A	A	B	X
Ob3	A	A	B	C	Y
Ob4	C	B	A	C	X
Ob5	A	A	B	C	Z
Ob6	C	A	A	B	X
Ob7	A	B	C	C	X
Ob8	C	B	A	C	Z
Ob9	B	C	A	B	Y
Ob10	C	A	A	B	X

(j) **Core**: Core is the set of attributes that is common to all reducts formed for an information system. In case of Table 7.1, the two reducts that can be formed are $R1 = \{A1, A2, A5\}$ and $R2 = \{A3, A4, A5\}$. Hence, core is the set of one attribute $\{A5\}$ that is common in both the reducts $R1$ and $R2$. If we remove the core set of attributes from the reduct, it will hamper the equivalence class structures formed from the information table. Hence, core can be also regarded as the indispensable attribute of an information system.

7.1.2 Measures of Rough Set Approximations

The two standard numerical measures as suggested by Pawlak for characterizing the imprecision of rough set approximations are accuracy and roughness. These two measures in rough set theory are often used in evaluation of rules of data mining and machine learning.

(a) **Accuracy:** The accuracy of approximation for a rough set S is given by:

$$\text{Accuracy}(S) = \frac{|\underline{Z}S|}{|\overline{Z}S|}$$

where $S \neq \emptyset$, and $|\cdot|$ represents the cardinality of a set. This accuracy value, which lies within the range 0–1, indicates how closely the rough set approximates the target set. Clearly, when $\overline{Z}S = \underline{Z}S$, the accuracy value is 1, and the approximations is considered perfect. Alternatively, when $\underline{Z}S = 0$ (empty), the accuracy value is also 0.

(b) **Roughness**: The roughness measure for a rough set S is given by:

$$\text{Roughness} (S) = \frac{|\overline{Z}S - \underline{Z}S|}{|\overline{Z}S|} = \frac{|\text{BR}(S)|}{|\overline{Z}S|}$$

As can be seen from the above equation, the roughness measure is related to the notion of BR of a set. The roughness measure can be also calculated in terms of accuracy of approximation as follows:

$$\text{Roughness} (S) = 1 - \text{Accuracy}(S)$$

Example 7.1 Considering Table 7.2, for set $S = \{s | A3(s) = 1\}$, the accuracy and roughness measures can be calculated as follows:

$$\text{Accuracy} (S) = \frac{|\{\text{Ob2},\text{Ob3}\}|}{|\{\text{Ob2},\text{Ob3},\text{Ob5},\text{Ob6},\text{Ob7},\text{Ob8}\}|} = \frac{1}{3}$$

$$\text{Roughness} (S) = \frac{|\{\text{Ob5},\text{Ob6},\text{Ob7},\text{Ob8}\}|}{|\{\text{Ob2},\text{Ob3},\text{Ob5},\text{Ob6},\text{Ob7},\text{Ob8}\}|} = \frac{2}{3}$$

As can be seen from the derived values, Roughness $(S) = 1 - \text{Accuracy}(S) = 1 - \frac{1}{3} = \frac{2}{3}$.

The roughness measure can be compared to be the standard Marczewski–Steinhaus distance between the lower and upper approximations. Pawlak stated that the accuracy measure is "*intended to capture the degree of completeness of our*

Table 7.2 A simple information table.

Object	A1	A2	A3
Ob1	1	1	2
Ob2	1	2	1
Ob3	1	3	1
Ob4	2	1	2
Ob5	2	2	2
Ob6	2	3	1
Ob7	2	2	1
Ob8	2	3	2

knowledge about the set X," whereas the roughness measure *"represents the degree of incompleteness."* These two numerical measures of rough set theory help in estimating imprecision of the approximate characterization of a set.

7.2 Using Rough Sets for Information System

To analyze data, rough set theory uses a simple data representation scheme called the information system. In such a system, an information table is studied to find the indiscernibility among objects. Each cell of the information table gives the value of an object on an attribute. An information table can be expressed in the form:

$$T = [U, A, \{V_a \mid a \in A\}, \{I_a \mid a \in A\}]$$

where, U is the finite, nonempty set called the Universe, and consists of all objects or entities. Here, A is the nonempty set of all attributes, V_a is the nonempty set of values for an attribute $a \in A$, and I_a is the information function that maps objects or entities in U with values in V_a. Typically, in an information system, rows represent objects and columns represents attributes. If the information function I_a is missing for one or more objects, the information table is said to be incomplete.

Example 7.2   Table 7.2 shows a simple information table of the form $T = \{U, A, V_a, I_a\}$ where, i.e., $A = \{A1, A2, A3\}$, O is the set of all objects, i.e., $O = \{Ob1, Ob2, Ob3, Ob4, Ob5, Ob6, Ob7, Ob8\}$. V_{a1} refers to the set of values for attribute A1 and can be written as $V_{A1} = \{1, 2\}$. Similarly, $V_{A2} = \{1,2,3\}$ and $V_{A3} = \{1,2\}$. The information function $I_{A1}(Ob1) = 1$, Similarly, $I_{A2}(Ob3) = 3$, $I_{A3}(Ob4) = 2$, and so on.

Now, if two attributes – A1 and A2 – are taken into consideration, such that $A = \{A1, A2\}$, we get six equivalence classes – {Ob1}, {Ob2} {Ob3}, {Ob4}, {Ob5, Ob7}, and {Ob6, Ob8} – in which each *equivalence class* has the same set of values for all the considered attributes. Again, if we consider a set of only two attributes such that $A = \{A1, A3\}$, then, we get only four equivalence classes – {Ob1}, {Ob2, Ob3}, {Ob4, Ob5, Ob8}, and {Ob6, Ob7}. The selection of attributes for set A becomes the deciding factor for the formation of equivalence classes. This leads to an indiscernible relation, which is itself an equivalence relation formed by the intersection of some equivalence relations. Two objects are indiscernible (equivalent) if and only if they consist of the same set of values for every attribute considered in set A. In Table 7.2, the set {Ob5, Ob7} is indiscernible in terms of attributes {A1, A2}. Again, the set {Ob1, Ob2, Ob3} is indiscernible in terms of attribute {A1}.

In general, for an information system $F = \{U, A\}$, then any $A' \subseteq A$, the A' – indiscernibility relation $\text{IR}(A')$ will be:

$$\text{IR}(A') = \{(s, s') \in U^2 \mid \forall a \in A', a(s) = a(s')\}$$

Here, the equivalence classes of the A'-indiscernibility relation are denoted by $[s]_{A'}$. If $(s, s') \in A'$, then objects s and s' are indiscernible from each other for considered set of attributes from A'.

From Table 7.2, the indiscernibility classes for $A = \{A1, A2\}$ are $\{Ob1\}$, $\{Ob2\}$, $\{Ob3\}$, $\{Ob4\}$, $\{Ob5, Ob7\}$, and $\{Ob6, Ob8\}$. Now, for set $S = \{s \mid A3(s) = 1\}$, we have, the set as $\{Ob2, Ob3, Ob6, Ob7\}$. In this case, the lower and upper approximations will be:

Z-lower : $\underline{Z}S = \{Ob2, Ob3\}$

Z-upper : $\overline{Z}S = \{Ob2, Ob3, Ob6, Ob7, Ob8, Ob5\}$

Therefore, the BR, the PR, and the NR for the above case will be:

$\text{BR}(S) = \overline{Z}S - \underline{Z}S = \{Ob6, Ob7, Ob8, Ob5\}$

$PR = \text{Z-lower} : \underline{Z}S = \{Ob2, Ob3\}$

$\text{NR} = U - \overline{Z}S = \{Ob1, Ob4\}$

7.3 Decision Rules and Decision Tables

A decision table is like an information table but contains two types of attributes – the condition attribute and the decision attribute. In rough set theory, a decision table is represented by $T = \{U, A, C, D\}$, where U is the nonempty finite Universe set, A is the set of all attributes, C is the set of condition attributes, and D is the set of decision attributes such that $C, D \subset A$. Table 7.3 illustrates a decision table for customer information of a bank that have availed a loan. In the table, the condition attributes are `Marital_Status` and `Age_Group`, and the decision attribute is `Loan_Paid`.

From each row of a decision Table A, condition can be formed by checking whether the condition attributes are satisfied or not. However, many a times, decision rules having the same conditions may give different decisions. In such a case, decision rules are said to be *conflicting* or *inconsistent*. In case the decision rules having the same conditions give same decisions, the rules are said to be *nonconflicting* or consistent. For example, for *Customer_id* 102 and 106 (rows 2 and 6), the values of condition attributes are the same (*Married* and 31-40), but the decision attribute values of these two records differ – *Yes* for Customer_Id 102 and *No* for Customer_Id 107. Hence, the decision rule is *conflicting* in this case.

Table 7.3 A decision table for bank loan.

Customer_Id	Marital status	Age group	Loan paid
101	Single	31–40	No
102	Married	31–40	Yes
103	Divorced	41–50	No
104	Single	41–50	Yes
105	Single	31–40	No
106	Married	31–40	No
107	Married	41–50	Yes

Decision rules are also called as "if...then..." rules, as these rules can be written in the form of "if...then" statements. For example, if we consider row 1 from Table 7.3, it can be represented as an implication:

```
if (Marital_Status, Single) and (Age_Group, 31-40), then
     (Loan_Paid, No)
```

Similarly, if we consider row 8 from Table 7.3, it can be represented as another logical implication:

```
if (Marital_Status, Married) and (Age_Group, 31-40) then
     (Loan_Paid, Yes)
```

Such set of decision rules occurring in a decision table form a decision algorithm.

7.3.1 Parameters of Decision Tables

A decision table can generate many parameters of interest such as consistency factor, certainty factor, and coverage factor.

7.3.1.1 Consistency Factor

A decision table, as a whole, may be considered as consistent or inconsistent based on whether all the decision rules formed from the decision table are consistent or inconsistent. This is found by measuring the consistency factor $\text{Con}(C, D)$, where C refers to the condition attributes, and D refers to the decision attributes. $\text{Con}(C, D)$ is found by checking the number of consistent rules formed compared to the number of all the rules of the table. If $\text{Con}(C, D) = 1$, it can be concluded that the decision table is consistent, whereas if $\text{Con}(C, D) \neq 1$, the decision table is inconsistent. For instance, from Table 7.3, we can calculate that

$$\text{Con}(C, D) = 5/7 = 0.714$$

as there are two inconsistent rules for *Customer_Id* 102 and 104 out of a total of seven rules of the table.

7.3.1.2 Support and Strength

If we consider $C = \{c_1, c_2, c_3, \dots, c_n\}$ and $D = \{d_1, d_2, d_3, \dots, d_n\}$ such that for every $s \in U$, a sequence

$$c_1(s), c_2(s), \dots, c_n(s), d_1(s), d_2(s), \dots, d_m(s)$$

is determined and called as a decision rule induced by s in table T, and denoted by

$$c_1(s), c_2(s), \dots, c_n(s) \rightarrow d_1(s), d_2(s), \dots, d_m(s)$$

In such a case, the support of a decision rule, which indicates the number of identical decision rules in a decision table, can be calculated as:

$$\text{Support}_s(C, D) = |\, C(s) \cap D(s)\, |$$

Considering Table 7.3, where the condition attributes (C) are `Marital_Status` and `Age_Group`, and the decision attribute (D) is `Loan_Paid`, the value of support for a decision table can be calculated as

$$\text{Support}_s(C, D) = 2$$

This value is calculated based on the following identical rule fetched from Table 7.3.

```
(Marital_Status, Single) ^ (Age_Group, 31-40) →
     (Loan_Paid, No)
```

Once the support value is known, we can also find the strength of a decision rule as:

$$\text{Strength}_s(C, D) = \frac{|C(s) \cap D(s)|}{|U|} = \frac{\text{Support}_s(C, D)}{|U|}$$

Again, considering Table 7.3, where the condition attributes (C) are `Marital_Status` and `Age_Group`, and the decision attribute (D) is `Loan_Paid`, the value of strength of a decision table for $|U| = 7$ can be calculated as:

$$\text{Strength}_s(C, D) = \frac{2}{7} = 0.2857.$$

7.3.1.3 Certainty Factor

The certainty factor Cert(A, B) is a conditional probability that is interpreted as the frequency of objects having the property B in the set of objects having the property A. The certainty factor of a decision rule, denoted by $\text{Cert}_s(C, D)$, can be expressed in the form:

$$\text{Cert}_s(C, D) = \frac{|C(s) \cap D(s)|}{|C(s)|} = \frac{\text{Support}_s(C, D)}{|C(s)|} = \frac{\text{Strength}_s(C, D)}{\lambda(C(s))}$$

where, $C(s) = \emptyset$ and $\lambda(C(s)) = \frac{|C(s)|}{|U|}$. Based on the certainty factor, a decision rule can be considered as certain or uncertain. If $\text{Cert}_s(C, D) = 1$, the decision rule is said to be certain; if $0 < \text{Cert}_s(C, D) < 1$, the decision rule is said to be uncertain.

Again, considering Table 7.3, where the condition attributes (C) are `Marital_Status` and `Age_Group`, and the decision attribute (D) is `Loan_Paid`, the certainty value can be calculated as:

$$\text{Cert}_s(C, D) = \frac{|C(s) \cap D(s)|}{|C(s)|} = \frac{2}{2} = 1$$

7.3.1.4 Coverage Factor

The coverage factor $\text{Cov}(A, B)$ is a conditional probability that is interpreted as the frequency of objects having the property A in the set of objects having the property B. The coverage factor of a decision rule, used for estimation of quality of a decision rule, is denoted by $\text{Cov}_s(C, D)$ where, $D(s) = \emptyset$ and $\lambda(D(s)) = \frac{|D(s)|}{|U|}$, and can be expressed in the form:

$$\text{Cov}_s(C, D) = \frac{|C(s) \cap D(s)|}{|D(s)|} = \frac{\text{Support}_s(C, D)}{|D(s)|} = \frac{\text{Strength}_s(C, D)}{\lambda(D(s))}$$

Again, considering Table 7.3, where the condition attributes (C) are `Marital_Status` and `Age_Group`, and the decision attribute (D) is `Loan_Paid`, the coverage value can be calculated as

$$\text{Cov}_s(C, D) = \frac{|C(s) \cap D(s)|}{|D(s)|} = \frac{2}{4} = 0.5$$

Let us consider another case to understand these parameters of a decision table clearly. For this, let us consider the decision table given in Table 7.4 , for each decision rule the support value is provided in the last column for a total of 500 instances in the table, i.e., $|U| = 500$. This support value of a decision rule indicates the number of instances available in the table for that decision rule. For instance, Rule 3

```
(Marital_Status, Single) ^ (Age_Group, 31-40) →
    (Loan_Paid, Yes)
```

has a total of 10 instances out of the total of 500 instances of the table.

For each decision rule of Table 7.4, the values of strength, certainty factor, and coverage factor is given in Table 7.5. It can be seen that the sum total of strength for all the decision rules of a decision table is 1.

7.3.2 Probabilistic Properties of Decision Tables

The parameters of a decision table (discussed in Section 7.3.1) lead to some important probabilistic properties as discussed next. If we again consider

Table 7.4 Support values of a decision table for bank loan.

Decision rule	Marital status	Age group	Loan paid	Support
1	Single	31–40	No	150
2	Single	41–50	Yes	40
3	Single	31–40	Yes	10
4	Married	31–40	Yes	140
5	Married	31–40	No	10
6	Married	41–50	Yes	70
7	Divorced	31–40	No	80

Table 7.5 Strength, certainty, and coverage values of decision rules.

Decision rule	Strength	Certainty	Coverage
1	0.30	0.94	0.63
2	0.08	1.0	0.15
3	0.02	0.06	0.04
4	0.28	0.93	0.54
5	0.02	0.07	0.04
6	0.14	1.0	0.27
7	0.16	1.0	0.33

$C = \{c1, c2, c3, \ldots, cn\}$ and $D = \{d1, d2, d3, , \ldots, , dn\}$ such that a decision rule is induced by s in table T for every $s \in U$ and is denoted by $c1(s)$, $c2(s)$, $\ldots$, $cn(s) \rightarrow d1(s)$, $d2(s)$, $\ldots$, $dm(s)$. This decision rule can also be written as $Cs \rightarrow D$ such that $\Omega = C(s)$, $\psi = D(s)$, and $\lambda(C(s)) = \frac{|C(s)|}{|U|}$. In that case, the following probabilistic properties will be valid for any decision table.

If we consider Table 7.4, the probabilistic property (7.1) can be proven by considering Rules 1 and 3, for which the value of the certainty factor sums up to 1.

$$\sum_{q \in \Omega} \mathrm{Cert}_q(C, D) = 1 \tag{7.1}$$

Similarly, the property (7.2) can be proven from Table 7.4 by considering Rules 1, 5, and 7 (where the decision attribute value is "*No*") for which the value of the coverage factor sums up to 1.

$$\sum_{q \in \psi} \text{Cov}_q(C, D) = 1 \tag{7.2}$$

Formulae (7.3) and (7.4) together are referred to as *probability theorem* that relates to the strength of decision rules. Here, strength typically refers to the level of dependency or significance between the conditions (antecedents) and the class (consequent) of the rule. Strong rules have a higher level of certainty in their conclusions, while weak rules might have a lower level of certainty.

$$\lambda(C(s)) = \sum_{q \in \psi} \text{Strength}_q(C, D) \tag{7.3}$$

$$\lambda(D(s)) = \sum_{q \in \Omega} \text{Strength}_q(C, D) \tag{7.4}$$

Formulae (7.5) and (7.6) together are referred to as *Bayes' theorem*, which is a powerful tool for reasoning about uncertainty. Bayesian reasoning can be applied to decision rules in order to incorporate new evidence and update probabilities.

$$\text{Cert}_s(C, D) = \frac{\text{Cov}_s(C, D). \; \lambda(D(s))}{\sum_{q \in \psi} \text{Cov}_q(C, D).\lambda(D(y))} = \frac{\text{Strength}_s(C, D)}{\lambda(C(s))} \tag{7.5}$$

$$\text{Cov}_s(C, D) = \frac{\text{Cert}_s(C, D). \; \lambda(C(s))}{\sum_{q \in \Omega} \text{Cert}_q(C, D).\lambda(C(y))} = \frac{\text{Strength}_s(C, D)}{\lambda(D(s))} \tag{7.6}$$

It can be noticed that it is good enough to know the value of strength of that decision rule to calculate the certainty and coverage factors of a decision rule.

7.4 Application Areas of Rough Set Theory

Rough sets can be applied in various fundamental and important application areas for several research experiments and diagnosis. Its relevance and prominence have been realized in various real-life applications. Few such application areas, such as classification, clustering, medical diagnosis, image processing, and speech analysis are briefly discussed in this section.

7.4.1 Classification

Dimensionality reduction for complex datasets is usually handled by appropriate feature selection to reduce the high complexity of data. Attribute reduction or feature selection has always been considered as an important preprocessing step for removing irrelevant data and increasing data accuracy. Feature selection for dimensionality reduction can be targeted by finding a minimal subset of attributes that provides the same classification as the entire dataset.

The minimal subset, called as reduct in Rough Set theory, provides the minimal relevant features for making a correct decision for classification. However, finding reducts for a dataset is considered as a NP-hard problem, and researchers have worked on this area to find near-optimal solutions for this issue. For instance, if the total number of features is "n," the total number of candidate subsets will be 2^n, and this will result in an exhaustive search even for a moderate value of "n." Hence, the lesser the number of features chosen, the faster will be the execution time for classification (Figure 7.2).

In the feature selection process using rough set theory, every time a new subset is generated, it is compared with the previous best subset generated. This process is repeated until a predefined number of iterations are reached or a predefined number of features are selected. In the best case, the process is stopped when adding or removing a feature does not yield a better subset of features. At the end, the selected best features are validated using standard evaluation tests.

The Rough Set Exploration System (RSES) tool can be used for calculation of reducts using the concept of rough set theory. RSES is a graphical user interface (GUI)-based package and can perform the following sequence of steps, as shown in Figure 7.3, based of the rough set approach of analysis of data. Here is a general guideline on how you might use RSES to calculate reducts:

(a) **Download and install RSES**: Obtain the latest version of RSES from its official website or repository. Follow the installation instructions provided for your operating system.
(b) **Load your dataset**: Open RSES and load the dataset you want to work with. Typically, datasets are loaded from text files or CSV files.
(c) **Define attributes and decision attributes**: In RSES, specify which attributes are condition attributes and which one is the decision attribute. This will be necessary for reduct calculation.

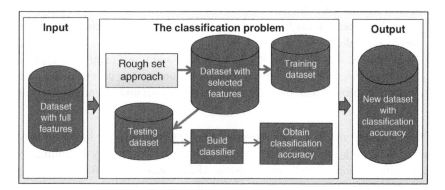

Figure 7.2 The standard classification problem.

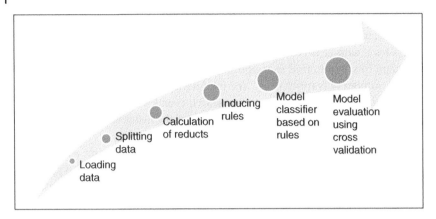

Figure 7.3 Sequence of steps used by RSES tool.

(d) **Calculate reducts**: To calculate reducts using RSES, follow these steps:
   i. Select the "Attributes" or "Feature Selection" section in the RSES interface.
   ii. Choose the dataset you loaded earlier.
   iii. Specify the condition attributes and decision attribute.
   iv. Select an algorithm for reduct calculation. RSES might offer different algorithms such as Quick Reduct Algorithm (QRA) or Genetic Algorithm (GA).
   v. Initiate the reduct calculation process by clicking a "Calculate" or "Find Reducts" button.
(e) **View and analyze reducts**: Once the reduct calculation is complete, RSES will likely display a list of reducts or a single reduct, depending on the algorithm used. You can analyze the reducts generated to understand the minimal subsets of attributes that preserve the decision-making capability of the original dataset.
(f) **Save Results**: You might have the option to save the calculated reducts or analysis results for further reference.
(g) **Experiment and Explore**: RSES might offer additional features to explore other rough set concepts, perform rule induction, analyze dependencies, and more. Experiment with these features to deepen your understanding of rough set theory.

Keep in mind that the steps provided are a general guideline based on how similar tools work, and the actual interface and options might vary depending on the specific version of RSES you are using. Always refer to the official documentation or user guides provided by the RSES developers for detailed and accurate instructions.

7.4.2 Clustering

The theory of rough sets has been widely accepted and used for classification, and it has been equally found favorable in applications of clustering. Clustering algorithms are mainly used in data mining and several other application areas, such as marketing and bioinformatics. In most of the real-time practical clustering approaches, the clusters do not have crisp boundaries as an object or node may belong to more than one cluster. This results in overlapping clusters in which an object may belong to more than one node. For instance, a particular symptom, say headache, may belong to both the clusters of diagnoses – migraine and sinus. Hence, the concept of rough sets can be incorporated in various existing standard clustering techniques, as it can deal with overlapping objects efficiently. In this section, we will discuss applications of k-means clustering to rough set theory, as k-means clustering is one of the most frequently used clustering algorithms in real-life domain.

In rough clustering, the upper and lower approximations necessary follow some of the basic rough set properties such as:

i. An object v can be a member of at most one lower approximation.
ii. If an object v is a member of a lower approximation of a set, it will be also a part of its upper approximation. This results in the lower approximation of the set being a subset of its corresponding upper approximation.
iii. If an object v is not a member of any lower approximation, it will belong to two or more upper approximations. This results in an object belonging to more than one BR.

In k-means clustering, "k" number of clusters is formed from "n" objects, in which the objects are represented by q-dimensional vectors. Initially, the clustering technique begins by randomly choosing "k" objects as the centroids of the k clusters. An object is considered to belong to one out of the "k" clusters by finding the minimum value of the distance $D(v, c)$ between the object vector $v = (v_1, v_2, v_3, ..., v_x, ..., v_q)$ and the cluster vector $c = (c_1, c_2, c_3, ..., c_x, ..., c_q)$. The distance $D(v, c)$ is then calculated as:

$$c_x = \frac{\sum_{v \in c} v_x}{|c|}, \text{where } 1 \leq x \leq q$$

where, $|c|$ is the size of cluster c. The calculation of distance is repeated many a times until the centroids of clusters get stabilized. This is logically realized when the centroid values are almost identical in both the previous iteration and the current iteration.

Rough sets approach is incorporated in k-means clustering by including the concepts of lower and upper approximations. In such a case, the centroids calculation for k-means clustering using rough set approach is done as shown:

if $\underline{Z}S \neq \phi$ and $\overline{Z}S - \underline{Z}S = \phi$

$$c_x = \frac{\sum_{v \in \underline{Z}S} v_x}{|\underline{Z}S|}$$

else if $\underline{Z}S = \phi$ and $\overline{Z}S - \underline{Z}S \neq \phi$

$$c_x = \frac{\sum_{v \in (\overline{Z}S - \underline{Z}S)} v_x}{|\overline{Z}S - \underline{Z}S|}$$

else

$$c_x = p_{lower} \times \frac{\sum_{v \in \underline{Z}S} v_x}{|\underline{Z}S|} + p_{upper} \times \frac{\sum_{v \in (\overline{Z}S - \underline{Z}S)} v_x}{|\overline{Z}S - \underline{Z}S|}$$

where $1 \leq x \leq q$. The two parameters p_{lower} and p_{upper} relates to the importance of lower and upper approximations, respectively, and the sum of p_{lower} and p_{upper} results in the value 1. While conducting experiments, various pairs of values of (p_{lower}, p_{upper}) can be applied such as, (0.60, 0.40) and (0.70, 0.30).

After conducting the experiment several times with varying values of p_{lower} and p_{upper}, the process can be stopped when the resulting intervals will provide good representations of clusters. However, the above centroid calculation will result in conventional k-means centroid calculation if the lower and upper approximations are found to be equal as shown in first condition when $\overline{Z}S - \underline{Z}S = \phi$.

The next step to be followed for k-means clustering using rough set approach is to find whether each object belongs to either lower approximation or upper approximation of a cluster. An object "v" will be assigned to a lower approximation of a cluster, when the distance between "v" and the center of the particular cluster is the smallest compared to the distances of the remaining other cluster centers.

Let us consider the distance $D(v, c_x)$ between a vector v and the centroid of a cluster c_x. Now, to determine the membership of object v, the following two steps are to be followed:

i. Find the nearest centroid (refer to Figure 7.4) by considering:

$$D_{min} = D(v, c_x) = \min_{1 \leq j \leq k} D(v, c_x)$$

ii. Check if further centroids are not significantly farther away than the closest one. For checking this, let us consider $T = \{u: D(v, c_u)/D(v, c_x) \leq threshold$ and $u \neq x\}$. In such a case:
   a. If $T = \phi$, then there is no other centroid that is similarly close to object v.
   b. If $T \neq \phi$, then there is at least one other centroid that is similarly close to object v.

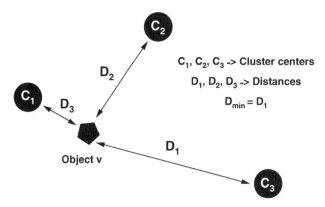

Figure 7.4 Determining the nearest centroid for an object.

By considering the above two steps, the following rule can be applied for an object v to the approximations:

```
if T≠φ
        v ∈ ZS(c_u)  and  v ∈ ZS(c_x),  ∀  u∈T
else
    v ∈ ZS(c_x)   and  v ∈ ZS(c_x)
```

The rough clustering approach forms clusters in which an object can belong to more than one cluster. The rough K-means described above has augmented the traditional k-means clustering technique by considering real-life instances of cluster formation in which objects do belong to more than one cluster.

7.4.3 Medical Diagnosis

Medical diagnostic rules can be modeled with the concept of rough set theory, as such diagnosis is based on imprecision and uncertainty. As seen before, rough set theory works well while dealing with imprecise and uncertain data. Moreover, medical data is less pliable to fixed formulae, as most of the time it is difficult to assign initial assumptions.

Rough set approach allows analyzing medical data without any such initial assumptions. For instance, magnetic resonance imaging (MRI) scans used in medical analysis can be studied by correlating the *base histogram* of the images to lower approximation and the encrustation with the upper approximation.

The rough set approach builds pattern matching system to these MRI images to provide a meaningful diagnosis through the images.

The concept of decision rules and decision trees, as discussed in Section 7.3, can also be applied in case of medical data analysis. For this, let us consider the decision table as given in Table 7.7. In the table, the condition attributes are {Headache, Temperature, Heartbeat}, and the decision attribute is {Flu}.

Now if we consider a relation A as:

$A = \{$Headache, Temperature, Heartbeat$\}$, then,

Indiscernibility$(A) = \text{IR}(A) = \{\{P1, P8\}, \{P2, P3\}, \{P4\}, \{P5, P6\}, \{P7\}\}$.

Again, if we consider a set $S = \{s|\text{Flu}(s) = \text{"Yes"}\}$, we have, the set as {P1, P2, P3, P7}. In this case, the lower and upper approximations will be:

Z-lower : $\underline{Z}S = \{P2, P3, P7\}$

Z-upper : $\overline{Z}S = \{P1, P8, P2, P3, P7\}$

Therefore, the BR, the PR, and the NR for the above case will be:

$\text{BR}(S) = \overline{Z}S - \underline{Z}S = \{P1, P8\}$

$PR = Z\text{-lower} : \underline{Z}S = \{P2, P3, P7\}$

$NR = U - \overline{Z}S = \{P4, P5, P6\}$

We have also studied in the previous section of this chapter that a decision table, as a whole, may be considered as consistent or inconsistent, based on whether all the decision rules formed from the decision table are consistent or inconsistent. This is found by measuring the consistency factor $\text{Con}(C, D)$, where C refers to the condition attributes, and D refers to the decision attributes. From Table 7.5, we can calculate that

$\text{Con}(C, D) = 6/8 = 0.75$

as there are two inconsistent rules for *Patient* P1 and P8, out of a total of eight rules of the table.

Again, considering the condition attributes as {Headache, Temperature, Heartbeat} and the decision attribute as {Flu}, the value of support for the decision Table 7.5 will be:

$\text{Support}_s(C, D) = 4$

This value is calculated based on the following two identical rules fetched from Table 7.5.

```
(Headache, Yes) ^ (Temperature, High) ^ (Heartbeat,
     Abnormal)→ (Flu, Yes)


(Headache, Yes) ^ (Temperature, Normal) ^ (Heartbeat,
     Abnormal)→ (Flu, No)
```

Table 7.6 An exemplary decision table containing patient details.

Patient	Headache	Temperature	Heartbeat	Flu
P1	Yes	High	Normal	Yes
P2	Yes	High	Abnormal	Yes
P3	Yes	High	Abnormal	Yes
P4	No	High	Normal	No
P5	Yes	Normal	Abnormal	No
P6	Yes	Normal	Abnormal	No
P7	Yes	Low	Normal	Yes
P8	Yes	High	Normal	No

The various decision rules that can be formed by considering the three condition attributes and the one decision attribute of Table 7.6 are mentioned below:

Rule 1: *(Headache, Yes) ^ (Temperature, High) ^ (Heartbeat, Normal) -> (Flu, Yes)*
Rule 2: *(Headache, Yes) ^ (Temperature, High) ^ (Heartbeat, Normal) -> (Flu, No)*
Rule 3: *(Headache, Yes) ^ (Temperature, High) ^ (Heartbeat, Abormal) -> (Flu, Yes)*
Rule 4: *(Headache, No) ^ (Temperature, High) ^ (Heartbeat, Normal) -> (Flu, No)*
Rule 5: *(Headache, Yes) ^ (Temperature, Normal) ^ (Heartbeat, Abnormal) -> (Flu, No)*
Rule 6: *(Headache, Yes) ^ (Temperature, Low) ^ (Heartbeat, Normal) -> (Flu, Yes)*

Now, the support $Support_s(C, D)$, the strength $Strength_s(C, D)$, the certainty factor $Certs(C, D)$, and the coverage factor $Cov_s(C, D)$ of each of the five decision rules for Table 7.6 is calculated as shown in Table 7.7.

The certainty factors from Table 7.7 lead us to the following conclusions:

(a) 50% of the patients who have headache and high temperature but normal heart beat suffer from flu.
(b) 50% of the patients who have headache and high temperature but normal heart beat may not suffer from flu.
(c) 100% of the patients who have headache, high temperature, and an abnormal heart beat suffer from flu.

Table 7.7 Support, strength, certainty, and coverage values of all decision rules.

Decision rule	Support	Strength	Certainty	Coverage
Rule 1	1	0.125	0.5	0.25
Rule 2	1	0.125	0.5	0.25
Rule 3	2	0.250	1.0	0.5
Rule 4	1	0.125	1.0	0.25
Rule 5	2	0.250	1.0	0.5
Rule 6	1	0.125	1.0	0.25

(d) 100% of the patients who do not have headache but high temperature and a normal heart beat do not suffer from flu.

(e) 100% of the patients who have headache but normal temperature and an abnormal heart beat do not suffer from flu.

(f) 100% of the patients who have headache, low temperature, and a normal heart beat suffer from flu.

In this way, the inverse decision rules can also be formed using the coverage factor values. Thus, rough set theory can be used to form decision algorithms by classifying the information system into lower and upper approximations. This kind of research study can be applied to form an accurate and reliable expert system that can help physicians build a diagnosis system.

7.4.4 Image Processing

Rough set theory can be applied to handle many challenges in the field of image processing such as image segmentation, image compression, and clustering. The concept of rough sets for image processing is mainly used for either analysis or manipulation of a digitized image. For this, an image is granuled for extracting subsets of images that fall under similar clusters. The concept of granules (equivalence classes) is related to indiscernibility relation that partitions the universe based on similarity of attributes of objects.

Let us now discuss one of the core application areas of rough sets used in image processing, which is image segmentation. Image segmentation partitions a digital image into multiple segments. This process cluster pixels into separate image regions that can be helpful for image recognition, image compression, and for many other image processing techniques. Colored images are segmented using rough set theory by encrustation of histogram called as histon. The histon can be

Figure 7.5 Algorithmic steps for image segmentation.

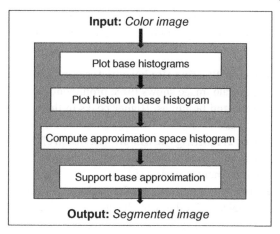

considered as the superset of a basic histogram and is basically a contour plotted on top of an existing histogram. It can be correlated with the upper approximation of a set that indicates that all the elements belonging to this set consist of the same segment having similar color values.

One of the standard algorithms for image segmentation of color images is discussed below, which consists of four basic steps as illustrated in Figure 7.5.

- **Step 1**: Considering the three primary color components – red, green, and blue – the histogram is to be plotted for each color component (can follow the procedure for plotting of one-dimensional entities). These histograms are often referred to as base histograms.
- **Step 2**: Plot the histon of the base histogram. For this, pixels with similar color values are to be found and accordingly grouped to form regions with similar color. A sphere of similar color points is formed as given by the formula:

$$(x-r')^2 + (y-g')^2 + (z-b')^2 = R^2$$

where, R represents the radius of the sphere of the region in the neighborhood of a pixel having color intensities as (r', g', b'). By considering the value of R, a set of histons will be built based on varying degree of color intensity.
- **Step 3**: Carry out the segmentation of the troughs and valleys for the histon. This is done since the histon can accentuate the regions having similar color values by differentiating the regions with respect to dissimilar color values.
- **Step 4**: Consider the segments formed by the Green histon as the primary segments, and support the segments with the segments obtained from Red and Blue histons. The green component of a color is the most important, and also the human eye is more receptive toward the green component of white light.

Let us consider an example to further illustrate the steps involved in image segmentation using rough set theory. For this, we consider a grayscale image of a landscape.

- **Step 1: Plotting the base histogram**: Assume that the base histogram of the grayscale image shows three prominent peaks, indicating the presence of sky, trees, and buildings. Higher peaks in the histogram might indicate regions of interest.
- **Step 2: Plotting the histon**: The histon of the base histogram reveals that there are transitions in pixel intensity frequencies at certain points, suggesting potential segment boundaries.
- **Step 3: Segmentation of troughs and valleys for the histon**: Identify three troughs and valleys in the histon, indicating potential segmentation points. Troughs and valleys represent regions of the image where there are transitions in pixel intensity frequencies. These transitions can be interpreted as potential boundaries between segments. Each trough and valley suggest a potential segmentation point.
- **Step 4: Primary segments**: The segments formed by the histon troughs and valleys correspond to the primary segments, representing different regions of the image. These segments are labeled as sky, trees, and buildings.

Rough set theory might be considered in cases where image data exhibits significant uncertainty or vagueness, which requires handling indiscernibility and imprecision.

7.4.5 Speech Analysis

Speech signal is mainly used for pattern matching for which some preprocessing steps are applied (as given in Figure 7.6), namely:

- signal preprocessing
- feature extraction, and,
- vector quantization
- **Vector quantization (VQ)**: This step is mainly used for data compression and is mainly applied to form a discrete or semi-continuous hidden Markov model (HMM) based speech recognition system. VQ is treated as simplification of scalar quantization to vector quantization. For this, the VQ encoding–decoding techniques are used. The role of VQ encoder is to encode a set of n-dimensional data vectors with a small subset C, which is known as the codebook. The elements of C are represented as C_i, and are called as codevectors or codewords. Next, the index i of codevector is passed to the decoder for the decoding process based on the table look-up procedure.

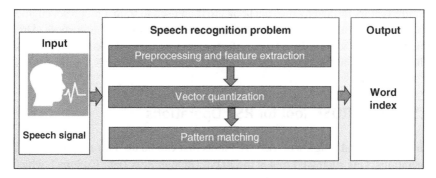

Figure 7.6 The standard speech recognition process.

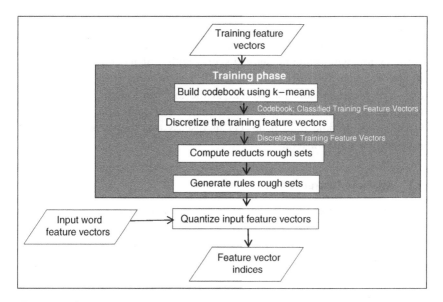

Figure 7.7 Rough set-based vector quantizier.

A hybrid approach of building vector quantizer has been built using the concept of k-means and rough sets (refer to Figure 7.7). The testing of the vector quantizer showed good performance in terms of recognition rate and time. In this vector quantization approach, in the training phase, the k-means clustering algorithm is used in the training phase to form a cluster of training feature vectors. The best representing vector is chosen for each cluster to form the codebook.

Since only the use of k-means clustering technique results in building a final codebook that is highly dependent on the initial codebook, the rough set theory has been augmented with k-means clustering to solve this issue. The classified feature vectors formed by the codebook are then used to train a rough set engine. A discretization algorithm to deal with discrete data is used for this purpose. After this, the discretized classified training feature vectors are used to compute reducts. The classification rules are then generated to classify input words feature vectors.

7.5 Using ROSE Tool for RST Operations

There are several rough set-based GUI tools that can be used for rough set-based operations. One such GUI tool is the ROSE (ROugh SEts Data Explorer), which is a software mainly used for implementing basic elements of rough set. ROSE is designed as an easy point and click, menu-driven, user-friendly tool for data exploration and analysis.

ROSE accepts information table as input data that consists of condition attributes and decision attribute(s). The input data is actually stored in a plain text file by following some predefined syntax with a filename having extension .ISF (Information System File). The ROSE tool window is divided into four parts – the *Menu bar* and the *Toolbar* at the top, the *Console* window at the bottom, the *Methods Tree* window in the middle left pane, and the *Project List* window in the middle right pane. Let us discuss two simple rough set-based opeartions using ROSE2 tool.

7.5.1 Attribute Discretization

The automatic discretization of continuously valued attributes can be carried out using the ROSE tool as a preprocessing step for handling dataset. The ROSE tool uses the Fayyad & Irani's MDL method for data discretization for creating a manageable number of discrete values for each attribute from a large number of contiguous values for any attribute. For example, the age attribute can be categorized into three sets of intervals – *young* (all values less than 30 years), *middle-aged* (30–50 years), and *old* (above 50 years).

There can be two reasons for carrying out data discretization.

- Handling large values of contiguous data for attributes is difficult for carrying out any kind of data analysis or mining. Smaller range of discrete values is more manageable for human interpretation of data.
- In many learning fields of data mining, such as induction rules and association rules, only discrete values of data are handled. For this, before any machine learning process begins, the continuous attributes are needed to be encoded for attribute discretization.

A typical discretization process carries out four essential steps:

(a) Sorting all the continuous values of the attributes to be discretized
(b) Choosing a cut-point for splitting the continuous values into intervals.
(c) Splitting or merging the intervals of continuous values
(d) Choosing a stopping criterion for the discretization process to complete or end.

Data can be discretized using the ROSE tool by choosing any dataset having continuously valued attribute. The dataset in the ROSE2 software is stored using the filename extension "*.ISF.*" Initially, an in-built dataset can be selected from the menu *Project > Add File(s) to Project*. For attribute discretization of an information table, the BANK.ISF dataset is selected that contains 66 records having six attributes. This is done by choosing *Project > Add File(s)* menu *to Project*. The content of the dataset can be accessed in ROSE2 software by right-clicking on the icon of the dataset and choosing the *View* option (as shown in Figure 7.8).

The discretization process can be carried out for the BANK.ISF dataset using the ROSE2 tool by choosing *Preprocessing > Discretization > Local* option from the *Methods Tree* window. The *Local* option in the *Methods* window has to be dragged and dropped on the BANK.ISF icon available in the *Project List* window. This will result in opening a dialog box, as shown in Figure 7.9, for choosing the decision attribute.

Once the "Ok" button with default options is clicked, an icon with the filename BANK-LOCAL.ISF appears in The Projects List window that contains the dataset having discretized valued attributes. The dataset is partially visible in Figure 7.10.

7.5.2 Finding Lower and Upper Approximations

As discussed in the beginning of this chapter, rough sets are identified by approximations, namely the lower approximation and the upper approximation, as well as the BR (as illustrated in Figure 7.1). Hence, identifying the lower and upper approximations is a primary task in solving any rough set-based modeling technique, which can be easily found by using the ROSE2 GUI tool.

For finding approximations of an information table, the MUSHROOM.ISF dataset is selected that contains 8124 records having 22 attributes. This is done by choosing *Project > Add File(s)* menu *to Project*. The content of the dataset can be accessed in ROSE2 software by right-clicking on the icon of the dataset and choosing the *View* option (as shown in Figure 7.11).

One of the primary tasks in rough set-based approach is finding the lower and upper approximations of the dataset. As explained in Section 7.1.1 of this chapter, the lower approximation ($\underline{Z}S$) of a set S with respect to relation Z is the set of all objects that are assured to be classified as S with respect to Z. Again, the upper

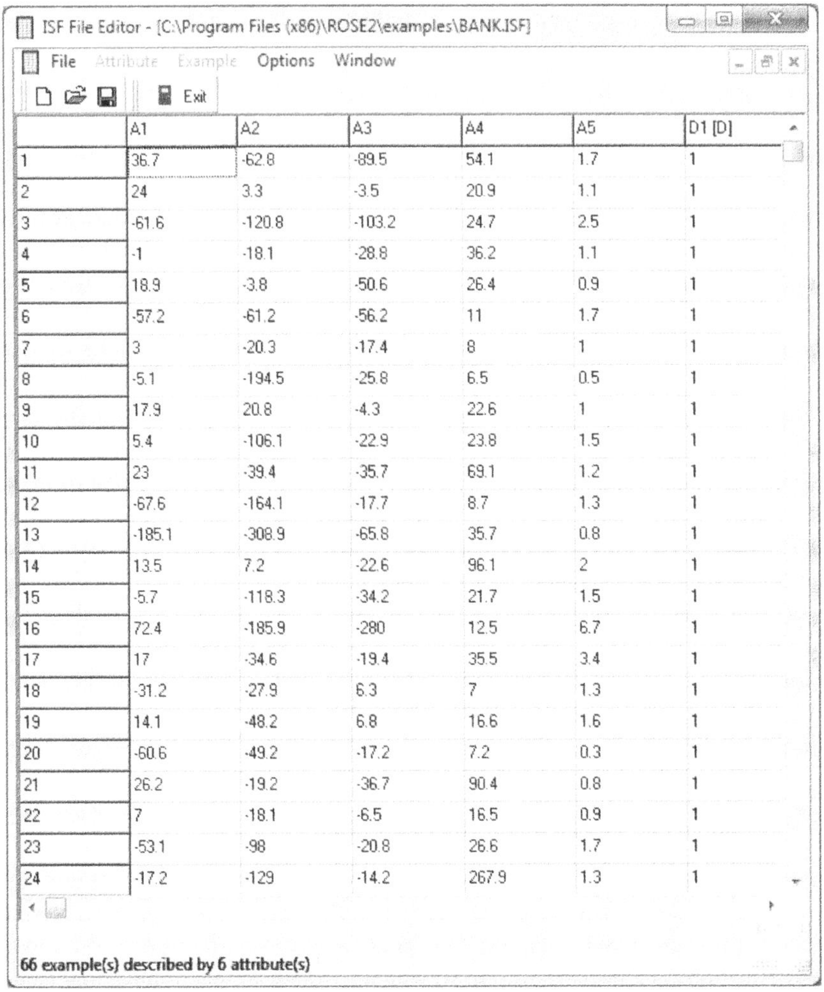

	A1	A2	A3	A4	A5	D1 [D]
1	36.7	-62.8	-89.5	54.1	1.7	1
2	24	3.3	-3.5	20.9	1.1	1
3	-61.6	-120.8	-103.2	24.7	2.5	1
4	-1	-18.1	-28.8	36.2	1.1	1
5	18.9	-3.8	-50.6	26.4	0.9	1
6	-57.2	-61.2	-56.2	11	1.7	1
7	3	-20.3	-17.4	8	1	1
8	-5.1	-194.5	-25.8	6.5	0.5	1
9	17.9	20.8	-4.3	22.6	1	1
10	5.4	-106.1	-22.9	23.8	1.5	1
11	23	-39.4	-35.7	69.1	1.2	1
12	-67.6	-164.1	-17.7	8.7	1.3	1
13	-185.1	-308.9	-65.8	35.7	0.8	1
14	13.5	7.2	-22.6	96.1	2	1
15	-5.7	-118.3	-34.2	21.7	1.5	1
16	72.4	-185.9	-280	12.5	6.7	1
17	17	-34.6	-19.4	35.5	3.4	1
18	-31.2	-27.9	6.3	7	1.3	1
19	14.1	-48.2	6.8	16.6	1.6	1
20	-60.6	-49.2	-17.2	7.2	0.3	1
21	26.2	-19.2	-36.7	90.4	0.8	1
22	7	-18.1	-6.5	16.5	0.9	1
23	-53.1	-98	-20.8	26.6	1.7	1
24	-17.2	-129	-14.2	267.9	1.3	1

Figure 7.8 The BANK.ISF dataset.

approximation ($\overline{Z}S$) of a set S with respect to relation Z is the set of all objects that can be possibly classified as S with respect to Z. The lower and upper approximations are given by:

$$Z\text{-lower} : \underline{Z}S = \{s \in U : [s]_Z \subseteq S\}$$

$$Z\text{-upper} : \overline{Z}S = \{s \in U : [s]_Z \cap S \neq \emptyset\}$$

The approximations can be computed from the MUSHROOM.ISF dataset using the ROSE2 tool by choosing *Preprocessing > Approximations* option from the

Figure 7.9 Dialog box for local discretization process.

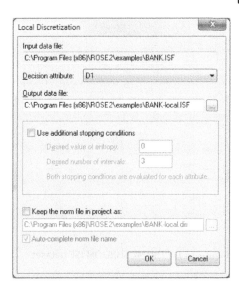

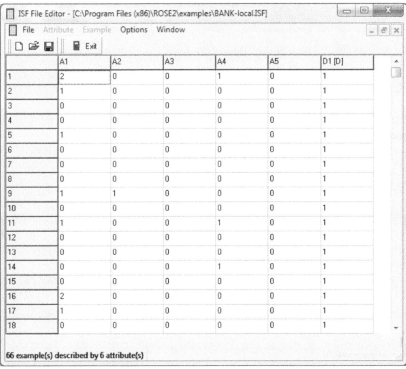

Figure 7.10 Display of BANK.ISF dataset (having discretized values for all attributes).

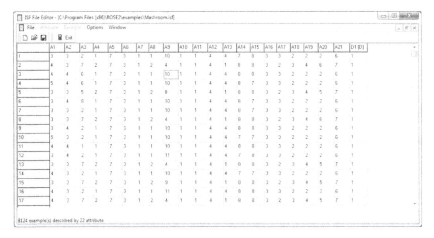

Figure 7.11 The MUSHROOM.ISF dataset.

Figure 7.12 Dialog box for finding approximations.

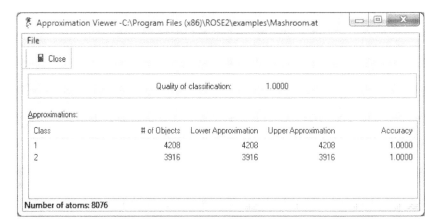

Figure 7.13 Display of approximations in the approximation viewer window.

Methods Tree window. The *Approximations* option in the *Methods* window has to be dragged and dropped on the MUSHROOM.ISF icon available in the *Project List* window. This will result in opening a dialog box, as shown in Figure 7.12, for choosing the decision attribute.

Once the "Ok" button with default options is clicked, the list of classes, the number of objects in each class, and their corresponding lower and upper approximation values are displayed as shown in Figure 7.13. The result also shows a classification accuracy of 1.0, which is 100%.

Exercises

A) Choose the correct answer from among the alternatives given:

a) The concepts of rough sets were introduced in the field of computer science by
   i) Dominik Slezak
   ii) Zdzisław I. Pawlak
   iii) Dennis Ritchie
   iv) James Gosling

b) _____ region is basically the difference between the upper and the lower approximations.
   i) Positive
   ii) Negative
   iii) Boundary
   iv) Approximation

c) The _____ region is the same as the lower approximation of a set.
   i) Positive
   ii) Negative
   iii) Boundary
   iv) Approximation

d) The _____ is the complete set of objects that are possibly members of a target set "*S*."
   i) Lower approximation
   ii) Upper approximation
   iii) Approximation space
   iv) Boundary region (BR)

e) Core is the set of attributes that is common to all _____ formed for an information system.
   i) Decision rules
   ii) Equivalence relations
   iii) Reducts
   iv) Approximation sets

f) For a given set "*S*," if the lower approximation is equal to its upper approximation, the accuracy and roughness measures will be equal to
   i) 0 and 0
   ii) 1 and 1
   iii) 1 and 0
   iv) 0 and 1

g) For measuring the consistency factor, the two types of attributes to be considered are _____
   i) Simple attributes and multiple attributes
   ii) Simple attributes and complex attributes
   iii) Composite attributes and distributed attributes
   iv) Condition attributes and decision attributes

B) Answer the following questions:

1) What is a rough set? For which applications can rough set theory be used?
2) Define the following terms:
   i) Approximation space
   ii) Lower approximation
   iii) Upper approximation
   iv) Boundary region (BR)
   v) Positive region (PR)
   vi) Negative region (NR)
3) What is meant by core and reduct? Mention any three reducts for the given Table A. Also, find the upper approximation, lower approximation, boundary region (BR), positive region (PR), and negative region (NR) for Table A.

Table A An information table.

Patient_ID	Blood Pressure	Chest Pain	Cholesterol	Heart Problem
P1	High	Yes	High	Yes
P2	High	Yes	High	Yes
P3	High	No	High	No
P4	High	Yes	High	Yes
P5	High	Yes	Low	No
P6	Normal	No	High	No
P7	Normal	Yes	No	No
P8	High	No	No	No
P9	High	No	High	Yes
P10	Normal	Yes	No	No

4) For each rule of Table A, find the support, strength, certainty factor, and coverage factor.

5) Why can a boundary region (BR) be empty? Mention any three important properties each for upper approximation and for lower approximation of a set *S*.

6) What does an information table contain? How are equivalence classes formed from an information table?

7) Mention any four important probabilistic properties of a decision table.

8) Explain the two main accuracy measures of rough set approximations.

9) For Table A, calculate the accuracy and roughness measures. What do these values signify?

10) What do the certainty factor and coverage factor signify? When can a decision rule be considered certain?

11) What does the strength of a decision rule signify? What can be the possible range of values for the strength of a decision rule? What should be the sum total value of the strength of all decision rules of a decision table?

12) What is the role of reduct in the classification process? Explain, in detail, the process of feature set selection using rough set approach.

13) Differentiate between basic k-means clustering and rough set-based k-means clustering.

14) What is meant by histon? How can rough set concept be used for segmentation of a colored image?

15) Discuss any two important application areas of rough set theory.

16) Consider a simple binary dataset given below:

```
dataset = [
{"attr1": 1, "attr2": 0},
{"attr1": 0, "attr2": 1},
{"attr1": 1, "attr2": 1},
{"attr1": 0, "attr2": 0},
]
```

Explain the process for finding the lower and upper approximations for this dataset using the ROSE tool.

17) Develop a rough clustering algorithm that groups similar objects based on their lower and upper approximations in a dataset.

18) Given the below dataset, consider the decision attribute to be *"Exam Result"* and the set of condition attributes as *{Attendance, Study Hours}*.

Student ID	Attendance	Study Hours	Exam Result
1	Good	Low	Pass
2	Poor	Medium	Pass
3	Good	High	Pass
4	Poor	Medium	Fail
5	Good	High	Fail

Calculate the attribute reduction for the given set of condition attributes using the discernibility matrix approach. Show your calculations step by step.

8

Hybrid Systems

Hybrid systems in soft computing offer a flexible and powerful approach to problem solving, allowing for robust and efficient solutions in complex domains where traditional methods may fall short. Their ability to adapt, learn, and optimize makes them particularly valuable for addressing real-world challenges with varying levels of complexity and uncertainty. For instance, a hybrid system may use fuzzy logic to handle uncertain inputs, neural networks (NNs) for pattern recognition, and evolutionary algorithms to optimize the system's parameters. The specific combination and integration of techniques depend on the problem at hand and the desired outcome. This chapter focusses on hybrid systems, and its importance and applications in soft computing.

8.1 Introduction to Hybrid Systems

Hybrid systems in soft computing refer to the integration or combination of different soft computing techniques or methodologies to solve complex problems. Soft computing encompasses a set of computational techniques that are inspired by human-like or biological processes, allowing for flexible and adaptive problem-solving approaches. Hybrid systems leverage the strengths of multiple soft computing methods to overcome limitations and enhance performance in addressing real-world challenges.

Some commonly used soft computing techniques that can be integrated into hybrid systems include fuzzy logic, artificial neural network, evolutionary computation, and swarm intelligence. Hybrid systems in soft computing aim to leverage the complementary strengths of these techniques to tackle diverse challenges. By integrating multiple approaches, hybrid systems can handle uncertainty, complexity, and nonlinearity in problem domains that may be difficult for individual methods alone.

Principles of Soft Computing Using Python Programming: Learn How to Deploy Soft Computing Models in Real World Applications, First Edition. Gypsy Nandi.
© 2024 The Institute of Electrical and Electronics Engineers, Inc. Published 2024 by John Wiley & Sons, Inc.

In the context of hybrid systems in soft computing, various types of hybrid systems can be classified based on their characteristics and functionality. Here are a few commonly recognized types of hybrid systems:

(a) **Sequential Hybrid Systems:** Sequential hybrid systems involve the combination of different soft computing techniques in a sequential manner. The output of one technique serves as the input to another, forming a pipeline or a cascaded structure. For example, a sequential hybrid system might employ fuzzy logic for preprocessing, followed by NNs for feature extraction, and, finally, genetic algorithms (GAs) for optimization.

(b) **Embedded Hybrid Systems:** Embedded hybrid systems refer to the integration of soft computing techniques into a larger existing system or framework. In this type of hybrid system, soft computing methods are embedded or incorporated into traditional algorithms or systems to enhance their capabilities. For example, incorporating a fuzzy logic controller into a conventional control system or embedding NNs within a decision support system.

(c) **Auxiliary Hybrid Systems:** Auxiliary hybrid systems use one soft computing technique as an auxiliary or supporting tool to improve the performance of another technique. The auxiliary technique assists in enhancing the effectiveness, efficiency, or robustness of the primary technique. For instance, using GAs to tune the parameters of an artificial neural network or using fuzzy logic to guide the exploration of an evolutionary algorithm. Figure 8.1 illustrates the three types of hybrid systems, namely, (a) sequence hybrid system, (b) embedded hybrid system, and (c) auxiliary hybrid system.

(d) **Cooperative Hybrid Systems:** Cooperative hybrid systems involve the collaboration and cooperation of multiple soft computing techniques or models to jointly solve a problem. These techniques work in parallel, and share information or intermediate results to arrive at a final solution. Examples include swarm intelligence algorithms, where multiple individuals in the swarm contribute to finding optimal solutions collectively.

(e) **Ensemble Hybrid Systems:** Ensemble hybrid systems combine the predictions or outputs of multiple individual soft computing models to produce a final result. Each individual model may use a different algorithm or technique, and the ensemble system aggregates their outputs to make a collective decision. Ensemble methods like bagging, boosting, or stacking are examples of this type of hybrid system.

Applications of neurogenetic systems span various domains, including pattern recognition, data mining, optimization, control systems, image and signal processing, and bioinformatics. These hybrid systems have been successfully employed in tasks, such as classification, regression, prediction, optimization, and feature selection.

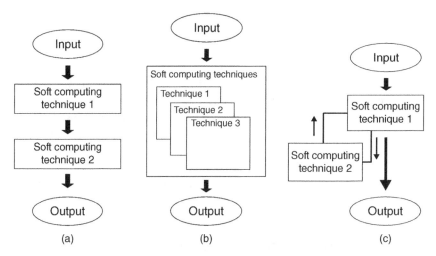

Figure 8.1 (a) Sequential hybrid system, (b) embedded hybrid system, and (c) auxiliary hybrid system.

Hybrid systems may exhibit characteristics of multiple types. The specific type of hybrid system used depends on the problem at hand, the available techniques, and the desired outcome. The objective is to leverage the strengths of different soft computing approaches and create synergistic solutions that outperform individual methods.

8.2 Neurogenetic Systems

Neurogenetic systems, also known as neurogenetic hybrid systems, combine the principles and techniques of NNs and GAs. These hybrid systems integrate the ability of NNs to learn and adapt with the optimization capabilities of GAs, resulting in powerful problem-solving frameworks.

NNs, NNs, as discussed in chapter 3 and chapter 4 of this book, are biologically inspired computational models that consist of interconnected nodes or neurons. They are capable of learning from data and making predictions or decisions based on learned patterns. NNs excel in tasks such as pattern recognition, classification, regression, and function approximation. They can capture complex nonlinear relationships, and adapt their internal weights and biases through a learning process.

On the other hand, GAs (as discussed in Chapter 6) are optimization algorithms inspired by natural evolution and genetic principles. They use techniques such as selection, crossover, and mutation to evolve a population of candidate solutions over generations. GAs are effective in searching for optimal or near-optimal solutions in complex, high-dimensional, and multimodal search spaces.

The integration of NNs and GAs in neurogenetic systems offers several advantages. NNs can learn from training data and adjust their internal parameters (weights and biases) to fit the patterns in the data. This ability allows them to adapt to changing environments or evolving problem scenarios. GAs provide a global search capability, exploring a wide range of potential solutions. They are effective in finding optimal or near-optimal solutions, especially in complex and multimodal search spaces. While NNs excel in local pattern recognition and generalization, GAs excel in global exploration and optimization. By combining these techniques, neurogenetic systems leverage the complementary strengths of both the approaches.

8.2.1 GA-based Weight Determination of Multilayer Feed-forward Net

GA-based weight determination of a multilayer feed-forward neural network is an approach that uses a GA to optimize the weights of the neural network. This technique combines the principles of GAs, which are inspired by the process of natural selection, with the structure and learning capabilities of a feed-forward neural network.

In a multilayer feed-forward neural network, information flows in a forward direction from the input layer, through one or more hidden layers, and finally to the output layer. The weights associated with the connections between neurons determine the strength of the connections, and play a crucial role in the network's ability to learn and make accurate predictions.

The GA-based weight determination method involves the following steps:

(a) **Encoding:** Each solution in the population represents a set of weights for the neural network. The weights are encoded as a chromosome or a string of binary values, where each value corresponds to a weight in the neural network.
(b) **Initialization:** A population of candidate solutions (chromosomes) is randomly generated. Each chromosome corresponds to a set of weights for the neural network.
(c) **Evaluation:** Each chromosome is decoded to obtain a set of weights. The neural network is then trained using these weights on a training dataset, and the performance of the network is evaluated using a fitness function. The fitness function measures how well the neural network performs on the task at hand, such as classification accuracy or mean squared error.
(d) **Selection:** Chromosomes with higher fitness values have a higher probability of being selected for reproduction, mimicking the process of natural selection.

Common selection methods include tournament selection, roulette wheel selection, or rank-based selection.

(e) **Crossover:** The selected chromosomes undergo crossover, where portions of their genetic material (weights) are exchanged to create new offspring solutions. Crossover promotes exploration of the search space and helps in combining beneficial characteristics from different parent solutions.

(f) **Mutation:** In order to introduce diversity into the population and prevent premature convergence, random changes (mutations) are applied to the offspring solutions. These changes alter the weights of the neural network randomly.

(g) **Replacement:** The new offspring solutions (with possible mutations) replace some of existing solutions in the population based on their fitness. This ensures that the fitter individuals have a higher chance of survival and passing their genetic material to the next generation.

(h) **Termination:** The GA iterations continue until a stopping criterion is met, such as reaching the maximum number of generations or obtaining a solution that meets the desired fitness threshold.

(i) **Final Solution:** The GA process results in a final set of weights for the neural network, which represents an optimized solution based on the given fitness function.

The GA-based weight determination approach allows for the automatic optimization of weights in a multilayer feed-forward neural network, enabling the network to learn and adapt to complex patterns in the data. By leveraging the evolutionary principles of GAs, this technique can find weights that lead to improved network performance and better generalization on unseen data.

To illustrate the GA-based weight determination of a multilayer feed-forward neural network for a binary classification problem, let us consider a dataset with two input features ($X1$ and $X2$) and a binary target variable (y). We want to train a neural network with one hidden layer and one output neuron to classify the data points into two classes (0 or 1). The first step is to encode the weights of the neural network as a chromosome consisting of binary values. For simplicity, let us assume that the neural network has three input neurons, two hidden neurons, and one output neuron. The chromosome would have 15 binary values: 3 for hidden-input layer weights, 2 for hidden-output layer weights, and 10 for bias values.

Next, a population of candidate solutions (chromosomes) is randomly generated, each representing a set of weights for the neural network. Each chromosome is decoded to obtain the weights for the neural network. The neural network is trained using these weights on the training dataset, and its performance is evaluated using a fitness function such as classification accuracy or cross-entropy loss. Chromosomes with higher fitness values have a higher probability of being selected for reproduction. The tournament selection can be used, where a subset of chromosomes is randomly selected, and the one with the highest fitness is chosen for reproduction. The selected chromosomes undergo crossover, where portions of their genetic material (weights) are exchanged to create new offspring solutions. For example, single-point crossover can be performed by randomly selecting a crossover point and swapping the genetic material beyond that point between the parent chromosomes.

Random changes (mutations) are applied to the offspring solutions to introduce diversity. This could involve flipping individual bits in the chromosome, which corresponds to small changes in the weights. The new offspring solutions replace some of the existing solutions in the population based on their fitness. The fitter individuals have a higher chance of survival and passing their genetic material to the next generation. The GA iterations continue until a stopping criterion is met, such as reaching the maximum number of generations or obtaining a solution that meets the desired fitness threshold. The GA process results in a final set of weights for the neural network, which represents an optimized solution based on the given fitness function.

Program 8.1 illustrates the Python code that demonstrates the GA-based weight determination of a multilayer feed-forward neural network using the DEAP library. A detailed explained of the code is given next:

(a) **Data Preparation:**
   - The code begins by generating a synthetic binary classification dataset using the `make_classification()` function from scikit-learn.
   - The dataset is then split into training and testing sets using the `train_test_split()` function.

(b) **Evaluation Function (`evaluate()`):**
   - This function takes an individual (a chromosome) as input and evaluates its fitness.
   - It creates a feed-forward neural network with the specified weights.
   - The neural network is trained on the training dataset, and the accuracy of predictions is calculated.
   - The fitness of the individual is calculated based on the accuracy.

(c) **Initialization:**
   - The code initializes the GA toolbox using the DEAP library.
   - It defines the optimization problem by creating `FitnessMax` and Individual classes using the `creator.create()` function.
   - The toolbox is then registered with the necessary functions, such as initialization of individuals and populations, evaluation, and genetic operators.

(d) **Genetic Algorithm Loop:**
   - The code sets the number of generations and population size.
   - It creates an initial population of individuals using the `population()` function.

- The GA loop starts, where each generation undergoes the following steps:
  - o The fitness of each individual in the population is evaluated using the *evaluate()* function.
  - o The selection operator (*toolbox.select()*) is applied to select individuals for the next generation.
  - o Crossover and mutation operators (*toolbox.mate()* and *toolbox.mutate()*) are applied to create new offspring.
  - o The population is replaced with the offspring.

  The loop continues for the specified number of generations.

(e) **Best Individual and Evaluation:**
  - The best individual from the final population is selected using the *tools.selBest()* function.
  - The best individual's weights are evaluated on the test set using the *evaluate()* function to obtain the test accuracy.

(f) **Output:**
  - The code prints the best individual (chromosome) found during the evolution process.
  - It also prints the test accuracy achieved by the best individual on the unseen test data.

Program 8.1 *GA-based Weight Determination of Multilayer Feed-forward Net*

```
import numpy as np
from sklearn.datasets import make_classification
from sklearn.model_selection import train_test_split
from sklearn.metrics import accuracy_score
import random
from deap import algorithms, base, creator, tools

# Generate a synthetic binary classification dataset
X, y = make_classification(n_samples=1000,
n_features=2, n_informative=2,
n_redundant=0, random_state=42)

# Split the dataset into training and testing sets
X_train, X_test, y_train, y_test = train_test_split(X, y,
test_size=0.2, random_state=42)

# Define the evaluation function for the neural network
def evaluate(individual):
    # Create the feed-forward neural network with specified weights
    # Assume the network has 2 input neurons, 2 hidden neurons, and
    # 1 output neuron
    w_input_hidden = np.array(individual[:4]).reshape((2, 2))
    w_hidden_output = np.array(individual[4:6]).reshape((2, 1))
```

```
    # Calculate the outputs of the neural network
    hidden_layer_output = np.dot(X_train, w_input_hidden)
    hidden_layer_activation = 1 / (1 + np.exp(-hidden_layer_
        output))
    output_layer_output = np.dot(hidden_layer_activation, w_hidden_
        output)
    output_layer_activation = 1 / (1 + np.exp(-output_layer_
        output))

    # Calculate the accuracy of predictions
    y_pred = np.round(output_layer_activation)
    accuracy = accuracy_score(y_train, y_pred)

    return accuracy,

# Define the optimization problem
creator.create("FitnessMax", base.Fitness, weights=(1.0,))
creator.create("Individual", list, fitness=creator.FitnessMax)

# Initialize the genetic algorithm toolbox
toolbox = base.Toolbox()

# Define the possible values for weights in the neural network
toolbox.register("attr_float", random.uniform, -1, 1)

# Define the structure of an individual (a chromosome)
toolbox.register("individual", tools.initRepeat, creator.Individual,
toolbox.attr_float, n=6)

# Define the population structure
toolbox.register("population", tools.initRepeat, list, tool-
box.individual)

# Define the evaluation function
toolbox.register("evaluate", evaluate)

# Define the genetic operators
toolbox.register("mate", tools.cxTwoPoint)
toolbox.register("mutate", tools.mutGaussian, mu=0, sigma=0.2,
indpb=0.1)
toolbox.register("select", tools.selTournament, tournsize=3)

# Set the number of generations and population size
num_generations = 10
population_size = 100

# Create the initial population
population = toolbox.population(n=population_size)

# Run the genetic algorithm
```

```
for generation in range(num_generations):
    # Evaluate the fitness of each individual in the population
    fitnesses = toolbox.map(toolbox.evaluate, population)
    for ind, fit in zip(population, fitnesses):
        ind.fitness.values = fit

    # Select the next generation individuals
    offspring = toolbox.select(population, len(population))

    # Apply crossover and mutation operations
    offspring = list(map(toolbox.clone, offspring))
    for child1, child2 in zip(offspring[::2], offspring[1::2]):
        if random.random() < 0.5:
            toolbox.mate(child1, child2)
            del child1.fitness.values
            del child2.fitness.values

    for mutant in offspring:
        if random.random() < 0.1:
            toolbox.mutate(mutant)
            del mutant.fitness.values

    # Replace the population with the offspring
    population[:] = offspring

# Select the best individual from the final population
best_individual = tools.selBest(population, k=1)[0]

# Evaluate the best individual on the test set
test_accuracy = evaluate(best_individual)[0]

print("Best Individual:", best_individual)
print("Test Accuracy:", test_accuracy)
```

The output of Program 8.1 is displayed next. The output of the code includes the best individual, represented by a list of weights (chromosome), and the corresponding test accuracy achieved by the neural network with those weights. The best individual represents the optimized weights for the multilayer feed-forward neural network. These weights should result in a higher accuracy on the test set compared to other individuals in the final population.

```
Best Individual: [0.0678403418233603, 0.04174335906052762,
                  0.4597601600227963, -0.7659771052317565,
                  0.6354974130832376, -0.6133952438054482]
Test Accuracy: 0.86875
```

The actual output may vary due to the stochastic nature of the GA. The performance of the algorithm depends on various factors such as the dataset, the configuration of the GA, and the specific problem being solved.

It's important to note that the success of GA-based weight determination depends on various factors such as the choice of fitness function, population size, selection, crossover, and mutation strategies. Experimentation and fine-tuning of these parameters are often required to achieve optimal results for a specific problem domain.

8.2.2 Neuroevolution of Augmenting Topologies (NEAT)

Neuroevolution of Augmenting Topologies (NEAT) is a powerful algorithmic approach that combines NNs and evolutionary algorithms to automatically evolve artificial NNs. NEAT was introduced by Kenneth O. Stanley and Risto Miikkulainen in 2002.

NEAT aims to address the challenges associated with training NNs by evolving both the structure and weights of NNs simultaneously. It starts with a population of simple NNs and evolves them over generations, allowing for the discovery of more complex and effective neural network architectures. The key features of NEAT include:

- **Genetic Encoding:** NEAT uses a specific genetic encoding scheme to represent NNs as genomes. Each genome represents an individual neural network. Genomes consist of a set of nodes and connections. Nodes represent neurons, and connections represent the synapses between neurons.
- **Historical Markings:** NEAT employs historical markings to maintain the genealogy of genomes across generations. This helps in tracking the origin and lineage of genes, enabling crossover and mutation operations to be applied effectively.
- **Innovation Numbers:** Each gene in NEAT is assigned a unique innovation number to track its historical origin. Innovation numbers are used to match genes during crossover, allowing for the preservation of similar structural components in the offspring.
- **Speciation:** NEAT incorporates speciation, which groups genomes into species based on their similarity. Speciation promotes diversity and prevents premature convergence by allowing separate populations to explore different regions of the search space.
- **Complexification:** NEAT starts with the minimal initial network structure, and evolves it by adding nodes and connections over generations. This allows for the incremental development of complex NNs.
- **Crossover and Mutation:** NEAT applies both crossover and mutation operators to evolve NNs. Crossover combines genes from two parent genomes, while mutation introduces small changes to the genomes. These operations enable the exploration of different network structures and weights.

By combining these features, NEAT can effectively explore the space of possible neural network architectures and optimize them for specific tasks. It allows for the automatic discovery of neural network structures that perform well on a given problem. NEAT has been successfully applied to various tasks, including control problems, game playing, robotics, and more. It has demonstrated the ability to evolve NNs that outperform hand-designed architectures in several domains. Overall, NEAT provides a flexible and powerful framework for automatically evolving NNs, allowing for the discovery of novel and efficient solutions to complex problems.

Program 8.2 shows a simple Python code to demonstrate a simple implementation of NEAT to evolve feed-forward NNs for solving a specific task through crossover and mutation. The program defines a simple feed-forward neural network structure using the *NeuralNetwork* class. It has an *__init__* method that initializes the input size, output size, and random weights for the network. It also has a predict method that performs the forward pass of the neural network. A fitness function, *fitness_function*, is defined to evaluate the performance of each neural network. In this example, it calculates the mean squared error (MSE) between the neural network's predictions and the target values for a set of input examples.

The *evolve_neural_networks* function handles the NEAT evolution process. It takes the number of generations as input. The function initializes the input size, output size, and an empty population list to hold the NNs. A for loop is used to generate an initial population of NNs. In this example, 10 NNs are created with random weights. Another 'for loop' in the program code runs for the specified number of generations. Inside the loop, the fitness of each neural network in the population is evaluated using the *fitness_function*. The fitness scores are stored in a list called *fitness_scores*.

The *fitness_scores* list is sorted based on the fitness scores in descending order. This is done using the sort method and a lambda function as the sorting key. The population list is then updated by extracting the NNs from the sorted *fitness_scores* list. The top-performing NNs (parents) are selected from the population. In this example, the top five NNs are chosen as parents. New NNs (children) are created through crossover and mutation. For each child, two parents are randomly selected without replacement using *random.sample*.

The weights of the children are obtained by averaging the weights of their parents and adding a random mutation. The old population is replaced with the new one, which consists of the parents and children. The best fitness score in the current generation is printed. It is obtained from the first element of the sorted *fitness_scores* list. The *evolve_neural_networks* function is called with the specified number of generations.

Program 8.2 *NEAT to Evolve Feedforward Neural Networks*

```python
import numpy as np
import random

# Define a simple feedforward neural network structure
class NeuralNetwork:
    def __init__(self, input_size, output_size):
        self.input_size = input_size
        self.output_size = output_size
        self.weights = np.random.randn(input_size, output_size)

    def predict(self, inputs):
        return np.dot(inputs, self.weights)

# Define a fitness function to evaluate the performance of each
  neural network
def fitness_function(neural_network):
    inputs = np.array([[0, 0], [0, 1], [1, 0], [1, 1]])
    targets = np.array([[0], [1], [1], [0]])
    predictions = neural_network.predict(inputs)
    return -np.mean((predictions - targets) ** 2)   # Negative mean
        squared error as fitness

# NEAT evolution process
def evolve_neural_networks(num_generations):
    input_size = 2
    output_size = 1

    population = []   # List to hold neural networks

    # Generate an initial population of neural networks
    for _ in range(10):
        neural_network = NeuralNetwork(input_size, output_size)
        population.append(neural_network)

    for generation in range(num_generations):
        # Evaluate the fitness of each neural network in the
          population
        fitness_scores = []
        for neural_network in population:
            fitness_score = fitness_function(neural_network)
            fitness_scores.append((neural_network, fitness_score))

        # Sort the population based on fitness scores
          (descending order)
        fitness_scores.sort(key=lambda x: x[1], reverse=True)
        population = [neural_network for neural_network, _ in
          fitness_scores]
```

```
# Select the top performing neural networks (parents)
parents = population[:5]

# Create new neural networks (children) through crossover
  and mutation
children = []
for _ in range(5):
    parent1, parent2 = random.sample(parents, 2)  # Select
        two parents without replacement
    child = NeuralNetwork(input_size, output_size)
    child.weights = (parent1.weights + parent2.weights) / 2
        # Crossover
    mutation = np.random.randn(input_size, output_size)
        # Mutation
    child.weights += mutation
    children.append(child)

# Replace the old population with the new one (parents +
  children)
population = parents + children

# Print the best fitness score in the current generation
best_fitness = fitness_scores[0][1]
print(f"Generation {generation}: Best Fitness =
  {best_fitness:.4f}")

# Run the NEAT evolution for 10 generations
evolve_neural_networks(num_generations=10)
```

The output of Program 8.2 is displayed next. The output indicates the progress of the NEAT evolution process over the specified number of generations. Each line displays the current generation number and the corresponding best fitness score achieved by the top-performing neural network in that generation.

The fitness score represents the performance of the neural network in minimizing the mean squared error (MSE) between its predictions and the target values. The best fitness score should generally improve over the generations, as the evolution process aims to optimize the NNs. However, keep in mind that the exact values and trends may vary due to the random initialization and mutation steps in the process.

```
Generation 0: Best Fitness = -0.5670
Generation 1: Best Fitness = -0.3788
Generation 2: Best Fitness = -0.3788
Generation 3: Best Fitness = -0.3735
Generation 4: Best Fitness = -0.3735
Generation 5: Best Fitness = -0.3518
Generation 6: Best Fitness = -0.3518
```

```
Generation 7: Best Fitness = -0.3518
Generation 8: Best Fitness = -0.3518
Generation 9: Best Fitness = -0.3518
```

By observing the best fitness scores, one can assess how well the NEAT algorithm is progressing in optimizing the NNs for the given task. In a more complex NEAT implementation, additional information such as the neural network topology, the connections between nodes, and other parameters could also be tracked and analyzed during the evolution process.

8.3 Fuzzy-Neural Systems

Fuzzy-Neural systems, also known as Neuro-Fuzzy systems, are hybrid intelligent systems that combine fuzzy logic and artificial neural networks (ANNs). These systems leverage the strengths of both fuzzy logic and NNs to address complex problems that may have uncertainty, imprecision, and nonlinearity. Figure 8.2 shows the block diagram of a Fuzzy-Neural system that uses the fusion of fuzzy logic and NNs to create a hybrid system that can handle uncertainty and imprecision.

- **Fuzzy Logic:** Fuzzy logic is a mathematical framework for dealing with imprecise or uncertain information. Unlike classical logic, where elements are either true or false, fuzzy logic allows for intermediate values between true and false, represented by linguistic terms like `"very hot"` or `"somewhat cold"`. Fuzzy logic uses membership functions to assign a degree of membership to each linguistic term, which indicates how well an input belongs to a particular fuzzy set.
- **Artificial Neural Networks (ANNs):** ANNs are computational models inspired by the structure and function of the human brain. They consist of

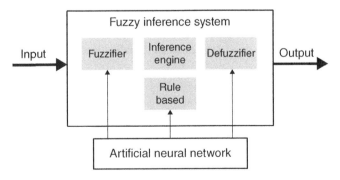

Figure 8.2 Block diagram of a Fuzzy-Neural system.

interconnected nodes (neurons) organized into layers, including an input layer, one or more hidden layers, and an output layer. Each connection between neurons has a weight, which is adjusted during training to learn the relationships between input and output data.

The fusion of fuzzy logic and NNs aims to create systems that can handle uncertainty, imprecision, and nonlinearity in data. The key components of a Fuzzy-Neural system include:

(a) **Fuzzification:** The process of converting crisp inputs into fuzzy linguistic terms using membership functions.
(b) **Inference:** Fuzzy inference applies fuzzy rules to make decisions based on the fuzzified input. These rules are often expressed in the form of IF-THEN statements, where the IF part involves conditions on input variables, and the THEN part includes the conclusions or actions.
(c) **Defuzzification:** The defuzzification process converts fuzzy output values obtained from the inference step back into crisp values, suitable for decision making or control actions.

Fuzzy-Neural systems can handle uncertain or imprecise data effectively, making them suitable for real-world applications where data may not be crisp. NNs in the system can learn from data and adjust their parameters, allowing the system to adapt and improve performance over time.

The combination of fuzzy logic and NNs allows the system to model complex, nonlinear relationships in the data. Fuzzy-Neural systems have been successfully applied to various fields, including control systems, pattern recognition, forecasting and prediction, and decision support. Overall, Fuzzy-Neural systems offer a powerful approach for handling uncertainty and complexity in data, making them valuable tools in a wide range of real-world applications.

8.3.1 Fuzzy Neurons

Fuzzy neurons, also known as fuzzy logic neurons, are a specific type of neuron used in Fuzzy-Neural systems, which combine fuzzy logic and artificial neural networks (ANNs). These neurons play a crucial role in handling imprecise or uncertain data in the input and output layers of the fuzzy-neural system. To get an overview of fuzzy neurons, it is important to understand the core terms and techniques related to fuzzy neurons:

(a) **Fuzzification:** The main function of fuzzy neurons is fuzzification. Unlike traditional neurons in standard ANNs, fuzzy neurons do not use fixed numeric inputs. Instead, they accept linguistic values (e.g., `"very hot"`, `"moderate"`, `"cold"`) and convert them into fuzzy membership values.

These membership values represent the degree to which the input belongs to particular linguistic terms or fuzzy sets. Fuzzification is achieved using membership functions, which map the input values to membership degrees.

(b) **Membership Functions:** Membership functions are fundamental to fuzzy neurons. They define the degree of membership for each linguistic term or fuzzy set. These functions can take various shapes, such as triangular, trapezoidal, or Gaussian, depending on the specific application. The fuzzy neuron evaluates the input against the membership functions and calculates the membership degrees for each linguistic term.

(c) **Fuzzy Inference:** After fuzzification, the fuzzy neuron performs fuzzy inference to process the fuzzy input and make decisions. Fuzzy inference involves applying fuzzy rules that describe how to combine the fuzzified inputs to produce the desired output. These rules are typically expressed in IF-THEN format and are determined based on expert knowledge or data-driven learning.

(d) **Defuzzification:** The final step in fuzzy neurons is defuzzification, which converts the fuzzy output obtained from fuzzy inference back into crisp values. Defuzzification can be achieved using various methods, such as centroid, mean of maxima, or weighted average.

Program 8.3 shows the Python code to demonstrate fuzzy neuron for temperature control. In this code, fuzzy logic is used to control the air conditioning system based on the temperature input. The program starts by defining three fuzzy membership functions: `membership_cold`, `membership_moderate`, and `membership_hot`. These functions represent the degree of membership of the input temperature to the linguistic terms `"Cold"`, `"Moderate"`, and `"Hot"`, respectively. Triangular membership functions are used for simplicity.

Next, the program defines fuzzy inference rules using the `fuzzy_or` and `fuzzy_and` functions. The `fuzzy_or` function represents the logical OR operation, and the `fuzzy_and` function represents the logical AND operation. The rule-based fuzzy inference determines the strength of activation for each linguistic term based on the input temperature's membership values. After fuzzy inference, the program performs defuzzification to convert the fuzzy output values back into crisp values. The centroid method is used for defuzzification, which calculates the center of mass of the fuzzy set. The result is a crisp value representing the degree of activation of the air conditioning system.

The `fuzzy_neuron` function combines the fuzzification, fuzzy inference, and defuzzification steps. It takes the input temperature as an argument, fuzzifies it using the membership functions, applies fuzzy inference rules, and performs defuzzification to obtain the air conditioning system's output. The `fuzzy_not` function represents the logical NOT operation, which complements the membership value (`1 - x`). The `main` function demonstrates the use of the fuzzy neuron. It sets the input temperature to 25 °C and calls the `fuzzy_neuron` function to calculate the degree of activation for the air conditioning system.

Program 8.3 *Fuzzy Neuron for Temperature Control*

```python
import numpy as np

# Fuzzy membership functions
def membership_cold(x):
    if x <= 20:
        return 1.0
    elif x > 20 and x < 25:
        return (25 - x) / (25 - 20)
    else:
        return 0.0

def membership_moderate(x):
    if x > 20 and x < 25:
        return (x - 20) / (25 - 20)
    elif x >= 25 and x <= 30:
        return 1.0
    elif x > 30 and x < 35:
        return (35 - x) / (35 - 30)
    else:
        return 0.0

def membership_hot(x):
    if x >= 30 and x <= 35:
        return (x - 30) / (35 - 30)
    elif x > 35:
        return 1.0
    else:
        return 0.0

# Fuzzy inference using "OR" operator
def fuzzy_or(*args):
    return max(args)

# Fuzzy inference using "AND" operator
def fuzzy_and(*args):
    return min(args)

# Defuzzification using the centroid method
def defuzzification(result):
    total_area = sum(result)
    if total_area == 0:
        return None
    else:
        return sum(i * result[i] for i in range(len(result))) / \
            total_area
```

```python
# Fuzzy neuron for temperature control
def fuzzy_neuron(input_temp):
    cold_value = membership_cold(input_temp)
    moderate_value = membership_moderate(input_temp)
    hot_value = membership_hot(input_temp)

# Rule-based fuzzy inference
    air_cold = fuzzy_or(fuzzy_and(cold_value, fuzzy_or(fuzzy_and(1,
    fuzzy_not(moderate_value)), fuzzy_and(1, fuzzy_not(hot_value)))),
    fuzzy_and(moderate_value, fuzzy_or(fuzzy_and(1, fuzzy_not
    (cold_value)), fuzzy_and(1, fuzzy_not(hot_value)))))

    air_moderate = fuzzy_or(fuzzy_and(moderate_value, fuzzy_or
    (fuzzy_and(1, fuzzy_not(cold_value)), fuzzy_and(1, fuzzy_not
    (hot_value)))),
    fuzzy_and(hot_value, fuzzy_or(fuzzy_and(1, fuzzy_not(cold_value)),
    fuzzy_and(1, fuzzy_not(moderate_value)))))

    air_hot = fuzzy_or(fuzzy_and(hot_value, fuzzy_or(fuzzy_and(1,
    fuzzy_not(cold_value)), fuzzy_and(1, fuzzy_not(moderate_value)))),
    fuzzy_and(cold_value, fuzzy_or(fuzzy_and(1, fuzzy_not
    (moderate_value)), fuzzy_and(1, fuzzy_not(hot_value)))))

        # Defuzzification
        result = [0] * 100
        for i in range(100):
         result[i] = fuzzy_or(air_cold * membership_cold(i),
           air_moderate * membership_moderate(i), air_hot *
           membership_hot(i))

        return defuzzification(result)

# Helper function for "NOT" operator
def fuzzy_not(x):
    return 1 - x

# Main function to demonstrate the fuzzy neuron
def main():
    input_temp = 25   # Input temperature in degrees Celsius

    # Fuzzy inference
    air_conditioning = fuzzy_neuron(input_temp)
    print(f"Input Temperature: {input_temp}°C")
    print(f"Air Conditioning Output: {air_conditioning:.2f}")

if __name__ == "__main__":
    main()
```

The output of Program 8.3 is displayed next. The input temperature is set to 25 °C. The fuzzy neuron applies the fuzzy inference rules to determine the degree of activation for each linguistic term (cold, moderate, and hot) based on the input temperature's membership values. Since the input temperature falls within the range where "Moderate" has the highest membership value (around 1), the fuzzy neuron activates the "Moderate" air conditioning level. The output from the defuzzification step represents the degree of activation for the air conditioning system, with 0 indicating no activation and 100 indicating full activation.

```
Input Temperature: 25°C
Air Conditioning Output: 15.79
```

The air conditioning output (15.79, in the given output) will be a numeric value between 0 and 100, indicating the degree of activation for the air conditioning system. The higher the value, the more the air conditioning system will be activated.

The code shows a simplified demonstration of a fuzzy neuron for temperature control. In real-world applications, more sophisticated membership functions and fuzzy rules would be used for accurate control. The example provides a basic understanding of how fuzzy neurons can be used for control systems based on fuzzy logic principles.

Overall, fuzzy neurons are essential components of Fuzzy-Neural systems, providing the capability to handle uncertain and imprecise data effectively, making them valuable tools in various real-world applications.

8.3.2 Adaptive Neuro-fuzzy Inference System (ANFIS)

Adaptive Neuro-Fuzzy Inference System (ANFIS) is a hybrid intelligent system that combines the adaptability of NNs and the interpretability of fuzzy logic. ANFIS is specifically designed for function approximation and inference tasks, and it can be used for modeling complex systems, rule-based reasoning, and decision making.

ANFIS was introduced by Jang in 1993 as an extension of Takagi–Sugeno fuzzy inference systems to address the challenges of rule tuning and fuzzy membership function parameter optimization. The system automatically adjusts its parameters using a learning algorithm based on input–output data to achieve accurate modeling and inference. ANFIS consists of five layers, which are discussed next.

(a) **Fuzzification Layer:** The first layer of ANFIS is the fuzzification layer, where each input data point is converted into fuzzy membership degrees using membership functions. The membership functions represent the degree of membership of the input data to different linguistic terms.

(b) **Rule Layer:** The rule layer computes the firing strength of each rule. Each rule corresponds to a combination of fuzzy membership degrees from the fuzzification layer. The firing strength represents the activation level of each rule, given the input data.

(c) **Rule Consequent Layer:** The rule consequent layer computes the output of each rule using the consequent part of the fuzzy rules. In ANFIS, the Takagi–Sugeno fuzzy model is used, which expresses the rule's consequent as a linear function of the input variables.

(d) **Normalization Layer:** The normalization layer calculates the normalized firing strength of each rule. It ensures that the sum of all normalized firing strengths is equal to 1, providing a weighted average for the final output.

(e) **Defuzzification Layer:** The defuzzification layer calculates the overall output of the ANFIS model based on the weighted averages of the outputs from the rule consequent layer.

The ANFIS model employs a hybrid learning algorithm that combines gradient descent and least-squares estimation to adaptively adjust the parameters (weights and fuzzy membership function parameters) of the system. This learning process minimizes the error between the ANFIS model's predicted output and the target output from the training data.

Program 8.4 illustrates the Python code used to demonstrate the use of Adaptive Neuro-Fuzzy Inference System (ANFIS). The program is a simplified implementation of an ANFIS model to predict outputs from inputs using Gaussian membership functions and gradient descent for parameter adaptation.

The `gaussmf` function defines a Gaussian membership function, which is used for fuzzification in ANFIS. It takes *x*, mean, and sigma as input and returns the Gaussian membership values. The `predict_anfis` function is responsible for predicting the ANFIS output, given the input *x* and the ANFIS rules. It loops through the fuzzy rules, calculates the Gaussian membership values for each rule using `gaussmf`, and aggregates the weighted contributions to predict the output.

The `train_anfis` function trains the ANFIS model using a gradient descent approach. It initializes two fuzzy rules with initial parameters (`mean`, `sigma`, and `coeff`). The training process iterates for a specified number of epochs. In each epoch, it calculates the prediction using the current rules, and updates the rule coefficients to minimize the error between the predicted and actual output. Random input data *x* is generated for demonstration purposes. Additionally, random noise is added to the sine function to create the output data *y*.

The `train_anfis` function is called with the generated input *x* and output *y*. The ANFIS model is trained for 50 epochs with a learning rate of 0.1. The trained

ANFIS rules are used to predict the output values for the input data x. The program prints the actual output values y and the predicted output values y_pred for comparison. The output of the program will show the actual and predicted output values for the random data generated.

Program 8.4   *ANFIS Model for Parameter Adaptation*

```
import numpy as np

def gaussmf(x, mean, sigma):
    return np.exp(-0.5 * ((x - mean) / sigma) ** 2)

def predict_anfis(x, rules):
    y_pred = np.zeros_like(x)
    for i in range(len(rules)):
        w = gaussmf(x, rules[i]['mean'], rules[i]['sigma'])
        y_pred += rules[i]['coeff'] * w
    return y_pred

def train_anfis(x, y, num_epochs=10, learning_rate=0.01):
    rules = [
        {'mean': 2.0, 'sigma': 1.0, 'coeff': 0.0},
        {'mean': 8.0, 'sigma': 1.0, 'coeff': 0.0}
    ]

    for epoch in range(num_epochs):
        y_pred = predict_anfis(x, rules)
        error = y - y_pred

        for i in range(len(rules)):
            w = gaussmf(x, rules[i]['mean'], rules[i]['sigma'])
            delta_coeff = learning_rate * np.sum(w * error)
            rules[i]['coeff'] += delta_coeff

    return rules

# Generate random data for demonstration
np.random.seed(0)
x = np.random.rand(100) * 10
y = np.sin(x) + np.random.normal(scale=0.1, size=x.shape)

# Train the ANFIS model
trained_rules = train_anfis(x, y, num_epochs=50, learning_rate=0.1)

# Predict using the trained model
y_pred = predict_anfis(x, trained_rules)
# Print the comparison of actual and predicted values
print("Actual Values:", y)
print("Predicted Values:", y_pred)
```

The output of Program 8.4 is given next. The output displays arrays containing the actual output values *y* and the predicted output values `y_pred`. These values are compared for each corresponding input *x* generated earlier. The predicted values (`y_pred`) are generated using the trained ANFIS model, which has learned the fuzzy rules and their coefficients from the training data. The actual values (*y*) were generated by adding random noise to the sine function.

```
Actual Values: [-0.83041379   0.85357806 -0.20621284 -0.89448679
 -0.74008257   0.36444128
 -0.82603257   0.46760626 -0.31734381 -0.53326634   0.95768151
 -0.71609827
 -0.54607402   0.26567484   0.68774382   0.83581937   0.2018593
  1.06914918
  1.01007045   0.70307721 -0.16527418   0.85577159 -1.12228985
  1.09575455
  ...  ...
  ...  ...
 -0.70127374   0.55302958 -0.96779522   0.65272999 -0.3813023
  0.16312885
  0.0480033    0.41291054   1.05389453   0.70569158   0.14158738
  1.03426159
 -0.48632557   0.13076826   0.86114029   0.04868543]

Predicted Values: [0.03887846 0.60248083 0.12368996 0.03569268
 0.0748561    0.26333568
 0.054973     0.56655902 0.22620021 0.16821455 0.86029187 0.02593326
 0.05962261 0.39227757 0.3935936   0.47814501 0.17961804 0.81851582
 0.84289224 0.67560622 0.17511972 0.86321178 0.03242002 0.84703316
  ...  ...
  ...  ...
 0.05774434 0.73005164 0.0236153   0.51515769 0.07092542 0.37421111
 0.44764113 0.35843257 0.71646345 0.60828348 0.60621484 0.89138577
 0.08891431 0.17926032 0.82783941 0.13425097]
```

Since a simple ANFIS implementation is used with just two fuzzy rules and random data, the prediction accuracy may not be high. In practice, ANFIS models with more fuzzy rules and real-world data would be used for better results. The purpose of this program is to demonstrate the basic concept of Adaptive Neuro-Fuzzy Inference System (ANFIS), where the ANFIS model learns to map inputs to outputs by adapting fuzzy rules based on the training data.

ANFIS has found applications in various fields, including function approximation, system modeling and control, times series prediction, and pattern recognition. ANFIS automatically adjusts its parameters based on the input–output data, making it adaptable to different problems. ANFIS is a powerful and versatile technique that combines the strengths of fuzzy logic and NNs, making it suitable for a wide range of applications where interpretability and adaptability are essential.

8.4   Fuzzy-Genetic Systems

Fuzzy-Genetic Systems, also known as Genetic-Fuzzy systems or Fuzzy-Genetic algorithms (FGAs), are hybrid intelligent systems that combine the principles of fuzzy logic and GAs. These systems aim to leverage the strengths of both fuzzy logic and GAs to tackle complex problems involving uncertainty, imprecision, and optimization.

- **Fuzzy Logic:** Fuzzy logic is a mathematical framework for dealing with imprecise or uncertain information. Unlike classical logic, which deals with crisp binary values (true or false), fuzzy logic allows for intermediate values between true and false, represented by linguistic terms such as `"very hot"`, `"moderate"`, or `"cold"`. Fuzzy logic uses membership functions to assign a degree of membership to each linguistic term, indicating the level of truth for a given input.
- **Genetic Algorithms (GAs):** GAs are search and optimization techniques inspired by the process of natural selection. They are used to find approximate solutions to complex optimization problems by mimicking the principles of biological evolution, such as selection, crossover, and mutation. In a GA, potential solutions (individuals) to a problem are encoded as chromosomes, and these chromosomes are subjected to evolution and selection over multiple generations to find the best solution (fittest individual).

The fusion of fuzzy logic and GAs in Fuzzy-Genetic systems allows for the representation and handling of uncertainty in the chromosomes. Fuzzy logic provides a means to evaluate the fitness of individuals in the population based on imprecise or fuzzy data, enabling more robust and adaptive optimization. The components of Fuzzy-Genetic systems include the following:

(a) **Encoding and Chromosomes:** The solution space of the optimization problem is encoded into chromosomes. These chromosomes represent potential solutions and contain genetic information that can be subjected to genetic operators.
(b) **Fuzzy Evaluation and Fitness Function:** In Fuzzy-Genetic systems, the fitness function evaluates the fitness of individuals in the population using fuzzy logic. Fuzzy membership functions are employed to map the chromosome's genetic information to linguistic terms, representing the degree of truth for each linguistic term. The fuzzy fitness function considers the degree of membership of each linguistic term to determine the overall fitness of an individual.
(c) **Genetic Operators:** Genetic operators, such as selection, crossover, and mutation, are applied to the population of chromosomes in the same way as traditional GAs. These operators drive the evolution process to create new generations of individuals based on the fitness evaluation.

Fuzzy-Genetic systems are more robust and adaptive in handling uncertainty and imprecision compared to traditional GAs. The integration of fuzzy logic allows for a more flexible and interpretable representation of the optimization problem. The hybrid nature of Fuzzy-Genetic systems often leads to improved convergence to optimal or near-optimal solutions.

Fuzzy-Genetic systems have been applied to various real-world problems, including system optimization, rule-based systems, and pattern recognition. Overall, Fuzzy-Genetic systems offer a powerful approach to tackle complex problems with uncertainty, making them valuable tools in optimization, control, and decision-making applications.

One real-time example of Fuzzy-Genetic systems is the optimization of traffic signal timings in an urban traffic control system. Urban traffic control systems aim to efficiently manage traffic flow at intersections to minimize congestion, reduce travel time, and improve overall traffic efficiency. One critical aspect is optimizing traffic signal timings for different phases (`green`, `yellow`, `red`) to ensure smooth traffic flow. For fuzzy modeling, the system defines linguistic terms (e.g., `"low"`, `"medium"`, `"high"`) to represent traffic density, queue length, and vehicle speed at an intersection. Membership functions are created to map the sensor data (such as vehicle count) to these linguistic terms. Traffic control experts create a set of fuzzy rules based on their domain knowledge. For example, rules like `"IF traffic density is high AND queue length is low, THEN increase green signal duration"` can be formulated.

Fuzzy logic is used to evaluate the degree of truth for each fuzzy rule based on the current sensor data. The system performs fuzzy inference to compute the appropriate green signal duration for each phase based on the fuzzy rule firing strengths. The green signal durations obtained from the fuzzy inference are considered as chromosomes in the GAs. The fitness function is designed to measure the performance of the signal timings based on traffic flow efficiency metrics, such as average travel time, average waiting time, and queue length.

Genetic operators (selection, crossover, and mutation) are applied to the chromosome population. The GA evolves multiple generations to search for the best combination of signal timings that optimize the fitness function. The Fuzzy-Genetic system iterates between fuzzy inference and genetic evolution, until it converges to an optimal or near-optimal solution for the traffic signal timings.

Program 8.5 uses Python code to explain Fuzzy-Genetic system. The purpose of this program is to demonstrate the integration of fuzzy logic and GAs to optimize a simple quadratic objective function. The program defines a simple objective function called `objective_function(x)`, which is a quadratic function (x `** 2 - 4 * ` x ` + 4`). The goal is to minimize this function using the

Fuzzy-Genetic system. The program then defines fuzzy membership functions for the input variable *x* and the output variable (fitness).

In this example, three triangular membership functions (*low*, *medium*, and *high*) are created for each variable. The *fuzzify* function takes a crisp value *x_value* and returns a list of membership degrees for each linguistic term (*low*, *medium*, and *high*). The *defuzzify* function takes a fuzzy output value (*fitness_value*) and converts it into a crisp value using the centroid defuzzification method.

The Fuzzy-Genetic system is initialized using the *ga* function from the *geneticalgorithm* library. It specifies the objective function, dimension (number of variables) as 1, variable type as '*real*' (continuous), and variable boundaries as *varbound*, which is set to [-10, 10] in this example. The *algorithm_param* dictionary sets the parameters for the GA, such as population size, mutation probability, and crossover probability.

The program runs the GA to find the optimal value of *x* that minimizes the objective function. The optimization process continues for a maximum of 100 iterations (*max_num_iteration*). The best solution found is stored in the solution variable. After optimization, the program displays the optimized value of *x* and the corresponding value of the objective function (*fitness*). It also displays the membership degrees for the optimized *x* in the fuzzy sets (*low*, *medium*, and *high*).

Program 8.5 *Fuzzy-Genetic System to Optimize a Simple Quadratic Objective Function*

```
import numpy as np
import skfuzzy as fuzz
from geneticalgorithm import geneticalgorithm as ga

# Function to be optimized (minimized)
def objective_function(x):
    return x ** 2 - 4 * x + 4

# Fuzzy logic membership functions for input variables
x = np.arange(-10, 11, 1)
x_membership_low = fuzz.trimf(x, [-10, -10, 0])
x_membership_medium = fuzz.trimf(x, [-10, 0, 10])
x_membership_high = fuzz.trimf(x, [0, 10, 10])

# Fuzzy logic membership functions for output variable (fitness)
fitness = np.arange(0, 50, 1)
fitness_membership_low = fuzz.trimf(fitness, [0, 0, 25])
fitness_membership_medium = fuzz.trimf(fitness, [0, 25, 50])
fitness_membership_high = fuzz.trimf(fitness, [25, 50, 50])

# Fuzzification (mapping input to fuzzy membership degrees)
```

```
def fuzzify(x_value):
    return [
        fuzz.interp_membership(x, x_membership_low, x_value),
        fuzz.interp_membership(x, x_membership_medium, x_value),
        fuzz.interp_membership(x, x_membership_high, x_value)
    ]

# Defuzzification (mapping fuzzy output to crisp value)
def defuzzify(fitness_value):
    return fuzz.defuzz(fitness, fitness_membership_medium, 'cen-
troid')

# Fuzzy-Genetic System
varbound = np.array([[-10, 10]])
algorithm_param = {'max_num_iteration': 100, 'population_size': 10,
'mutation_probability': 0.1, 'elit_ratio': 0.01, 'parents_portion':
0.3, 'crossover_probability': 0.5,
'crossover_type': 'uniform', 'max_iteration_without_improv': None}
model = ga(function=objective_function, dimension=1,
variable_type='real', variable_boundaries=varbound,
function_timeout=20, algorithm_parameters = algorithm_param)

# Running the optimization
model.run()

# Obtaining the optimized solution
solution = model.output_dict

# Display the result
x_optimized = solution['variable']
fitness_optimized = solution['function']
print("Optimized Value of x:", x_optimized[0])
print("Optimized Value of the Objective Function:",
fitness_optimized)

# Display membership degrees for the optimized x
membership_degrees = fuzzify(x_optimized[0])
print("Membership Degrees for the Optimized x:")
print("Low:", membership_degrees[0])
print("Medium:", membership_degrees[1])
print("High:", membership_degrees[2])
```

The output of Program 8.5 will vary slightly in each run due to the stochastic nature of GAs. However, it will generally display the following details, and only the values may differ in each run.

```
The best solution found:
 [2.02769079]

Objective function:
 0.0007667798834551931
```

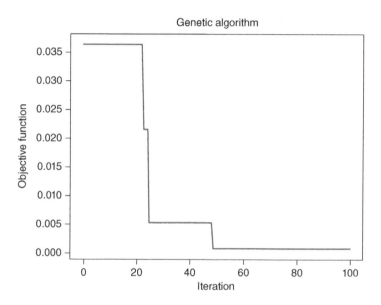

```
Optimized Value of x: 2.027690790589201
Optimized Value of the Objective Function:
    0.0007667798834551931
Membership Degrees for the Optimized x:
Low: 0.0
Medium: 0.79723092094108
High: 0.2027690790589201
```

Here, in the output, the optimized value of x is the value of x that minimizes the objective function (x ** 2 - 4 * x + 4). The optimized value of the objective function is the fitness value corresponding to the optimized value of x, which is the result of evaluating the objective function at the optimal x. Next, the membership degrees for the optimized x are the membership degrees for the optimized x in the fuzzy sets (low, medium, and high). They indicate the degree of truth for each linguistic term based on the optimized value of x. The fuzzy logic membership functions provide a more flexible and interpretable representation of the optimization problem, and the GA adapts to find the optimal solution based on the fuzzy fitness evaluation.

8.5 Hybrid Systems in Medical Devices

Hybrid systems in medical devices refer to the integration of different technologies and components to create advanced medical devices that can perform a variety of functions with increased efficiency and versatility. These devices combine elements from various disciplines, such as electronics, mechanics, software, and biological components, to address specific medical challenges and improve patient outcomes. The goal is to create smarter, more adaptive, and interconnected medical devices that can cater to individual patient needs and offer personalized healthcare solutions. Here are some key aspects of hybrid systems in medical devices:

(a) **Integration of Sensors and Actuators:** Medical devices often rely on sensors to monitor physiological parameters, such as heart rate, blood pressure, temperature, and oxygen levels. Actuators are used to provide therapeutic interventions, such as drug delivery or adjustments to medical equipment settings. Hybrid medical devices can combine different sensors and actuators to provide real-time data for diagnosis and treatment.

(b) **Connectivity and Data Sharing:** Hybrid medical devices can be equipped with wireless communication capabilities, allowing them to connect to other devices, medical networks, or centralized monitoring systems. This enables seamless data sharing and remote monitoring, facilitating continuous healthcare monitoring and analysis.

(c) **Adaptive and Closed-Loop Control:** Hybrid medical devices can incorporate closed-loop control systems that adjust their parameters based on real-time feedback from the patient's condition. These adaptive systems can optimize treatment and maintain specific physiological variables within desired ranges.

(d) **Software and Algorithms:** Hybrid medical devices often employ sophisticated software and algorithms to process sensor data, perform computations, and make intelligent decisions. This could include AI-based algorithms for diagnosing medical conditions or optimizing treatment plans.

(e) **Implantable Hybrid Devices:** Some hybrid medical devices are designed to be implanted inside the body to provide ongoing monitoring or treatment. These devices may have a mix of biological and electronic components, ensuring compatibility and long-term functionality.

(f) **Assistive and Prosthetic Devices:** Hybrid systems are also used in the development of assistive devices and prosthetics. Combining mechanical components with sensors and control systems allows for more natural and intuitive interactions with the user.

(g) **Robotics in Surgery:** Robotic surgical systems are a prime example of hybrid medical devices. Surgeons can use these systems to perform minimally invasive procedures with enhanced precision and dexterity, reducing patient trauma, and improving surgical outcomes.

(h) **Personalized Healthcare:** Hybrid medical devices have the potential to offer personalized healthcare solutions tailored to individual patients.

By integrating patient-specific data and AI capabilities, these devices can adapt treatments and interventions to suit unique medical needs.

(i) **Wearable Health Technology:** Many wearable health devices, such as smartwatches and fitness trackers, incorporate hybrid systems to measure vital signs, track physical activity, and even provide health alerts or reminders.

Overall, hybrid systems in medical devices represent a promising avenue for advancing healthcare technology. By merging various technologies and disciplines, these devices can improve diagnostics, treatment, and patient care, leading to better medical outcomes and enhancing the quality of life for patients. However, the development of such devices requires careful consideration of safety, regulatory compliance, and ethical considerations to ensure their effective and responsible use in healthcare settings.

Explaining hybrid systems in medical devices requires a more theoretical and conceptual approach rather than actual Python code, as the implementation of medical devices involves specialized hardware, electronics, and regulatory considerations. However, a simplified Python code example is provided in Program 8.6 that illustrates a basic hybrid system concept that can be used for medical analysis.

Let's consider a hypothetical scenario where we create a simple hybrid medical device simulation that involves monitoring a patient's heart rate and delivering medication if the heart rate exceeds a certain threshold. Program 8.6 uses Python code to represent the simulation of the hybrid system. The Python code begins by importing the required modules, which in this case are random and time. These modules will be used to simulate heart rate measurements and medication delivery delays, respectively.

- Defining the `HeartRateSensor` class: The `HeartRateSensor` class represents a hypothetical heart rate monitoring device or sensor. For simplicity, heart rate measurements is simulated using the `random.randint(60, 100)` function, which generates a random integer between 60 and 100. In a real medical device, this would be replaced with actual sensor data acquisition.

- Defining the `MedicationDeliverySystem` class: The `MedicationDeliverySystem` class represents a hypothetical medication delivery system. In this example, we simulate medication delivery by printing a message and introducing a 2-second delay with `time.sleep(2)`. In a real medical device, this class would interface with a medication delivery mechanism.

- Defining the `HybridMedicalDevice` class: The `HybridMedicalDevice` class is the main class that brings together the heart rate sensor and the medication delivery system. It initializes instances of the `HeartRateSensor` and `MedicationDeliverySystem` classes in its constructor.

- The `monitor_heart_rate` method: The `monitor_heart_rate` method is the core of our simulation. It simulates the continuous monitoring of the heart rate and delivers medication if the heart rate exceeds a certain threshold (in this case, 90 beats per minute).

In the main block, an instance of the *HybridMedicalDevice* class named *hybrid_device* is created. The *monitor_heart_rate* method is then called with five iterations so as to run the simulation for five iterations. Since the heart rate measurements are simulated, each iteration will show a random heart rate value between 60 and 100 (inclusive). If any of these random values exceed 90, the medication delivery will be triggered with a 2-second delay.

Program 8.6   *Hybrid System for Heart Rate Analysis*

```
import random
import time

class HeartRateSensor:
    def measure_heart_rate(self):
        # Simulate heart rate measurement (replace this with real
           sensor data)
        return random.randint(60, 100)

class MedicationDeliverySystem:
    def deliver_medication(self):
        print("Delivering medication...")
        # Simulate the medication delivery process
        time.sleep(2)
        print("Medication delivered.")

class HybridMedicalDevice:
    def __init__(self):
        self.heart_rate_sensor = HeartRateSensor()
        self.medication_delivery_system =
            MedicationDeliverySystem()

    def monitor_heart_rate(self, iterations=10):
        for _ in range(iterations):
            heart_rate = self.heart_rate_sensor.measure_heart_
               rate()
            print(f"Heart rate: {heart_rate}")

            if heart_rate > 90:   # Threshold for medication
                delivery
                self.medication_delivery_system.deliver_
                    medication()

            time.sleep(1)

if __name__ == "__main__":
    hybrid_device = HybridMedicalDevice()
```

```
hybrid_device.monitor_heart_rate(iterations=5)    # Set the
    desired number of iterations
```

A sample output for Program 8.6 is displayed next. In the given output, the heart rate exceeded 90 twice, and the medication was delivered on those occasions. The simulation runs for five iterations (as specified by *iterations*=5), and the program terminates after the 5th iteration.

```
Heart rate: 80
Heart rate: 93
Delivering medication...
Heart rate: 62
Heart rate: 87
Heart rate: 95
Delivering medication...
Heart rate: 68
Heart rate: 72
Heart rate: 74
```

This program is a highly simplified simulation to demonstrate the concept of a hybrid medical device. In real-world medical devices, the heart rate monitoring and medication delivery systems would be much more sophisticated and closely regulated to ensure patient safety and effectiveness.

Now, let's discuss another program to discuss about hybrid systems in medical devices. Program 8.7 shows the Python code for a hybrid rehabilitation device that is simulated to assist patients with their physical rehabilitation by monitoring their movement using an accelerometer and providing feedback through an actuator. The accelerometer measures acceleration during the exercise, and the actuator provides feedback to the patient, such as vibration or resistance, if the acceleration exceeds a certain threshold.

(a) Defining the *Accelerometer* class: The *Accelerometer* class represents a hypothetical sensor used to measure acceleration during a patient's rehabilitation exercise. For simplicity, acceleration measurements is simulated using a fixed value of 0.5 m/s^2. In a real medical device, this would be replaced with actual sensor data.

(b) Defining the *Actuator* class: The *Actuator* class represents a hypothetical component that provides feedback to the patient during their rehabilitation exercise. In this example, feedback is simulated by printing a message and introducing a 1-second delay with time.sleep(1). In a real medical device, the actuator may vibrate or apply resistance to guide the patient's movements.

(c) Defining the *HybridRehabilitationDevice* class: The *HybridRehabilitationDevice* class is the main class that brings together the accelerometer and the actuator. It initializes instances of the Accelerometer and *Actuator* classes in its constructor.

(d) The *perform_rehabilitation* method: The *perform_rehabilita-*
tion method is the core of the simulation. It simulates a rehabilitation
exercise session that lasts for a specified duration (default is 5 seconds).
Within a loop, the accelerometer measures the acceleration during the
exercise, and the result is printed. If the measured acceleration exceeds a
threshold value of 0.7 m/s^2 (hypothetical value for this example), the
actuator provides feedback by printing a message and introducing a 1-second
delay.

In the main block, an instance of the *HybridRehabilitationDevice* class
named *rehab_device* is created. The *perform_rehabilitation* method is
then called with duration=10, specifying that a rehabilitation exercise session
is being simulated that will last for 10 seconds. Since the accelerometer's measurements are simulated with a fixed value of 0.5 m/s^2, the output will repeatedly
display this acceleration value. However, when the hypothetical threshold of 0.7
m/s^2 is exceeded, the actuator will provide feedback by printing a message and
introducing a 1-second delay.

Program 8.7 *Hybrid System for Physical Rehabilitation Analysis*

```
import time

class Accelerometer:
    def measure_acceleration(self):
        # Simulate acceleration measurement (replace this with real
          sensor data)
        return 0.5  # Example: Simulated acceleration value of
          0.5 m/s^2

class Actuator:
    def provide_feedback(self, force):
        print(f"Applying force: {force:.2f} N")
        # Simulate the actuator providing feedback (e.g.,
          vibrating or resisting)
        time.sleep(1)
        print("Feedback applied.")

class HybridRehabilitationDevice:
    def __init__(self):
        self.accelerometer = Accelerometer()
        self.actuator = Actuator()

    def perform_rehabilitation(self, duration=5):
        start_time = time.time()
        while time.time() - start_time < duration:
            acceleration = self.accelerometer.measure_
              acceleration()
```

```
print(f"Acceleration: {acceleration:.2f} m/s^2")

# If acceleration is above a certain threshold,
  provide feedback
if acceleration > 0.7:
    self.actuator.provide_feedback(acceleration * 10)

time.sleep(0.5)

if __name__ == "__main__":
    rehab_device = HybridRehabilitationDevice()
    rehab_device.perform_rehabilitation(duration=10)
```

A sample output for Program 8.7 is displayed next. In the given output, the acceleration exceeds the threshold (0.7 m/s^2) twice, triggering the actuator to provide feedback. The simulation runs for 10 seconds (as specified by duration=10), and the program will terminate after the 10-second duration.

```
Acceleration: 0.50 m/s^2
Acceleration: 0.50 m/s^2
Acceleration: 0.50 m/s^2
Acceleration: 0.60 m/s^2
Acceleration: 0.70 m/s^2
Acceleration: 0.75 m/s^2
Applying force: 7.50 N
Feedback applied.
Acceleration: 0.50 m/s^2
Acceleration: 0.55 m/s^2
Acceleration: 0.65 m/s^2
Acceleration: 0.70 m/s^2
Acceleration: 0.75 m/s^2
Applying force: 7.50 N
Feedback applied.
```

It is to be noted that this is a simplified simulation to illustrate the concept of a hybrid medical device in rehabilitation. In real-world medical devices, the accelerometer's measurements and actuator's feedback would be more advanced, and the rehabilitation program would be customized to suit the patient's specific needs under professional guidance.

Hybrid systems play a pivotal role in addressing sustainability challenges. From smart grids to hybrid renewable energy systems, researchers are leveraging the versatility of hybrid systems to optimize energy management, enhance efficiency, and reduce environmental impact. The medical field, too, has greatly benefited from hybrid systems. The integration of sensors, actuators, and AI algorithms in medical devices has led to personalized healthcare solutions, improved diagnostics, and more effective treatment plans.

As technology continues to advance, hybrid systems will remain at the forefront of research and development. Their ability to bridge the gap between continuous and discrete dynamics, adapt to changing conditions, and optimize system behavior will undoubtedly drive innovation across diverse industries, and shape the future of intelligent and interconnected systems.

In conclusion, the study of hybrid systems is not only fascinating but also essential for meeting the challenges of an increasingly complex and interconnected world. Embracing the potential of hybrid systems opens up new frontiers in research, engineering, and technology, empowering us to create smarter, more efficient, and adaptive systems that enhance our lives and reshape the world around us.

Exercises

A) Choose the correct answer from among the alternatives given:

a) A type of hybrid system that uses one soft computing technique as a supporting tool to improve the performance of another technique:

   i) Sequential hybrid system

   ii) Embedded hybrid system

   iii) Auxiliary hybrid system

   iv) Ensemble hybrid system

b) What is the primary goal of using a genetic algorithm (GA) for weight determination in a Multilayer Feed-forward Neural Network?

   i) To minimize the number of hidden layers in the network.

   ii) To maximize the number of neurons in the output layer.

   iii) To find the optimal set of weights that minimizes the network's error function.

   iv) To increase the learning rate of the network.

c) What is the role of a fitness function in the genetic algorithm?

   i) It determines the probability of a genetic mutation occurring.

   ii) It measures how well an individual solution performs the task at hand.

   iii) It controls the crossover operation between parents.

   iv) It keeps track of the total number of generations in the algorithm.

d) In NEAT, how are neural network structures represented?

   i) As a fixed, predefined architecture.

   ii) As a direct acyclic graph (DAG) with no recurrent connections.

   iii) As a single-layer perceptron.

   iv) As a stack of fully connected layers.

e) What is speciation in the context of NEAT?

   i) The process of selecting the best-performing neural networks.

   ii) The technique of adding new layers to the neural network.

iii) The process of dividing the population into species based on their similarity.

iv) The process of gradually reducing the size of the neural network over generations.

f) Fuzzy-Neural systems combine the principles of fuzzy logic and neural networks to:

i) Process crisp inputs and generate crisp outputs.

ii) Handle only binary classification tasks.

iii) Represent knowledge in the form of rules and linguistic variables.

iv) Implement complex mathematical operations efficiently.

g) Which of the following techniques is used to represent membership functions in fuzzy neurons?

i) Heaviside function

ii) Step function

iii) Sigmoid function

iv) Gaussian function

h) Which statement best describes the purpose of the `"defuzzification"` process in fuzzy neurons?

i) To convert fuzzy output into crisp values

ii) To calculate the error gradient during backpropagation

iii) To initialize the connection weights in the neural network

iv) To combine fuzzy inputs into a single fuzzy output

i) Which technique is commonly used to update the connection weights in Fuzzy-Neural networks during training?

i) Gradient Descent

ii) K-Means Clustering

iii) Random Forest

iv) Breadth-First Search

j) What is the main function of the *"Fuzzification Layer"* in an ANFIS architecture?

i) It converts the crisp inputs into fuzzy sets using membership functions.

ii) It updates the connection weights during training.

iii) It calculates the output using a defuzzification method.

iv) It applies the activation function to the weighted sum of inputs.

k) What is the primary function of the *"Consequent Layer"* in ANFIS?

i) It converts the fuzzy rule outputs into crisp values.

ii) It calculates the overall error of the system.

iii) It performs the forward pass during training.

iv) It normalizes the fuzzy rule firing strengths.

l) Which of the following is a key advantage of ANFIS?
   i) It requires a large amount of labeled data for training.
   ii) It can only handle linear relationships between input and output variables.
   iii) It provides interpretable and explainable results.
   iv) It is not suitable for real-time applications.

m) In a Fuzzy-Genetic system, what does the "genetic" component refer to?
   i) Using DNA sequences to represent fuzzy sets.
   ii) Applying the principles of heredity and natural selection to evolve solutions.
   iii) Using statistical genetics to analyze fuzzy rule performance.
   iv) Integrating genetic data into fuzzy logic controllers.

n) Which step of the Fuzzy-Genetic system involves encoding the fuzzy rules into chromosomes?
   i) Crossover
   ii) Mutation
   iii) Selection
   iv) Encoding

o) What is the role of the fitness function in a Fuzzy-Genetic system?
   i) To evaluate the suitability of fuzzy rules for a specific problem
   ii) To calculate the probability of crossover and mutation operations
   iii) To represent the degree of fuzziness in the input data
   iv) To transform continuous variables into discrete values

B) **Answer the following questions:**
   1) Describe the concept of Neurogenetic systems and how they combine neural networks with genetic algorithms for problem solving.
   2) Discuss the role of genetic algorithms in Neurogenetic systems and how they contribute to the optimization of neural network parameters.
   3) Provide examples of real-world applications where Neurogenetic systems have been successfully employed, and explain their benefits in those applications.
   4) Explain the role of fuzzy logic in Fuzzy-Neural systems and how it helps in generating linguistic rules and membership functions for the neural network.
   5) Discuss the advantages of Fuzzy-Neural systems over traditional neural networks in tasks that involve dealing with fuzzy or vague data.
   6) Compare and contrast Neurogenetic and Fuzzy-Neural systems in terms of their approaches, advantages, and specific problem domains where each is best suited for implementation.

7) Explain the learning process in ANFIS. How are the parameters of the fuzzy sets and the neural network weights adapted during the training phase to optimize the model's performance?

8) Discuss the advantages and limitations of ANFIS compared to other machine learning models, such as traditional fuzzy systems, neural networks, or support vector machines. In what scenarios does ANFIS excel, and when might other models be more appropriate choices?

9) What is Neuro Evolution of Adaptive Topologies (NEAT), and how does it differ from traditional neuroevolution or genetic algorithms for evolving neural networks?

10) Describe the key components and steps involved in the NEAT algorithm. How does it maintain innovation and prevent premature convergence during the evolution process?

Index

a

Activation Function (AF)   81
  binary step AF   81
  leaky ReLU   88
  linear AF   83
  ReLU AF   85
  sigmoid/logistic AF   84
  SoftMax AF   90
  tanh AF   87
AlexNet   131
ANFIS   307
Angular Fuzzy Sets   53
ANN Learning Rule   91
Ant Colony Optimization   15, 233
Antecedent   1
Approximation space   257
Artificial Bee Colony   16
  confidence   27
  minimum confidence   27
  minimum support   27
  support   27
Artificial Neural Network   11, 75
Association Analysis   26
Attribute discretization   280
Autoencoders   149
Average Pooling   129
Axon   10–11, 75

b

Bayesian Inference (BI)   168
Bayesian Machine Learning   191
Bayesian Network   171
Bayesian Structure Learning   178
Bayes Theorem   168
Belief Network   171
Bias   100
Binary Fuzzy Relation   45
Binary Step Activation Function   81
Boundary Region   258

c

Chaos Theory   30
Chromosome   198
Classification   21
Clustering   25, 271
  centroid-based clustering   25
  density-based clustering   25
  distribution-based clustering   25
  hierarchical clustering   25
Collective Sorting   228
Collective Transport   230
Competitive Learning Rule   95
Conditional Independence   172
Conditional Random Field Learning   177

Principles of Soft Computing Using Python Programming: Learn How to Deploy Soft Computing Models in Real World Applications, First Edition. Gypsy Nandi.
© 2024 The Institute of Electrical and Electronics Engineers, Inc. Published 2024 by John Wiley & Sons, Inc.

Consequence   1
Constrained-Based Method   178
Contrastive Divergence   177
Control Action   1
Convolutional Neural Network
     125
   convolutional layer   126
   feature map   126
   kernel/filter   126
   pooling   128
Correlation Learning Rule   94
Crisp Set   35
Crossover   204
   multi-point crossover   204
   one-point crossover   204
   partially mapped crossover   205
   uniform crossover   204

d

Decision Rule   263
Decision Table   263
   certainty factor   265
   consistency factor   264
   coverage factor   266
   probabilistic properties   266
   strength   265
   support   265
Deep Learning   123–125
Defuzzification   58
   centroid method   60
   maxima methods   62
   max-membership principle   58
   mean-max membership   59
   weighted average method   61
Delta Learning Rule   94
Dendrite   10–11, 75
DenseNet   131
Differential Equation   18
Division of Labor   229

e

Efficient Net   131
Equivalence Class   257
Equivalence Relation   256
Evidential Reasoning   30
Evolutionary Computing   12
Evolutionary Programming   13
Evolutionary Strategies   14
Expectation Maximization   177
Expected Values   165

f

Feature Map   126
Feature Selection   268
Feedback Neural Network   111
Feed-Forward Neural Network   98
Filter/Kernel   126
Fitness Function   199
Foraging Behavior   228
Fuzzification   58
Fuzzy c-Means   62
Fuzzy Computing   7, 35–37
Fuzzy Genetic Systems   311
Fuzzy Membership Functions   38,
     46–49
Fuzzy Neural Systems   302
Fuzzy Neuron   303
Fuzzy Set   35, 37–38
Fuzzy Set Operations   41
Fuzzy Set Properties   42

g

Gaussian Membership Function   48
Generative Adversial Network   144
Genetic Algorithms   17, 56–57, 197
   chromosome   198
   crossover   204
   fitness function   199
   mutation   205

parent selection   200
population initialization   144
GoogleNet   131

h
Hard Computing   2
Hebbian Learning Rule   93
Hidden Layer   76
Hidden Markov Model   178
HNN Algorithm   116
Hopfield Neural Network   116
Human Expertise   5
Hybrid Computing   3–4
Hybrid Systems   289
  auxiliary hybrid systems   290
  embedded hybrid systems   290
  sequential hybrid systems   290

i
Image Processing   276
Indiscernibility Relation   263
Inductive Reasoning   57

j
Job-Shop Scheduling

k
Kernel/Filter   126
Kohonen   113
  best matching unit   114
  self-organizing map   113

l
Leaky ReLU Activation Function
  88
Learning Rule   91
  competitive learning rule   95
  correlation learning rule   94
  delta learning rule   94
  Hebbian learning rule   93

Outstar learning rule   95
  perceptron learning rule   93
LeNet   130
Linear Activation Function   83
Linear Regression   23
Logistic Activation Function   84
Logistic Regression   23
Long Short-Term Memory Network
  139
Lower Approximation   257

m
Machine Learning   19, 191
Mapping Function   1
Markov Decision Process   186
Markovian Network   171
Markov Random Field   172
Maximum Likelihood Estimation
  177
Max Pooling   129
McCulloch-Pitts ANN Model   96
Medical Devices   315
Medical Diagnosis   273
Membership Function   9–10, 35
Membership Value Assignments   49
Multi-Layer Perceptron   103
Mutation   205
  bit flip mutation   206
  inverse mutation   207
  random resetting   206
  scramble mutation   207
  swap mutation   207

n
NEAT   298
Negative Region   259
Neural Network   10, 53–56
Neurogenetic Systems   291
Neuron   10–11, 75

o

Odds   162
Optimization Algorithm   235
Outstar Learning Rule   95

p

Parameter Learning   177
Particle Swarm Intelligence   15
Pawlak Rough Set   255
Perceptron   99
    multi-layer perceptron   103
    single-layer perceptron   99
Perceptron Learning Rule   93
Pheromone   227
Pooling   128
    average pooling   129
    max pooling   129
Population-Based Algorithms   197
Positive Region   259
Probabilistic Models   191
Probabilistic Reasoning   29, 159
Probability   159
Probability Perspectives   165
    axiomatic approach   167
    classical approach   166
    empirical approach   166
    subjective approach   167

r

Radial Basis Function Network   107
Random Experiment   160
Random Variables   160
    continuous random variables   161
    discrete random variables   161
Recurrent Neural Network   137
Reduct   259
Regression   22
    Lasso regression   23
    linear regression   23

logistic regression   23
    polynomial regression   23
    Ridge regression   23
    support vector regression   24
Reinforcement Learning   28
ReLU   85
ResNET   131
Risks   162
ROSE Tool   280
Rough Set Theory   255
    accuracy   261
    roughness   260

s

Sample Space   162
Self-Organization   231
Self-Organizing Map   111
Semi-Supervised Learning   27
Sigmoid Activation Function   84
Sigmoidal Membership Function
    48
Single-Layer Perceptron   99
Singleton Membership Function
    46
SoftMax Activation Function   90
Soma   10–11, 75
Speech Analysis   278
Stigmergy   229
Supervised Learning   20
Swarm Intelligence   15, 225
Synapse   10–11, 75

t

Tanh Activation Function   87
Test Accuracy   136
Test Loss   136
Threshold Logic Unit   11
Trapezoidal Membership Function
    48

Travelling Salesman Problem   212, 236
Triangular Membership Function   46

u

Unsupervised Learning   24
Upper Approximation   258

v

Vector Quantization   278
Vehicle Routing Problem   216
VGGNet   131

w

Weighted Average Method   61
Weights   11, 50, 75
Weight Tuning   77

z

Zadeh, Lofti A.   1, 7, 35
    fuzzy computing   7, 35–37
    soft computing   1
Zdislaw Pawlak   255
    rough set theory   255

Printed and bound by CPI Group (UK) Ltd, Croydon, CR0 4YY

27/10/2024

14580669-0004